GIS *Tutorial*
for Marketing

Population of Selected Countries

Bosworth

FRED L. MILLER

D1611564

ESRI Press
REDLANDS, CALIFORNIA

ESRI Press, 380 New York Street, Redlands, California 92373-8100

Copyright © 2007 ESRI
All rights reserved. First edition 2007

10 09 08 07   1 2 3 4 5 6 7 8 9 10

Printed in the United States of America

Library of Congress Cataloging-in-Publication Data
Miller, Fred L., 1949–
      GIS tutorial for marketing / Fred L. Miller.
         p.   cm.
      Includes indexes.
      ISBN 978-1-58948-079-7 (pbk. : alk. paper)
      1. Marketing—Data processing. 2. Geographic information systems. I. Title.
   HF5415.125.M55   2007
   658.800285—dc22   2007007441

Ask for ESRI Press titles at your local bookstore or order by calling 1-800-447-9778. You can also shop online at www.esri.com/esripress. Outside the United States, contact your local ESRI distributor.

ESRI Press titles are distributed to the trade by the following:
In North America:
Ingram Publisher Services
Toll-free telephone: (800) 648-3104
Toll-free fax: (800) 838-1149
E-mail: customerservice@ingrampublisherservices.com

In the United Kingdom, Europe, and the Middle East:
Transatlantic Publishers Group Ltd.
Telephone: 44 20 7373 2515
Fax: 44 20 7244 1018
E-mail: richard@tpgltd.co.uk

Cover design by Amaree Israngkura
Interior design by Jennifer Galloway

Contents

Acknowledgments

I would like to thank all who contributed so significantly to the publication of this book.

The exercises in this book were used by students at Murray State University and Bellarmine University prior to their compilation in this volume. Professors Glynn Mangold and Terry Holmes at Murray State University and Professor Joan Combs Durso at Bellarmine University used them in their courses. Their comments and those of their students were very helpful in revising and refining the exercises.

I am grateful to Deborah Webb, director of the Community Farm Alliance in Lexington, Kentucky, who graciously allowed me to use descriptions of that organization and its activities in chapter 5, thus extending the reach of the book to include a not-for-profit community organization.

Most exercise data is extracted from the rich demographic and Community Tapestry lifestyle segmentation data included in the ESRI Business Analyst product, and is used here with permission of the product managers. I appreciate their willingness to share this data with me and those who will learn to use it more effectively through this book.

Finally, many thanks to the members of the ESRI Press team who contributed so much to this effort. Ann Johnson and Judy Hawkins were invaluable in initiating and shaping the project. Shauna Neidigh did a wonderful job in the initial editing of the book. Amy Collins's willingness to step into the project at midstream and her dedication to its timely completion were the bedrock of our efforts. Rob Burke's careful reading and testing of the exercises and his insightful suggestions for improvement were very beneficial. Michael Law provided invaluable cartographic assistance, while Brent Roderick provided guidance for my use of Community Tapestry data. Colleen Langley and Jennifer Galloway contributed their editing and design skills. Carmen Fye and Kathleen Morgan were of great help in securing the necessary data permissions. The readers of this book will benefit immeasurably from the talents and professionalism of this team and its members.

I dedicate this book to Linda, Bettye, Les, Fran, Jack, Josh, Les and Jess,
whose love and support made it possible.

Preface

GIS Tutorial for Marketing provides readers a broad-based, hands-on resource for learning how to use geographic information system (GIS) tools in marketing. It includes software exercises that support several different courses in the university marketing curriculum.

This book may be used as:

1. *A supplemental resource for use in several different marketing courses*
   In this scenario, marketing professors will select relevant chapters to include in their courses, and students will develop GIS skills systematically as they progress through the marketing curriculum. In this context, chapter 1 serves as an ArcGIS introduction and review, while chapter 2 provides the same functions relative to the Community Tapestry lifestyle segmentation system. The remaining chapters are designed to be independent rather than sequential. Thus, they may be completed in whatever order students encounter them as they move through their academic program.

   In this approach, the ArcGIS 9.2 trial software that students receive with the book will likely expire before they complete all of the exercises. They will still, however, be able to work with university labs hosting ArcGIS 9.2 software. In addition, course professors at institutions with ESRI site licenses may order student editions of ArcGIS software from ESRI by following the appropriate link at *http://www.esri.com/esripress/gistutorialmarketing*. This option allows students to complete course assignments on their personal computers.

2. *An application resource for a dedicated marketing course*
   In this scenario, *GIS Tutorial for Marketing* provides the practical exercises for a single marketing course focusing on GIS applications in the field. In this context, students should complete chapters 1 and 2 first, then the remaining chapters in the order deemed most appropriate by the course instructor.

   A CD of instructor resources including implementation guidelines, sample syllabi, introductory PowerPoint presentations for each major chapter, and sample answers to the questions in each chapter is available for instructors using either approach. These materials can be ordered from *http://www.esri.com/esripress/gistutorialmarketing*.

3. *A self-study resource for marketing professionals who wish to develop GIS knowledge and skills*
   This scenario is appropriate for learners who wish to independently develop GIS skills in marketing, focusing on those chapters most relevant to their professional interests. They should begin with chapters 1 and 2, then proceed in the order they deem most beneficial.

This book comes with one CD that contains the data used in chapter exercises and one DVD that contains a 180-day trial version of ArcGIS 9.2. (If you already have ArcGIS 9.2 on your computer, you only need to install the data.) Instructions for installing the two discs are provided in appendix B.

Introduction

The software exercises in this book are designed for ArcGIS 9.2. They work with any license level (ArcView, ArcEditor, or ArcInfo). To complete one of the exercises, you must have the Network Analyst extension. This extension is included with the trial software found at the back of the book. The trial software will expire 180 days from the date of the initial installation.

The data CD in the back of the book contains the GIS data required to complete the exercises, including a copy of the 2006 Community Tapestry Demonstration product from ESRI.

Everything happens somewhere.

But in marketing does it make any difference where?

More often than not it does.

Stores, offices, and warehouses have locations. Customers have addresses, shopping patterns, and preferred travel modes. Sales representatives are assigned to geographic territories to service their accounts effectively and efficiently. Suppliers and intermediaries have distribution centers, transportation networks, and supply chains. Promotional media have geographic coverage areas. Even in cyber marketing, where transactions occur regardless of location, firms must ship purchased products, meet delivery schedules, and provide customer service. In addition, where online customers live can provide insight into their demographic characteristics, values, and shopping patterns.

Understanding the spatial dimension of marketing and marketing analysis can enhance a firm's ability to serve its customers, improve firm performance, and create a competitive advantage. The three-pronged premise of this book is that: (1) virtually all aspects of marketing have a spatial dimension; (2) geographic information system (GIS) technology provides valuable tools in managing this dimension; and (3) marketing managers who use these tools will be more successful.

This book provides a systematic path for learning GIS throughout most of your marketing courses. This will provide you a broad-based understanding of the technology and how to apply it in the real world.

What is GIS?

ESRI, developer of the ArcGIS software you will use in this book, offers the following definition of GIS.

> "An integrated collection of computer software and data used to view and manage information about geographic places, analyze spatial relationships, and model spatial processes. A GIS provides a framework for gathering and organizing spatial data and related information so that it can be displayed and analyzed."[1]

If you have ever used an interactive Web mapping service (such as Google Earth), there is much you will find familiar as you work within a GIS environment. GIS facilitates the representation of geographic or spatial knowledge, most commonly presented in maps. But GIS is much more than digital mapping. As with most information systems, you can use GIS to organize and store data, manipulate data, facilitate data analysis, and create data presentation formats such as tables, charts, and reports.

1. T. Wade and S. Sommers. *A to Z GIS*. Redlands, Calif.: ESRI Press, 2006.

Using GIS to address common business problems enables exciting approaches to making sound business decisions. You can geographically display virtually any dataset with a spatial component, offering a fresh perspective on business information. You can also integrate that data with other spatial data to provide more comprehensive approaches to business problems. For example, integrating a map of possible sites for your new plant with workforce, floodplain, and transportation maps can avoid costly mistakes.

GIS also provides tools for analyzing the spatial dimension of business information. Basic questions such as "Where are my stores? My customers? My distribution centers? My sales force? My competitors?" are inherently spatial and crucial to understanding the business enterprise. However, the greater value of spatial analysis is in its ability to answer more strategic questions such as "Where should I place my next store to better serve customers? Where do our most attractive prospects live? How can we communicate with them? What is the most efficient structure for our sales territories?" Further, the inherently visual representation of this information in GIS creates strong communication capabilities as well, affording executives a more comprehensive basis for making business decisions.

What is ArcGIS?

The ArcGIS Desktop product is composed of two primary applications: ArcCatalog and ArcMap. ArcCatalog is the application you would use for managing your data. ArcMap is the application to use for displaying, navigating, and manipulating data. In this book you will only work with the ArcMap application.

ArcGIS Desktop has three license levels: ArcView, ArcEditor, and ArcInfo. ArcEditor offers additional capabilities over ArcView, and ArcInfo offers the full extent of the software's capabilities. This book is designed for the ArcView license, meaning every task can be accomplished by any ArcGIS user, no matter what license they have.

ArcGIS provides an impressive array of functionality. ESRI also provides additional applications, called extensions, that extend the capabilities of the standard software package. They provide functionality that is vital for users in specialized fields. Many organizations use these extensions in facilities management, supply chain management, and customer service operations.

One such extension is Network Analyst, which you will use in chapter 9 to determine the best route for a series of sales calls. Network Analyst is used extensively in routing applications for sales representatives, service technicians, repair crews, and emergency response teams.

Another extension, Business Analyst, is designed specifically for use as a tool for business and marketing planning. It includes a set of tools for customer profiling, market segmentation, market area analysis, and opportunity prospecting. Further, it incorporates a very extensive demographic dataset of the United States at levels of geography ranging from national and state levels to census block groups. Most of this data includes measures from the 2000 U.S. Census, updated estimates of current year values, and five-year projections. Business Analyst also includes Community Tapestry data for use in lifestyle segmentation analysis. Data on businesses and shopping centers is also provided for use in competitor analysis.

Many Business Analyst features build on the procedures, tools, and data you will use in this book. Indeed, the demographic and Community Tapestry data you will be using are from Business Analyst. Should you encounter this extension in your workplace, you will recognize many of the applications and be able to incorporate them into your workflow.

The role of GIS in marketing

Given this general definition of GIS and its usefulness in business decision making, what are the applications in marketing? Though the specific GIS tools and procedures are vast, there are four essential capabilities they provide:

1. Enhanced spatial insight into marketing data.
2. Greater potential for visualization in marketing analysis.
3. The addition of powerful spatial analysis tools to the marketer's toolbox.
4. Enhanced communication capabilities in marketing reports and presentations.

Let's explore each of these capabilities briefly.

Spatial insight

In many cases the spatial dimension of marketing data provides additional insight and understanding to the marketer. Consider the following example of World Treasures, a fictional online store covered in chapter 6. Using a list of electronic newsletter subscribers from its online store, the organization has identified high concentrations of users by ZIP Code in the state of New York. The table below lists the number of subscribers by ZIP Code.

Record*	ZIP Code*	Subscribers
16	10021	300
239	11234	296
264	11375	294
364	11746	290
373	11758	290
240	11235	268
50	10314	252
316	11572	250
313	11566	246
215	11209	244
234	11229	238
18	10023	226
338	11710	216
305	11554	208
405	11803	208
63	10463	204
200	11040	196

This information is both relevant and actionable. By targeting these ZIP Codes in a direct mail campaign, the firm can increase its response rate. However, the table tells only part of the story. Consider the map on the next page that displays New York ZIP Codes and shows where the segments are located.

Target ZIP Codes for the World Treasures Direct Mail Campaign

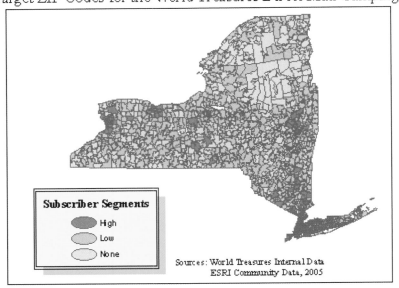

While the geographic concentration of attractive ZIP Codes cannot be seen in the table, it is obvious on the map. This insight would allow World Treasures to support its campaign with promotional techniques targeted at these concentrations.

Visualization

With some marketing decisions, spatial information does more than merely provide insight; it is a crucial component of the decision-making process. Consider the following situation from Meiers Home Furnishings, a fictional firm covered in chapter 4. To understand the competitive environment for its two stores, the firm has developed a list of furniture stores in the Chicago area. The table below is a sample of that data.

StoreID'	Store Type	Annual Sales
1	Independent	$2 Mil or Less
2	Natl Chain	$2 Mil or Less
3	Independent	$2 Mil or Less
4	Independent	$2 Mil or Less
5	Natl Chain	$2 Mil or Less
6	Independent	$2 Mil or Less
7	Loc/Regl Chain	$2 Mil or Less
8	Loc/Regl Chain	$2 Mil or Less
9	Independent	$2 Mil or Less
10	Independent	$2 Mil or Less
11	Natl Chain	$2 Mil or Less
12	Independent	$2 Mil or Less
13	Loc/Regl Chain	$2 Mil or Less
14	Independent	$2 Mil or Less
15	Independent	$2 Mil or Less

While the information in the table is important, its true significance is hard to assess without considering the spatial component. Which competing stores are closest and, therefore, present the greatest competition to the two stores? The following map provides that answer at a glance with its display of competitors relative to the Lombard Street and Pulaski Street stores' market areas. The map's visual representation makes the relevant information much clearer.

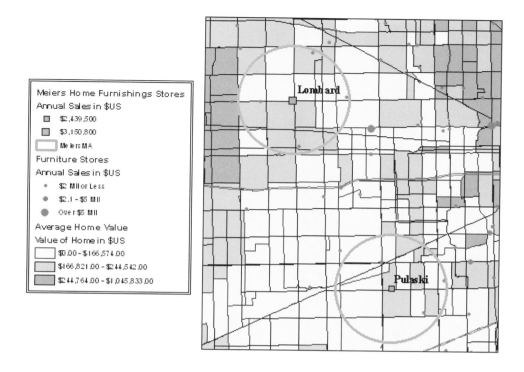

Spatial analysis

In some situations, the spatial dimension can be analyzed to derive valuable new information. Consider this example from Outdoor Living Inc., a fictional company covered in chapter 3. The firm's budget allows it to participate in four outdoor recreation shows in the Tampa, Florida area. The map below displays the stores that sponsor such shows and the geographic distribution of Outdoor Living's target families across the city. Assuming that outdoor shows will typically draw new prospects from a two-mile radius, the challenge is to identify the four shows that best provide that opportunity to high concentrations of the firm's targeted families. This problem is inherently spatial. Its solution requires the tools available in GIS.

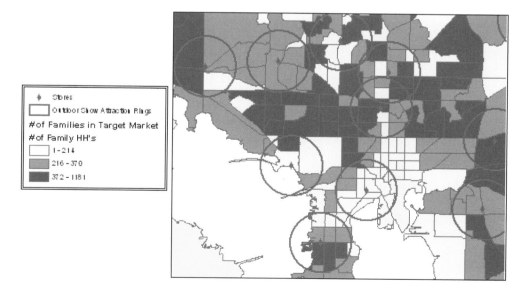

Communication

GIS tools can greatly enhance the communication value of marketing reports and presentations. This is an extension of the visualization value discussed above. Incorporating maps into marketing reports can effectively communicate the spatial dimension of marketing analyses. Maps, along with text, tables, and charts, allow researchers to more clearly communicate relationships and interactions within their studies.

Consider the following map from the Community Farm Alliance (CFA), covered in chapter 5. One of CFA's central goals is to increase the availability of locally produced foods to low-income consumers. When it targets grocery stores to carry its products, it must also consider the accessibility of these stores to low-income consumers. This map displays the ZIP Codes in Lexington, Kentucky with the highest percentages of families living below the poverty line (depicted in dark blue). The city's grocery stores are displayed with orange dots representing their size. The light blue dots are grocery stores that have been targeted by CFA and lie within the ZIP Codes with the highest levels of poverty. Listing these stores in a table does nothing to communicate their geographic distribution. However, the map instantly communicates where the grocery stores are located in the area of interest.

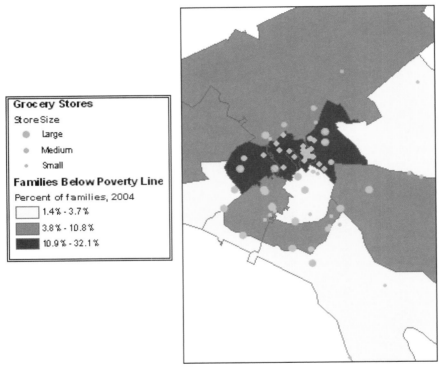

These are the major contributions of GIS tools to marketing analysis. You will gain firsthand experience with all of them as you progress through this book.

What will you learn in this book?

This book contains a series of chapters that illustrate GIS applications in marketing. Two of the chapters are general orientations: one to GIS software and the other to the Community Tapestry system, a lifestyle segmentation tool that is used extensively in developing marketing strategies. Each of the seven remaining chapters is related to a marketing class in your curriculum. As you complete them you will broaden your understanding of the subject matter of each class while you learn to use GIS tools in that dimension of the marketing field.

Chapter 1: Seeking and Evaluating Marketing Opportunities
An orientation to ArcMap

In this chapter, you will explore the basic tools, functions, and features of the ArcMap interface. You will use these tools as you help Silver and Stones, a Santa Fe jewelry store, understand its competitive environment and evaluate marketing opportunities.

You should complete this introductory chapter before you attempt any of the course-specific chapters. You may also wish to revisit this lesson as a refresher course between subsequent chapters.

Chapter 2: Working with Community Tapestry Data
An orientation to the lifestyle segmentation system

The Community Tapestry system is a lifestyle segmentation system that classifies U.S. residential areas into 65 neighborhood segments with distinct demographic and lifestyle characteristics. The Community Tapestry system is very useful for customer profiling and market targeting. In this chapter, you will use this system to help Silver and Stones, the same Santa Fe jewelry store you worked with in the introductory chapter, develop a direct marketing campaign to expand its customer base.

Because this chapter provides an introduction to the Community Tapestry system, you should complete it before starting chapters 4 or 5, as they require use of the Community Tapestry system as well.

Chapter 3: Developing a Targeted Promotional Campaign
Course: Principles of Marketing

Outdoor Living Inc., a manufacturer of recreational and camping equipment, has introduced a new product designed to appeal to families with little camping experience. The firm has defined its target market segment and must now tailor its promotional campaign to reach them. You will use GIS tools to focus three distinct components of that campaign on clusters of targeted families in Florida.

Chapter 4: Planning a Merchandising Strategy
Course: Consumer Behavior

Meiers Home Furnishings has a problem in its Chicago market. Its retail expansion to a second location has not met expectations, though the site for the second store was painstakingly selected based on the demographic similarity of its market area to that of the first store. Could the problem be differing lifestyle segments in the market areas of the two stores? You will use the Community Tapestry segmentation system to answer this question and to help match the merchandising strategy of each store to the lifestyle characteristics of its customers.

Chapter 5: Developing an Integrated Marketing Communication Program
Course: Promotional Management/Advertising/Integrated Marketing Communication

The Community Farm Alliance (CFA) is a nonprofit organization of Kentucky farmers. It wishes to convince Kentucky grocery stores and restaurants to offer locally produced food products and Kentucky consumers to buy them. CFA's initial target is Lexington, Kentucky. You will use GIS tools to design an integrated marketing communication program with both business-to-business and business-to-consumer components to achieve this goal.

Chapter 6: Prospect Profiling
Course: Marketing Research/eCommerce/Internet Marketing

World Treasures, Inc. is an online retailer specializing in traditional crafts and art objects produced by artisans around the world. It wishes to implement a direct catalog marketing program to customers who are interested in these products but unwilling to buy them online. It believes the best customer prospects for the new program are Web site users who have subscribed to the firm's electronic newsletter but never purchased items from the Web site. Using the state of New York as the test market, you will use GIS tools to profile this group of prospects and find concentrations of them in New York's ZIP Codes. Thus, World Treasures will be able to lower the cost of the strategy while increasing its response rate.

Chapter 7: International Market Assessment and Expansion
Course: International/Global Marketing Management
Personal Management Development (PMD) is a provider of multimedia, online managerial training programs. It specializes in preparing women with technical backgrounds to assume managerial positions in their organizations. The firm wishes to build upon its success in the United States by expanding into international markets. To do so, it must identify the country markets that offer the highest probability of success. In this international market assessment process, you will use GIS tools to screen country markets based on demographic and cultural characteristics to identify those that best match PMD's selection criteria.

Chapter 8: Retail Site Selection
Course: Retailing/Retail Management
Better Books is a book retailer with two stores in the San Francisco area. The firm wants to build on its success by opening a third store in the city. It is seeking a location that serves a customer base similar to that of its most successful store while minimizing the sales the new location will draw from the two existing stores. You will use GIS tools to help Better Books profile the characteristics of its current market areas and identify a third location that will meet the firm's objectives.

Chapter 9: Managing Sales Territories
Course: Personal Selling/Sales Management
Northwest's Best is a new wine distributor in the Portland, Oregon area. The firm has secured exclusive distribution rights in this area from a group of vineyards in Washington and Oregon. It will sell the wines of these vineyards to restaurants and liquor stores in the Portland region. To do so, it must design a sales territory system for its three-person sales force and develop systems for serving each territory efficiently. You will use GIS tools to recommend a sales territory system to the firm and to determine the optimal route for sales calls within the territories.

How will you learn?

Aside from chapters 1 and 2, which consist of introductory exercises, the other seven chapters are formal projects for designated fields of marketing. If you are using this book as a supplemental resource for several marketing classes, you will complete these projects when you take the related courses. They are not designed to be sequential. In other words, you will encounter them whenever you take the corresponding course in your academic schedule.

To facilitate learning in this type of environment, each chapter follows a common structure. In this way, you will be familiar with the structure whenever you encounter these projects in your academic career. This structure includes the following components, designed to help you understand the relevance of the chapter for your marketing class and the contribution GIS brings to that area of marketing.

Learning objectives
The learning objectives at the beginning of each chapter tell you exactly what you can expect to learn about using GIS in the context of a specific marketing application.

Marketing scenario

Each chapter is based on a detailed marketing scenario. These scenarios cover a range of organizations, geographic areas, and marketing problems. Each poses a common, real-world marketing situation and identifies the decisions or recommendations required in that situation. As you move through the project, you will use GIS tools to systematically construct an appropriate response to the central problem of the case.

Background information

This component relates the marketing scenario to the content of the relevant course. It identifies the course concepts embodied by the case and their relationship with GIS technology. Information about GIS data and processes may also be found here.

Data dictionary

Most chapters include a data dictionary table, which provides descriptive information about the data you will use in the exercises.

Exercises

In each chapter, you will perform step-by-step exercises using ArcGIS software. Each exercise provides detailed instructions for performing relevant GIS analysis, and contains result graphics periodically so you can make sure you're on the right track. As you progress through each exercise, you will not only become more familiar with GIS, but you will also develop a solution for the problem presented in the marketing scenario.

Additional applications

The GIS exercises incorporated into these chapters are designed to help you learn the basic skills relevant to a particular type of analysis. In each area, however, the capabilities of GIS go well beyond these basic skills. This section of each chapter will provide a greater appreciation of those capabilities by describing specialized applications in the field as well as specific examples of organizations that have implemented unique GIS solutions to their advantage. Thus, this section will give you a more complete sense of the potential role of GIS in the field of marketing being discussed in the chapter.

Project report

Chapters 3 through 9 are accompanied by a digital project report template in the form of a Microsoft Word document that will help you prepare your final project report.

The report template document contains the chapter's exercise titles as well as the report questions associated with that exercise. As you complete each exercise, you may record your answers to these questions in the body of the template, thus building your project report as you proceed. In addition, each chapter requires you to design one or more exhibits, which may be a map, graph, or table. The report template tells you where and how to insert these exhibits.

As you proceed through the chapter, your report will take shape as you record your answers and insert required exhibits. This allows you to complete assigned exercises and prepare the report concurrently. As you work through several chapters, you will become quite adept at the process. This will allow you to concentrate your attention on the GIS skills you are learning and report your results clearly and efficiently.

How will you encounter GIS in your career?

Organizations are increasingly recognizing the value of GIS throughout their operations. As a result, they are developing enterprise-level solutions that integrate GIS tools within their information infrastructures. As these technologies develop, GIS applications will become more integrated and widely distributed, but they will also be disaggregated. That is, select components, tools, or applications will be extracted from comprehensive GIS systems, integrated with other information technology tools in the enterprise suite, and distributed across the enterprise using application servers or, in many cases, the Web.

As a result, when you encounter GIS applications in your organization they might be in one or more of several forms. The most common are described below. The chapters in this book will help you recognize and use GIS tools in whatever form you find them.

Desktop or networked GIS systems

If you use this book with the included software installed on a home computer, you will be using ArcGIS as a stand-alone product in a desktop environment. If you work in a computer lab, you may be using a network installation of the same product, depending on the configuration and procedures at your institution.

This may also be the configuration you use when you encounter GIS software in your career. This would be the case in firms that have licensed the ArcGIS product either as a standard component of their organization's software load, or as a network tool that can be accessed on demand by users on the organization's network. Either way, the interface, functions, and features of the system will closely resemble those taught in this book.

Specialized GIS applications based on the ArcGIS framework

You may encounter the GIS tools you work with here in the context of specialized software packages within your organization. The most common applications for these packages are market area analysis, site selection, real estate marketing, sales territory management, facilities management, and routing applications. Business partners of GIS software companies developed many of these systems, which are built upon the standard software platforms of those companies. ESRI, for example, has several hundred business partners, many of whom build specialized applications as extensions of ArcGIS. Their users encounter the familiar ArcGIS interface, but have access to the specialized tools provided in the business partner's system. In these systems the basic interface and toolset you use in this book will be augmented with functions and processes designed by the business partner to produce the specialized application. Several chapters reference these specialized systems in their additional applications and resources section.

Integrated into enterprise information systems

This configuration can take two forms. In the first, users of desktop or networked GIS systems use standard tools to access data stored in enterprise databases and information systems. For example, the ESRI ArcSDE server product provides multiple GIS users with direct access to very large relational databases containing shareable data, thereby facilitating the application of GIS analysis to a wide array of enterprise data. The World Treasures scenario presented in chapter 6 simulates this type of integration with the electronic newsletter subscriber database imported from the firm's Web server.

In the second type of configuration, you might encounter GIS tools integrated into your organization's proprietary information systems. From a developer's perspective, GIS systems are comprehensive collections of objects, or discrete chunks of programming code that perform specific tasks. In addition to integrated packages, GIS software firms also license direct access to these GIS objects. Developers within other organizations can then selectively use the objects they need within their own applications. For example, the ESRI MapObjects system is a collection of GIS and mapping objects that developers can selectively embed in their applications to extend their spatial capabilities.

You might also encounter GIS applications in Web-based services that you access with a browser. For example, ArcGIS Server is a Web-based GIS that allows firms to distribute GIS functionality to both internal and external users with Internet access. Therefore, a proprietary system for customer analysis within your organization may well include some of the GIS tools used in this book even though the full ArcGIS package is not available to you.

On-demand, Web-based applications

In this alternative, the user organization does not host the GIS tools, functions, and data, but rather obtains them on GIS software companies' servers. In this configuration, firms contract for access to services hosted by GIS suppliers and integrate these tools into their own applications. In this scenario your encounter with GIS tools might occur in one of two ways.

In the first, you would directly access GIS software that has been configured for on-demand, Web-based access. For example, the ESRI Business Analyst system is not only a desktop extension; it is also available as Business Analyst Online. This is a cost-effective option for firms whose need for Business Analyst capabilities is intermittent.

In the second, your organization would access Web-based GIS tools and data for use in its own applications. ESRI ArcWeb Services offers this capability by hosting both GIS applications and datasets. When client organizations develop their Web site, they access ArcWeb Services for GIS components. This arrangement frees clients from the time and expense of maintaining large datasets and updated software. If these services are deployed in your firm's intranet, they would be incorporated into the information technology tools available to you. If they are deployed through your organization's Internet presence, they would be available to customers, suppliers, and the general public.

Off we go

Now you have a better idea of the purpose and structure of this book. You have a broad understanding of the types of GIS skills you will learn and how they can enhance decision making in various fields of marketing. You also know the various contexts in which you might work with GIS tools throughout your career.

You're ready. Let's get started.

CHAPTER 1

Seeking and Evaluating Marketing Opportunities

An orientation to ArcMap

In this chapter you will use ArcGIS software (specifically the ArcMap application) to explore the business environment and evaluate two potential growth strategies for Silver and Stones*, a jewelry retailer in Santa Fe, New Mexico. In so doing, you will learn how to use the ArcMap graphical user interface of menus, buttons, and tools to perform GIS operations.

* This is a fictional company and scenario, created for educational purposes only. Any resemblance to actual persons, events, or corporations is unintended.

Learning objectives

In the following marketing opportunity analysis exercises, you will use ArcGIS to:

1. Display demographic characteristics of a geographic region on a map
2. Display competitors and their characteristics on a map
3. Identify attractive customer prospects for a sales promotion program
4. Query a database to identify potential business partners

Marketing scenario

Silver and Stones, Inc., is a jewelry store in Santa Fe, New Mexico. The firm specializes in original pieces of jewelry crafted from silver and gemstones by Southwest Native American artisans as well as contemporary local silversmiths. Each piece is unique and comes with a certificate of originality and authenticity signed by the artisan who crafted it.

Silver and Stones's primary market is tourists in the four-season Santa Fe recreational area. The store is located near a busy tourist shopping area. This shopping area includes several other jewelry stores and souvenir shops. Owners Bill and Belle Buell wish to distinguish Silver and Stones from competitive stores with unique pieces that offer tourists distinctive mementos of their Santa Fe experience, and they have been successful with this approach. Though Silver and Stones's jewelry is priced higher than jewelry in local competing stores, many tourists return to the store each time they vacation in the area and some have become regular customers. Indeed, the Buells maintain a mailing list of these customers and send them offers with a quarterly newsletter. Though this is the firm's largest block of customers, the Buells wish to expand this market further. Chapter 2 involves a direct marketing program aimed at these customers and similar prospects. However, the firm also wishes to increase efforts to attract additional Santa Fe tourists. Specifically, the Buells wish to focus on tourists staying at local bed and breakfast (B&B) establishments. This objective is based on research indicating that B&B patrons tend to spend more on vacation and to seek out unique souvenir items more than tourists who stay at hotels or resorts.

In addition to tourists, about a third of Silver and Stones customers are local Santa Fe residents, many of whom are collectors of the unique pieces the store offers. The Buells want to increase sales to these prospects through in-store sales or, alternatively, with sales booths at the annual Santa Fe Film Festival in December and the Southwestern Association for Indian Art's Indian Market each August. They wish to analyze geographic concentrations of local jewelry buyers to determine the appropriate approach to this market.

Background information

A core function of any business is the unending search for marketing opportunities that the firm can exploit profitably. Environmental scanning and opportunity analysis are fundamental components of the planning process that supports these efforts. These are the tools firms use to monitor their environments for opportunities and evaluate alternative strategies for exploiting them. In this chapter, you will perform these functions for Silver and Stones. As you do, you will also be getting familiar with the ArcGIS product, specifically, the ArcMap application.

ArcMap is an indispensable software application for assessing the spatial dimension during environmental scanning and opportunity analysis. You will use ArcMap to display Silver and Stones's marketing environment and to help assess two potential strategies for increasing sales. Though you will not complete a formal report as required by chapters 3 through 9, you will make recommendations relative to these growth strategies.

This introductory chapter should be completed before you proceed to any of the other chapters. In addition, you may use it as a review tool should you need a software refresher lesson in between the other chapters.

Data dictionary

Silver and Stones Santa Fe data dictionary	
Attribute	**Description**
For CensusTracts	
TOTPOP_CY	Total population, 2004
JewelryHH	Average jewelry purchased by household, 2004
DOMTAP	Dominant Community Tapestry segment, 2004
For Competitors (Hypothetical)	
Type	Jewelry store or souvenir shop
Ownership	Independent, local chain, or national chain
SalesLevel	Approximate annual sales range
For BedAndBreakfasts (Hypothetical)	
Rooms	Number of guest rooms available
For SFStreets	
Name	Street name
Source: ESRI Business Information Solutions, 2005	

Exercise 1.1 Environmental scanning

For retailers like Silver and Stones, the spatial component of environmental scanning is very important. Concentrations of potential customers, whether they are local residents or tourists visiting the area, constitute significant opportunities. Larger retailers in the vicinity can draw retail traffic, but direct competitors in the area pose potential threats. ArcGIS is a valuable tool in assessing these factors. Thus, in this exercise, you will:

- Display the geographic distribution of Santa Fe's population and jewelry purchases
- Display the location of the city's souvenir shops, competing jewelry stores, and bed and breakfast inns
- Assess the competitive environment in the vicinity of Silver and Stones's store

Open an existing map

1   **To launch ArcMap, from the Windows taskbar, click Start > All Programs > ArcGIS > ArcMap.**

Depending on how the software has been installed or which Windows operating system you are using, there may be a slightly different navigation menu from which to open ArcMap.

2   **If you see a start dialog box, click the "An existing map" option. Otherwise, click the Open button on the ArcMap Standard toolbar.**

3   **Browse to the location of the GISMKT folder (e.g., C:\ESRIPress\GISMKT), double-click the SilverStonesSF folder, then click the SilverStonesSF1 map document to select it.**

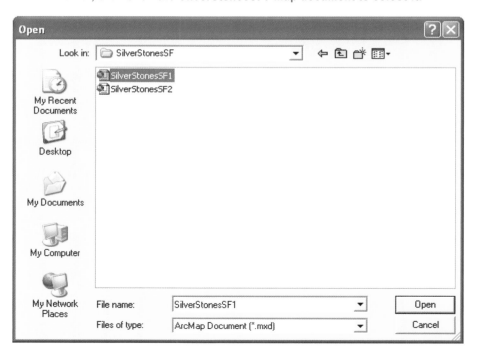

4   **Click Open.**

This is a map of the Santa Fe metropolitan area.

Standard toolbar

Tools toolbar

Table of contents

Display area

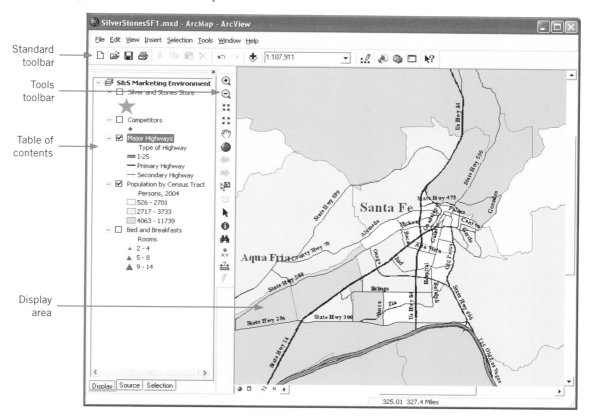

Display map layers

A digital map is composed of layers. You can see the layers listed in the table of contents on the left side of the window. The table of contents contains five layers in all. Each one contains features (points, lines, and polygons) that can be displayed in the map display area. Notice the check boxes next to the layer names in the table of contents. When the box is checked, the layer is visible in the display area. Currently only two layers are visible in the map. One of those layers represents Santa Fe metropolitan area census tracts. Each tract is drawn in a different color depending on its population. A layer of the area's major highways is also turned on. You can turn any of the layers on and off in the table of contents by clicking their check boxes.

Turn layers off and on

1   Click the check box next to the Silver and Stones Store layer to turn it on (a check mark appears in the check box).

The store appears on the map as a purple star.

2   Now turn on the Competitors and Bed and Breakfasts layers.

The Competitors layer appears as dots on the map. The Bed and Breakfasts layer, however, does not appear even though the layer has been turned on. This is because the Population by Census Tract layer is covering the points of the Bed and Breakfasts layer.

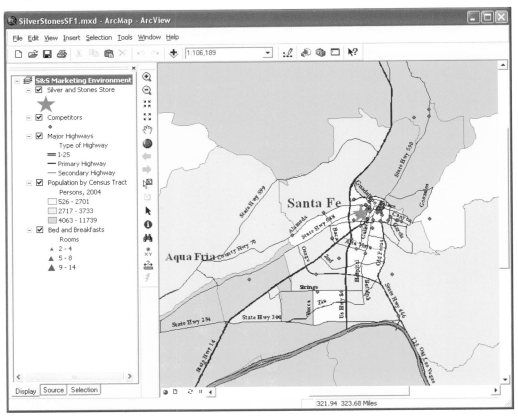

ArcMap displays layers from the bottom of the table of contents to the top. Layers on the bottom draw first, and the top layer draws last. In this case, the Population by Census Tract layer, composed of big blocks of color, obscures the points of the Bed and Breakfasts layer.

You can easily change the order of layers in the table of contents.

Change the display order of layers

1 In the table of contents, click Bed and Breakfasts and hold down the mouse button. Drag the Bed and Breakfasts layer to a position above the Population by Census Tract layer, then release the mouse button.

You are now able to see the Bed and Breakfasts layer.

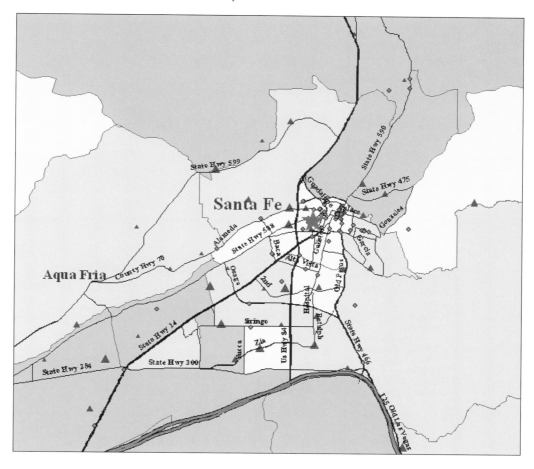

Note that the triangle symbols representing the bed and breakfasts are sized according to the number of rooms, while the Competitors features are all represented by a single green dot. In the next step you will learn how to alter the Competitors symbols to make the map more informative.

Change the appearance of features

Competitors of Silver and Stones are represented by one symbol. However, there are two types of competitors included in the layer—jewelry stores and souvenir shops. This difference is significant to the Buells. While jewelry stores can be direct competitors, souvenir shops are a bit different. Though they sell some jewelry, the quality does not match that offered by the jewelry stores. Thus, tourists will often be attracted to the idea of jewelry in a souvenir shop, but decide to purchase higher quality items at a jewelry store. In addition, souvenir shops tend to draw tourist traffic to an area, which benefits all the other nearby retailers.

For these reasons, you will change the display of the Competitors layer so that the jewelry stores get one symbol and souvenir shops get another.

Change a layer's symbology

1   In the table of contents, double-click Competitors (or right-click the layer and select Properties). The Layer Properties dialog box opens.

2   Click the Symbology tab. In the Show area, click Categories, then click Unique values.

3   Under Value Field, make sure Type is chosen. If it's not, click the drop-down arrow and choose Type from the list.

4   Click the Add All Values button to display all the values for the Type attribute. Then uncheck the box next to <all other values>.

Your dialog box should match the one below, except you may see different colors since ArcMap assigns random default colors.

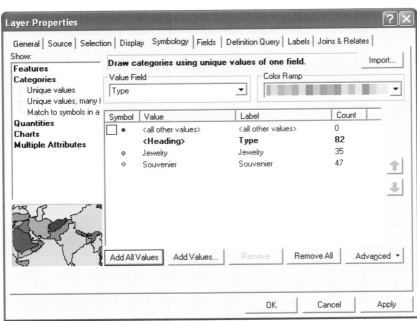

The two categories of competitors each now have a different point symbol. The points are very small and may be difficult to discern on the map, so you will give them more appropriate symbols.

5 Double-click the small circle to the left of the Jewelry heading to display the Symbol Selector dialog box.

6 Click the Circle 1 symbol to select it. In the drop-down box for Color, select Poinsettia Red as the symbol color (or some other shade of red you like). For the Size setting, use the arrows to set the number to 8.00.

7 When your dialog box matches the graphic below, click OK to apply these settings and close the Symbol Selector dialog box.

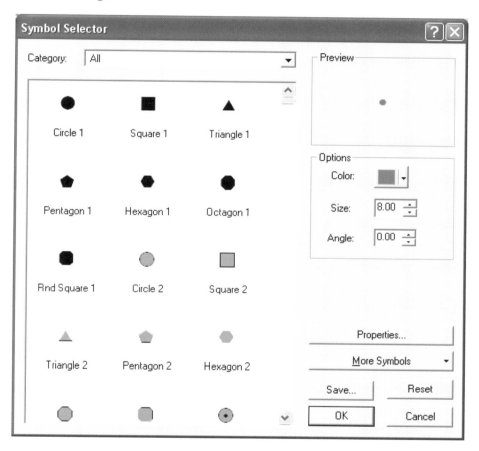

8 Now double-click the Souvenir symbol and change it to: Square 1, Electron Gold (or another orange), size 8. Click OK.

9 Click OK to close the Layer Properties and update the Competitors layer with these two new symbols.

The map now displays jewelry and souvenir shop competitors in circles and squares, providing more information about the competitive environment.

Add and display a new layer

The map now displays most of the information you desire for Silver and Stones, its competitors, and area B&Bs. The underlying demographic layer presents data on population by census tracts. Though this information is useful, the same dataset has other attributes that are more relevant. The data dictionary reveals that the same census dataset contains an attribute reporting purchases of jewelry by household per census tract. This attribute is much more relevant to Silver and Stones. You will add another layer and symbolize it to display jewelry sales on the map.

Add a new layer

1   **Click the Add Data button.** ✦

2   **In the Add Data dialog box, navigate to the \GISMKT\SilverStonesSF folder and double-click the SilverStonesSF.mdb geodatabase to open it and view its contents.**

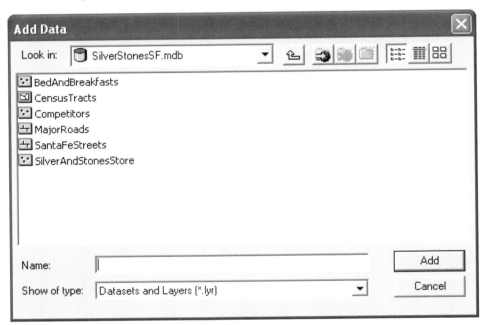

A geodatabase is simply a Microsoft Access format file that contains geographic data as well as tabular data. A geodatabase then is filled with tables. However, some of the tables have a geographic field. This field is sometimes called the Shape field or the Geometry field. It contains the geometric description of the points, lines, or polygons that can be drawn on a map in ArcMap. If a table contains a Shape field, that table is called a feature class.

Any feature class in a geodatabase becomes a layer when added to a map. Now that you have the geodatabase open you can see that it contains six feature classes. You can tell they are feature classes because the icon to their left represents either some points, lines, or polygons. BedAndBreakfasts, Competitors, and SilverAndStonesStore are point feature classes. MajorRoads and SantaFeStreets are line feature classes. And CensusTracts is a polygon feature class.

You are going to add the CensusTracts feature class to the map next.

3   Click the **CensusTracts** feature class, then click Add to add the layer to the map.

You see the new layer, but every one of the census tract polygons is symbolized with a single random color. You will change the layer's symbology so that each census tract draws in a color that represents its jewelry purchase information.

Change a layer's symbology

1   Double-click the CensusTracts layer to open its Layer Properties dialog box.

2   Click the General tab and for Layer Name enter **Jewelry Purchases**.

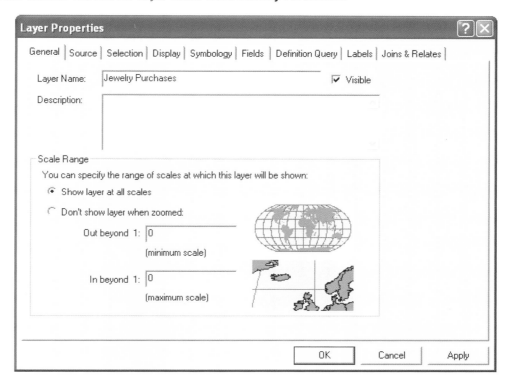

3   Click the Symbology tab. In the Show area, click Quantities, and then under Quantities click Graduated colors.

4   In the Fields area, click the drop-down arrow next to Value and select the JewelryHH field, which contains the values for average jewelry purchases by household in each census tract.

5   Click the drop-down arrow next to Color Ramp; scroll through the options and choose a light green to dark green color ramp.

The census tracts layer now has five ranges of numbers, called classes, and each class has a different colored symbol. The darker the symbol color the higher the level of household purchases of jewelry.

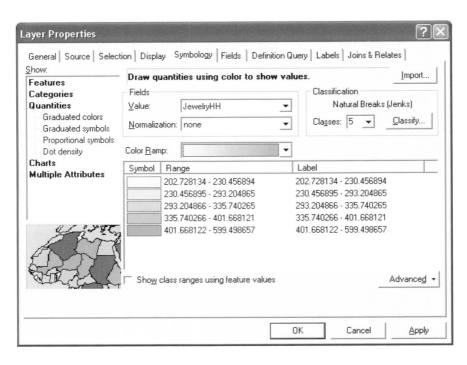

The more classes there are the harder it can be to understand the map. So you will change the number of classes from five to three. That way the layer will show High, Medium, and Low spending areas, making the information easier to understand.

6 **In the Layer Properties dialog box, click the Classify button to display the Classification dialog box.**

7 **For Method, click the drop-down arrow and select Quantile.**

8 **For Classes, select 3.**

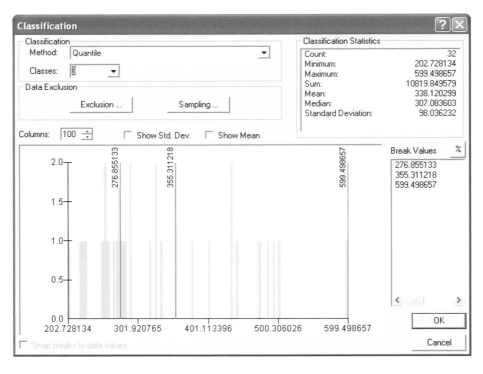

With these settings, you have specified that this layer will display in three classes based on household jewelry purchases by census tract. The quantile method means that each class will contain roughly the same number of census tracts. There are thirty-two tracts, so there will be ten or eleven in each of the three classes. This classification scheme is similar to that of the population layer.

9   Click OK to return to the Label Properties dialog box.

You will now adjust the classification labels for the layer's legend.

10   Under the Color Ramp area you see three column headings: Symbol, Range, and Label. You can click on any of these to change some properties. You want to change the format of the labels, so click the Label heading, then click Format Labels to open the Number Format dialog box. (Note: Do not click the Labels tab at the top of the Layer Properties dialog box. If you do so inadvertently, click the Symbology tab to return.)

11   In the Category area, click Currency.

12   Click OK to return to the Layer Properties dialog box.

13   At the bottom of the Layer Properties dialog box, check the box next to "Show class ranges using feature values."

The values in the Range column change and now show actual values from the JewelryHH field in the CensusTracts attribute table. The gaps between the highest values in one class and the lowest values in the next class indicate that no features have values for this attribute in that range.

14 Click **OK** to close the Layer Properties dialog box and to display the layer's revised settings in the map.

15 Turn off the Population by Census Tract layer.

Edit legend title

1 In the table of contents, click the attribute name JewelryHH under the Jewelry Purchases layer. After the name is selected, click it again to make the name editable. (Note: If your second click is too quick, the Properties dialog box will open. Click Cancel, then try again, clicking more slowly to reach the edit function.)

2 Replace JewelryHH with **$US per HH, 2004**. Press the Enter key to complete the name change.

The resulting map displays the average household jewelry purchases per census tract, jewelry stores and souvenir shops, and B&B locations with triangles sized per number of available rooms.

The map now contains all the information you require to complete your analysis. However, its current scale makes it difficult to see the detail of Silver and Stones's competitive environment. You will use the ArcMap navigation tools to alter the extent of the display area.

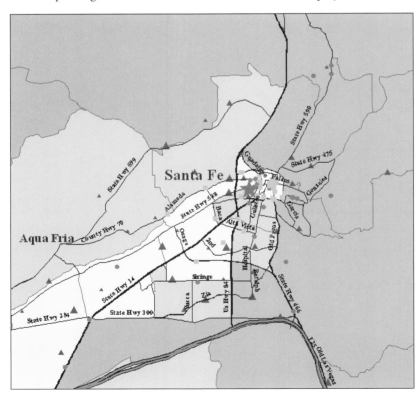

Explore the map

Use the fixed zoom buttons

ArcMap offers several ways to zoom in and out on a map. You will use them as you explore Silver and Stones's competitive environment.

1   Locate the Fixed Zoom In and Fixed Zoom Out buttons on the Tools toolbar. This toolbar may be docked at the side or top of your screen, or in between the table of contents and map display area.

2   Click the Fixed Zoom In button three times.

With each click the display zooms in on the center of the map. Repeated clicks will continue zooming in.

3   To reverse this process, click the Fixed Zoom Out button. Repeat until you reach the scale you desire.

Use the standard zoom tools

The Zoom In and Zoom Out tools allow you to focus on precisely the area of the map you wish. You will use them to view the area immediately surrounding the Silver and Stones store.

1   Locate the Zoom In and Zoom Out tools on the Tools toolbar.

2   Click the Zoom In tool to select it. In the map display area click and drag to draw a rectangle around the purple star. When the rectangle contains the area you wish to see, release the mouse button.

The map zooms in on the Silver and Stones store. You can now see the store's nearest competitors (Note: Your map will not be identical to the one in the graphic below, but it will reflect the rectangle you defined with the tool.)

You will set a bookmark here so you can return to this view later in the chapter.

3   From the main menu bar, click View, then point to Bookmarks, then click Create. In the Spatial Bookmark window, replace Bookmark 1 with **SS Store**, then click OK.

4   Click the Zoom Out tool to select it. Click and drag the tool in the map and release it. The map zooms out to a wider display.

Zoom to a specific layer

ArcMap also allows you to perform zoom operations directly on layers in the table of contents. This allows you to observe the geographic extent of any single layer.

1   In the table of contents, right-click the Silver and Stones Store layer, then click Zoom to Layer.

The map zooms to this layer. As there is only one feature in the layer, the map now shows the immediate vicinity of this store in detail.

2   Repeat this operation with the Bed and Breakfasts layer.

As this layer contains several features distributed around the Santa Fe area, the map now shows a greater portion of the area.

Move between extents you have viewed

As you use these tools to zoom in and out on the map, you are changing the extent (the visible geographic area) of the map. ArcMap records these changes and allows you to navigate between them using the Next and Previous Extent buttons.

1   Locate the Previous Extent ⬅ and Next Extent ➡ buttons on the Tools toolbar. (Note: The Next Extent button will be grayed out until you employ the Previous Extent button.)

2   Click these buttons as you wish to move back and forth between the map extents you have viewed.

3   Click the Full Extent button 🌐 to zoom all the way out to see every layer. You may use this button at any time to return directly to the full extent of the map.

Zoom quickly with the mouse scroll wheel

1   Click anywhere on the map, then roll the scroll wheel of your mouse to zoom in and out.

Try more navigation tools

When exploring a map with the zoom operations, you may wish to move between different portions of the map. The Pan tool and Overview window can help.

1 **Zoom to the Silver and Stones Store layer.**

You will use a pan operation to view adjacent map areas.

2 **Click the Pan tool ✋ to select it. In the map display area, click and hold a point on the map, then drag the Pan tool in any direction to pan the map.**

3 **Zoom to the extent of the Bed and Breakfasts layer.**

As you move around the map, it is difficult to see the relationship between the zoomed extent you are seeing and the overall map. The Overview window allows you to pan around the map while retaining the full extent perspective.

4 **From the main menu bar, click Window > Overview.**

The Overview window appears. In it, the current extent of the map is depicted with a red rectangle with red hatch marks on top of a small rendition of the full extent of the map. The rectangle indicates the area that you are zoomed in on. You can change the map display by moving into the Overview and clicking and dragging the red rectangle or by resizing it.

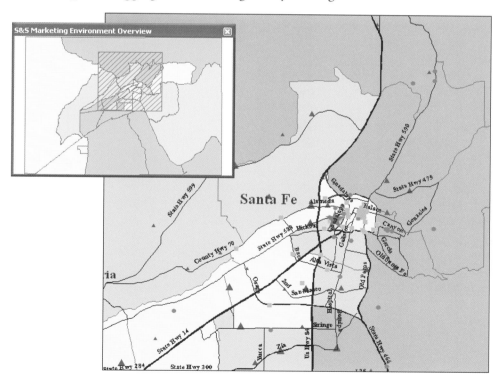

5 **Using the Overview window, explore various areas of the map. Close the window when you are finished.**

While viewing one portion of the map, you may want to explore other areas without zooming the entire map. The Magnifier window provides this capacity.

6   From the main menu bar, click Window > Magnifier.

The Magnification window opens. Look to the immediate east of the Silver and Stones store. You will see a cluster of competitors that are difficult to distinguish. You will use the Magnifier window to zoom in on them further.

7   Click and hold the left mouse button in the blue border at the top of the Magnifier window. A set of crosshairs appears in the center of the window. Drag the window until this targeting device covers the area of the map that contains a concentration of competitors, then release the mouse button.

The target area now appears in the Magnifier window at the level of magnification indicated. You may use it to explore smaller regions of the map in more detail as you examine Silver and Stones's competitors. Leave this window open for the next step.

Identify features and measure distances

While several souvenir stores are near Silver and Stones, only one of them has annual sales of over $1 million. This level of volume will produce tourist traffic for Silver and Stones, so you wish to identify it and determine its distance from the store. You will use the Identify and Measure tools to perform these tasks.

1   The map view should be zoomed to the area surrounding Silver and Stones store and the Magnifier window should be open (you can move it to the edge of the map for easier viewing). If this is not the case, from the main menu click View > Bookmarks, then click the SS Store bookmark you created earlier.

2   Click the Identify tool 🛈 on the Tools toolbar. The Identify window opens.

3   Move the tool over the map display area to see the Identify icon. Position the cursor over a competitor's location and click it.

The Identify window now displays all the attributes of the competitor that you clicked.

4   Position the Magnifier window over a concentration of competitors. You can click on a competitor with the Identify tool in either the map display area or in the Magnifier window. Click on a few competitors in either place to see their attributes.

5   Now use the Identify tool to display the attributes of some souvenir shops near Silver and Stones until you find the one with a sales level of $1 million or more. Use the Magnifier window if you wish. Note the location of this store. Close the Identify and Magnifier windows.

You will use the Measure tool to determine the distance from the high-dollar souvenir shop to Silver and Stones.

6   Zoom in on the map so you can see both Silver and Stones and the high-dollar souvenir shop. Click the Measure tool ⟷ on the Tools toolbar.

7   With the Measure tool active, click the Silver and Stones point, and then click the souvenir shop.

The Measure tool creates a line between the two locations. The distance is reported in the Measure dialog box.

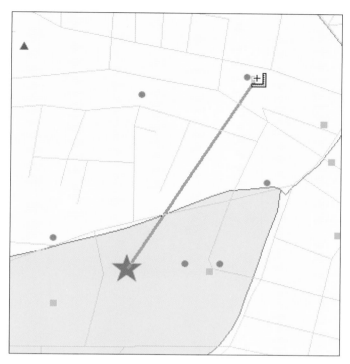

This is the straight line distance between the two points. Tourists traveling between these sites, however, would most likely walk or drive along the city streets. Because the map currently contains only a layer of major highways (not all streets), you could approximate this distance by tracing the likely path tourists will follow. Instead you will add a layer of city streets and then trace a path over those streets.

8   Close the Measure dialog box.

9   Click the Add Data button.

10   In the Add Data dialog box, navigate to \GISMKT\SilverStonesSF\SilverStonesSF.mdb to open it.

11   Click the SantaFeStreets feature class and then click Add to add the layer to the map.

Whenever you add a new layer to a map, it's assigned a random color. So you will change the color of the streets to a gray color.

12   In the table of contents, right-click the line symbol under SantaFeStreets. In the color palette, choose Gray 30%.

13   Turn off the Major Highways layer to make the map appear less cluttered.

Now that you have the local city streets, you can make a more appropriate measure of the distance between the two stores.

14 Position the cursor over Silver and Stones and click. Move to the nearest street and click again. Follow the local city streets, clicking at each intersection where you want to make a turn. Try to create the shortest path to the large souvenir store. If at any time you make a mistake, or just want to try to create a shorter path, simply double-click the map to clear the tool and then start another path. For the last segment, position the cursor over the souvenir store and click a final time.

The path you created should resemble the one below.

Note that, in this case, the segment and total lengths are different. The segment value reports the length of the last segment in the path you traced. The total value is the total distance from one store to the other. Not surprisingly, it is a bit longer than the direct path between the two stores.

15 Double-click to terminate the measure operation. Close the Measure dialog box.

16 Click the Select Elements tool ⬉ to return to the default pointer.

17 You may use the navigation tools as you wish to complete your exploration of Silver and Stones's environment. When you are finished, click the Full Extent button to return to the full extent of all layers in the map.

Save the map document

You have completed this exercise.

1 Save your map file as SilverStonesSF1_fl.mxd (replace f and l with your first and last initials). To do so, from the main menu bar click File > Save As. Navigate to your **\GISMKT\SilverStonesSF** folder, type **SilverStonesSF1_fl** as the file name, and click Save.

Exercise 1.2   Opportunity analysis

As you have seen, GIS is an important environmental scanning tool, adding spatial insight to a firm's understanding of its business situation. GIS has an equally important role in opportunity analysis, the evaluation of alternative marketing strategies for feasibility and profitability. Both integrate traditional business data with the spatial capabilities of GIS. Initially, they allow marketers to extend traditional data analysis to include a spatial dimension. More significantly, they facilitate analyses in which the spatial component is the key factor in a marketing decision. You will use both these approaches as you evaluate marketing opportunities for Silver and Stones. Specifically, in this exercise, you will:

- Display the geographic distribution of household jewelry purchases in the Santa Fe area and evaluate two alternative strategies for reaching local households with high purchase levels
- Display the geographic distribution and size of bed and breakfast inns near the Silver and Stones store and assess the feasibility of serving the tourists who stay at these inns with a shuttle bus service

Open an existing map

1   In ArcMap, click File > Open. Browse to the location of the GISMKT folder (e.g., **C:\ESRIPress\ GISMKT**), double-click the **SilverStonesSF** folder, then double-click **SilverStonesSF2.mxd**.

In this map document, the table of contents includes six layers, four of which are turned on. The map displays jewelry purchases by census tract in the Santa Fe area, Silver and Stones, the competitors, and the bed and breakfasts. The highways and population layers are turned off.

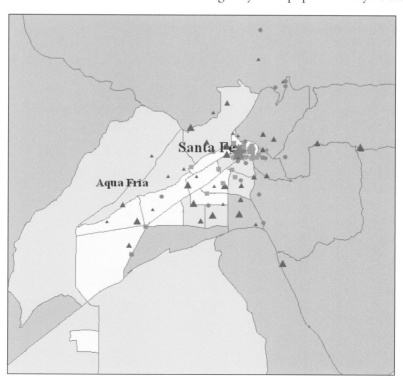

Evaluate strategies to increase customer base

Your first task will be to evaluate a proposal to increase the number of customers in the Santa Fe area. The Buells are considering the following two approaches.

Strategy 1 would concentrate on traditional promotional efforts in the community surrounding Silver and Stones. Advertising would feature specially priced items and invite prospects to visit the store to purchase them. This strategy is appropriate if most attractive prospects live in the vicinity of Silver and Stones.

Strategy 2 would concentrate on attracting new customers through sales booths at community events such as the Santa Fe Film Festival and the Southwestern Association for Indian Art's Indian Market. The Buells would mail flyers to prospective customers throughout the Santa Fe area offering a 10 percent discount for purchases at the Silver and Stones booth. The hope is that prospects would seek out the booth and develop an interest in the firm's products, which they might then purchase at the booth or in the store. This strategy is appropriate if attractive prospects live beyond the immediate vicinity of the store.

As you can see, the choice between these strategies depends upon the geographic distribution of the most attractive prospects. You will use ArcMap to analyze that distribution and recommend a strategy.

Select features by attributes

The Buells consider their most attractive prospects to be households that purchase a lot of jewelry. The current map displays the average annual purchases of jewelry per household in Santa Fe's census tracts. Notice that the top classification, which contains one third of these census tracts, begins with a value of about $380. To target the households with the highest levels of jewelry purchases, the Buells wish to use a higher threshold: specifically, $400 per year. You will use the ArcMap Select by Attributes operation to select census tracts with this level of spending.

1   Right-click the Jewelry Purchases layer and click Open Attribute Table to display the attribute table for the layer.

The attribute table contains demographic data for Santa Fe's census tracts. Because it is a table, you may perform standard queries against it to select records of interest. In this case, you wish to select census tracts with JewelryHH attribute values of 400 or higher.

2   In the table, scroll to the right if necessary to find the JewelryHH attribute.

3   Click the Options button, then Select by Attributes. (Note: If you can't see the Options button, expand the attribute table.)

The Select by Attributes dialog box opens. You will build a query for selecting the appropriate census tracts. The query will appear in the white box near the bottom of the dialog box.

4   In the area displaying the layer's attributes, scroll through the list and double-click [JewelryHH] to start the query.

5   Click the greater than operator (>) to add it to the query.

6   Position the cursor just to the right of the > sign in the query box, and type **400**.

The query should read [**JewelryHH**] > **400** and the dialog box should match the graphic below.

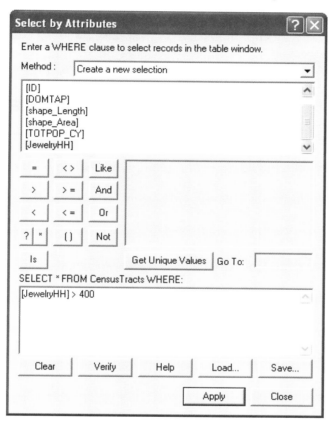

7   Click Apply, then click Close to run the query and close the dialog box.

Examine the effects of this operation on the attribute table and map. In the table, the selected records are highlighted. The number of selected records is reported at the bottom of the table. On the map, the corresponding features are also highlighted. With this simple query, you have determined which and how many census tracts are the most attractive, and even more significantly, where they are located relative to Silver and Stones.

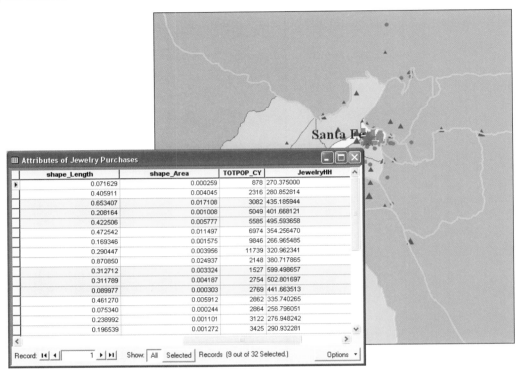

You have the information you need to make your recommendation. Do so by answering these questions. (Move the attribute table so it doesn't obscure the map if you need to.)

 Are the most attractive prospective customers located in the immediate vicinity of the Silver and Stones store? Based on this conclusion, which strategy do you recommend to the Buells?

8 To unselect the census tracts in the attribute table and on the map, from the main menu bar, click Selection, then click Clear Selected Features.

9 Close the attribute table.

You have completed your analysis of this marketing opportunity.

Evaluate the B&B shuttle proposal

You will evaluate the second strategy, designed to increase sales to tourists. Based on market research data, the Buells are considering a plan to target guests at bed and breakfast inns in the Santa Fe area. The program would include displays of Silver and Stones's items in each inn and a free shuttle service offering guests transportation to the store and back. The objectives of the program are to increase in-store sales and to expand the firm's database of tourist customers who also purchase by mail.

The Buells have imposed some constraints on the initial trial of the shuttle program. To cover additional personnel and transportation costs, the program must service a minimum of 80 guest rooms in all. However, to efficiently serve customers, the program should include no more than 25 inns, all of which should be within a two-mile radius of Silver and Stones.

Your task is to determine the feasibility of the bed and breakfast shuttle proposal given these constraints.

Select features spatially

Your first step is to identify the bed and breakfast inns within the requisite two miles of Silver and Stones. To do so, you will perform a spatial selection.

1   Turn off the Competitors layer and zoom in to the area around Silver and Stones.

2   On the main menu, click Selection, then click Select by Location.

3   In the Select by Location dialog box, confirm that the first option is set to "select features from."

4   For the second option, click the check box next to Bed and Breakfasts.

5   For the next drop-down, choose "are within a distance of."

6   Select the Silver and Stones Store for the next option.

7   Confirm that the Apply a buffer option is checked, enter a value of **2** for the buffer distance, and select Miles as the buffer unit.

The Select by Location dialog box should look like the first graphic on the next page.

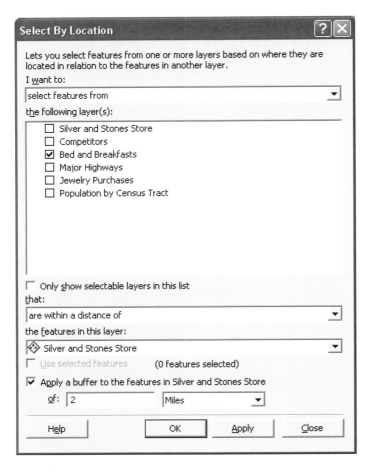

8   **Click Apply, then Close to perform the selection and close the dialog box.**

9   **From the Selection menu, choose Zoom to Selected Features to zoom the map to the B&B inns included in your selection.**

Your map should look like the graphic below. It displays the selected inns and their proximity to Silver and Stones. If you wish, you may use the Measure tool to determine the distance of any individual inn from the store.

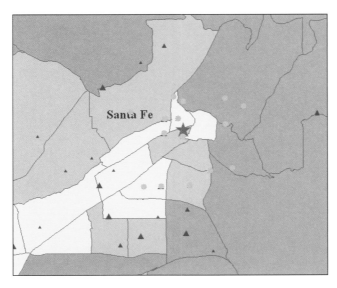

Calculate statistics on selected features

You have identified the B&B inns that meet the spatial constraint of the Buell's proposal. You must now determine if they meet the quantitative constraints.

1 Right-click the Bed and Breakfasts layer and click Open Attribute Table.

2 In the attribute table, click the Selected button to view only the selected records.

The selected inns are highlighted and their number reported at the bottom of the table.

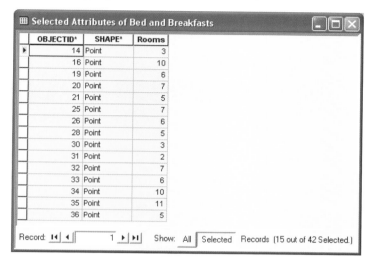

To calculate the number of guest rooms available in the selected B&Bs you will use the Statistics function.

3 Right-click the header cell at the top of the Rooms column, then click Statistics to calculate summary statistics on the values of this attribute for the selected features.

The results are reported in the Selection Statistics window. The Count field reports the number of B&Bs selected and the Sum field reports the total number of rooms in these inns. Use this information to answer the following questions about the feasibility of the Buells' shuttle proposal.

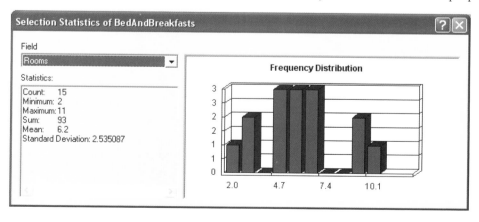

How many B&B inns are within two miles of the Silver and Stones store? How many total guest rooms are available in these inns? Do these values meet the constraints imposed by the Buells? Based on this information, is the B&B shuttle proposal feasible?

4   Close the Statistics window and attribute table.

Save the map document

You have completed your analysis of this marketing opportunity.

1   Save your map file as **SilverStonesSF2_fl.mxd** (replace f and l with your first and last initials) in your **\GISMKT\SilverStonesSF** folder.

2   To close ArcMap, click File > Exit.

Congratulations! You have completed the introductory project.

The primary objective of this chapter has been to familiarize you with the ArcMap interface and basic tools. This foundation will enable you to successfully complete the other chapters in this book.

In this chapter, you observed the value of GIS operations in environmental scanning and opportunity analysis, perhaps the two central components of strategic marketing planning. Indeed, several of the chapters in this book are extensions of these two processes augmented with additional concepts and tools from the various fields in the marketing discipline.

In the interest of simplicity, this chapter has used limited datasets to perform these functions. As you develop your GIS skills with this book, you will encounter more extensive data and more sophisticated analyses.

It's time to really dive into your exploration of GIS applications in marketing. Enjoy your journey.

CHAPTER 2

Working with Community Tapestry Data

An orientation to the lifestyle segmentation system

This chapter provides an introductory overview of the Community Tapestry lifestyle segmentation system. It is based on the Community Tapestry demonstration CD, which has been integrated into the data CD for this book. In the following exercises you will use this system to develop a direct marketing program for the Silver and Stones* jewelry store in Santa Fe, New Mexico. You will learn how to use the Community Tapestry tools to determine the values, behaviors, and purchasing patterns of different lifestyle segments and to use this information to develop effective marketing strategies.

Note: You should read this chapter and complete the exercises before undertaking chapters 4 or 5, which use the Community Tapestry system and assume familiarity with it.

* This is a fictional company and scenario, created for educational purposes only. Any resemblance to actual persons, events, or corporations is unintended.

Learning objectives

In order to develop a direct marketing program, in the following exercises you will use the Community Tapestry system to:

1. Select attractive Community Tapestry segments for a product or service
2. Identify the dominant Community Tapestry segments to which existing customers belong
3. Identify segment values, behaviors, and purchasing patterns relevant to the marketing program
4. Identify geographic concentrations of Community Tapestry segments that present growth opportunities

Marketing scenario

If you recently completed the first chapter in this book, you will recall that Silver and Stones, Inc., is a jewelry store in Santa Fe, New Mexico, specializing in original pieces of jewelry crafted by local artisans. Each piece is unique and comes with a certificate of originality and authenticity signed by the artisan who crafted it.

Silver and Stones's primary market is tourists in the four-season Santa Fe recreational area. The store is located near a busy tourist shopping area in Santa Fe that includes several other jewelry stores and souvenir shops. Owners Bill and Belle Buell have been successful in distinguishing Silver and Stones from competing stores with unique pieces that offer tourists distinctive mementos of their Santa Fe experience. Despite higher prices, many tourists return to the store each time they vacation in the area and many have become regular customers. The Buells cultivate this loyalty by asking each customer to provide an address to which they send a quarterly newsletter. Each edition features silversmiths who design pieces for Silver and Stones, with pictures and descriptions of the pieces they have designed.

The Buells wish to increase sales by adding a database marketing program using a direct-mail campaign that targets prospects across the United States. Direct-mail materials will be shorter and more focused than the newsletter, describing a few selected items to recipients and inviting them to order by mail, phone, or the firm's transactional Web site. Current newsletter recipients will be the foundation of the marketing database. However, the Buells wish to extend the database to other households across the country who share the lifestyle patterns and values of their newsletter subscribers. In this chapter, you will use the Community Tapestry system to assist the Buells in this project.

Background information

The Community Tapestry segmentation system is a product of ESRI. It classifies households in the United States into 65 distinct lifestyle segments. The system combines demographic data with housing, lifestyle, and purchasing behavior information to produce rich profiles of its 65 segments. This provides marketers greater insight into the motivation and behavior of their customers and prospects, something that is not possible with purely demographic segmentation systems.

Community Tapestry is enhanced even further when combined with Market Potential Indexes (MPIs) based on data from Mediamark Research Inc. These indexes report Community Tapestry segment behaviors on an extensive range of attitudes, lifestyle activities, media habits, and purchasing patterns. Specific indexes are included for a range of consumer product categories. As all the indexes are based on a standard value of 100, which represents the national average across all households for that behavior, the patterns of a Community Tapestry segment relative to a set of behaviors are immediately clear. For example, if the MPI for the 04-Boomburbs segment on the behavior "Heavy newspaper reader" is 125, it means that households in this segment are 25 percent more likely than the national average to read newspapers heavily. Therefore, newspapers would be a good medium for communicating with these households. Similarly, the variations in behavior between households in two or more Community Tapestry segments allow marketers to tailor offerings to a defined set of values and behaviors. This is, in fact, what you will do in this exercise for Silver and Stones.

Exercise 2.1 Explore the Community Tapestry demonstration

To use the Community Tapestry system as an effective marketing tool, you must understand its structure, the segments it contains, and the rich data it provides on the purchasing behavior of segments. Thus, in this exercise, you will:

- Run the Community Tapestry demonstration
- View demographic summary tables and profiles of Community Tapestry segments
- Select Community Tapestry segments and compare their demographics, values, and jewelry purchasing patterns

Start the demonstration

1   Open Windows Explorer by right-clicking Start at the lower left corner of your computer screen, then choosing Explore.

2   Navigate to the directory to which you installed the data for this book and expand the **GISMKT** folder, then click and expand the **CommunityTapestry** subfolder.

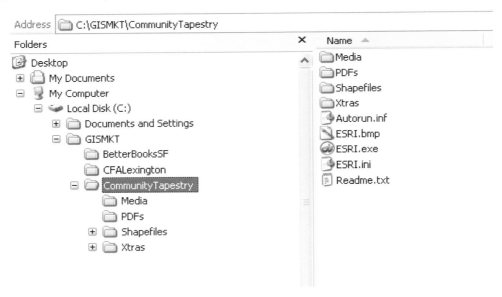

3   Double-click ESRI.exe. This opens the main menu for the Community Tapestry demonstration. (Note: If you do not see file extensions, click Tools > Folder Options, then click the View tab. Make sure the option to "Hide extension for known file types" is not checked.)

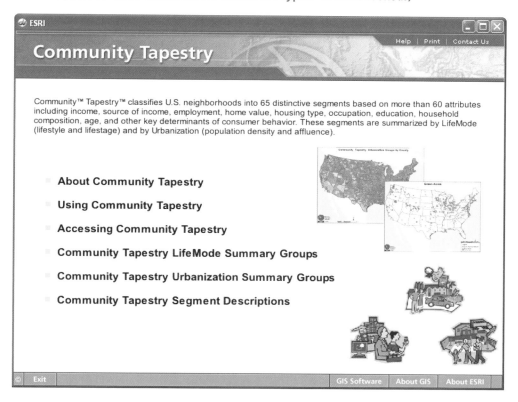

Learn about the Community Tapestry system

1   Click About Community Tapestry and read the overview of the Community Tapestry classification system, including the two associated PDF documents. When you are finished, click Home to return.

2   Click Using Community Tapestry to view a list of possible applications for the Community Tapestry system. When you have finished reading, click Home to return.

The list of applications you just saw includes some of the tasks you will perform for Silver and Stones.

View a summary table of the 65 Community Tapestry segments

1   Click Community Tapestry Segment Descriptions, then Community Tapestry Summary Table to open a PDF document containing a summary table of the 65 Community Tapestry segments and their major demographic characteristics.

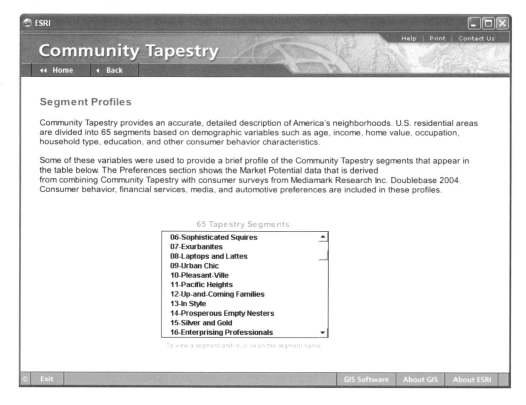

	Households	Population	2000-05 Annual Pop Change (%)	Housing Type	Household Type	Average HH Size	Median Age	Diversity Index	Median HH Income	Median Net Worth	Median Home Value	Home Ownership Rate (%)
United States	112,448,901	298,727,898	1.14	--	--	2.59	36.3	58	$49,747	$107,683	$163,247	68
01: Top Rung	802,659	2,367,843	1.05	Single Family	Married Couple Families	2.90	42.3	30	$178,988	$556,393	$1,014,599	93
02: Suburban Splendor	1,907,187	5,840,963	1.90	Single Family	Married Couple Families	3.04	40.5	32	$114,508	$309,337	$408,069	94
03: Connoisseurs	1,605,955	4,330,830	0.86	Single Family	Married Couple Families	2.65	45.4	33	$118,478	$357,276	$664,514	91
04: Boomburbs	2,147,878	8,700,629	4.64	Single Family	Married Couples w/Kids	3.11	33.8	43	$103,743	$191,055	$308,664	92
05: Wealthy Seaboard Suburbs	1,610,431	4,611,985	0.83	Single Family	Married Couple Families	2.82	41.7	41	$93,130	$270,317	$444,838	91
06: Sophisticated Squires	2,937,666	8,923,775	2.01	Single Family	Married Couple Families	3.02	37.4	36	$80,531	$215,636	$244,491	92
07: Exurbanites	2,689,891	7,370,717	1.53	Single Family	Married Couple Families	2.71	43.6	25	$83,181	$259,020	$255,894	91
08: Laptops and Lattes	1,156,482	2,176,859	0.56	Multi-Unit Rentals	Singles: Shared	1.82	38.1	47	$90,996	$272,019	$705,451	41
09: Urban Chic	1,536,409	3,762,923	1.00	Single Family; Multi-Units	Mixed	2.40	41.4	47	$84,821	$262,669	$633,033	70
10: Pleasant-Ville	1,979,844	5,781,387	0.78	Single Family	Married Couple Families	2.88	39.4	56	$73,003	$198,413	$326,530	86
11: Pacific Heights	719,450	2,335,263	0.80	Single Family; Townhome	Married Couple Families	3.21	38.4	78	$76,030	$211,043	$573,585	72
12: Up and Coming Families	3,203,786	9,494,339	4.10	Single Family	Married Couples w/Kids	2.95	31.9	50	$68,395	$120,053	$185,532	86
13: In Style	2,780,811	6,869,159	1.56	Single Family; Townhome	Mixed	2.43	39.3	39	$67,847	$186,597	$231,775	72
14: Prosperous Empty Nesters	2,102,727	5,137,571	0.76	Single Family	Married Couples w/No Kids	2.38	47.2	25	$66,162	$224,591	$197,759	88
15: Silver and Gold	1,015,118	2,136,623	2.90	Single Family/Seasonal	Married Couples w/No Kids	2.07	58.5	19	$66,546	$275,971	$326,610	86

2   Scroll through this table, noting the names of the Community Tapestry segments along with their size and demographic characteristics. When you are finished, close the PDF.

View segment profiles

1   Back in the Community Tapestry system, click Segment Profiles. This page lists the 65 Community Tapestry segments in a box at the bottom of the window.

2   Scroll through the segment names, then click on one of your choice to open its segment
    description.

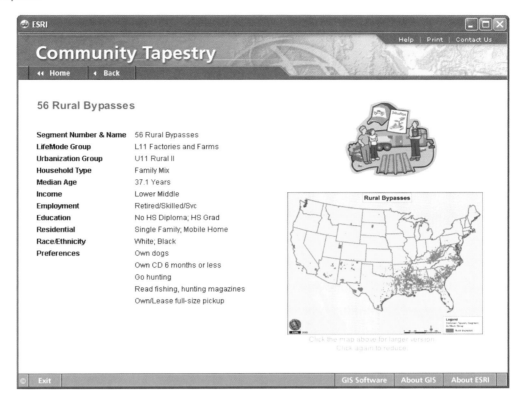

The description window displays a summary of the segment you have chosen. In the lower right
corner of the window is a map displaying the distribution of this segment by block group across the
United States.

3   Click on the map to expand it. Click again to return to the segment summary window.

4   Repeat this operation to view several segment summaries (click the Back button to see the list
    of segments).

You are now familiar with the Community Tapestry neighborhood classification system. You will
now use the demographic and Market Potential Indexes stored with the Community Tapestry
system to compare the characteristics and behaviors of selected segments.

Compare demographic characteristics

1   Choose two Community Tapestry segments you wish to compare.

2   Open the Community Tapestry Summary Table (click Home, Community Tapestry Segment Descriptions, Community Tapestry Summary Table) to view the demographic characteristics of the segments you selected. Record the appropriate values in the table on page 38, under the section labeled Demographic measures.

This side-by-side comparison provides some sense of the demographic differences among the Community Tapestry segments. However, the greater value of the system lies in the insights it provides into differences in values, behaviors, purchasing patterns, and media habits. To reveal these dimensions of the Community Tapestry system, you will use the Market Potential Indexes included in the system.

Compare Market Potential Indexes

1   From the main menu of the Community Tapestry system, click Community Tapestry Segment Descriptions, then click Market Potential Indexes.

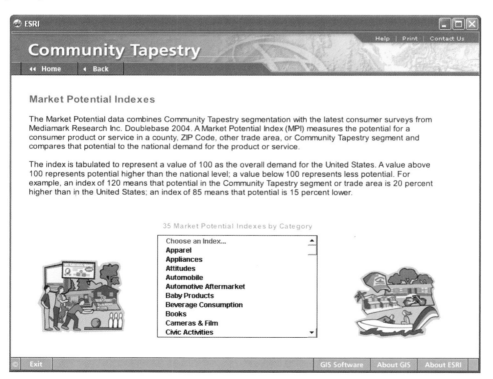

Read the description of the Market Potential Index system. Note that it compares the values and behaviors of Community Tapestry segments based on an index system with a base of 100, which represents the national average. If a segment has a value greater than 100 for an MPI, the residential households in that segment are more likely than the national average to report that value or behavior. A value less than 100 indicates that the households are less likely than the national average to report that behavior.

You will find some relevant MPI values for the two groups you have selected so you can better compare the groups.

2 For each of the two segments you are comparing, record the MPI values for the items listed in the table on the following page. You should already have recorded the demographic measures. For example, the first category you want to explore is "Attitudes." In the Market Potential Indexes box, click Attitudes. In the window that appears, find the place where the attitude item and your segment meet in the matrix, then record that value in the table. Use the Back button to access a new category.

Community Tapestry segment (number and name)		
Demographic measures		
Household Type		
Average Household Size		
Median Age		
Diversity Index		
Median Household Income		
Median Net Worth		
Home Ownership Rate		
Market Potential Indexes		
Attitudes category		
Consider self very conservative		
Consider self middle of the road		
Consider self very liberal		
Leisure Activities/Lifestyle category		
Went to beach in last 12 months		
Danced/went dancing in last 12 months		
Dine out once a week		
Attended movies in last 6 months		
Went to zoo in last 12 months		
Media category		
Heavy viewer of daytime TV		
Heavy viewer of prime-time TV		
Heavy magazine reader		
Heavy newspaper reader		
Heavy radio listener		
Shopping category		
Ordered any item by phone/mail/Internet last 12 months		
Apparel category		
Bought fine jewelry in last 12 months		
Spent on fine jewelry in last 12 months, < $400		
Spent on fine jewelry in last 12 months, $400–$749		
Spent on fine jewelry in last 12 months, $750+		
Spent on fine jewelry in last 12 months, sterling		

 What differences do these values reveal relative to the demographics, values, behaviors, and shopping patterns of the two Community Tapestry segments you have selected?

Your exploration of the Community Tapestry system is complete.

Exercise 2.2 Integrate Community Tapestry data into marketing strategies

You are now familiar with the information included in the Community Tapestry system and how it can be used to identify differences in demographics, lifestyle activities, and purchasing patterns between segments. You will now use the Community Tapestry tools to develop potential marketing strategies for expanding the sales of Silver and Stones. Thus, in this exercise you will:

- Develop three different marketing strategies for Silver and Stones using the Community Tapestry system
- Choose the best strategy and use Market Potential Indexes to plan a direct marketing program

Select Community Tapestry segments as target markets and identify geographic concentrations

In the first strategy, the Buells would identify Community Tapestry segments with favorable purchasing patterns for jewelry, seek out geographic concentrations of those segments, and devise marketing strategies to serve them.

1 From the home page of the Community Tapestry demonstration system, click Community Tapestry Segment Descriptions, then click Market Potential Indexes.

2 On the Market Potential Indexes page, click the Apparel category, and in the new page scroll to the fine jewelry items near the bottom of the list.

3 Focus on the item Spent on fine jewelry in the last 12 months, $750+. Scroll to the right through the values of the 65 segments. Identify the one with the highest value for this measure.

 Which segment has the highest value for this measure? What is the MPI measure for this group?

4 Click Back, Home, Community Tapestry Segment Descriptions, Segment Profiles to reach the Segment Profiles list. Find 10 - Pleasant-Ville in the list, and click it to view the profile of this segment.

5 Click the map to enlarge it. Note the concentrations across the country.

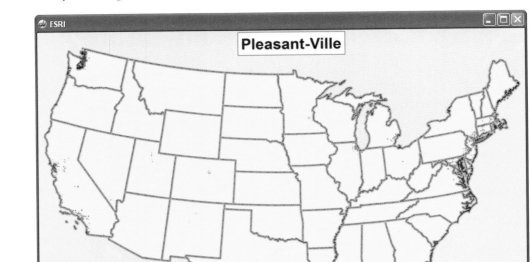

The map displays where concentrations of Pleasant-Ville households are across the country. Armed with this information, the Buells could choose to reach these potential customers with additional retail sites in these locations or a range of direct marketing approaches targeting the ZIP Codes of these concentrations with specific offers, print catalogs, and a transactional Web site.

The weakness of this approach is that the selection of a target segment is largely speculative. That is, households in the 10 - Pleasant-Ville segment are a strong market for fine jewelry in general, but not necessarily for the Silver and Stones product line in particular. In this approach, the firm selects segments that *might* be good customers rather then identifying segments that *are* good customers. The other two strategies avoid this weakness.

Identify dominant Community Tapestry segments in current market area

The second strategy assumes that the majority of customers for a retail store reside in the proximity of that store. This approach is very commonly used in retail market area analysis. Once a firm understands the characteristics of the customers it is serving, it can increase sales by improving its offerings to those customers and by seeking concentrations of similar customers in other geographic areas.

1   Review the map below, taken from chapter 1, which also featured Silver and Stones. The store's location is indicated by the purple star. It is displayed over a thematic map that indicates the dominant Community Tapestry segment of the census tracts in the Santa Fe area. The DOMTAP field in the Identify window displays the number of the dominant Community Tapestry segment in the census tract where the Silver and Stones store is located. Record the number for this segment in the Market-area-based strategy column of the table on page 43.

2   Working in the Market-area-based strategy column of the table, use the Community Tapestry Summary Table PDF and the Market Potential Indexes feature of the Community Tapestry system to find and record the dominant segment name, the demographic measures, and the MPI values for the indicated items. You will repeat this process for the next strategy.

This approach can be very profitable for traditional retailers. Identifying characteristics of the market areas of successful stores can be a very fruitful way of selecting additional retail sites and using direct marketing approaches to reach customers with similar characteristics. Indeed, these approaches are illustrated in several chapters of this volume.

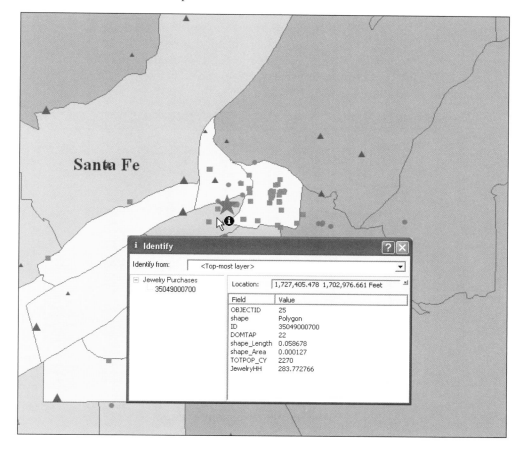

However, the approach can also have weaknesses. The difficulty lies in the assumption that a retailer's primary customers live within proximity of the store. In the case of Silver and Stones, however, the target customers for the expansion project are tourists who visit the city on vacation. Thus, the assumption of a geographically compact market area may not be appropriate in this case. This does not mean that their customers do not share similar demographic and lifestyle characteristics, but merely that the firm must use another method to discover them. You will explore such a method in the third marketing strategy option.

Identify dominant Community Tapestry segments among current customers

The third strategy assumes that the current customers of a retail establishment provide a profile for identifying new prospects. This approach is particularly useful in this case, as the target customers for Silver and Stones's sales expansion project are tourists who do not live in the Santa Fe area. Since the company maintains an address database of many of its customers, it can use this information to develop its customer profile.

The key piece of information in this case is ZIP Code data, which is used to match customers with Community Tapestry data. In this process, each customer in the Silver and Stones customer database is assumed to belong to the dominant Community Tapestry segment of the ZIP Code area in which he or she lives. Using ArcGIS software, the matching process is achieved with a table join operation based on the ZIP Code field. You will have a chance to execute this operation in later chapters.

Once the association is created, the firm can look for concentrations of Community Tapestry segments in its customer base through a summary operation on the dominant Community Tapestry segment field. A graph based on the joined data table, shown below, displays the Community Tapestry concentrations visually.

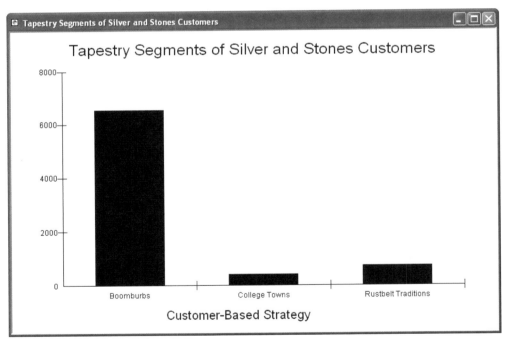

1   Review the graph above. Use it to identify the largest Community Tapestry segment among Silver and Stones customers. Record the number and name of this segment in the Customer-based strategy column of the table on the following page.

2   Working in the Customer-based strategy column of the table, use the Community Tapestry Summary Table PDF and the Market Potential Indexes feature of the Community Tapestry system to find and record the demographic measures and MPI values for the indicated items.

Community Tapestry segment (number and name)	Market-area-based strategy _____	Customer-based strategy _____
Demographic measures		
Household Type		
Average Household Size		
Median Age		
Diversity Index		
Median Household Income		
Median Net Worth		
Home Ownership Rate		
Market Potential Indexes		
Attitudes category		
Consider self very conservative		
Consider self middle of the road		
Consider self very liberal		
Leisure Activities/Lifestyle category		
Went to beach in last 12 months		
Danced/went dancing in last 12 months		
Dine out once a week		
Attended movies in last 6 months		
Went to zoo in last 12 months		
Media category		
Heavy viewer of daytime TV		
Heavy viewer of prime-time TV		
Heavy magazine reader		
Heavy newspaper reader		
Heavy radio listener		
Shopping category		
Ordered any item by phone/mail/Internet last 12 months		
Apparel category		
Bought fine jewelry in last 12 months		
Spent on fine jewelry in last 12 months, < $400		
Spent on fine jewelry in last 12 months, $400–$749		
Spent on fine jewelry in last 12 months, $750+		
Bought fine jewelry in last 12 months, sterling		

Use the graph and table above to answer the questions on the following page.

Does the dominant Community Tapestry segment in the market-area-based strategy match that of the customer-based strategy? Which best reflects the composition of the firm's tourist customer base? Why?

Use Market Potential Indexes to plan direct marketing program

Once you have identified the target segment for Silver and Stones's new marketing program, you may use the MPI system to fine-tune the offering. Specifically, you may use the system to identify specific media behaviors and buying patterns. As an example, use the system to answer the following questions about the preferred Community Tapestry segment you identified above.

From the Media category: What two types of magazines do households in this segment read most frequently? Which two sections of daily newspapers would reach them most effectively?

From the Internet category: Does the segment use the Internet several times a day? Has it ordered items from the Internet in the last 12 months?

From the Yellow Pages category: Does the segment purchase goods by phone or mail from catalogs? How much has the segment spent on phone and mail orders in the past 12 months?

How will this information help Silver and Stones promote its direct marketing program? How appropriate is such a program for reaching this segment? Is it likely to increase sales? Explain your conclusion.

Review the Community Tapestry system

1   Return to the home screen of the Community Tapestry demonstration system and click Using Community Tapestry to reach the page describing the potential applications of this system. You visited this page at the beginning of this chapter.

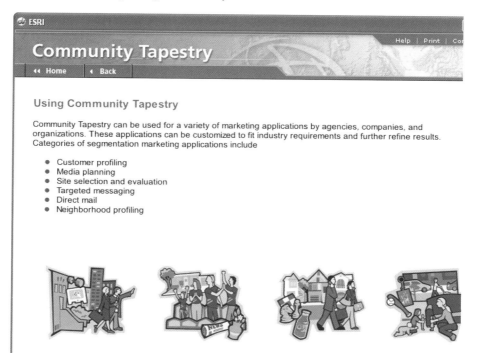

In designing a sales expansion strategy for Silver and Stones, you have performed several of these applications. First, you saw how using ArcGIS to associate each customer with a Community Tapestry segment and then summarize the number of customers in each segment creates a Community Tapestry profile of the customer database. In this exercise, you did not perform the actual data association, but you examined the results in the form of a graph. This allowed you to identify the Community Tapestry segment that will be the target of the direct marketing program. This is a customer profiling application of the Community Tapestry system.

Once the desirable segment is identified, the next step would be to design the communication message for the direct marketing campaign. For this task you would use the MPI values related to attitudes and lifestyle activities to craft the specific message for the audience. This is a targeted messaging application of the Community Tapestry system.

The next step is to communicate the selected message to the target audience. This would be done via direct mail and media promotion. The direct-mail campaign would be aimed at ZIP Codes in which the targeted Community Tapestry segment is dominant. These specific areas would be identified using ArcGIS software. Then you would be able to send mailings aimed at the areas highlighted in the concentration map for this segment, shown on the next page. This is a direct-mail application of the Community Tapestry system.

Media promotion will be used to supplement the direct-mail campaign and convince prospects to order online, by phone, or by mail. You used the MPI Media category to determine the appropriate media for this campaign. This is a media planning application of the Community Tapestry system.

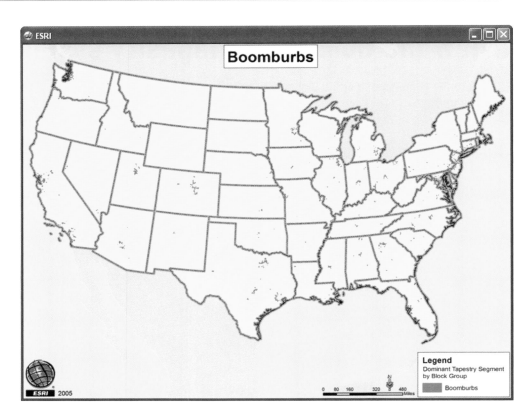

The Buells wish to pursue a direct marketing growth option focusing on the 04-Boomburbs segment whose members visit their store as tourists. However, many retailers find that their best customers are those who live near the store in which they shop. In this situation, the Community Tapestry system is relevant to the growth strategy of opening additional retail stores. In general, this approach creates a profile of the market area for an existing successful store, and then seeks out additional geographic areas whose profile matches this model.

When you identified the dominant Community Tapestry segment in the census tract in which Silver and Stones is located, you were using a simplified approach to the neighborhood profiling application of the Community Tapestry system.

Once the model retail store profile is identified (in this case, that of the 22 - Metropolitans segment), the firm would seek out geographic concentrations of that target segment. This process again relies on the Community Tapestry segment concentration map. This is a site selection and evaluation application of the Community Tapestry system.

2   Close the Community Tapestry demonstration system and any other open windows.

Congratulations! You have completed the Community Tapestry project.

In these exercises, you explored the major applications of the Community Tapestry system and used them to understand Silver and Stones customers more fully. Your knowledge of this system will also help you with the Meiers Home Furnishings and Community Farm Alliance exercises found in chapters 4 and 5, both of which use Community Tapestry data to devise marketing strategies. These chapters illustrate how marketers can use the rich consumer data in the Community Tapestry system to serve customers more effectively and profitably.

CHAPTER 3

Developing a Targeted Promotional Campaign

Course: Principles of Marketing

This chapter involves implementing a market segmentation program. You will plan the promotional campaign for Outdoor Living Inc.'s* new recreational product in the Florida market. The firm makes camping and recreational equipment and has introduced a new, moderately priced camper to attract middle-income families who are new to camping. To be successful, the firm must reach concentrations of targeted customers with its promotional campaign for the new product. You will learn how to use GIS tools to achieve this goal with each of the three components of this campaign: advertising, direct mail, and outdoor shows sponsored by recreational stores.

* This is a fictional company and scenario, created for educational purposes only. Any resemblance to actual persons, events, or corporations is unintended.

Learning objectives

To maximize the effectiveness of the promotional campaign in Florida, you will learn how to use ArcGIS to:

1. Create map symbology to display population demographics
2. Select target Florida families for advertising and direct-mail components of a promotional campaign using appropriate geographic units and demographic attributes
3. Select Tampa-area recreational stores with outdoor shows based on their location relative to target market households
4. Design maps to communicate and support your recommendations

Marketing scenario

Outdoor Living Inc. manufactures a wide range of products for recreational outdoor living. The product line ranges from small, one-person tents for backpackers to large tents for camping and enclosed awnings for large gatherings.

The firm's newest product, the Conestoga, is a modular camper tent mounted on a small trailer for towing behind a vehicle. In addition to the pop-up tent commonly offered with competing products, it includes a modular enclosed "porch" that extends the unit with a covered space large enough for dining or recreation. In addition, the basic unit incorporates a patented compact kitchen unit that provides electricity, cooking, and washing facilities. The Conestoga also contains an integrated entertainment center with satellite television, DVD, and advanced audio capabilities. The unit is exceptionally light, easily maintained, and simple to set up and take down. It is designed to make outdoor living quick, comfortable, and easy for families with children.

The features and convenience of the Conestoga make it ideal for a family new to camping. In addition, innovative design and production techniques allow Outdoor Living to offer the model at an attractive price point. Therefore, Outdoor Living plans to focus its marketing efforts on families in a middle-income range in hopes of attracting them to the recreational pleasures of camping. Ideally, they will be satisfied with their experience and become lifelong campers and consumers of Outdoor Living products.

For these reasons, Outdoor Living has chosen to supplement its national advertising campaign with more focused efforts to reach new consumers in its target market. Specifically, the firm plans to: (1) conduct local television and newspaper advertising in markets with high concentrations of target customers; (2) reach targeted consumers via direct mail with price incentives; and (3) demonstrate the benefits of the new product in outdoor shows at outlets serving its targeted consumers.

Within this strategy the key to success is identifying concentrations of prospects who fit the profile of the product's target segment: families with incomes of $35,000 to $60,000. As sales manager for the southeastern U.S. region, your tasks are to identify geographic concentrations of target customers and design your promotional activities to reach them efficiently. You have chosen to begin this process with the state of Florida and have acquired data on population, family size, income, and market segmentation measures for the state.

Background information

Market segmentation is one of the most powerful tools in the marketing field. It allows firms to identify specific groups of consumers based on their common characteristics and design marketing offerings custom tailored to their needs and preferences. Successful use of segmentation tools allows marketers to enhance brand image, build customer loyalty, and decrease price sensitivity, all of which contribute to long-term sales and profits.

Market segments are defined using a wide range of segmenting dimensions including demographic, socioeconomic, lifestyle, benefit, and usage measures. The choice of segmenting dimensions depends upon several factors, including competitive conditions in the product market, the availability and cost of relevant data, and the market position of the firm's brand.

However segments are defined and analyzed, for segmentation strategies to be successful, marketers must be able to effectively reach targeted consumers with promotion, products, and services. In most cases, this requirement implies a spatial dimension to the implementation of a segmentation strategy. To reach customers, marketers must know where they are. Further, different distribution and promotional approaches require that marketers analyze customer location in different ways. This chapter illustrates that concept.

Outdoor Living has defined its target market as families with incomes between $35,000 and $60,000. Though this appears to be a straightforward definition, it does include judgments about buying behavior for the Conestoga. As a demographic variable, *families* is one of several measures of population units, and refers to people who reside together and are related to each other by birth, marriage, or adoption. *Population,* another measure, is defined as the total number of people residing in a geographic area, whatever their living arrangement. *Households* include people who are residing together whether or not they are related to each other. Thus, families are included in households, but not all households are families. You may get more information about families from the dataset by comparing the total family population measure with the total population measure. The ratio of these two measures is the total percentage of the population living in family units. Outdoor Living's focus on families reflects the judgment that family units, not individuals or households of unrelated people, will be the purchasing unit for the Conestoga product.

The income dimension of Outdoor Living's target segment reflects the firm's perception of the general income boundary between the categories in its product mix. Families with lower levels of income will be more attracted to Outdoor Living's tent products, while those with higher levels will be more attracted to motorized recreational vehicles. Remember that these boundaries are not fixed, but represent behavioral tendencies among target consumers.

This combination of measures is captured in two variables in the dataset: number of families in the target market (the total number of families in the designated income range) and percentage of families in the target market (the number of target market families as a percentage of all families in a geographic area). Each of these measures is useful in the process of planning Outdoor Living's promotional campaign.

In this planning process, you will also use several different geographic units. Each represents a different approach for dividing larger geographic units into smaller ones for purposes of understanding the distribution of a population characteristic. You will begin the process with political units of geography—the state of Florida and its counties.

Another type of unit is the ZIP Code system that the U.S. Postal Service uses to facilitate mail delivery. As ZIP Code boundaries can change over time, postal geographies are not as valuable for longitudinal research as are census geographies (described below), which, though not permanent, are relatively more stable. However, from a marketing perspective, ZIP Code level analysis is useful because it is actionable. That is, attractive ZIP Codes are more easily targeted with direct-mail tools than are units of census geography.

Census geography units are created by the U.S. Census Bureau to administer and report its decennial census of the country. The most basic units of census geography for which data is reported are:

- Census tracts, which are subdivisions of counties
- Census block groups, which are subdivisions of census tracts
- Census blocks, which are subdivisions of census block groups

Census tracts were originally drawn to reflect some degree of internal demographic similarity, though this has often been eroded by natural patterns of population migration. They also vary in size, though the average census tract population is about 4,000. However, because census tract boundaries remain relatively stable over time, this unit is useful for tracking long-term change in population patterns. The census tract is the unit of census geography included in Outdoor Living's promotional planning analysis.

The Census Bureau and commercial marketing data suppliers also use several other geographic units to report population characteristics. Core Based Statistical Areas are population centers with integrated economic, transportation, and communication systems that often cross county or even state boundaries. They include Metropolitan Statistical Areas (larger urban and suburban areas surrounding a city of 50,000 or more, or a general urban area of 100,000 or more) and Micropolitan Statistical Areas (urban and suburban areas around a population center of 10,000 to 50,000). Some commercial marketing data firms also collect and report data for a geographic unit that they themselves define. Nielsen Media Research's Designated Market Areas is an example of this type of geographic unit.

Outdoor Living Florida data dictionary	
Attribute	**Description**
For State, Counties, ZIPCodes and HillsboroughCensusTracts	
TOTPOP_CY	Total population, 2004
FAMPOP_CY	Family population, 2004
FAMHH_CY	Family households, 2004
AVGFMSZ_CY	Average family size, 2004
PCI_CY	Per capita income, 2004
NumFamInTM	Number of families in target market, 2004
PctFamInTM	Percentage of families in target market, 2004
For MajorCities	
AreaName	City name
Capital	State capital (yes or no)
For OutdoorStoresShows	
StoreName	Name of outdoor store
Source: ESRI Community Data, 2005	

Exercise 3.1   Explore demographic characteristics

To maximize the effectiveness of your promotional campaign, you must focus your resources on geographic concentrations of your target customers. To prepare for this analysis, you must explore demographic variations among Florida's geographic areas. Thus, in this exercise, you will:

* Load, display, and explore maps of Florida
* View thematic maps of Florida's counties and their demographic characteristics
* Examine data distribution in densely populated areas

Open an existing map

1   **From the Windows taskbar, click Start > All Programs > ArcGIS > ArcMap.**

Depending on how the software has been installed or which Windows operating system you are using, there may be a slightly different navigation menu from which to open ArcMap.

2   **If you see a Start dialog box, click the "An existing map" option. Otherwise, click the Open button on the Standard toolbar.**

3   **Browse to the location of the GISMKT folder (e.g., C:\ESRIPress\GISMKT), double-click the OutdoorLivingFL folder, then click the OutdoorLivingFL1 map document and click Open.**

When the map opens, several layers appear in the table of contents and a map of Florida appears in the map display area. The visible layers represent the state of Florida and its major cities. The Total Population by County, Average Family Size by County, and Per Capita Income by County layers represent demographic information about Florida's counties, but are not currently visible. The Tampa Area Per Capita Income layer contains income data by census tract in the Tampa area, and is also currently not visible.

Display map layers

The table of contents contains several items, called layers, each of which represents features that can be displayed on the map. You can view the layers by turning them on and off (clicking their check boxes).

Change the display order of layers

In ArcMap, layers draw from the bottom of the table of contents up. Thus, the top layer can obscure layers underneath it. The State of Florida layer is at the top of the table of contents thereby covering all the other layers. So even though the Cities layer is turned on, you can't see the city markers because the state polygon is covering them. You can reorder layers in the table of contents by dragging them from one position to another.

1   In the table of contents, click **Major Cities** and hold down the mouse button.

2   Drag **Major Cities** to the top of the table of contents, then release the mouse button.

The symbols for the Major Cities layer now appear on top of the State layer.

Turn layers on and off

1   Turn off the State layer.

2   Turn on the Total Population by County layer.

 In general, what parts of the state contain the highest population measures?

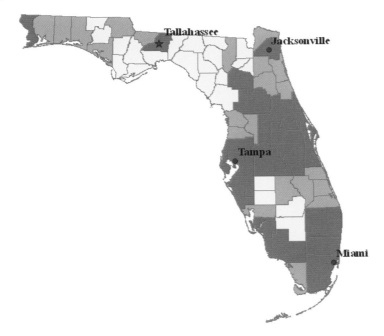

3   Now turn on the Major Cities and Per Capita Income by County layers and turn all other layers off.

Explore demographic characteristics with thematic layers

Thematic layers allow you to display selected attributes of features in a map format. They are useful in analyzing and communicating the distribution of demographic characteristics within a region of interest. In this task, you will explore the variations of population, household size, and income among Florida's counties. To do so, you will turn the various county data layers on and off, allowing you to review the distribution of population, household size, and income.

Identify data for specific counties

You may use the Identify tool to click on a feature, like a county, and display its attribute information.

1   From the Tools toolbar, click the Identify tool. ⓘ

2   Click inside the county southwest of Miami.

This county flashes briefly and the Identify window displays all the attributes for this county, Monroe County. You may use this tool to review the attributes of any other counties you wish. Consult the data dictionary to determine the meaning of attribute names.

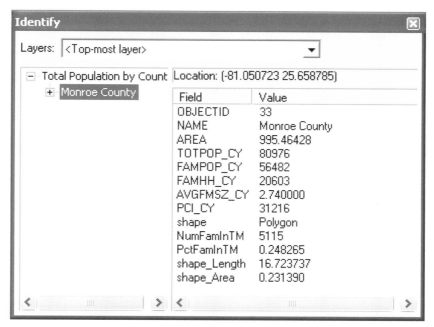

3   Close the Identify window.

4   Turn off the Per Capita Income by Country layer, and turn on the Average Family Size by County layer. Observe the data distribution of this layer. When you're finished, turn on the Total Population by County layer.

Change the data represented by a layer

The Total Population by County layer displays the number of people in each county. However, Outdoor Living's target market is defined as families. Therefore, the number of family households in an area is a more relevant market measure than is total population. Thus, you must revise the Total Population by County layer to display this attribute.

1　Double-click the Total Population by County layer (or right-click the layer and select Properties).

2　Click the General tab. For Layer Name, enter **Family Households by County**. Don't click OK—that will close the Layer Properties dialog box, and you have more properties to change.

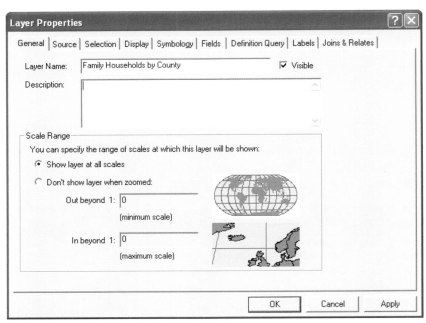

3　Click the Symbology tab. In the Value field, select the appropriate attribute. (Use the data dictionary to identify the attribute name for the Family Households measure.)

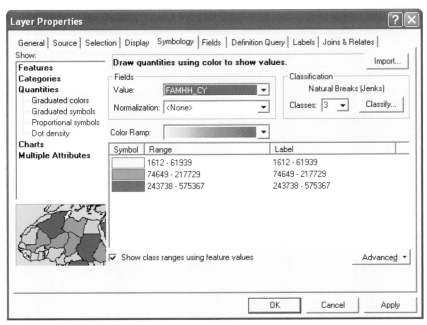

4   Click OK.

5   In the table of contents, click the word FAMHH_CY under the layer name, then click again to make it editable. Replace FAMHH_CY with **Families**. (Note: If your second click is too quick, the Layer Properties dialog box will open. Click Cancel, then try again, clicking more slowly to reach the edit function.)

The resulting map displays the number of family households in each of Florida's counties. This data is more directly related to the firm's target market than total population.

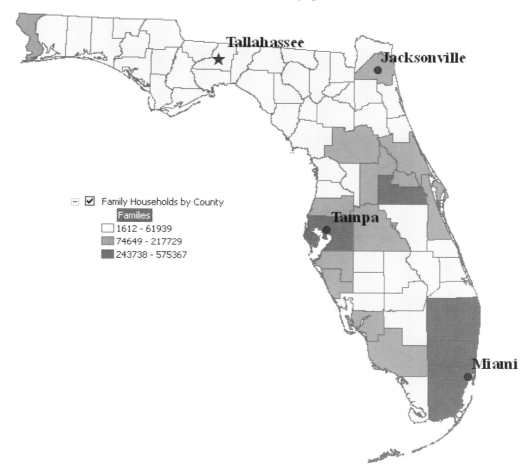

Display data distribution in smaller areas

You have observed attribute variation between Florida's counties. With ArcMap you may also explore variations within smaller geographic areas. Consider the Tampa region as an example.

1 Click the check boxes to the left of the layers in the table of contents to display only the Major Cities, Tampa Area Per Capita Income, and Per Capita Income by County layers. (Turn all other layers off.)

2 Right-click the Tampa Area Per Capita Income layer and click Zoom To Layer to zoom in and center the map display on the Tampa area.

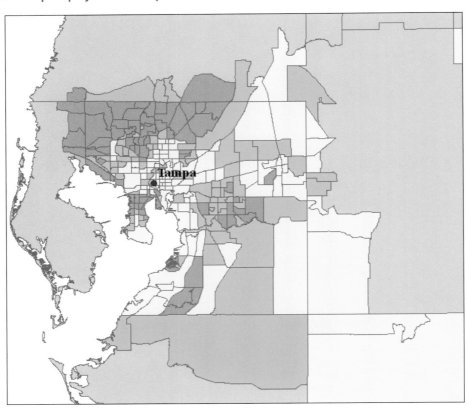

3   Turn off the Tampa Area Per Capita Income layer.

Compare this view with the previous view. This view indicates that the counties within the Tampa region fall within the middle income classification. However, the previous view reveals that many of the census tracts in the area fall into the upper and lower classifications. Further, some census tracts in the region have levels of per capita income that are significantly lower than any of Florida's counties, while other census tracts have levels that are significantly higher. Exploring these relationships allows you to understand the distribution of Outdoor Living's target market not only between counties but between the census tracts of a metropolitan area.

Update report and save map document

1   Use your observations of the maps you have displayed to answer the question below. Summarize your answer in the appropriate section of the project report template (OutdoorLivingFL_ReportTemplate.doc) which you will find in your \GISMKT\OutdoorLivingFL folder.

What do you observe about the geographic distribution of family households, family size, and income in Florida's counties?

2   Save your map file as OutdoorLivingFL1_fl.mxd (replace f and l with your first and last initials). To do so, from the File menu, choose Save As. Navigate to your \GISMKT\OutdoorLivingFL folder, type OutdoorLivingFL1_fl.mxd as the file name, and click Save.

Exercise 3.2 Select counties for local advertising campaign

Local advertising media such as newspapers, radio, and television stations provide broad coverage of their local markets. Media costs are for insertions or time slots. While costs vary with audience size, they are not determined directly on a per-household basis, as direct-mail costs are. For these reasons, counties are the appropriate geographic units for the local advertising campaign and the number of target market families in each is the appropriate market measure. The budget for the local advertising campaign will support ten county markets. You will select the specific counties for the campaign based on the total number of families in the target market residing in each county. Thus, in this exercise, you will:

- Identify the ten Florida counties with the largest number of families in the target market
- Design a map that identifies these counties and their location
- Calculate the total number of target market families that will be exposed to the campaign in these counties

Open an existing map

1   In ArcMap, open the **OutdoorLivingFL2** map document found in your **\GISMKT\OutdoorLivingFL** folder.

The map contains two layers: an outline of Florida and its major cities.

Add and display a new map layer

This analysis requires a map layer depicting the distribution of Outdoor Living's target market across Florida's counties. Recall that the target market is families with annual incomes between $35,000 and $60,000. Your first step is to add and display this map layer.

Add a map layer

1   Click the Add Data button. ✛

2   In the Add Data dialog box, navigate to the **OutdoorLivingFL** geodatabase found in your **\GISMKT\ OutdoorLivingFL** folder.

3   Double-click the geodatabase to open it. Click **Counties**.

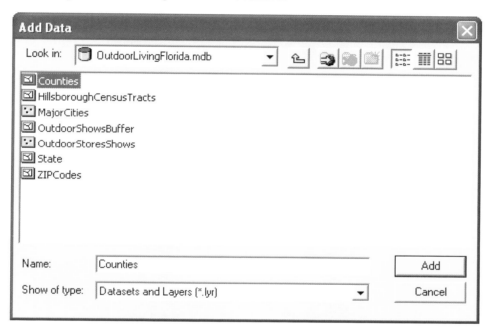

4   Click Add to add the Counties feature class as a new layer to the map.

The resulting map displays Florida's counties; however, every county is the same color. You will change the layer's symbology so that each county's color represents the correct attribute value.

Edit a map layer's symbology

1 Double-click the Counties layer in the table of contents (or right-click the layer and select Properties).

2 Click the General tab and enter **Number of Families in Target Market** as the new layer name.

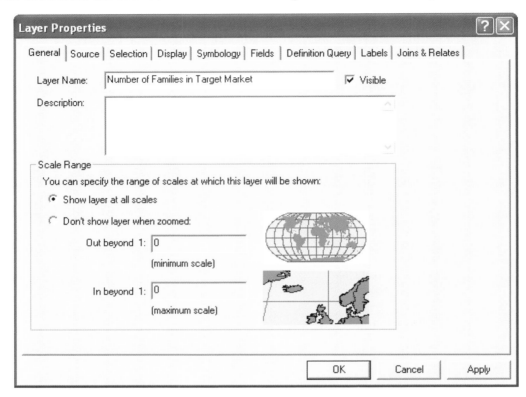

3 Click the Symbology tab. In the Show area, click Quantities, then click Graduated colors.

4 Select the appropriate attribute name in the drop-down box in the Value field. (You can use the data dictionary to identify the attribute name for the number of families in target market measure.)

5 Click the "Show class ranges using feature values" check box to define classification ranges using actual values from the layer's attribute table.

6   Select any color scheme using the drop-down box in the Color Ramp field.

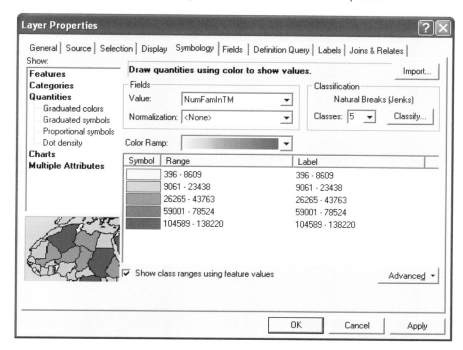

These settings specify which attribute value will be used to display the layer and how it will be displayed. Next you will designate how many classes will be used to display the data.

7   While still in the Layer Properties dialog box (on the Symbology tab), click the Classify button to display the Classification dialog box.

8   For the Method option, click the drop-down arrow and choose Quantile.

9   For the Classes option, choose 4.

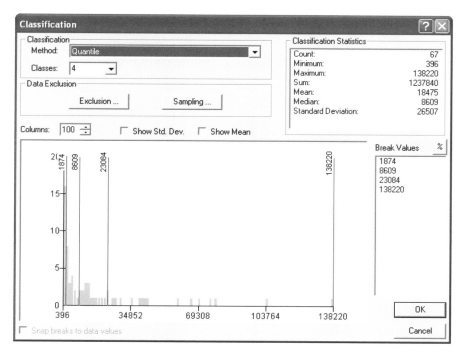

With these settings, you have specified that this layer will display in 4 classes, each containing a roughly equal number of counties. Note in the Classification Statistics area that Florida has 67 counties. So 16 or 17 counties will be in each of the 4 classes.

The highest class will be composed of the top 10 counties that will be included in the initial promotional campaign, as well as another 6 or 7 counties to include in the campaign should additional funds become available.

10 Click **OK** to assign the 4 classes. Click **OK** again to complete the layer symbolization process.

The resulting map displays the distribution of Outdoor Living's target market across Florida counties.

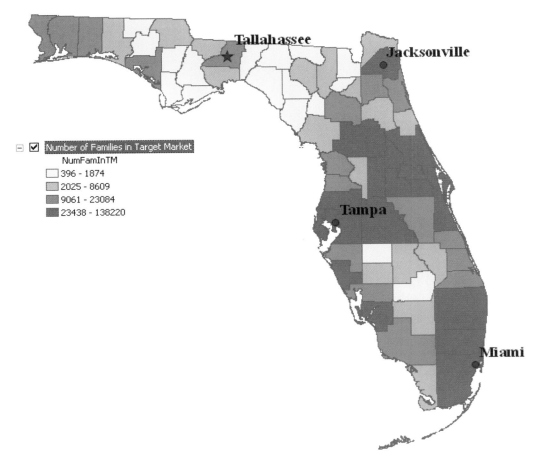

The class of counties with the highest values contains the 10 counties you are seeking in this task. You will now identify them specifically.

Analyze data in attribute tables

You can view a layer's data by opening its attribute table. You will sort, select, and calculate summary statistics on attributes in the counties layer table to learn the names of the top ten counties.

Sort and select counties based on attribute values

Your first task is to identify the ten Florida counties with the highest number of families in Outdoor Living's target market. You will do so by sorting and selecting records in the layer's attribute table.

1   In the table of contents, right-click the Number of Families in Target Market layer, and click Open Attribute Table.

The attribute table contains the data for each county feature in the layer.

2   Scroll horizontally through the table to find the NumFamInTM attribute, then right-click the column header cell and select the Sort Descending option.

This sorts the feature values for this attribute from highest to lowest.

3   Click the small gray box to the immediate left of the first record in the table to select it.

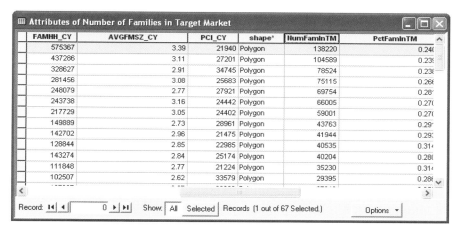

This record turns blue to indicate that it is selected. If you look on the map, you will see that the corresponding county polygon is also selected and drawn in blue. You may need to move the attribute table to see the table and map simultaneously.

4   In the same manner, select several records in the attribute table and then view the changes on the map.

5   To select multiple features, click the small gray box to the immediate left of the topmost feature and hold your mouse button down. Move the mouse pointer down the column of boxes to select the first ten features in the table. Alternatively, you can press and hold the Ctrl key as you click each record.

Note that the counties are selected simultaneously on the map as well. These counties will be the target of your advertising campaign.

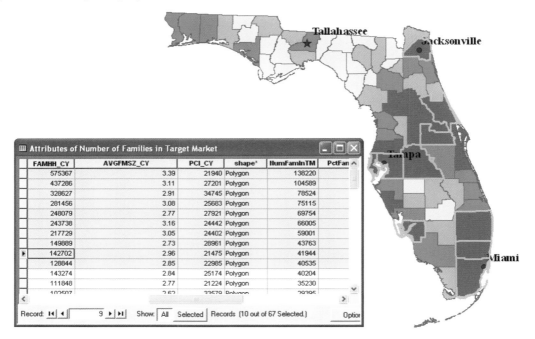

Calculate summary statistics for attributes

The final step in this exercise is to calculate the number of target market families that will be exposed to the advertising campaign. You will perform this step by calculating summary statistics for the relevant attribute in the attribute table.

1   Again find the NumFamInTM attribute, right-click the attribute name at the top of the column, then select Statistics. (Note: The top ten features for this attribute should still be selected in this table. If they are not, repeat step 5 above to select them. The summary statistics are only calculated for the selected records/features.)

In the Selection Statistics of Counties window, the Sum reports the total number of target market families in the ten selected counties. This is the number of families that will be exposed to Outdoor Living's advertising campaign.

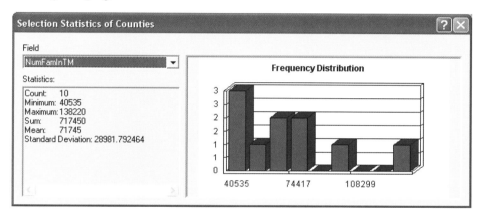

Update report and save map document

1   Use your map, attribute tables, and calculations to answer the questions below. Summarize your answers in the appropriate section of the project report template (OutdoorLivingFL_ReportTemplate.doc) which you will find in your \GISMKT\OutdoorLivingFL folder.

Which ten counties should be included in Outdoor Living's local advertising campaign? Why? How many target-market families will be reached by this campaign?

2   Close the statistics window and attribute table, and save your map file as **OutdoorLivingFL2_fl.mxd** (replace f and l with your first and last initials) in your **\GISMKT\OutdoorLivingFL** folder.

Exercise 3.3   Select ZIP Codes for direct-mail campaign

Direct mail offers customized communication with individual households that can easily be targeted by ZIP Code. Costs are based on the number of mailings and response rates are typically low. Thus, it is important that the highest possible percentage of recipients be target prospects. For these reasons, ZIP Codes are the appropriate geographic unit for the local advertising campaign, and the percentage of target market families is the appropriate market measure. The direct-mail budget for Florida will support a mailing to 750,000 households. You will select the ZIP Codes to be included in the mailing on the basis of the percentage of families in each that are in the target market. Thus, in this exercise, you will:

- Identify the ZIP Codes in Florida with the largest percentage of families in the target market
- Design a map that identifies these ZIP Codes and their location
- Calculate the total number of ZIP Codes and family households that will be included in the mailing
- Calculate the number of target market families who will receive mailings

Open an existing map

1   In ArcMap, open the **OutdoorLivingFL3** map document found in your **\GISMKT\OutdoorLivingFL** folder.

This map document contains three layers: a basemap of Florida, Florida's major cities, and ZIP Codes. The blank areas are national and state parks that are not assigned ZIP Codes.

Edit a layer's symbology

This map displays a ZIP Code layer, but it does not represent any data. You will edit this layer to display the percentage of families in each county that is in Outdoor Living's target market.

1 Double-click the ZIPCodes layer in the table of contents (or right-click the layer and select Properties).

2 Click the General tab and enter **Percent of Families in Target Market** as the new layer name.

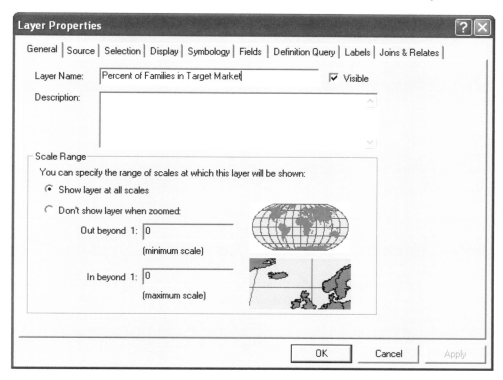

3 Click the Symbology tab. In the Show area, click Quantities, then click Graduated colors.

4 Select the appropriate attribute name in the drop-down box in the Value field. (You may use the data dictionary to identify the attribute name for the percentage of families in target market measure.)

5 Select a color scheme using the drop-down box in the Color Ramp field.

6 Click the "Show class ranges using feature values" check box to define classification ranges using actual values from the layer's attribute table.

These settings specify which attributes will be displayed in this layer and how the layer will appear.

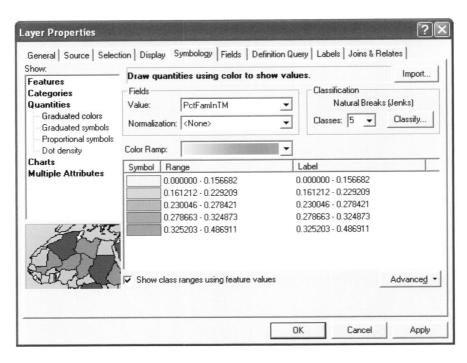

7   In the Symbology dialog box, click the Classify button to display the Classification dialog box.

8   For Method, choose Quantile.

9   For Classes, maintain the default value of 5.

These settings determine how many data classes will be displayed and how they will be determined. You have specified that the data will be displayed in quantiles. This means that each classification group will contain approximately one fifth of Florida's ZIP Codes. The group with the highest range of values for the attribute is the top 20 percent of ZIP Codes, the next group is the 20 percent of ZIP Codes with the next highest range of values, and so on through the classification groups.

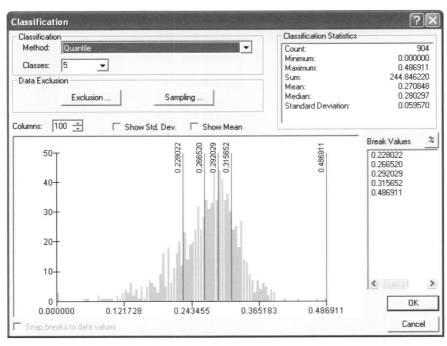

10 Click OK to return to the Symbology tab.

Note that the values for the class breaks are displayed as decimals with six decimal places. As these values are percentages, they should be displayed as such in the table of contents. You will specify these settings in the following steps.

11 Click the Label column header and then click Format Labels from the resulting menu to reach the Number Format dialog box. (Note: This is NOT the Labels tab in the Layer Properties dialog box, which serves a different function. If you clicked the Labels tab in error, click the Symbology tab and repeat the instruction above.)

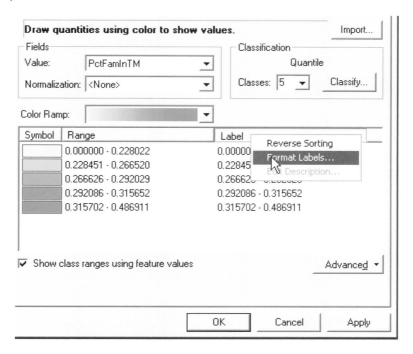

12 Under Categories, click Percentage, and click the option "The number represents a fraction. Adjust it to show a percentage."

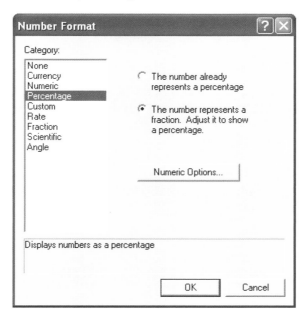

13   Click the Numeric Options button and, in the resulting dialog box, reduce the number of decimal places to 1.

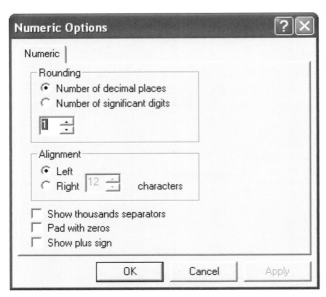

14   Click OK in each of the three dialog boxes to accept the changes.

The resulting layer displays the percentage of target market families in each of Florida's ZIP Codes. The map indicates which ZIP Codes have the highest concentration of target market families. You must now determine which of these ZIP Codes will be included in your 750,000-household mailing.

Analyze data in attribute tables

ArcMap allows you to analyze the data that underlies a layer by manipulating the layer's attribute table. You will use the attribute table tools to sort, select, and calculate summary statistics for this data.

Sort and select counties based on attribute values

As in the previous task, you will sort and select records in a layer attribute table to identify those you will target. However, as the number of ZIP Codes is so much greater, you will perform this selection by using an attribute query rather than selecting records manually.

1   In the table of contents, right-click the Percent of Families in Target Market layer, then select Open Attribute Table.

This layer's attribute table contains ZIP Code data for each of the features.

2   Scroll through the table to find the PctFamInTM attribute, right-click the column header, then select the Sort Descending option.

The records are sorted from highest to lowest.

To maximize the effectiveness of your direct-mail campaign, your 750,000 mailings should be sent to the ZIP Codes with the highest percentages of target market families. Therefore, you should select ZIP Codes from the top of this list down until you reach a total of 750,000 households. You will use the Select by Attributes function to accomplish this task.

3   At the bottom of the attribute table, click the Options button, then choose the Select by Attributes option. (Note: You may need to increase the size of the attribute table to see the Options button.)

4   In the resulting Select by Attributes dialog box, double-click the attribute name [PctFamInTM], then click the >= operator, then type .316 at the end of the equation in the Query box so that the full equation reads: [PctFamInTM] >= .316 (This is the minimum value of the highest quantile in the classification scheme.)

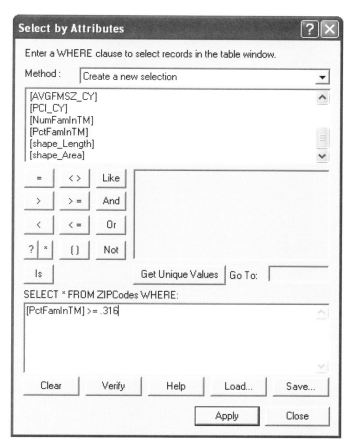

5 **Click Apply, then click Close.**

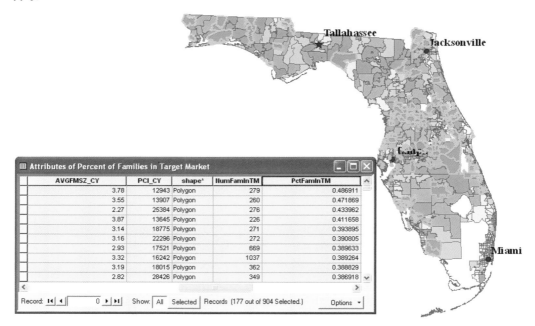

AVGFMSZ_CY	PCI_CY	shape*	NumFamInTM	PctFamInTM
3.78	12943	Polygon	279	0.486911
3.55	13907	Polygon	260	0.471869
2.27	25384	Polygon	276	0.433962
3.87	13645	Polygon	226	0.411658
3.14	18775	Polygon	271	0.393895
3.16	22296	Polygon	272	0.390805
2.93	17521	Polygon	669	0.389633
3.32	16242	Polygon	1037	0.389264
3.19	18015	Polygon	362	0.388829
2.82	28426	Polygon	349	0.386918

Records in the attribute table turn blue to indicate they are selected. The corresponding ZIP Codes are also highlighted in blue on the map.

You must now determine the number of ZIP Codes and family households that are contained in the selected ZIP Codes.

6 **Find the FAMHH_CY attribute, right-click the column header, then select the Statistics option to display the Selection Statistics of ZIPCodes window.**

In this window, the number of ZIP Codes selected is displayed as the Count while the number of family households in these ZIP Codes is displayed as the Sum.

 How many ZIP Codes are selected? How many family households will receive the mailing? Look at the sorted attribute table. Can the next highest ZIP Code be added to the selection without exceeding the 750,000-household limit?

You have determined how many family households will receive mailings in this campaign. You must now determine how many of these households fall within Outdoor Living's target market. To do so, you will repeat the Statistics calculation for the NumFamInTM attribute.

7 **Close the Statistics window. Find the NumFamInTM attribute, right-click the column header, then click Statistics to display the statistics of this attribute.**

In this window, the number of target market family households is displayed as the Sum.

Update report and save map document

1 Use your map, attribute tables, and calculations to answer the questions below. Summarize your answers in the appropriate section of the project report template.

 How many ZIP Codes and family households will be included in Outdoor Living's direct-mail campaign? Why? How many target-market families will be reached by this campaign?

2 Save the map document as **OutdoorLivingFL3_fl.mxd** (replace f and I with your first and last initials) in your **\GISMKT\OutdoorLivingFL** folder.

Exercise 3.4   Select stores for outdoor show demonstrations

Outdoor Living plans to feature its new product in outdoor and recreation shows in the major metropolitan areas of Florida. The budget will support four shows in the Hillsborough County portion of the Tampa area, and you will select the stores that will host the shows. Thus, in this exercise, you will:

- Examine the distribution of target market families in Hillsborough County
- Identify retail outlets that sponsor outdoor shows each year
- Select four stores for product demonstrations at outdoor stores

Open an existing map

1   In ArcMap, open the **OutdoorLivingFL4** map document from your **\GISMKT\OutdoorLivingFL** folder.

This map document contains four layers, including a thematic layer that represents the number of families in the target market for each Hillsborough County census tract, and a layer that represents the location of recreational stores that sponsor outdoor shows. A layer depicting two-mile rings around these stores is not turned on. There is also a state layer for Florida.

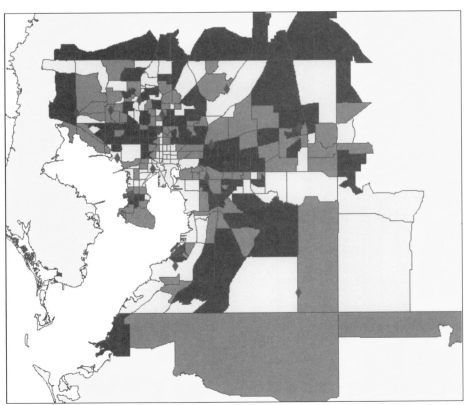

Explore stores and their surrounding areas

Note that the map displays the number of target market families in each of the area's census tracts. Review the distribution across this metropolitan area. The map also displays retail stores that sponsor outdoor shows where the new Conestoga model might be displayed. You can use the Identify tool to learn more about the locations of the stores.

1   Click the Identify tool 🛈 then click on one of the stores to display its attribute information in the Identify window.

2   Look at the attributes of other stores. As you move from store to store, observe the colors of the census tracts surrounding them to determine the number of target market families living near each store.

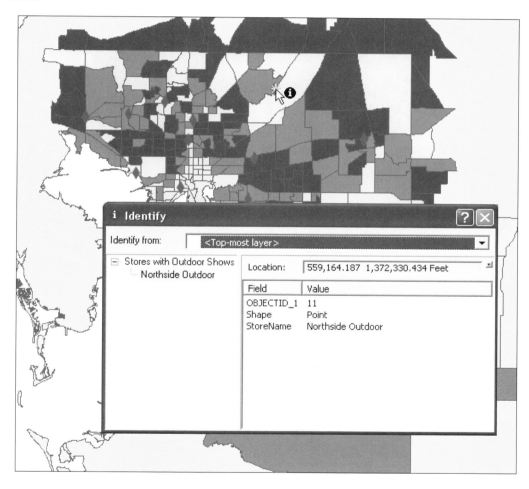

3   Close the Identify window when you're finished exploring.

Select specific stores for product demonstration at outdoor shows

Data from past outdoor shows suggests that most prospective buyers live within two miles of the show site. For this reason, you wish to view the areas where each outdoor show might draw these prospects.

1 Turn on the **Outdoor Show Attraction Rings** layer.

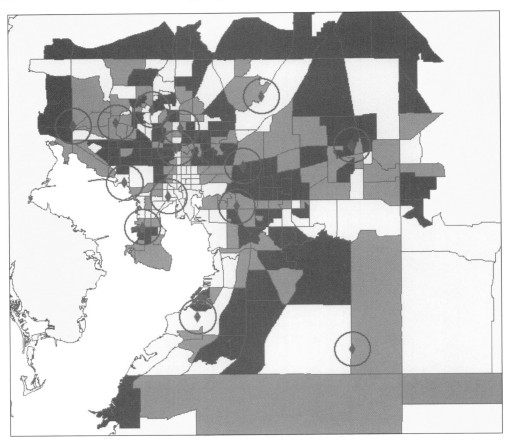

The resulting map displays a buffer ring with a two-mile radius around each outdoor show site.

2 Visually identify four stores that serve substantial numbers of target market families and are distributed across the Tampa area. Look for rings that contain several census tracts with high numbers of target market families and are geographically dispersed from each other. Your objective is to provide potential customers across the area an opportunity to view the Conestoga at a convenient outdoor show.

You will now use the map to display your selection.

3 In the table of contents, right-click the Stores with Outdoor Shows layer, then click Selection > Make This The Only Selectable Layer.

4 Click the Select Features tool ⬚ then click on a store of your choice. Notice that your selection is highlighted on the map.

5 Repeat this process with another store. When you select a second store, note what happens to the first store.

You will now use the multiple selection procedure to display the four stores you have selected for your outdoor store demonstrations.

6 With the Select Features tool active, click your first store again. Press the Shift key and hold it down. With the Shift key depressed, click your second chosen store.

7 Repeat this procedure to display your third and fourth selections.

The four selected stores are highlighted on the map. (Note: Although your map should be similar to that shown below, you may have made some different choices, which is OK.)

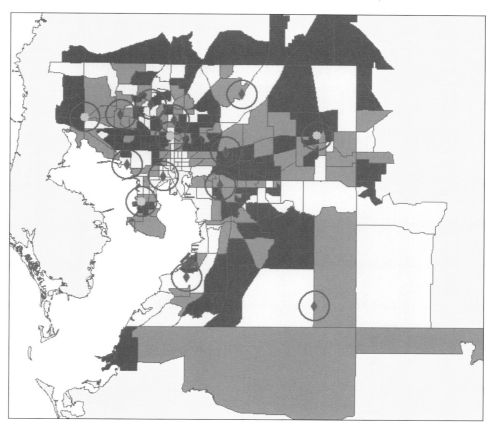

You will now export this map image and integrate it into the report template.

Export map and insert into your report

1   From the main menu bar, click File > Export Map to reach the Export Map dialog box. Navigate to your **\GISMKT\OutdoorLivingFL** folder. For File name, type **SelectedStores.emf**, then click Save to save the map document as a graphic file in EMF format to include in your report.

2   Locate the instructional text in brackets in the fourth section of the project report template for this chapter. Select this text, then from the main menu bar in Microsoft Word, click Insert > Picture > From File. Navigate to your **\GISMKT\OutdoorLivingFL** folder and select the **SelectedStores.emf** file. Click Insert to insert the picture into the report as exhibit 1. (Note: You may have to select and resize the image to fit the space provided.)

Update report and save map document

1   Use ArcMap tools and your map to answer the following questions. Summarize your answers in the appropriate section of the project report template.

Which four stores in this area have you selected to host outdoor show demonstrations? Why do you think this combination will be effective in attracting targeted customers?

2   Save the map document as **OutdoorLivingFL4_fl.mxd** (replace f and l with your first and last initials) in your **\GISMKT\OutdoorLivingFL** folder.

Exercise 3.5   Communicate and support your recommendations

You have completed the three components of your analysis and described your conclusions in the report template. You will now complete the report by summarizing your recommendations and providing maps to illustrate them. In this exercise you will:

* Restate your recommendations briefly
* Explain how geographic targeting will increase the effectiveness of each of the three components of your local marketing campaign in Florida
* Design two map layouts to support your analysis

Open an existing map

1   In ArcMap, open the **OutdoorLivingFL5** map document from your **\GISMKT\OutdoorLivingFL** folder.

This map contains four layers: a basemap of Florida, a layer displaying the state's major cities, a thematic layer displaying the number of families in the target market by county, and a thematic layer displaying the percentage of families in the target market by ZIP Code. The percentage layer is not turned on. This is the same map you created in exercise 3.2, and it identifies the ten counties you selected in that exercise as the focus of the advertising campaign.

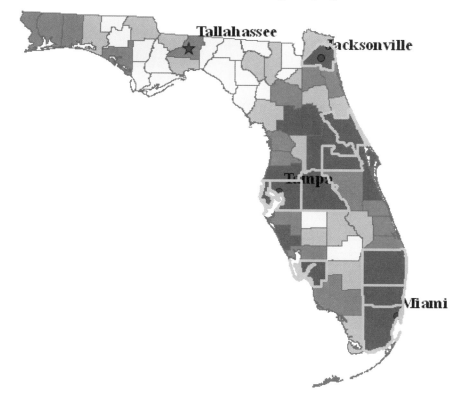

Create and edit a layout

In the first four exercises of this chapter, you used ArcMap as an analysis tool. In this exercise, you will use it as a communication tool by designing a map layout to support your report findings. A map layout is a collection of layers and other elements, such as legends, north arrows, scale bars, and text. You will use the ArcMap layout view to design a printable map, which you will use to increase the communication effectiveness of your entire marketing report.

1   **From the main menu bar, click View > Layout View.**

The map now appears in layout view with several additional elements added. Notice that the layout is a virtual piece of paper where you place and arrange elements to create a printable map suitable for a report, paper, article, or other presentation material.

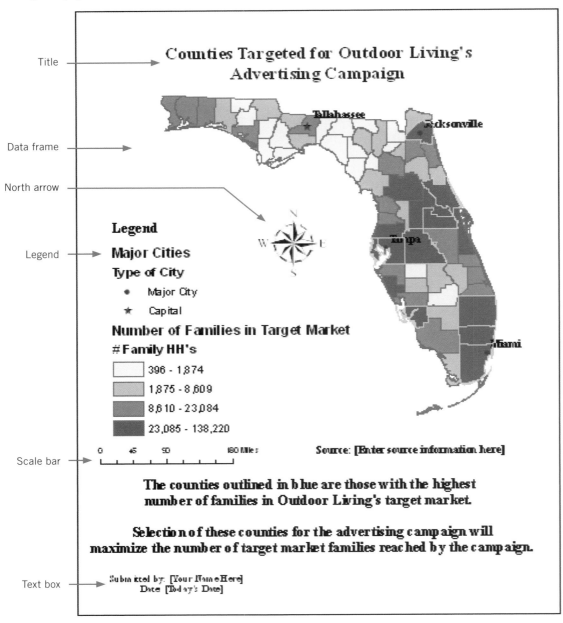

2   Review the various layout elements and note how they contribute to its communication value. To zoom in for a closer look, use the Zoom In tool on the Layout toolbar, which should have appeared when you switched to layout view. Although the tools on the Layout toolbar are similar to the navigation tools on the Tools toolbar, they are somewhat different, so familiarize yourself with each one.

The actual map illustrates the data frame, which includes all the layers you have been working with. A legend, north arrow, and scale bar all convey the meaning, orientation, and scale of the map to the reader. The three text boxes at the bottom contain data source information, the meaning of the selected features, the author, and creation date of the map—information readers require to evaluate the credibility of the map.

All the elements depict information about Florida's counties relative to the advertising campaign decision. However, the author and creation date information is incomplete. You must supply this information to complete your map for exhibit 2 in the report.

3   Notice the small text box at the bottom of the page that includes the Submitted by and Date elements. With the Select Elements tool click the text to select it. (A blue dashed line will appear around the text to show it has been selected.)

4   Right-click the selected text box and choose Properties.

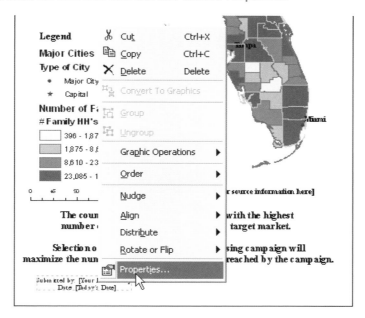

5   In the Properties dialog box, replace [Your Name Here] with your name, and replace [Today's Date] with the correct date. Click OK to accept the changes and close the dialog box.

Readers of your report must be able to ascertain the source and currency of the information it displays. You will edit the sources text box to provide this information.

6   Click the Sources text box just below the map, then right-click it and choose Properties. Replace the placeholder text with **ESRI Community Data, 2005**. Click OK.

Export the map layout document

The complete map is now ready to become exhibit 2 in your report. You will save it as a graphic file and insert it into the report template.

1   From the main menu bar, click File > Export Map to reach the Export Map dialog box. Navigate to your **\GISMKT\OutdoorLivingFL** folder. For File name, type **CountyAd.emf**, then click Save to save the map document as a graphic file in EMF format to include in your report.

2   In the project report template for this chapter, locate the page entitled Exhibit 2: County map for advertising campaign. Select the instructional text in brackets, then from the main menu bar in Microsoft Word, click Insert > Picture > From File. Navigate to your **\GISMKT\OutdoorLivingFL** folder and select the **CountyAd.emf** file. Click Insert to insert the picture into the report as exhibit 2. (Note: You may have to select and resize the image to display it on the same page as the title.)

Exhibit 2 of your report is now complete.

Edit data frame contents in layout view

To produce exhibit 3 of your report, you must edit the contents of the map to display the ZIP Codes that will be the focus of Outdoor Living's direct-mail campaign. To do so, you will edit the data frame and the map's title and text.

1   In the ArcMap table of contents, click the check boxes to turn off the Number of Families in Target Market layer and turn on the Percent of Families in Target Market layer. Now this layer displays in the data frame area of layout view.

This is the layer you created in exercise 3.3 to identify the ZIP Codes to be included in the direct-mail campaign. However, the selected ZIP Codes do not appear in the current map. To display them you must repeat the selection process you used in exercise 3.3.

2   Right-click the Percent of Families in Target Market layer, then click Open Attribute Table.

3   Click the Options button at the bottom of the attribute table, then choose Select by Attributes.

4   In the Select by Attributes dialog box, double-click the attribute name [PctFamInTM], then click the operator >=, then type **.316** at the end of the equation in the Query box so that the full equation reads: [PctFamInTM] >= .316. (This is the minimum value of the highest quantile in the classification scheme.)

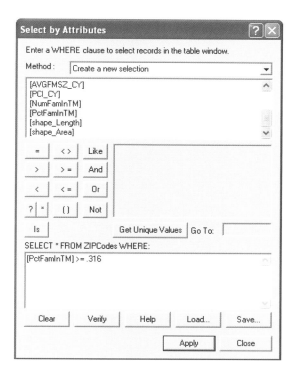

5   Click Apply, then close the dialog box.

The selected ZIP Codes now appear in the layout. (Note: If this is not the case, press the F5 key to refresh the view.) You must now edit the title and text to reflect the new content of the map.

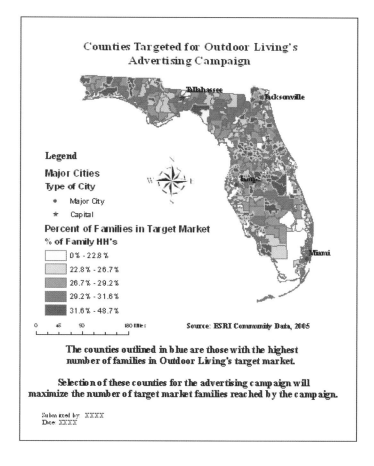

6   Open the properties for the title at the top of the layout page.

7   Replace the existing title text with **ZIP Codes Targeted for Outdoor Living's Direct Mail Campaign**. (Note: You may need to place a hard return after "Outdoor Living's" so the type will fit neatly on the page.)

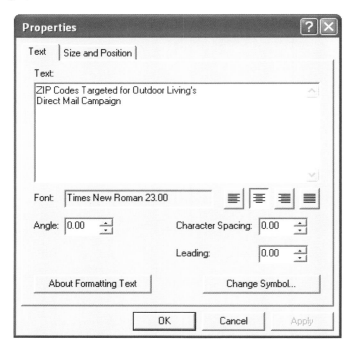

8   Click OK.

9   Open the properties for the large text box at the bottom of the page.

10 Delete the existing text and type: **The ZIP Codes outlined in blue are those with the highest percentage of families in Outdoor Living's target market. Selection of these ZIP Codes for the direct-mail campaign will maximize the number of target market families reached by the campaign.** (Note: You may need to manually enter hard returns by pressing the Enter key at the end of each line for the text to fit neatly on the page.) Click OK.

The resulting map now displays a title and explanatory text appropriate for the map's contents. It is ready to be exported and inserted into the project report.

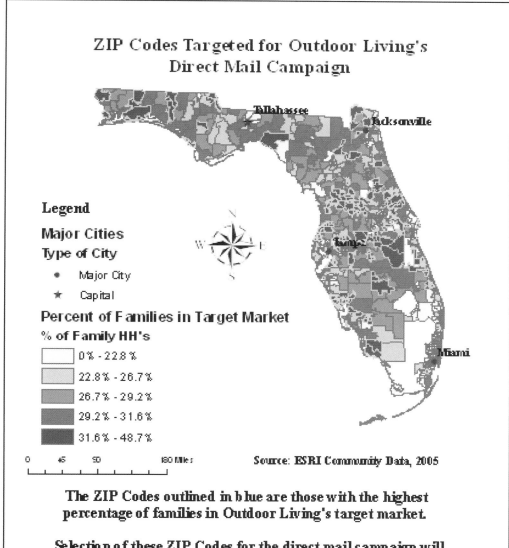

Export the new layout document

1   From the main menu bar, click File > Export Map. Navigate to your **\GISMKT\OutdoorLivingFL** folder. For File Name, type **ZIPMail.emf**, then click Save to save the map document as a graphic file in EMF format to include in your report.

2   In the project report template, locate the page entitled Exhibit 3: ZIP Code map for direct mail campaign. Select the instructional text, and from the main menu bar in Microsoft Word, click Insert > Picture > From File. Navigate to your **\GISMKT\OutdoorLivingFL** folder and select the **ZIPMail.emf** file, then click Insert to insert the picture into the report as exhibit 3. (Note: You may have to select and resize the image to display it on the same page as the title.)

Exhibit 3 of your report is now complete.

Update report and save map document

1   Use these map documents and your conclusions from prior exercises to complete the following task. Summarize your answer in the appropriate section of the project report template.

Restate your recommendations briefly and explain how geographic targeting will increase the effectiveness of each of the three components of your local marketing campaign in Florida.

2   Save the map document as **OutdoorLivingFL5_fl.mxd** (replace f and l with your first and last initials) in your **\GISMKT\OutdoorLivingFL** folder.

3   Close ArcMap.

Your written report with both map document exhibits is complete and ready for submission.

Congratulations! You have completed the Outdoor Living project.

Pause for a moment to consider what you have accomplished in this chapter. You have learned about various types of demographic measures and observed their distribution in the state of Florida at different levels of geography. You have used this data to identify concentrations of target customers for each of the three components of Outdoor Living's promotional campaign and designed map documents to communicate these results to an audience. In short, you have used ArcGIS as an effective analytical and communication tool in the market segmentation process.

Additional applications

This project covers the most fundamental marketing strategy of identifying target customers and focusing marketing efforts on concentrations of those customers. Though this process can be implemented with the simplified data used here, it becomes even more powerful when applied with sophisticated data and targeting techniques.

For example, while this project uses simple demographics of families within a specific income range, ESRI Business Information Solutions (ESRI BIS)[1] provides much more precise and complex analysis. Data is available on hundreds of additional variables, including ethnicity, income, household size and composition, housing ownership, housing value, net worth, type of employment, and educational attainment, among others. This data is available for a range of political, census, and postal geographies to support the needs of the analyst. In addition, several variables offer a range of historical values, current estimates, and future projections to support longitudinal study.

In addition to this wealth of demographic and socioeconomic data, ESRI BIS also offers extensive lifestyle data in the Community Tapestry Segmentation system. This system integrates demographic and socioeconomic information with lifestyle and purchasing data to provide profiles of 65 distinct neighborhood clusters. This system provides marketers with a more detailed understanding of the motivations, values, and lifestyles that underlie consumer purchasing patterns. Chapter 2 provides an overview of this system and its marketing applications. Chapters 4 and 5 use this system to develop marketing strategies responsive to these lifestyle variations.

ESRI Business Analyst, a software and data extension to ArcGIS, combines this extensive data collection with sophisticated analytical tools to support richer segmentation analysis. Working directly with customer files, an organization can create a profile of its best customers and then look across the United States for concentrations of prospective new customers who match that profile.

Several organizations use these capabilities to enhance their segmentation analysis. Galyans Sports and Outdoor stores, for example, uses its customer database integrated with demographic and Community Tapestry data from Business Analyst to focus its customer prospecting efforts.[2]

Similarly, Telefónica del Perú has implemented a GIS system that supports a wide range of its operations, from facilities management to customer service.[3] Among them is market analysis, in which thematic mapping is used to identify underserved areas of Peru, and attractive markets for wireless services among existing landline customers.

The *Arizona Republic* serves its advertisers by providing selective distribution of promotional materials to households with desired demographic characteristics, thus improving response rates and advertising effectiveness.[4] Advertisers can select ZIP Code level concentration or choose carrier routes within ZIP Codes to focus on target customers more closely. The *Washington Times* uses a similar approach to attract new subscribers. However, it focuses on lifestyle characteristics by targeting Community Tapestry segments in its marketing program.[5]

Western Exterminator also uses GIS tools to identify marketing opportunities in the metropolitan areas it serves.[6] The firm performs termite inspections that are required as part of home sales. By combining its internal records of inspections with home sales data by ZIP Code, the firm can identify ZIP Codes with high home sales and few inspections. These ZIP Code areas are growth opportunities for Western's inspection services.

As these examples illustrate, the business analysis capabilities that ArcGIS Desktop provides have tremendous value in the customer prospecting process. Identifying concentrations of target customers can improve the focus of promotional expenditures and help firms refine their products and hone their messages to find and serve their customers more effectively.

1. ESRI Business Information Solutions is currently known as ESRI Community Data.

2. Kevin Burgess, "Customer Analysis, Prospecting and Segmentation," ESRI Business GeoInfo Summit, June 2004.

3. Jim Baumann, "Are You Being Served," *Directions,* May 19, 2005.

4. Jay Visnansky, "Doing Market Focused Selling at the Arizona Republic," ESRI Business GeoInfo Summit, April 2005.

5. ESRI. "The Washington Times: GIS Increases Newspaper Subscriptions," Business Analyst product promotion brochure, 2005.

6. David Boyles, *GIS Means Business:Vol. 2,* Redlands, CA: ESRI Press, 2002.

CHAPTER 4

Planning a Merchandising Strategy

Course: Consumer Behavior

This chapter covers the role of GIS in merchandising strategies that focus on lifestyle segmentation. The retail expansion of Meiers Home Furnishings* in Chicago has not been as successful as planned. The market area for the firm's second store is quite similar demographically to that of its original store. Sales, however, have been disappointingly low. Why the difference? In this chapter you will learn how to use GIS tools and the Community Tapestry lifestyle segmentation system to analyze the demographic and lifestyle characteristics of market areas and customize marketing strategies according to these characteristics.

* This is a fictional company and scenario, created for educational purposes only. Any resemblance to actual persons, events, or corporations is unintended.

To design a merchandising strategy that is responsive to the market area of the struggling store, you will learn how to use ArcGIS to:

1. Create maps displaying population demographics and characteristics of the competitive environment
2. Define market areas for the two Meiers stores
3. Compare demographic characteristics and dominant Community Tapestry segments of the market areas
4. Analyze the values and purchasing patterns of the dominant segments using Market Potential Indexes
5. Customize the merchandising strategy of the Meiers store on Pulaski to the lifestyle, values, and purchasing patterns of its market area
6. Design maps to communicate and support your merchandising strategy recommendation

Marketing scenario

Meiers Home Furnishings is a family-owned retail furniture firm in the Chicago area. Its objective is to offer good quality, value-priced home furnishings to lower middle-class working families. Meiers defines this target market as families with incomes between $25,000 and $45,000 (in 2004) and with a high school education or less. It seeks to reach these customers with convenient, medium-sized retail stores in areas not served by large furniture stores or shopping centers.

The first Meiers store, opened by family patriarch Gunter Meiers on Lombard Street in 1954, was the firm's only outlet until three years ago. Then, granddaughter and current owner Ashley Meiers Johnson opened a second store near Pulaski Avenue. She chose this site because of the demographic similarity of the neighborhood with that of the original store. Specifically, Johnson sought a market area whose population was similar to that of the Lombard store in family structure, income, education, home ownership, and furniture purchasing patterns.

Sales for the first three years have been disappointing. Not only has the store produced lower sales levels, the mix of furniture items purchased has been quite different from that of the original store. As a result, Johnson is concerned that most of the furniture she is displaying is not attractive to her potential customers. This, in turn, increases her inventory carrying costs and, more importantly, causes her to lose sales that she could retain with the appropriate product mix. Further, she is puzzled that neighborhoods selected for their demographic similarity would display such significant variations in purchase patterns.

To address this problem, Johnson has directed you, as the new marketing manager for Meiers Home Furnishings, to reassess the original decision, to expand the consumer profile of the firm's stores, and, if necessary, to recommend a more appropriate marketing strategy. Further, she has approved your request to purchase additional demographic data, specifically, Community Tapestry profiles of the Lombard and Pulaski market areas and Market Potential Indexes based on consumer survey data from Mediamark Research Inc., provided by ESRI. You believe the additional demographic information and Community Tapestry lifestyle segmentation data might provide further insight into the differences, if any, between the Lombard and Pulaski market areas. Your approach will be to review the demographic characteristics of the two market areas and, if necessary, expand their profiles to include Community Tapestry data and relevant Market Potential Indexes.

You will use GIS tools to perform this business analysis for Meiers Home Furnishings and make recommendations for serving the customers of the Lombard and Pulaski stores more effectively.

Background information

Consumer purchasing decisions are complex behaviors influenced by a variety of personal, social, and situational factors. Consumer behavior is the field of marketing that seeks to understand these factors and their interactions in order to increase marketers' understanding of their customers. This understanding, in turn, is necessary for the design of marketing strategies that are responsive to consumer needs and purchasing behaviors. The situation Meiers Home Furnishings is facing illustrates the value of understanding the multifaceted aspect of consumer behavior.

The analysis begins with demographic data and an update of the demographic profile of the two market areas. This is a replication of the initial site selection decision that tests the continuing validity of the conclusion of demographic similarity. If that conclusion was incorrect or if population shifts over the past three years have eroded the demographic similarity of the market areas, then these factors might account for disappointing sales.

If the demographic similarities of the two market areas remain, you must examine other factors that contribute to the sales problem. Here you will use a second source—lifestyle data from the Community Tapestry segmentation system. Built by the ESRI data development team, Tapestry is the premier segmentation system available today. It is the culmination of a 30-year process of multivariate classification of households in the United States. The Community Tapestry system uses more than 60 variables from several sources to identify 65 discrete lifestyle segments. Households in each segment display similar demographic, lifestyle, and purchasing patterns. For a good introduction to the system, you should already have completed chapter 2: Working with Community Tapestry Data. That chapter explains how to access summary information, demographic profiles, and Market Potential Indexes for all 65 Community Tapestry segments.

More than 90 percent of households in the Lombard and Pulaski market areas fall into five of the 65 Community Tapestry segments. The distribution of these segments within the two market areas is included as a layer in the map documents you will use in the following exercises. You will compare this data to assess the differences in lifestyle patterns between the Lombard and Pulaski market areas.

If these market areas have different Community Tapestry distributions, you may understand their variations in purchasing patterns through a third source, purchasing behavior data from Market Potential Indexes. These measures indicate the frequency with which a particular group engages in a specific behavior compared with national averages. In this case, the groups are Community Tapestry segments. Market Potential Indexes are reported on a scale in which a score of 100 indicates that the group's value equals the national value. Scores above 100 indicate that the group's value is above the national value, while scores below 100 indicate the opposite.

As an example, a relevant behavior might be "Bought living room furniture in the past 12 months." While 30 percent of all households say they have done so, 36 percent of households in the Urban Chic Community Tapestry segment say they have done so. The Market Potential Index in this case is 120 [calculated as follows $((36/30)\times100)$], which indicates that Urban Chic households are 20 percent more likely to buy living room furniture annually than the population as a whole. If, on the other hand, 24 percent of the Exurbanites segment report this behavior, their Market Potential

Index would be 80, indicating that they are 20 percent less likely to buy living room furniture annually than is the population as a whole.

In this project, relevant Market Potential Indexes for furniture purchases are reported for each of the five Community Tapestry segments in the Lombard and Pulaski store areas. They provide more specific information about how variations in consumer lifestyle are reflected in purchasing behavior for specific products. You will use this information to recommend marketing strategy adjustments that will allow Meiers Home Furnishings to serve its customers more effectively.

Meiers Home Furnishings Chicago data dictionary	
Attribute	**Description**
For CensusTracts (ESRI)	
FAMHH_CY	Family households, 2004
AVGFINC_CY	Average family income, 2004
AVGVAL_CY	Average value of home, 2004
FURNPUR_CY	Total furniture purchases, 2004
For MajorRoads	
NAME	Name of road
Type	Type of road (limited access, primary highway, secondary highway)
For MeiersStores and FurnitureStores (Hypothetical)	
AnnualSales	Last year's sales
StoreType	Type of store by ownership
For MeiersFurnitureStores (Hypothetical)	
Location	Name of location
AnnualSales	Last year's sales
For ShoppingCenters (Hypothetical)	
SizInSqFt	Size of center in square feet of floor space
OccupancyRate	High, moderate, or low percent of available retail space occupied in past year
For MeiersMarketAreaDemographics (ESRI)	
Location	Store location
FAMHH_CY	Family households, 2004
AVGFINC_CY	Average family income, 2004
AVGVAL_CY	Average value of home, 2004
FurnFam	Furniture purchases per family
PctTM	Percentage of families in Meiers's target market
PctHSLess	Percentage of persons over 25 with a high school education or less
AvgFamSiz	Average family size
PctOwnHom	Percentage of families owning their home

For MeiersMarketAreaTapestry (ESRI)	
Location	Store location
	Number of households in each Community Tapestry segment 2004. Of the 65 Community Tapestry segments, these five account for over 90 percent of households in the Lombard and Pulaski market areas.
HH34	Number of Households in Family Foundations segment
HH45	Number of Households in City Strivers segment
HH47	Number of Households in Las Casas segment
HH51	Number of Households in Metro City Edge segment
HH64	Number of Households in City Commons segment[CEL1]
For TapestryMarketPotential	
BuyBehav	Buying behavior
HH34	Index for Family Foundations segment
HH45	Index for City Strivers segment
HH47	Index for Las Casas segment
HH51	Index for Metro City Edge segment
HH64	Index for City Commons segment
Source: ESRI, 2005; Community Tapestry Demonstration CD, 2006; MPI Data derived from MediaMark Research Inc., Doublebase 2004; hypothetical data for this exercise	

Exercise 4.1   Explore demographics and competition in Chicago

To understand the competitive situation of Meiers Home Furnishings, you must analyze its locations, those of competing furniture stores and shopping centers, and the relevant characteristics of the Chicago market. Thus, in this exercise, you will:

- Display maps of the Chicago area and its major roads
- Display the distribution of demographic characteristics across the area's census tracts
- Display the location and size of Chicago's furniture stores and shopping centers
- Display the locations and sales levels of the two Meiers stores

Open an existing map

1   **From the Windows taskbar, click Start > All Programs > ArcGIS > ArcMap.**

Depending on how ArcGIS and ArcMap have been installed or which Windows operating system you are using, there may be a slightly different navigation menu from which to open ArcMap.

2   **If you see a Start dialog box, click the "An existing map" option. Otherwise, click the Open button** **on the Standard toolbar.**

3   **Browse to the location of the GISMKT folder (e.g., C:\ESRIPress\GISMKT), double-click the MeiersChicago folder, then click the MeiersChicago1 map document and click Open.**

The map contains six layers, only three of which are currently visible in the map. One displays the location of Meiers Home Furnishings stores in Chicago. A second displays the location and size of Chicago's shopping centers, and a third the location and sales levels of competing furniture stores. A fourth layer displays the major roads in the Chicago area. The remaining two layers display the number of family households and average family income for the Chicago area census tracts.

Display layers

As stated above, not all of the layers appear in the map. You determine the information displayed in the map by turning layers on and off in the table of contents.

Turn layers off and on

1   Click the small check box to the left of the Shopping Centers layer to turn this layer on.

The shopping center point symbols vary in size based on each one's available square footage of shopping space. This allows you to assess the opportunities they create for Meiers in both location and size. Shopping centers with larger shopping areas offer shoppers more choices and generally draw them in greater numbers. This stream of shoppers creates an opportunity for Meiers, if the firm can entice them to visit their stores while they are in the area. Hence, shopping centers that are larger or nearer will create greater opportunities for crossover shoppers (those who are drawn to the area by the shopping center but visit other stores as well) than smaller, more distant stores. The symbols allow you to assess both factors simultaneously.

2   Click the small check box to the left of the Furniture Stores layer to turn this layer on.

Competing furniture stores now display on the map in symbols that represent their annual sales, which also allows you to assess their competitive position relative to Meiers stores.

3   Click the small check box to the left of the Family Households by Census Tract layer to turn it off (the check mark disappears).

4   Click the small check box to the left of the Average Family Income by Census Tract layer to turn it on.

The map below displays the results of these changes. Using these functions, you may explore the layers individually or in any combination you choose.

Add and display a new layer

Add a layer

The table of contents contains thematic layers with demographic characteristics. To complete your initial analysis, you must display a third characteristic, Average Home Value, and examine its distribution across Chicago's census tracts.

1 **Click the Add Data button.**

2 **In the Add Data dialog box, navigate to \GISMKT\MeiersChicago.mdb. Double-click the MeiersChicago geodatabase to open it and then click CensusTracts.**

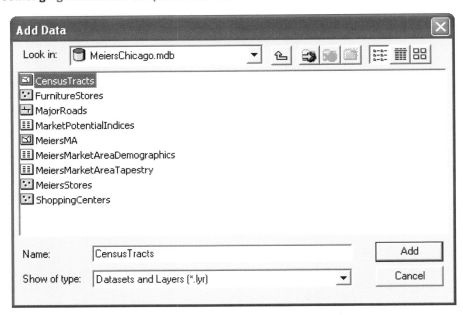

3 **Click Add to add the layer to the table of contents.**

The new layer is added to the table of contents and displays with a single color. You will now revise the properties of this layer to display average family home value.

Edit a layer's name and symbology

1   In the table of contents, double-click the CensusTracts layer (or right click the layer and select Properties).

2   Click the General tab and enter **Average Home Value by Census Tract** as the new layer name.

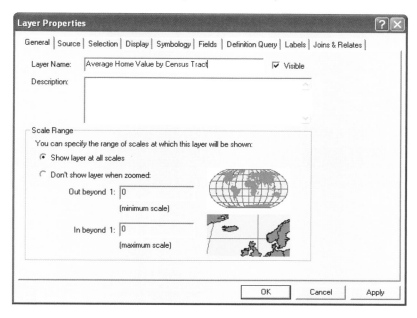

3   Click the Symbology tab. In the Show area click Quantities and then Graduated Colors.

4   In the drop-down box for the Value field select the appropriate attribute. (You can use the data dictionary to identify the attribute that reports average home value.)

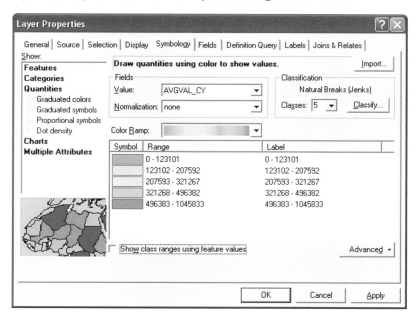

Notice that the ArcMap default classification system uses five classes assigned by natural breaks. You will change these settings to achieve consistency with the other census tract layers.

5   Click the Classify button to open the Classification dialog box.

6   For Method, choose Quantile.

7   For Classes, choose 3.

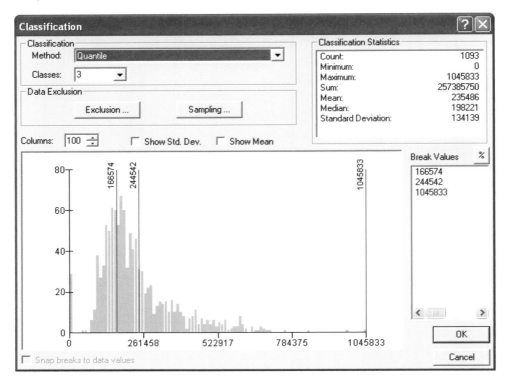

These options will cause the map to define three classes with a roughly equal number of census tracts in each. This is the same classification setting used by the other demographic layers in the map.

8   Click OK to return to the Layer Properties dialog box.

Format classification labels

You will now adjust the display of the classification labels in the map legend.

1   Click the Label heading in the Layer Properties dialog box, then click Format Labels to open the Number Format dialog box. (Note: Do not click the Labels tab at the top of this dialog box. If you do so inadvertently, click the Symbology tab to return.)

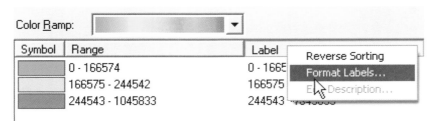

2   In the Category area, select Currency.

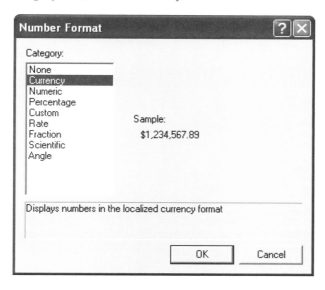

3   Click OK to return to the Layer Properties dialog box. Note that the labels now appear with $ signs and two decimal places.

4   Select a color scheme in the Color Ramp that will allow the Shopping Centers, Furniture Stores, and Major Roads layers to be clearly visible.

5   Check the box next to Show class ranges using feature values so that the classification ranges will be defined using actual values from the AVGVAL_CY field in the layer's attribute table.

The Symbology dialog box should look like this, though your choice of a color ramp might vary.

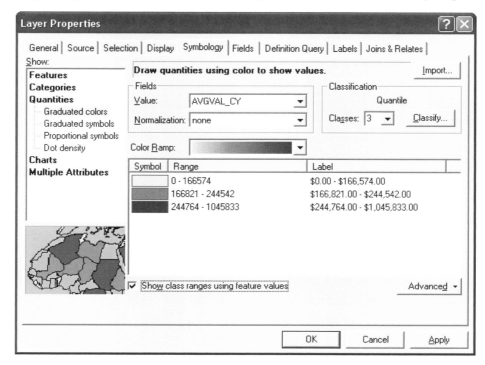

6   Click OK to close the Layer Properties dialog box and apply your changes.

The resulting layer displays the average home value in each of Chicago's census tracts. While it displays useful information, the map is cluttered and covers a larger geographic area than is relevant in the current analysis.

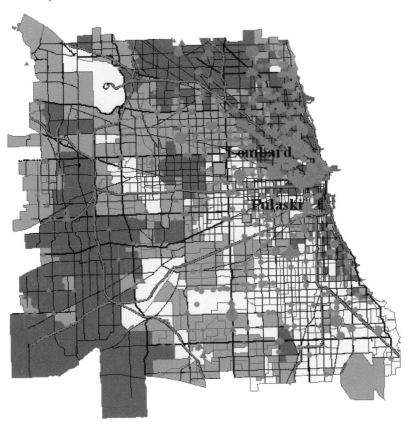

Change legend title

1   In the table of contents, click the attribute name AVGVAL_CY under the title to this layer, then click again to edit it.

2   Replace AVGVAL_CY with **Average Value in $US**. (Note: If your second click is too quick, the Properties dialog box will open. Click Cancel, then try again, clicking more slowly to reach the edit capability.)

Explore store locations

The Zoom In tool allows you to focus on a smaller area of a larger map. You will use it to concentrate your attention on the area surrounding the two Meiers stores.

Zoom to a specific area

1   Click the Zoom In tool 🔍 on the Tools toolbar to select it.

2   Zoom to a view that includes both of the Meiers stores.

The resulting map should display the area that surrounds the two stores. It should resemble the graphic below. (If you make a mistake, click the Previous Extent button ⬅ then zoom again.)

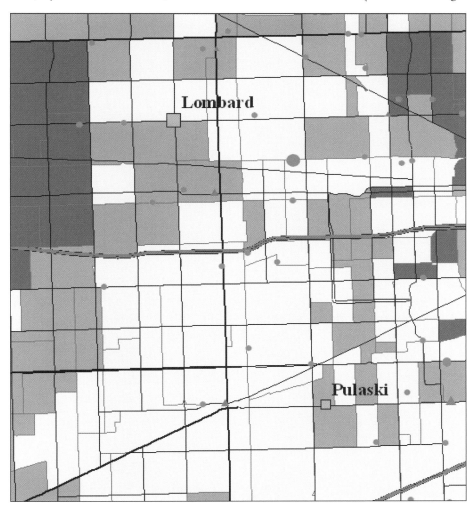

Select and identify features

The map displays shopping centers and furniture stores near the Meiers stores. These features affect the competitive environment in different ways. Shopping centers within a two-mile radius have a favorable impact, attracting shoppers who may visit Meiers while they are in the area. In contrast, furniture stores within one mile of the Lombard and Pulaski stores compete directly for sales with Meiers. You will select the shopping centers within two miles of Meiers locations and assess their impact, then repeat the process for furniture stores within a one-mile radius.

1 Click the Selection tab at the bottom of the table of contents.

2 From the layers list, check the Shopping Centers and Furniture Stores layers to set them as selectable layers, and uncheck all other layers.

3 Click the Display tab at the bottom of the table of contents to return to the display view.

4 On the main menu bar, click Selection, then Select by Location. Choose the options that will create a selection of shopping centers that are within a distance of two miles of Meiers Home Furnishings Stores.

The Select by Location dialog box should match the graphic below.

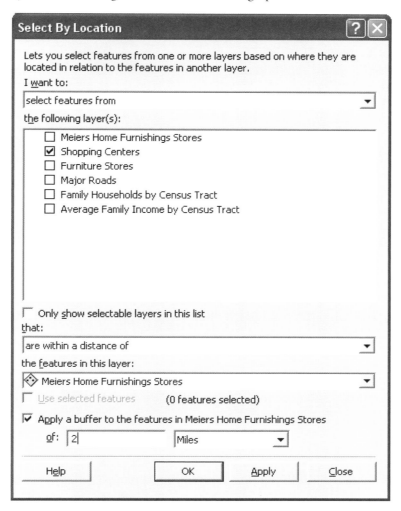

5   Click Apply, then Close.

The shopping centers within two miles of either Meiers store are highlighted on the map. You will use the Identify tool to learn more about them.

6   Click the Identify tool ⓘ to select it. This opens the Identify window.

7   For the Layers option at the top of the Identify window, click the drop-down arrow and choose Shopping Centers. Move the window as needed to view the map.

8   Click one of the selected shopping centers on the map. The attributes for this shopping center appear in the Identify window.

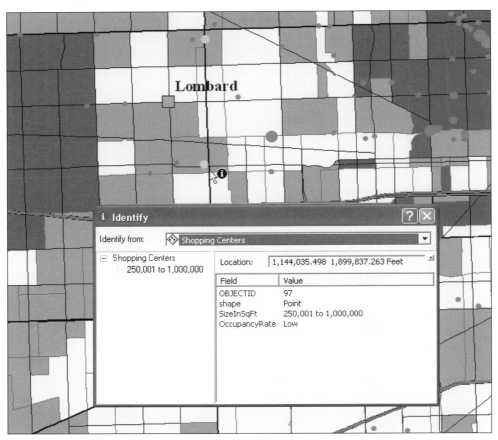

Note the OccupancyRate attribute, which reports the average monthly percentage of available space in the center occupied by retailers over the past year. This number is an indication of the attractiveness of the center to retailers. A high occupancy rate indicates that existing retailers are successful in the center and remain there, while new retailers move into the center quickly should vacancies occur. These centers attract more shoppers than do centers with moderate or low occupancy rates and, as a result, create greater crossover shopping opportunities for Meiers Home Furnishings. Recall that crossover shopping occurs when shoppers who are drawn to an area by one retail center (a shopping center) also visit other stores in the area (including Meiers Home Furnishings).

9   Use the Identify tool to review the attributes of the remaining selected shopping centers and their value in attracting shoppers to the Lombard and Pulaski locations.

10 On the main menu bar, click Selection, then Clear Selected Features. Now click Selection >
    Select by Location. Choose the options that will create a selection of furniture stores that are
    within one mile of Meiers Home Furnishings stores.

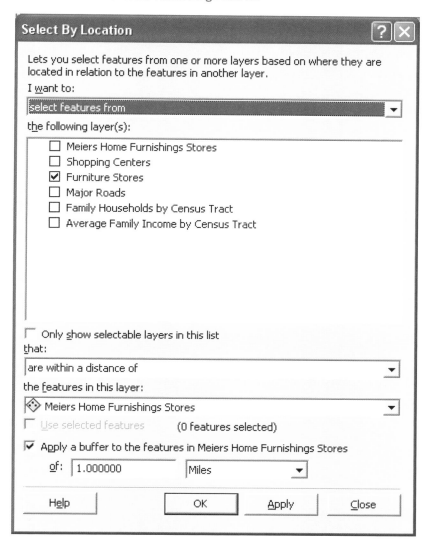

11 Click Apply, then Close.

12 Again use the Identify tool to review the attributes of the selected furniture stores and the
    competitive threat they pose to Meiers. (Note: Remember to choose Furniture Stores from
    the Layers drop-down list.) In general, the higher the level of sales, the greater the threat. In
    addition, chain stores generally have greater promotional resources than do independents and
    thus pose a greater threat.

Use this information to answer the report questions.

Update report and save map document

1   Use the map and the techniques you have learned to answer the questions below. Summarize your answer in the appropriate section of the project report template (MeiersChicago_ReportTemplate .doc), which you will find in your \GISMKT\MeiersChicago folder.

What do you observe about the geographic distribution of families, their income levels, and home values in Chicago? About the location of the two Meiers Home Furnishings stores relative to competitors, shopping centers, and major roads?

2   Save your map file as MeiersChicago1_fl.mxd (replace f and l with your first and last initials). To do so, click File on the main menu bar, then Save As. Navigate to your **\GISMKT\MeiersChicago** folder, type **MeiersChicago1_fl.mxd** as the file name, and click Save.

Exercise 4.2   Analyze market area demographic and Community Tapestry characteristics

To understand the customer base of the two Meiers stores, you must define the market areas of the stores and compare the demographic and lifestyle characteristics of the populations of these areas. Thus, in this exercise, you will:

* Define and display a simple one-mile ring market area for each store
* Compare the demographic and socioeconomic characteristics of the two market areas
* Compare the Community Tapestry composition of the two market areas

Open an existing map

1   In ArcMap, open the **MeiersChicago2** map document from your **\GISMKT\MeiersChicago** folder.

The extent of this map includes the area surrounding the two Meiers stores. The table of contents contains layers representing the Lombard and Pulaski stores, competing furniture stores, local shopping centers, major roads in the area, and average home values of Chicago area census tracts. The map also includes two data tables that contain demographic and Community Tapestry data for the market areas of Meiers Home Furnishings stores.

2   To see the data tables, click the Source tab at the bottom of the table of contents.

Define market areas for the Lombard and Pulaski stores

The current map allows you to see general characteristics of the locations of the two stores by displaying various demographic layers and observing their distribution relative to the stores. However, to make specific comparisons, you must focus on the market areas that each store serves. While market areas can be defined in many ways, in this exercise you will use a simple one-mile ring around each store to approximate the area in which most of its customers live. You will then be able to make direct comparisons of the demographic and lifestyle characteristics of the customers within the two market areas.

Create a buffer layer

1   Click the ArcToolbox button ![icon] on the Standard toolbar to open ArcToolbox.

2   Click the plus sign next to Analysis Tools to expand the toolbox, then expand the Proximity toolset to see the Buffer tool.

3   Double-click Buffer to open the tool's dialog box.

4   In the Buffer dialog box, click the drop-down arrow below the Input Features field, and select Meiers Home Furnishings Stores as the input features layer.

5 Click the Browse button to the right of the Output Feature Class field, navigate to **\GISMKT\ MeiersChicago\MeiersChicago.mdb**, and type **MeiersMarketAreas** for the name.

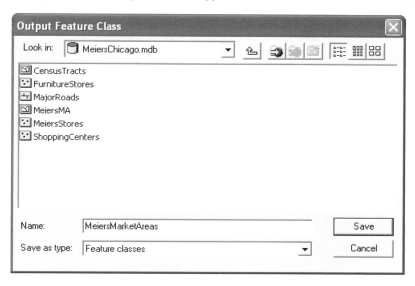

6 Click Save.

7 Back in the Buffer dialog box, enter **1** in the Linear unit field, and in the drop-down box to the right of this field, select Miles as the measurement unit.

The Buffer dialog box should look like the graphic below.

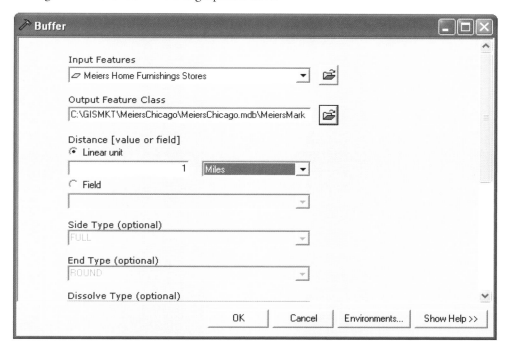

8 Click OK to run the buffer operation.

A progress window will display during the execution of this tool. It will notify you when the process is complete and the resulting buffer layer has been added to the table of contents and the map.

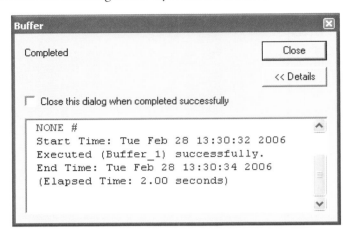

9 When the process is complete, if necessary, click Close to close the progress window.

10 Click the X in the upper right corner of ArcToolbox to close it.

The market areas of the two stores are now displayed on the map in the form of circles with a one-mile radius around the Lombard and Pulaski stores. The solid color of the circles obscures some of the layers below. You will adjust the display of the buffer layer to correct this.

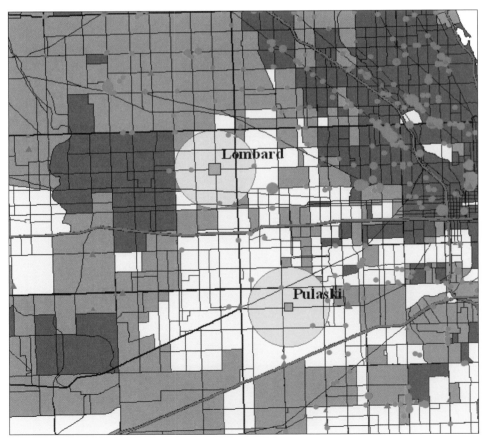

Change the display of a layer

First you will give the buffer layer a more descriptive name.

1   In the table of contents, double-click MeiersMarketAreas to open the Layer Properties dialog box. (Or right-click, then click Properties.)

2   Click the General tab, then enter **Meiers Store Market Areas** in the Layer Name field.

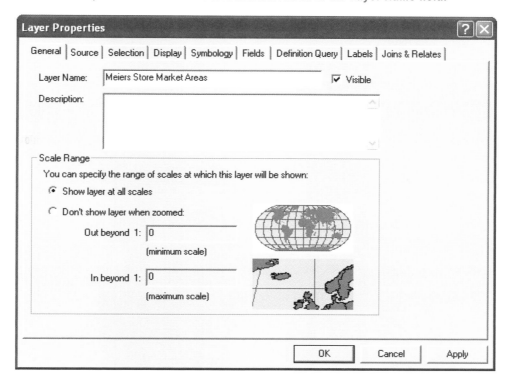

3   Click OK to change the layer's name.

Now you will change the layer's symbology.

4   Click the small, colored box below the Meiers Store Market Areas layer to open the Symbol Selector dialog box.

5   Click the arrow to the right of Fill Color and choose No Color to obtain a hollow, no-fill circle.

6   Click the up arrow in the Outline Width field to select an outline width of 2.

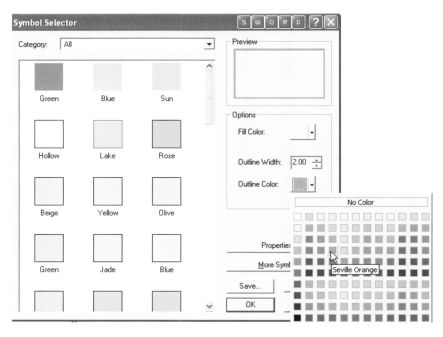

7   Click the arrow to the right of the Outline Color field and select Seville orange (row 4, column 4) as the color for the circle outlines.

8   Click OK to apply the new settings to the layer.

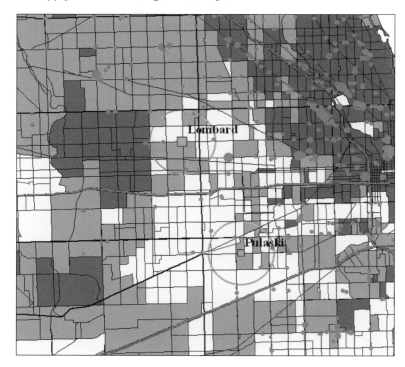

The resulting map displays the two stores, their market areas, and the surrounding features. Having defined the market areas, you are ready to compare their demographic and lifestyle characteristics.

Compare market area characteristics

At your request, Ms. Johnson has purchased demographic and lifestyle data for the market areas of the Lombard and Pulaski stores. This information is stored in the data tables you see at the bottom of the table of contents. You will use this data to compare the market areas of the two stores.

Compare demographic attribute values

1   In the table of contents, right-click the MeiersMarketAreaDemographics table, then click Open. (Note: If you don't see the table, click the Source tab at the bottom of the table of contents.)

This table contains the attribute values for the Lombard and Pulaski market areas.

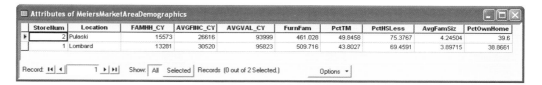

StoreNum	Location	FAMHH_CY	AVGFINC_CY	AVGVAL_CY	FurnFam	PctTM	PctHSLess	AvgFamSiz	PctOwnHome
2	Pulaski	15573	26616	93999	461.028	49.8458	75.3767	4.24504	39.6
1	Lombard	13281	30520	95823	509.716	43.8027	69.4591	3.89715	38.8661

2   Use the data dictionary to match the variable name to the demographic attribute. Write the values from the attribute table in the table below. To complete the last column, you must compare the values for the two store market areas. If the values for the Pulaski market area are within 15 percent of the values for the Lombard market area, you enter **X** in this column to indicate that they are similar. If the Pulaski values are within 10 percent of the Lombard values, enter **XX** in this column to indicate that they are *very* similar. To calculate the percentage difference, subtract the Lombard value from the Pulaski value and divide by the Lombard value. Multiply the result by 100 to express it as a percentage. Values may be positive or negative. If the magnitude is less than 15 but greater than 10, the market areas are classified as similar. If the magnitude is less than 10, the market areas are classified as *very* similar. For example, a value of -11 would be considered similar because 11 is between 10 and 15.

Demographic attribute	Lombard market area	Pulaski market area	Similar = X Very similar = XX
Family Households			
Avg Family Income			
Avg Home Value			
Furniture Purchases per Family			
% Families in TM			
% HS Educ or Less			
Avg Family Size			
% Families Owning Home			

If the demographic attribute values for the two stores differ enough, that might explain the performance variations of the stores. However, if they are similar or very similar, these variations are more likely related to lifestyle differences rather than demographics.

As a whole, are the characteristics of the market areas similar or dissimilar? Can performance variations in the stores be attributed to demographic differences in their market areas?

3   Close the attribute table.

Compare lifestyle attribute values

1 Now open the MeiersMarketAreaTapestry table.

If the demographic attribute values of the two market areas cannot explain variations in store performance, perhaps lifestyle factors can. The MeiersMarketAreaTapestry table contains the lifestyle data. Specifically, it reports the number of households in each market area that belong to the five most dominant Community Tapestry segments. Each such segment defines a group of people with similar demographics, lifestyle characteristics, values, and shopping patterns. If the Community Tapestry composition of the two market areas differs, their variations may explain the disappointing sales performance of the Pulaski store. It may also provide clues as to how the marketing strategy of that store may be adjusted to serve its market area more effectively.

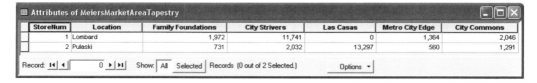

StoreNum	Location	Family Foundations	City Strivers	Las Casas	Metro City Edge	City Commons
1	Lombard	1,972	11,741	0	1,364	2,046
2	Pulaski	731	2,032	13,297	560	1,291

Record: ◄◄ ◄ 0 ► ►◄ Show: All Selected Records (0 out of 2 Selected.) Options ▾

This table contains the number of households in the Lombard and Pulaski market areas that belong to each of five Community Tapestry segments. More than 90 percent of households in the two market areas falls into one of these five segments.

2 Record the values from the attribute table in the table below.

Community Tapestry segment	Lombard market area	Pulaski market area
34: Family Foundations		
45: City Strivers		
47: Las Casas		
51: Metro City Edge		
64: City Commons		

Update report and save map document

1 Use the map and tables to answer the questions below. Summarize your answers in the appropriate section of the project report template (MeiersChicago_ReportTemplate.doc), which you will find in this chapter's data folder.

Are the demographic measures for the two areas similar? If similar, what does that tell you about the two market areas? How do the Community Tapestry compositions of the Lombard and Pulaski market areas differ?

2 Close the attribute table. Save the map document as **MeiersChicago2_fl.mxd** (replace f and l with your first and last initials) in your **\GISMKT\MeiersChicago** folder.

Exercise 4.3   Identify and compare dominant Community Tapestry segments

As the Lombard and Pulaski market areas have similar demographic profiles, the sales variation is more likely the result of differing lifestyle profiles between the market areas of the two stores. To understand this difference, you must identify the dominant Community Tapestry segment in each, and review the characteristics of those segments. Thus, in this exercise, you will:

- Design a graph of the Community Tapestry composition of the two market areas
- Compare the profiles of the dominant Community Tapestry segments in each market area

Open an existing map

1   In ArcMap, open the **MeiersChicago3** map document from your \GISMKT\MeiersChicago folder.

This map displays the Meiers stores on both Lombard and Pulaski, their market areas, and Chicago's major roads. It also displays the total annual value of furniture purchases for each of Chicago's census tracts. This map document also contains a table, called MeiersMarketAreaTapestry, that contains data on the major Community Tapestry segments in the market areas and the number of households in each.

2   If necessary, click the Source tab at the bottom of the table of contents to see the data tables.

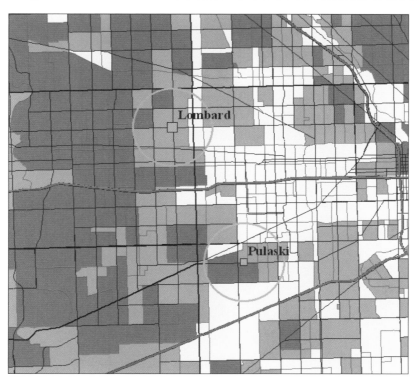

Design a graph from a data table

To display the Community Tapestry composition of the two market areas, you will design a graph based on the MeiersMarketAreaTapestry table.

1   From the main menu bar, click Tools > Graphs > Create.

2   In the Create Graph Wizard, maintain the default graph type of Vertical Bar.

3   For the Layer/Table option, choose MeiersMarketAreaTapestry.

4   For the Value field option, choose Family Foundations.

5   For X label field, choose Location.

6   Choose any custom color you like. Leave all other options set to their default values.

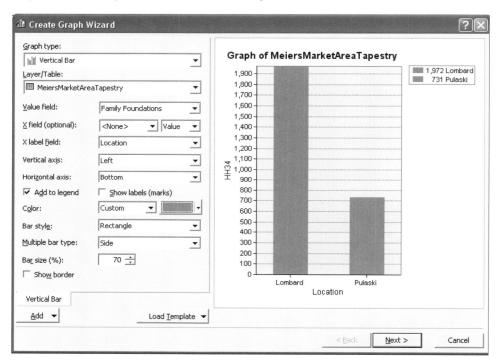

7   At the bottom of the window, click Vertical Bar to make it editable. Replace the default text with **Family Foundations**.

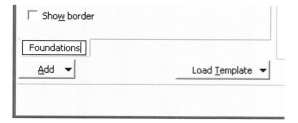

8   Click Add, then choose New Series.

9   Make sure the Layer/Table setting is correct. For Value field, choose City Strivers. Choose a custom color, then change Vertical Bar to **City Strivers**.

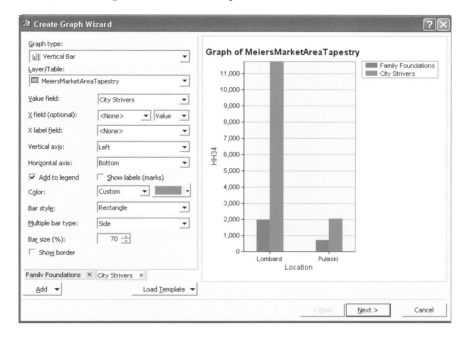

10   Repeat steps 8 and 9 three more times, choosing Las Casas, Metro City Edge, and City Commons for the value fields. Remember to choose a unique color and rename the bar each time.

11   When you're finished, click Next.

12   Change the title to **Meiers Market Area Community Tapestry Composition**.

13   Change the left axis title to **Households in each segment**.

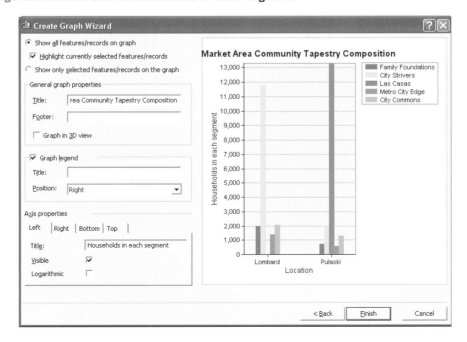

14   Click Finish.

The resulting graph should resemble this one, though your colors will vary. The tallest columns represent the Community Tapestry segments with the most households in each market area.

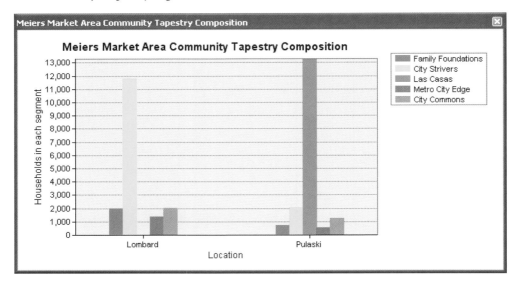

15   Right-click the title bar at the top of the graph window, then click Add to Layout to display this graph in layout view in addition to the active data frame.

Your screen now switches to layout view and the graph appears in addition to, and indeed on top of, the data frame. You may adjust the placement of both the data frame and the graph to improve the map's appearance.

16   Click the graph in the layout to select it. Use the cursor and handles of the graph box to resize it and/or move it. Repeat with the data frame so that the two elements do not overlap each other.

The graph is now displayed properly on the layout. You will work with layout view further in exercise 4.5.

17   On the main menu bar, click View > Data View to exit layout view.

Compare profiles of market area Community Tapestry segments

The table below contains summary profiles of the Community Tapestry segments that dominate each of these two market areas. These descriptions from ESRI provide insight into the values and lifestyles of the populations in the two market areas.

1   The Community Tapestry composition graph should be visible. If it is not, on the main menu bar, click Tools, Graphs, Meiers Market Area Community Tapestry Composition.

Which Community Tapestry segments are present in the Lombard market area? In the Pulaski market area? How does the numeric distribution of segments differ in the two market areas? Which is the dominant segment in each market area?

2   Review the summary descriptions of the dominant Community Tapestry segments in the Lombard and Pulaski market areas. Use this information to answer the report questions.

City Strivers Community Tapestry Segment Profile	
Segment Number & Name 45 City Strivers **LifeMode Group** L3 Metropolis **Urbanization Group** U2 Principal Urban Centers II **Household Type** Family mix **Median Age** 32.1 years **Income** Lower middle **Employment** Prof/mgmt/svc **Education** No HS diploma; HS grad **Residential** Mulitunit rental **Race/Ethnicity** Black **Preferences** Play tennis and basketball; Have personal education loan; Go dancing, attend dance performance; Watch syndicated TV shows; Leased last vehicle	City Strivers residents are urban denizens of densely settled neighborhoods in major metropolitan areas such as New York City and Chicago, Illinois. Most households are composed of a mix of family types. The median age is 32.1 years, and the median household income is $36,800. Employment is concentrated in the city, with half of employed residents working in the service industry, particularly in health care. Twenty-two percent are government workers. Unemployment is twice that of the U.S. level. Housing is mostly older, rented apartments in smaller, multiunit buildings. Primary spending is for groceries, baby products, and children's essentials. Residents enjoy going to dance performances, football and basketball games, and Six Flags theme parks. They listen to urban, all-news, and jazz radio formats, and watch TV, especially movies, sitcoms, news programs, courtroom TV and talk shows, tennis, and wrestling.
Source: ESRI Community Tapestry Demo CD, 2006	Source: *Community Tapestry: The Fabric of America's Neighborhoods.* ESRI White Paper, March 2006. Available at *http://www.esri.com/ tapestry.*

Las Casas Community Tapestry Segment Profile		
Segment Number & Name	47 Las Casas	Las Casas residents are the latest wave of western pioneers. Settled primarily in California, approximately half were born outside the United States. Young, Hispanic families dominate these households; 63 percent include children. This market has the highest average household size (4.27) among all the Community Tapestry segments. The median age is 25.4 years, and the median household income is $35,400. Most households are occupied by renters, although home ownership is at 42 percent. The median home value is $278,400. Housing is a mix of older apartment buildings, single-family homes, and town homes. This is a strong market for the purchase of baby and children's products. Residents enjoy listening to Hispanic radio, reading adventure stories, and playing soccer. Many treat their children to a family outing at a theme park, especially Disneyland. When taking a trip, Mexico is a popular destination.
LifeMode Group	L8 Global Roots	
Urbanization Group	U2 Principal Urban Centers II	
Household Type	Family mix	
Median Age	25.4 years	
Income	Lower middle	
Employment	Skilled/services	
Education	No HS diploma	
Residential	Mixed	
Race/Ethnicity	White; Hispanic	
Preferences	Buy children's products; Use federal savings bank; Play soccer and attend soccer games; Listen to Hispanic radio; Paid cash for last vehicle	
Source: ESRI Community Tapestry Demo CD, 2006		Source: *Community Tapestry: The Fabric of America's Neighborhoods.* *ESRI* White Paper, March 2006. Available at *http://www.esri.com/tapestry*.

Update report and save map document

1   Use the map, graph, and Community Tapestry summary table to answer the questions below. Summarize your answers in the appropriate section of the project report template.

How are the characteristics and values of the dominant segments in each of the market areas similar? How are they different? How might these differences affect their buying preferences for furniture?

2   Save your map file as **MeiersChicago3_fl.mxd** (replace f and l with your first and last initials) in your **\GISMKT\MeiersChicago** folder.

Exercise 4.4   Analyze buying behavior with Market Potential Indexes

The Community Tapestry profiles of the Pulaski and Lombard market areas provide insights into the differences between them. You wish to extend this analysis by reviewing the furniture-related purchasing behavior of the dominant segments in these market areas. Thus, in this exercise, you will:

- Design a data table to display the dominant Community Tapestry segments and their Market Potential Indexes

- Assess the different furniture buying patterns of the two dominant Community Tapestry segments

- Recommend revisions in marketing strategy for the Meiers store on Pulaski in response to these patterns

Open an existing map

1   Open the **MeiersChicago4** map document from your **\GISMKT\MeiersChicago** folder.

This map contains five layers: the Lombard and Pulaski stores, their market areas, Chicago's competing furniture stores, major roads, and a thematic layer that represents the average home value in each of the city's census tracts. In addition, there are two data tables. The first is the MeiersMarketAreaTapestry data table you used in the previous two exercises. The second, MarketPotentialIndexes, contains furniture-related market potential indexes for each of the five major Community Tapestry segments in the Meiers stores' market areas.

2   If necessary, to see the data tables, click the Source tab at the bottom of the table of contents.

Display table and change its display format

Open table and review its contents

1   **Right-click the MarketPotentialIndexes data table and click Open to view its contents.**

The table contains several furniture-related buying behaviors and the market potential indexes of those behaviors for each of the five major Community Tapestry segments in the Lombard and Pulaski market areas.

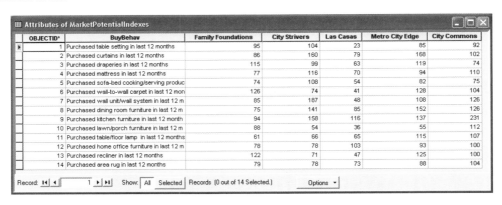

Review the values in this table. Recall that all values higher than 100 mean that a segment reports this behavior at a rate higher than the national average. As a result, you wish to focus on those values greater than 100.

In addition, the table reports results for all five segments. You wish to focus only on the dominant segments in the Lombard and Pulaski market areas. The dominant segment is the one with the highest number of households in the market area.

You will change the table's display format to display only the attributes relevant to your objectives.

Change the display format of a table

1   **In the table of contents, double-click the table (or right-click the table and select Properties) to display its properties.**

2   **Click the Fields tab to display information on the attributes contained in the table.**

You will adjust the field properties to display only the BuyBehav field and the values for the City Strivers and Las Casas segments.

3   **In the Name column, uncheck the ObjectID field to make it invisible. Do the same for the HH34, HH51, and HH64 fields.**

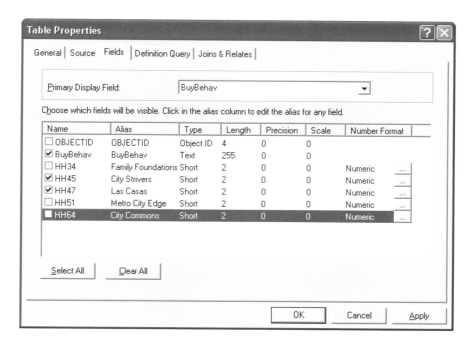

4   Click OK to close the dialog box and apply the new settings.

5   Again open the MarketPotentialIndexes table.

The table now displays only the Market Potential Indexes (MPI) values for the City Strivers and Las Casas segments. To study the buying behavior of a segment, you will sort the values in the table for that segment and focus your attention on those buying behaviors for which the segment has values of 100 or greater.

6   Right-click the City Strivers column header, then click Sort Descending to sort the table by this attribute in descending order.

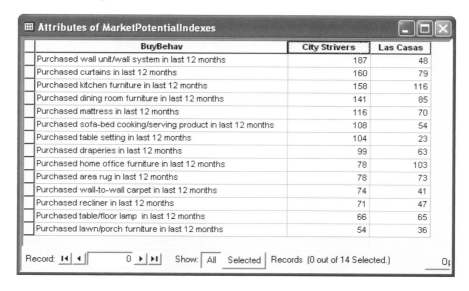

Note the buying behaviors with values greater than 100 and use them to answer the report questions.

7   Now right-click the Las Casas column header and choose Sort Descending.

Note the buying behaviors with values greater than 100 and use them to answer the report questions.

Update report and save map document

1   Use the table to answer the following questions. Summarize your answers in the appropriate section of the project report template.

How do the furniture buying patterns of the Las Casas Community Tapestry segment differ from those of the City Strivers segment? How will you adjust the merchandise mix in the Pulaski store to reflect these differences in buying patterns?

2   Close the table and save the map as **MeiersChicago4_fl.mxd** (replace f and l with your first and last initials) in your **\GISMKT\MeiersChicago** folder.

Exercise 4.5 Present your findings

You have performed demographic, Community Tapestry, and market potential comparisons of the Lombard and Pulaski market areas. To complete the analysis, you must use this information to recommend a merchandising strategy for the Pulaski store. Thus, in this exercise you will:

- Summarize your conclusions about the demographic, Community Tapestry, and market potential comparisons of the Lombard and Pulaski market areas
- Summarize your recommended marketing strategy adjustments for the Pulaski store
- Explain how your recommendations will improve customer satisfaction and sales at the Pulaski store
- Design a supporting map

Open an existing map

1   Open the **MeiersChicago5** map document from your **\GISMKT\MeiersChicago** folder.

This map opens in layout view. The table of contents contains seven layers and two data tables. The map displays a thematic map of family households by census tract in the vicinity of the two Meiers stores. A second thematic layer depicting average home values is also included in the map, but it is not currently turned on. The map also contains layers for the two Meiers stores, the market areas of those stores, shopping centers, furniture stores, and major roads in the area.

2   If necessary, to see the data tables, click the Source tab at the bottom of the table of contents.

In addition to the data frame, the layout view displays a graph and box in which you will place a table. The graph is the same Meiers Market Area Community Tapestry Composition graph you created in exercise 4.3. The table you will add is the Market Potential Indexes table you created in the previous exercise. Additional text and formatting have been added to these elements to improve their appearance and to explain their meaning.

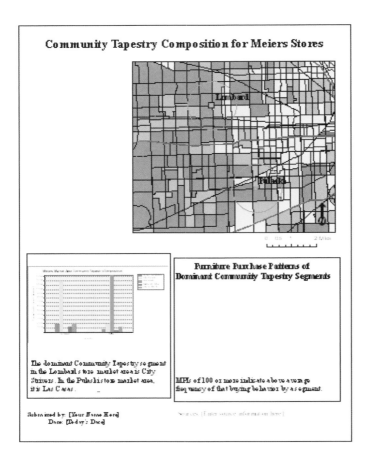

You will adjust the layers in the table of contents to display the thematic attribute and competition layer of your choice.

Edit the layout

1   **Click the check box to the left of the Family Households layer to turn it off. Click the check box next to the Average Home Value layer to turn it on.**

The Average Home Value layer is now visible in the map layout. In this manner, you may display the attribute you think is most relevant to your analysis.

2   **Now turn on the Shopping Centers and Furniture Stores layers. With both layers on, the resulting map may appear cluttered and confusing. To avoid this, decide which of the two layers is most relevant to the competitive environment of the two Meiers stores, and display that layer only.**

The resulting map will reflect your decisions about the relevance of the available layers.

3   **If you want to zoom in on the layout page for a better look, use the navigation tools on the Layout toolbar. The layout tools look similar to the tools on the Tools toolbar, but work differently as they help you to zoom in and out on the virtual piece of paper that makes up the layout.**

Add a table to the layout

Open table and adjust its display

Notice the box just below the map in layout view. It is designed to display an attribute table. You will open the appropriate table, select the records to display, and add it to layout view.

1 Right-click the MarketPotentialIndexes data table to open it and view its contents.

The table displays the MPI values for the City Strivers and Las Casas segments. You wish to include in the layout table all records with values of 100 or greater for either of the two segments, as these are the records most relevant to your recommended merchandising strategy.

2 Visually review the table to identify those buying behaviors with values of 100 or greater for either of the two visible Community Tapestry segments. Press the Ctrl key and hold it down. Click the small gray box to the immediate left of one of the records you have identified to select it. With the Ctrl key still pressed, repeat this operation for each of the buying behavior records that meet the selection criteria. If you select a nonqualifying record inadvertently, click it again with the Ctrl key still pressed to unselect it.

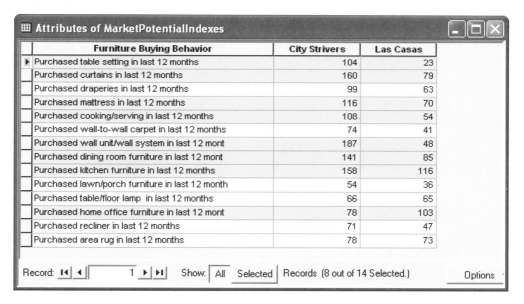

Furniture Buying Behavior	City Strivers	Las Casas
▶ Purchased table setting in last 12 months	104	23
Purchased curtains in last 12 months	160	79
Purchased draperies in last 12 months	99	63
Purchased mattress in last 12 months	116	70
Purchased cooking/serving in last 12 months	108	54
Purchased wall-to-wall carpet in last 12 months	74	41
Purchased wall unit/wall system in last 12 mont	187	48
Purchased dining room furniture in last 12 mont	141	85
Purchased kitchen furniture in last 12 months	158	116
Purchased lawn/porch furniture in last 12 month	54	36
Purchased table/floor lamp in last 12 months	66	65
Purchased home office furniture in last 12 mont	78	103
Purchased recliner in last 12 months	71	47
Purchased area rug in last 12 months	78	73

Record: ◄◄ ◄ 1 ► ►◄ Show: All Selected Records (8 out of 14 Selected.) Options

3 With all the appropriate records selected, click the Selected button at the bottom of the table to display only the selected records.

4   Right-click the Las Casas column header, then click Sort Descending to sort the table by this attribute in descending order.

5   Narrow the columns to ensure they will all be visible in the layout, as shown below. To do this, click the column dividers and drag to the left.

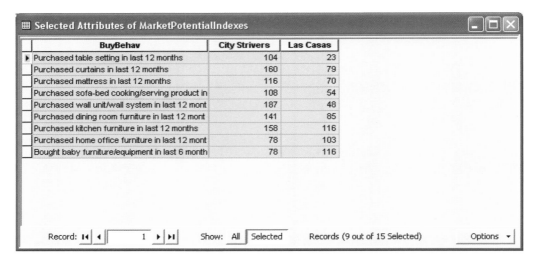

Selected Attributes of MarketPotentialIndexes

BuyBehav	City Strivers	Las Casas
▶ Purchased table setting in last 12 months	104	23
Purchased curtains in last 12 months	160	79
Purchased mattress in last 12 months	116	70
Purchased sofa-bed cooking/serving product in	108	54
Purchased wall unit/wall system in last 12 mont	187	48
Purchased dining room furniture in last 12 mont	141	85
Purchased kitchen furniture in last 12 months	158	116
Purchased home office furniture in last 12 mont	78	103
Bought baby furniture/equipment in last 6 month	78	116

Record: I◄ ◄   1   ► ►I   Show: All Selected   Records (9 out of 15 Selected)   Options ▾

Add table to layout

1   Click the Options button, then click Add Table to Layout. Close the table.

The table now appears in the layout, but not in the designated location. You will move the table into the designated box and resize it to fit.

2   Click the table to select it. Use the handles surrounding the table to resize it so it will fit in the open space. Drag and drop it to the correct location.

3   Click an empty area of the layout to unselect the table. (Note: If the data table does not fit the box, delete it, reopen the table, and repeat step 5 above to narrow the display fields further.)

The table now appears in the appropriate location on the layout.

Furniture Purchase Patterns of Dominant Community Tapestry Segments

BuyBehav	City Strivers	Las Casas
Purchased table setting in last 12 months	104	23
Purchased curtains in last 12 months	160	79
Purchased mattress in last 12 months	116	70
Purchased sofa-bed cooking/serving produc	108	54
Purchased wall unit/wall system in last 12 m	187	48
Purchased dining room furniture in last 12 m	141	85
Purchased kitchen furniture in last 12 month	158	116
Purchased home office furniture in last 12 m	78	103
Bought baby furniture/equipment in last 6 mo	78	116

MPIs of 100 or more indicate above average frequency of that buying behavior by a segment.

Add a legend to the layout

To understand the information displayed in a map, readers require a legend to explain the map's symbology. You will insert the legend to the left of the data frame on the layout.

1   On the main menu bar, click Insert > Legend to open the Legend Wizard.

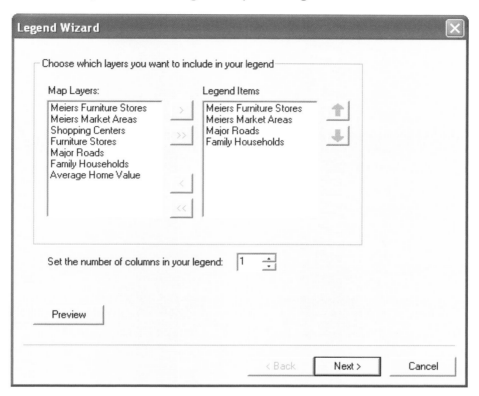

In the first panel of the Legend Wizard, you designate the layers you wish to appear in the legend. Available layers are listed in the box on the left while the layers that will appear in the legend are listed in the box on the right. To move a layer, click it to select it, then use the arrow indicators between the boxes to move it. The > button moves the selected layer from the left box to the right, while the >> button moves all layers from the left box to the right. Naturally, the < and << buttons perform the same functions in the reverse direction.

2   Move all additional layers you wish to display in the legend to the right box and move any you do not wish to display from the right box to the left. You may wish to maintain the current settings. When finished, click Next.

3   In the Legend Title text box, delete the word Legend, as your layers have their own titles and subtitles.

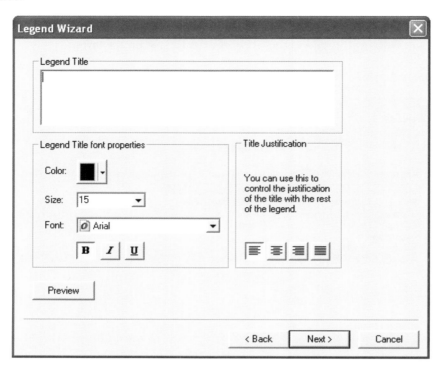

4   Click Next.

5   For the Border option, click the drop-down arrow and choose Double Line.

6   For the Drop Shadow option, click the drop-down arrow and choose Grey 20%.

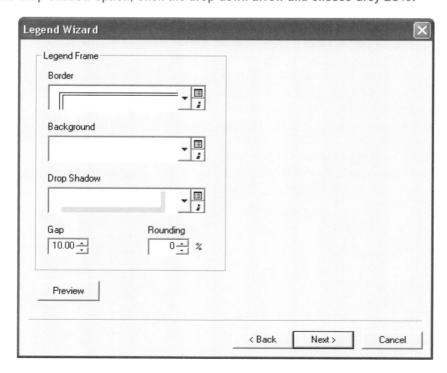

7   Click Next.

Step 4 of the Legend Wizard allows you to specify the size and shape of the color and line patches used in the legend. For this legend, the default values are acceptable.

8   Click Next.

Step 5 of the Legend Wizard allows you to specify the distance in points between the various items in the layer. For this legend, the default values are acceptable.

9   Click Finish to complete the legend and display it on the layout page.

10 As you've learned how to do, move the legend to the white space on the layout.

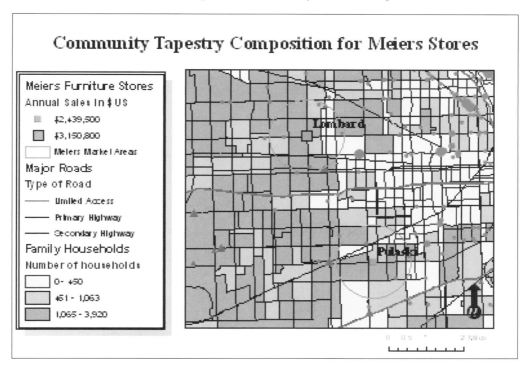

Add text to layout

1 Click the "Submitted by" text box at the bottom of the page to select it, then right-click and choose Properties.

2 In the Properties dialog box, replace the placeholder text with your name and today's date.

3 Click Apply, then OK to accept the changes.

4 Now select the "Sources" text box, then right-click and choose Properties. Replace the placeholder text with **ESRI Community Data, 2005** and on a second line **Mediamark Research Inc., Doublebase 2004.**

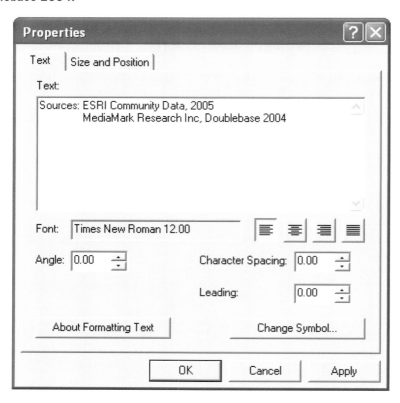

5 Click OK.

Layout view now displays the completed map that you will use as exhibit 1 in your report. You will now save it as a graphic file and insert it into the report template.

Export map and insert into your report

1 From the main menu bar, click File > Export Map to reach the Export Map dialog box. Navigate to your **\GISMKT\MeiersChicago** folder. For File Name, type **MATapestry.emf**, then click Save to save the map document as a graphic file to include in your report.

2 Open the report template for this chapter and navigate to the end of the document.

3 Locate the page entitled Exhibit 1: Meiers market areas. Select the instructional text in brackets, then from the main menu bar in Microsoft Word, click Insert > Picture > From File. Navigate to the **\GISMKT\MeiersChicago** folder and select the **MATapestry.emf** file. Click Insert to insert the picture into the report as exhibit 1. (Note: You may have to select and resize the image to display it on the same page as the title.)

Exhibit 1 of your report is now complete.

Update report and save map document

1 Use your previous analysis and the map layout you have created to perform the following task. Summarize your response in the appropriate section of the project report template.

 Summarize your conclusions about the demographic, Community Tapestry, and market potential comparisons of the Lombard and Pulaski market areas. Review the marketing strategy adjustments you recommend for the Pulaski store. Explain how your analysis and recommendations will improve customer satisfaction and sales at the Pulaski store.

2 Save the map document as **MeiersChicago5_fl.mxd** (replace f and l with your first and last initials) in your **\GISMKT\MeiersChicago** folder.

Congratulations! You have completed the Meiers Home Furnishings project.

Reflect for a moment on what you have learned in this chapter. You explored the demographic characteristics of the Chicago area in general and Meiers Home Furnishings market areas in particular. You evaluated the competitive environment of the firm's two stores relative to nearby shopping centers and competitors. Discovering that the market areas are demographically similar, you used the Community Tapestry segmentation system to determine that the dominant Community Tapestry segments of the two market areas differ. Finally, you used Market Potential Indexes relative to the dominant segments to craft a new merchandising strategy for the Pulaski store. You saw that consumer groups with similar demographic characteristics can differ in lifestyle and purchasing patterns, and you learned the value of integrating demographic data with lifestyle and purchasing behavior data when formulating marketing strategies.

Additional applications

In consumer behavior studies, lifestyle segmentation offers significant advantages over purely demographic segmentation techniques. This is true for two reasons. First, lifestyle segmentation data provides insight into the why of purchasing behavior, rather than simply the *whom* of demographic segmentation. Relationships between purchased products and consumers' beliefs, values, and life patterns are clearer. Second, when coupled with other patterns of consumer behavior, lifestyle data provides a more solid base of information for designing promotional messages and selecting media than do purely demographic measures.

Some lifestyle approaches are aimed at specific product markets or behaviors. For example, one study defines three lifestyle segments of Taiwanese consumers and identifies differences in their behavior relative to Internet advertising and purchasing.[1] A similar study defines five distinct lifestyle segments in the Australian wine markets and distinguishes the way these groups evaluate, purchase, and consume wine.[2] While these models are useful for the markets they cover, their general application across products is limited.

More comprehensive lifestyle approaches seek to define lifestyle clusters or segments in populations at the national or international level. Marketers may then evaluate these lifestyle segments as potential target markets or use them as tools to learn more about their existing customer base. One of the earliest systems was SRI International's VALS (Values and Life Styles) model and later its VALS 2 system, which divided consumers in the United States into eight lifestyle groups.[3] Claritas offers a more complex classification scheme in its PRIZM NE[4] system that identifies 67 distinct lifestyle segments in the United States. In addition, segments are aggregated into similar social groups and lifestage groups for marketers in search of broader classification systems.

The Community Tapestry segmentation system used in this chapter represents the fourth generation of market segmentation systems that began 30 years ago. Built in 2003 by the ESRI data development team, Community Tapestry classifies U.S. neighborhoods based on their demographic and socioeconomic characteristics. For a broader view of markets, these 65 segments are also aggregated into twelve LifeMode summary groups and eleven Urbanization summary groups. Commonalities of the LifeMode summary groups are lifestyle and life stage; similarities of the Urbanization summary groups are population density and affluence. This model is also extended with the Market Potential Indexes that you used to analyze the furniture purchasing patterns of the two dominant Community Tapestry segments.

Lifestyle segmentation tools have several applications for understanding consumers and developing responsive marketing strategies. In this project, you adjusted the merchandising mix of two stores that served different Community Tapestry segments based on their values and purchasing patterns. Other Market Potential Indexes allow you to extend this approach to the promotional component of the marketing mix as well.

Consider the following table that presents selected Market Potential Indexes for the City Strivers and Las Casas Community Tapestry segments.

Market Potential Indexes: Attitude, Media, and Activity Behaviors	Community Tapestry Segment	
	City Strivers	Las Casas
Consider self very middle-of-the-road	85	96
Consider self very liberal	143	93
Member of union	149	46
Attended movie in last 90 days > once per week	150	134
Attended dance performance in last 12 months	186	99
Played bingo in last 12 months	120	93
Participated in basketball	147	39
Participated in soccer	112	214
Heavy viewer of prime time television	113	115
Watch on television: pro basketball	159	57
Watch on television: soccer	138	171
Heavy newspaper reader	118	35
Read two or more daily newspapers	101	54
Read newspaper: home furnishings/garden section	91	27
Heavy magazine reader	103	78
Read automotive magazines	48	124
Read parenthood magazines	129	137
Read women's fashion magazines	162	135
Heavy radio listener	133	80
Radio listen format: religious	126	130
Radio listen format: oldies	36	117
Radio listen format: Hispanic	136	820
Source: ESRI Community Tapestry Demonstration CD, 2006. Data derived from MediaMark Research Inc., Doublebase 2004.		

The Market Potential Indexes for media exposure provide guidance as to where advertising aimed at these segments should be placed. The indexes report activities and interests to provide insight into how the message might be framed. For example, the City Strivers segment is more politically liberal, attends dance performances, participates in basketball, watches pro basketball and prime-time television, and listens to religious radio stations. The Las Casas segment is more politically moderate, watches movies frequently, relies on television more than other media, plays and watches soccer, and listens to Hispanic radio stations. Though this segment is not a heavy consumer of newspapers, magazines, or radio in general, there are specific programs and magazines which draw their attention.

ESRI ArcGIS Business Analyst extension provides some additional capabilities for lifestyle segmentation. First, it identifies dominant Community Tapestry groups at various levels of geography. This allows marketing analysts to view in thematic maps the segments they are serving within designated trade areas. This information, in turn, becomes a valuable tool for market prospecting, the process of identifying geographic concentrations of prospects with attractive demographic and lifestyle characteristics. For example, in the current project, if Meiers Home Furnishings devises a successful strategy for serving Las Casas households, it should consider expansion to other locations with concentrations of households in this segment. The prospecting tools in Business Analyst facilitate this type of analysis. The *Washington Times* uses this approach in its search for new subscribers in the Washington, D.C., area.[5] Subaru of America has applied these tools to target areas with attractive lifestyle characteristics for expansion of their dealer network.[6]

In short, lifestyle segmentation analysis confirms the value of these approaches in understanding consumer behavior and crafting responsive marketing mixes. This exercise shows how these tools provide additional insight into customer purchasing patterns to improve product merchandising decisions. It also discusses how this approach can inform other elements of the marketing mix and facilitate market prospecting as well.

1. Kenneth C. C. Yang, "A comparison of attitudes toward Internet advertising among lifestyle segments in Taiwan," *Journal of Marketing Communications* 10(3), 2004: 195–212.

2. Johan Bruwer, Elton Li and Mike Reic, "Segmentation of the Australian wine market using a wine-related lifestyle approach," *Journal of Wine Research* 13(3), 2002: 217–242.

3. Lewis C. Winters, "SRI announces VALS 2," *Marketing Research* 1(2), 1989: 67–69.

4. This system is described in Claritas's *My Best Segments* Web site at the following URL: *http://www.claritas.com/MyBestSegments/Default.jsp*

5. ESRI, "The Washington Times: GIS Increases Newspaper Subscriptions," Business Analyst product promotion brochure, 2005.

6. David Huffman, "Subaru of America, Inc. Targets Prime Markets Accurately and Efficiently," *Directions,* February 13, 2005.

CHAPTER 5

Developing an Integrated Marketing Communication Program

Course: Promotional Management/Advertising/ Integrated Marketing Communication

This chapter covers the role of GIS in promotional management. The Community Farm Alliance is a nonprofit organization of Kentucky farmers. It hopes to develop an integrated marketing communication program to convince selected grocery stores and restaurants in Lexington, Kentucky to carry their produce and Lexington consumers to buy their delicious, healthy, locally produced foods. Integrated marketing communication programs are comprehensive, multimedia promotional campaigns designed to ensure that firms communicate a consistent, coordinated message across their promotional activities. In that effort, you will use GIS tools and the Community Tapestry segmentation system to identify target groups of businesses and consumers and to develop media plans to communicate with them.

Learning objectives

To coordinate the components of an integrated marketing communication program, you will learn how to use ArcGIS to:

1. Create map symbology to display population and businesses characteristics
2. Select businesses for the push component of the campaign
3. Define and select groups of consumers for customized promotional messages
4. Select appropriate media for target Community Tapestry segments using Market Potential Indexes
5. Design maps to communicate and support your recommendations

Marketing scenario

The Community Farm Alliance (CFA) was founded in 1985 as a grassroots organization of Kentucky farmers. Its aim was to preserve the lifestyle and values of family farms in Kentucky through community education and political lobbying efforts. Through several farming crises and the gradual disintegration of the tobacco quota system that supported many of Kentucky's family farms, the organization has adjusted its objectives and strategies to meet the needs of Kentucky's farmers.

As federal tobacco price support programs have come to an end, CFA has turned its attention to helping Kentucky farmers respond to new market conditions and emerging trends in agricultural markets. As part of this effort it has expanded its membership to include urban residents interested in developing local sources of healthy foods. The organization is also trying to help former tobacco farmers find alternative revenue sources such as fruit and vegetable sales. This effort to direct food purchases to local suppliers also supports the local economy. One such initiative is the Local Independent Food Economy (LIFE) program that seeks to integrate locally produced foods into the food supplies of Kentucky's communities. The initial effort will focus on Lexington, an urban center of more than 260,000 people. The program's goal is to match farmers willing to produce fruit and vegetables for local consumption with grocery stores and restaurants willing to incorporate these products into their own offerings.

The program's first initiative, a downtown Farmers Market, is a successful outlet for locally produced foods. Though the market has been successful and is viewed positively throughout the city, its contribution to the community is limited by its size and single location. Therefore, CFA wishes to build upon this favorable image and expand its local foods program throughout the community.

To achieve this, CFA has designed an integrated marketing communication program focusing on a single message: Consumers can enjoy tastier, healthier foods by supporting local farmers. The objectives of the campaign are to convince food stores and restaurants to offer locally produced food to knowledgeable consumers.

The initial phase of the campaign included public relations activities to increase awareness of the program within the Lexington community. This effort began with designing a Web site describing the program, explaining the benefits of consuming local foods, and profiling selected farmers and their products. It also included distribution of materials at the Farmers Market, public service announcements for local media, and community outreach efforts to inform existing community organizations of the initiative. In addition, CFA designed and produced a logo, banners, and in-store signage for display by participating food stores and restaurants.

With this foundation complete, CFA is ready to implement the next stage of the campaign. This stage will involve both push and pull promotional strategies. Push strategies are aimed at wholesalers and retailers and are designed to convince them to stock and support local food products. In this case, the push strategy will be aimed at selected grocery stores and restaurants in the Lexington area. Pull strategies, on the other hand, are aimed at final consumers and are designed to motivate them to buy local food products from the outlets that offer them. In this case, the pull strategy will be aimed at Lexington residents, motivating them to buy locally produced food in grocery stores and restaurants.

The first goal of the push campaign is to identify locally owned grocery stores and convince them to carry locally produced fresh fruit and vegetables. The second goal of the push campaign is to convince locally owned restaurants in the Lexington area to serve dishes prepared with locally produced foods. This effort will focus on medium- to large-sized independent restaurants, providing them an advantage relative to chain operations through their ability to offer patrons dishes prepared from locally produced foods.

The pull component of the campaign uses business-to-consumer promotion. CFA will seek to understand the lifestyle patterns and media habits of Lexington consumers and develop a media strategy to reach them with its promotional message.

CFA wishes to apply GIS technologies to support this endeavor. Specifically, the organization wishes to analyze the geographic distribution of grocery stores and restaurants and to identify those that are the best prospects for the LIFE campaign. For the consumer level, the firm wishes to explore the geographic distribution and demographic characteristics of Lexington consumers and identify market segments for its advertising. Further, it wishes to use Community Tapestry segmentation analysis to select the advertising media most preferred by each segment.

In the context of this common message CFA also wishes to fine tune its communication to two specific groups of Lexington consumers. First, the organization is convinced that low-income consumers could improve their diets with fresh, local produce and wants to ensure that these consumers are aware of the availability of these foods in grocery stores. Second, CFA believes that frequent restaurant diners would be attracted to Lexington's independent restaurants by dishes prepared from local foods. Thus, the organization wishes to learn more about these groups, their lifestyles, and media patterns. The Community Tapestry system provides the mechanism for pursuing this analysis at the ZIP Code level in Lexington. You will use this system for recommending the promotional media most appropriate for each of these groups.

In the following exercises, you will use ArcMap application to perform these analyses for CFA and make recommendations for its business-to-business and business-to-consumer promotional programs.

Background information

Though typically associated with large national or international communication efforts, integrated marketing communication programs are equally applicable in smaller, local markets. In this case, CFA wishes to communicate the benefits of tasty, healthy foods from local farmers via its Web site, point of purchase displays, and local advertising. For the campaign to be successful, grocery stores and restaurants must be willing to sell food produced by CFA members. They must be convinced that Lexington's consumers desire these products and will seek them out. For this to occur, these consumers must be aware of the benefits of locally produced food as well as the grocery stores and restaurants where they can be purchased.

This interdependency between retailers and customers requires CFA to direct promotional efforts to both groups, hence the integration of the push and pull components of the campaign. The two components of the program support each other. The desire for locally produced food created by the pull campaign increases the incentives for grocery stores and restaurants to offer them. Similarly, the availability of locally produced foods in Lexington's grocery stores and restaurants affords consumers the opportunity to act on their desire to purchase these products. The campaign elements are further integrated in the common message of the benefits of tasty, healthy local foods, whether consumed at home or in restaurants.

CFA Lexington Area data dictionary	
Attribute	**Description**
For ZIPCodes (ESRI)	
TOTPOP_CY	Population, 2004
TOTHH_CY	Households, 2004
AVGHHSIZ_CY	Average household size, 2004
MEDAGE_CY	Median age, 2004
DIVINDX_CY	Ethnic diversity index, higher is more diverse, USA Avg = 54.6
PCTFAMBPL	Percentage of families living below poverty line, 2000
PctLTHS	Percentage of persons over 25 with less than high school education, 2004
PctHSSomCol	Percentage of persons over 25 with a high school degree or some college, 2004
PctColDeg	Percentage of persons over 25 with an associate degree or higher, 2004
FrtVegHH	Average expenditures on fruits and vegetables per household, 2004
RestaurantHH	Average expenditures in restaurants per household, 2004
For GroceryStores and Restaurants (Hypothetical)	
ZIP	ZIP Code in which the store is located
StoreSize	Size as a combination of annual sales and employment
Type	Type of store by ownership or product line
For TapestryData (ESRI)	
Emphasis	Promotional emphasis: Grocery or Restaurant
ZIPCount	Number of ZIP Codes in promotional emphasis
HH 04	Number of households in the Boomburbs segment, 2004
HH 12	Number of households in the Up-and-Coming Families segment, 2004
HH 22	Number of households in the Metropolitans segment, 2004
HH 32	Number of households in the Rustbelt Traditions segment, 2004
HH 33	Number of households in the Midlife Junction segment, 2004
HH 55	Number of households in the College Towns segment, 2004
For EmphasisMPIValues (ESRI)	
MediaBehavior	Media exposure behavior
HH 04	MPI value for Boomburbs segment, 2004
HH 12	MPI value for Up-and-Coming Families segment, 2004
HH 22	MPI value for Metropolitans segment, 2004
HH 32	MPI value for Rustbelt Traditions segment, 2004
HH 33	MPI value for Midlife Junction segment, 2004
HH 55	MPI value for College Towns segment, 2004
Source: ESRI Community Data, 2005; Community Tapestry Demonstration CD, 2006; MPI Data derived from MediaMark Research Inc., Doublebase 2004; hypothetical data for this exercise	

Exercise 5.1 Explore Lexington's food outlets and demographics

In this project you will analyze customer and demographic data at the ZIP Code level. To prepare for this analysis, you must examine a basemap of Lexington, Kentucky and relevant data to the project. Thus, in this exercise you will:

* Load and explore a basemap of Lexington that contains food outlets and demographic and purchasing data
* Add more demographic data to the project and give it meaningful symbology
* Create a map displaying bar graphs of educational attainment by ZIP Code

Open an existing map

1   To launch ArcMap, from the Windows taskbar, click Start > All Programs > ArcGIS > ArcMap.

Depending on how ArcGIS and ArcMap have been installed or which Windows operating system you are using, there may be a slightly different navigation menu from which to open ArcMap.

2   If you see an ArcMap start dialog box, click the "An existing map" option. Otherwise, click the Open button 📂 on the ArcMap Standard toolbar.

3   Browse to the location of the GISMKT folder (e.g., **C:\ESRIPress\GISMKT**), double-click the **CFALexington** folder, then select the **CFALexington1** map document and click Open.

The initial map includes six layers, two of which are visible. The visible layers display Lexington's highways and a thematic map of households by ZIP Code. The top two nonvisible layers contain information about grocery stores and restaurants in the city. The other two nonvisible layers contain additional demographic information at the ZIP Code level.

Visually examine map layers

The initial map provides a general orientation of Lexington and its major roads. It also provides some demographic information. You will examine other demographic characteristics by turning these demographic layers on and off.

1 Check the small white box to the left of the Families below Poverty Line layer to turn it on.

The map now displays the percentage of families living below the poverty line per ZIP Code.

2 Check the small white box to the left of the Purchases of Fruits and Vegetables layer to turn it on.

The map now displays average annual household purchases of fruits and vegetables per ZIP Code.

3   Turn on the Grocery Stores and Restaurants layers.

The map now displays the locations of the grocery stores and restaurants in Lexington. As these locations are hard to see at this scale, you will use several ArcMap operations to explore these layers in more detail.

Examine layers with navigation tools

Visually identify a portion of the map with several grocery stores and restaurants. By zooming in on an area, you can take a closer look at the distribution of the outlets.

1 **Click the Zoom In tool ⊕ to select it. Click and hold the mouse button near the area of the map that contains a concentration of grocery stores and restaurants. Drag the mouse to define the area you wish to view, and then release the mouse button.**

The map now shows a zoomed-in view of the distribution of grocery stores and restaurants. Observe the locations of these outlets relative to the city's major roads. Your map will differ based on the area you chose.

At this scale, you are viewing a small portion of the city. You may view adjacent areas by panning the map.

2 **Click the Pan tool 🖐 to select it. Click and hold a point on the map and drag the Pan tool to move across the map.**

3 **Continue using the navigation tools to explore the locations of food stores and restaurants in Lexington.**

4 **When you have completed your examination, click the Full Extent button ● to return the map display to its original extent.**

These navigation tools help you observe the distribution of Lexington's grocery stores and restaurants in general and relative to the city's major highways. Use your observations to answer the report questions at the end of this exercise.

Notice the mouse pointer as you work with the navigation tools. If you click while working with these tools, you might inadvertently make a change in the map. To avoid unintended effects, you can activate the Select Elements tool. This tool is used to select elements in the map without changing its extent or scale.

5   Click the Select Elements tool ▶ to activate it. This is how you return to the default pointer after using any of the navigation tools.

Add and display a new layer

You want to study the relationship between educational attainment and the other demographic attributes in the project. To do so, you will add two new layers to the map and symbolize them appropriately.

1   Turn off the Grocery Stores, Restaurants, and Highways layers.

The map now displays only the Purchases of Fruits and Vegetables layer. You will add two additional demographic layers to the study.

Add a layer

1   Click the Add Data button. ✛

2   Navigate to **\GISMKT\CFALexington\CFALexington.mdb**, the geodatabase for this project.

3   Double-click the database to view its feature classes, select **ZIPCodes**, and click Add to add the layer to the map.

The resulting map displays Lexington's ZIP Codes all in a single random color. That is, the ZIP Code layer displays no attribute data. You will change this by altering the layer's symbology.

Change a layer's symbology

1 Double-click the ZIPCodes layer (or right-click the layer and select Properties) to open the Layer Properties dialog box.

2 Click the General tab and enter **Purchases at Restaurants** as the new layer name.

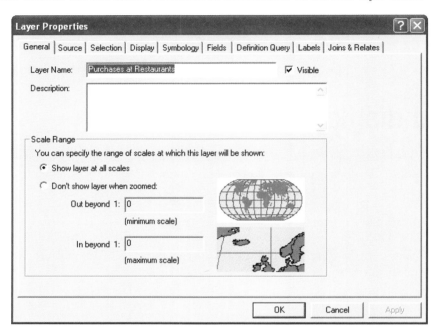

3 Click the Symbology tab.

4 Click Quantities, then Graduated Colors in the Show area.

5 Select the appropriate attribute name in the Value Field drop-down box. (Use the data dictionary to identify the attribute name for the Average expenditures in restaurants per household attribute.)

6 In the Color Ramp drop-down box, select a color scheme that differs from the other demographic layers and will allow the Grocery Stores and Restaurants layers to be discernible.

7 Check the "Show class ranges using feature values" option to define classification ranges using actual values from the dataset.

These settings specify what data will be displayed in this layer and how it will appear. You may also designate how many classes will be used to display the data and how the classes will be defined. You will adjust these settings to display three classes in a quantile system to make it consistent with the other demographic layers.

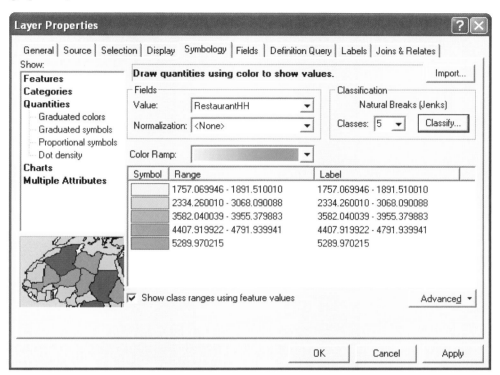

8   Click the Classify button to display the Classification dialog box.

9   Select Quantile in the Method drop-down box.

10 Select 3 in the Classes drop-down box.

With these settings you have specified that this layer will display in three classes, each containing a roughly equal number of ZIP Codes. As there are 14 ZIP Codes in the dataset, each class will contain either four or five records.

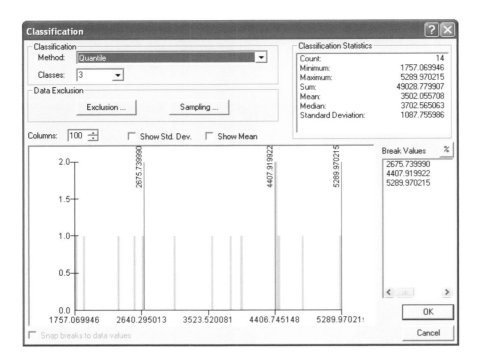

11 Click OK to return to the Symbology tab.

You will now adjust the display of classification labels in the map legend.

12 Click the Label button in the Layer Properties dialog box, then click Format Labels to open the Number Format dialog box. (Note: Do not click the Labels tab at the top of this dialog box. If you do so inadvertently, click the Symbology tab to return.)

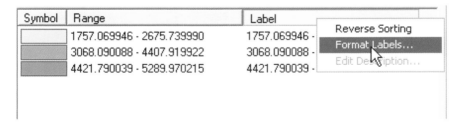

13 Select Currency in the Category field.

14 Click OK to return to the Layer Properties dialog box.

15 Click OK to close the Layer Properties dialog box and display the new settings in the map.

Change legend title

1 In the table of contents, click RestaurantHH, then click again to edit it.

2 Rename RestaurantHH to **$US per HH, 2004**. (Note: If your second click is too quick, the Properties dialog box will open. Click Cancel, then try again, clicking more slowly to reach the edit function.)

The resulting map displays annual household expenditures in restaurants by ZIP Code in Lexington You will now add to the project attribute data on educational attainment.

Add and display a new layer with bar graphs

1 Add the **ZIPCodes** layer to the map by repeating steps 1 through 3 in the Add a layer section beginning on page 145.

Design bar chart symbology for a layer

1 Double-click the ZIPCodes layer (or right-click the layer and select Properties) to open the Layer Properties dialog box.

2 Click the General tab and enter **Educational Attainment** as the new layer name.

3 Click the Symbology tab. In the Show area, click Charts and then click Bar/Column.

4 Click the attribute PctCollDeg in the Field Selection area in the center of the dialog box. Press the Ctrl key and select PctHSSC and PctLTHS, and then click the > button to the right of the Field Selection area to add these fields to the bar chart.

5 Select a chart color scheme that will be clearly visible when displayed on top of the other demographic layers in the map.

6 Click the Background symbol to open the Symbol Selector dialog box. Click the Fill Color drop-down button and select No color, which will create a transparent background for this layer.

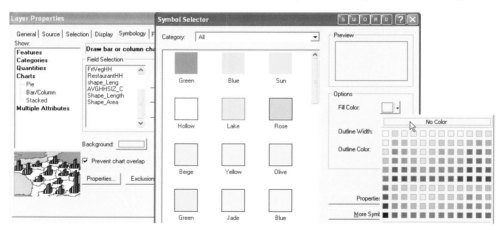

7 Click **OK** to return to the Symbology tab.

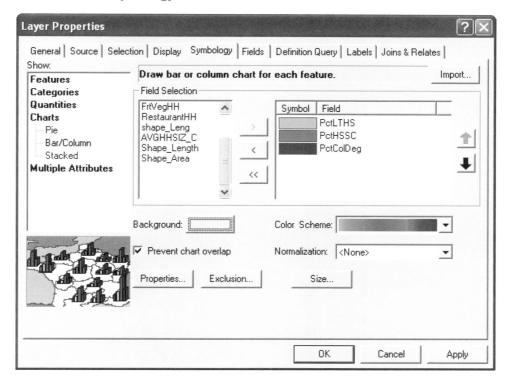

8 Click **OK** to close the layer properties and apply these settings to the layer.

Edit legend items

The map now contains a bar chart displaying the educational attainment of residents in each ZIP Code. However, the legend items are confusing to most readers. You will rename them to improve the communication value of the map.

1 In the table of contents, click the attribute name PctLTHS, then click again to edit it.

2 Rename PctLTHS to **Less than high school**. (Note: If your second click is too quick, the Properties dialog box will open. Click Cancel, then try again, clicking more slowly to reach the edit function.)

3 Repeat this procedure to rename PctHSSC to **HS degree or some college** and PctCollDeg to **College degree or higher**.

Note that the background of the Educational Attainment layer is transparent. Thus, you may view this bar chart layer and any of the other demographic layers simultaneously. This allows you to assess the relationship between educational attainment and any of the other attributes. Use the bar chart layer and the demographic layer to answer the report questions below.

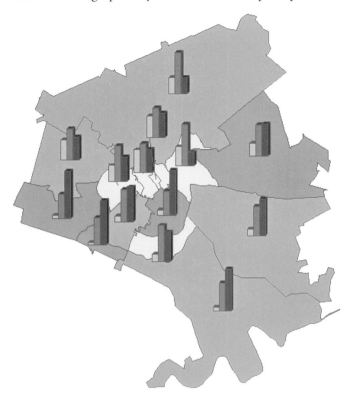

Update report and save map document

1   Use the maps you have designed to answer the following questions. Summarize your answers in the appropriate section of the project report template (**CFALexington_ReportTemplate.doc**), which you will find in your **\GISMKT\CFALexington** folder.

What do you observe about the geographic distribution of Lexington's grocery stores and restaurants in general? How does the distribution of stores and restaurants relate to the city's major highways? How does educational attainment appear to be related to poverty levels, purchases of fruits and vegetables, and expenditures in restaurants?

2   Save your map file as **CFALexington1_fl.mxd** (replace f and with your first and last initials). To do so, click File, then Save As in ArcMap. Navigate to your **\GISMKT\CFALexington** folder, type **CFALexington1_fl.mxd** as the file name, and click Save.

Exercise 5.2   Select grocery stores for the push campaign

The first objective of the CFA push campaign is to identify grocery stores and convince them to carry locally produced foods supplied by CFA members. Each participating store would be provided with identifying banners and shelf stickers for local foods. These stores will also be featured on CFA's Web site and in its press releases and consumer advertising. Thus, in this exercise you will:

- Display Lexington grocery stores by location and size
- Select the stores to be approached in the CFA push campaign
- Assess market coverage of selected stores in low-income ZIP Codes
- Create a map documenting these stores

Open an existing map

1   **Start ArcMap and open CFALexington2.mxd, found in your \GISMKT\CFALexington folder.**

This map contains three layers: Lexington's grocery stores, and two thematic layers showing a specific attribute by ZIP Code (families below poverty and purchases of fruits and vegetables).

Change the display of a layer

While the map displays the location of Lexington's grocery stores, it does not indicate their sizes. Your initial step will be to redesign the display of the grocery stores layer to reflect the size of each store.

1 **Double-click the Grocery Stores layer (or right-click the layer and select Properties).**

2 **Click the Symbology tab. Click Categories, then Unique values in the Show box.**

3 **Select StoreSize in the Value Field drop-down box.**

4 **Uncheck the box for <all other values> then click the Add All Values button to display the values for the StoreSize field.**

These settings will display stores by sales level using the small circles indicated. Though these symbols display the appropriate data, they are difficult to distinguish on the map. You will choose other symbols to make this layer clearer.

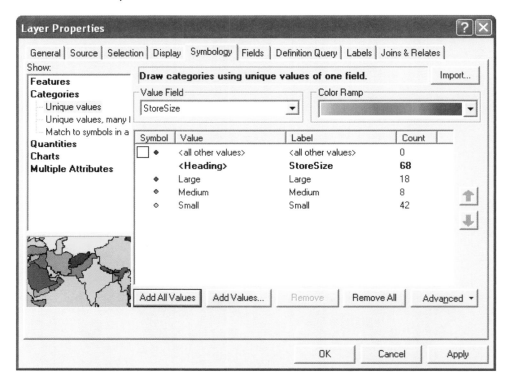

5 **Double-click the small circle to the left of the Large heading to display the Symbol Selector dialog box.**

6 **Click the Circle 1 symbol to select it. In the Color drop-down box, select Electron Gold (row 3, column 4) as the symbol color. Change the size to 16. Click OK to apply these settings and close the Symbol Selector dialog box.**

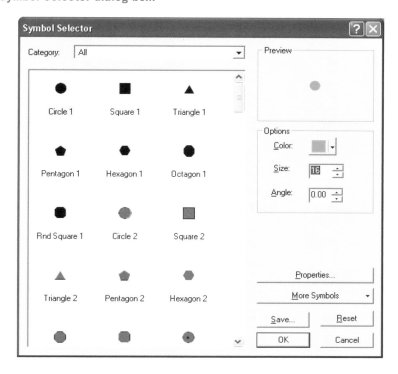

7 **Repeat this procedure for the remaining two symbols, selecting Circle 1 and Electron Gold. Make the Medium symbol size 12 and the Small symbol size 8.**

8 **Click OK to close the Layer Properties dialog box.**

The map now displays Lexington's grocery stores with symbols that reflect their size. This information allows you to assess the intensity of grocery store coverage more accurately.

Select CFA's target grocery stores

CFA plans to target locally owned grocery stores for three reasons. CFA believes that, in contrast to managers of national chain stores, owners of locally owned stores (1) have more authority to contract with local producers, (2) would be more likely to support local producers, and (3) would see the LIFE program as a competitive advantage relative to national chains.

CFA also wishes to make locally produced food products available in lower-income areas of Lexington. Consumers in these areas have not been frequent customers at the Farmers Market and tend to eat fewer fruits and vegetables than more affluent consumers. As CFA's promotional campaign will encourage these consumers to buy more local food products, it is important that they be able to find these products in their grocery stores.

To achieve these objectives you must select the appropriate grocery stores for the push campaign and assess the availability of these stores in lower-income ZIP Codes.

Select grocery stores by attribute

1   Right-click the Grocery Stores layer, then click **Open Attribute Table**.

2   In the attribute table, click the Options button, then click **Select by Attributes** to open the Select by Attributes dialog box.

3   Double-click **Type** to add it to the query box.

4   Click the **=** button to add it to the query box.

5   Click **Get Unique Values**, and double-click **'Local Grocery'** to add it to the query box.

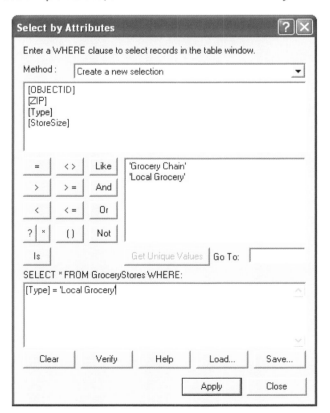

6   Click Apply to run the query, then close the Select by Attributes dialog box.

Notice the highlighted records in the table that correspond with the grocery store point features now highlighted on the map. The numbers at the bottom of the attribute table report how many grocery stores are in the Lexington area and how many of them have been selected. Take note of these numbers, as you will use them later.

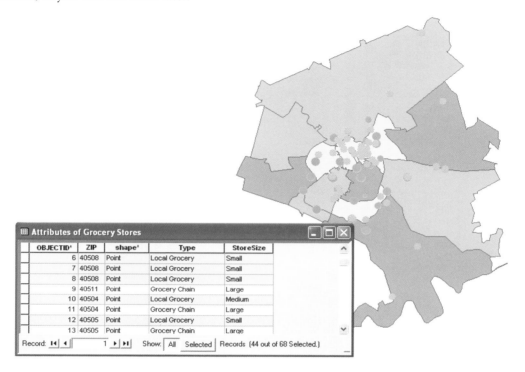

Select grocery stores in lower-income ZIP Codes by location and attribute

To determine the coverage of the selected stores in lower-income ZIP Codes, you will limit your current selection to those located in low-income areas.

1   Minimize the attribute table for the Grocery Stores layer, with its features still selected.

2   Turn off the Purchases of Fruits and Vegetables layer.

In the Families Below Poverty Line layer, the lowest-income ZIP Codes are those with the highest percentages of families living below the poverty line. The ZIP Codes in the highest classification for this attribute are those with values of 10.9 percent or higher. You will use this value to identify the ZIP Codes in which you wish to determine grocery store coverage.

3   Right-click the Families Below Poverty Line layer, then click Open Attribute Table.

4   In the attribute table, click the Options button, then click Select by Attributes to open the Select by Attributes dialog box.

5   Use the buttons and keyboard to enter **[PCTFAMBPL] >= 10.9** in the query box.

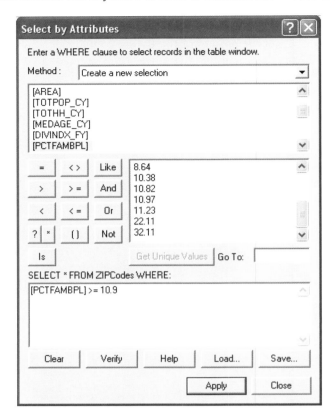

6   Click Apply to run the query, then close the Select by Attributes dialog box.

The selected features in the attribute table are highlighted as are the corresponding ZIP Codes on the map.

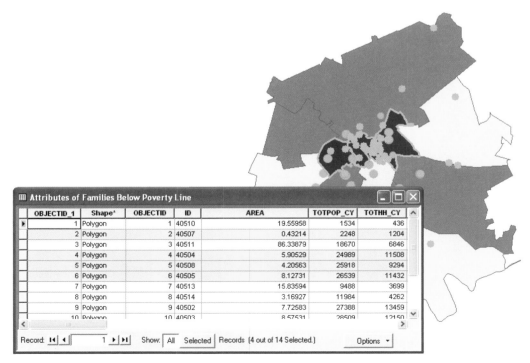

You will now select the grocery stores that are within these ZIP Codes.

7 Close the Families Below Poverty Line attribute table.

8 From the main menu bar, click Selection > Select by Location to open the Select by Location dialog box.

9 Under "I want to" choose the "select from the currently selected features in" option.

10 Check the Grocery Stores layer.

11 Under "that" choose "are contained by."

12 In the final drop-down menu, choose the Families Below Poverty Line layer.

13 Check the Use selected features box if it's not already checked. This limits the process to the four selected ZIP Codes in the Families Below Poverty Line layer.

With these settings, you have created an expression that says, "I want to select from the currently selected features in the Grocery Stores layer those features that are contained by the currently selected ZIP Codes in the Families Below Poverty Line layer."

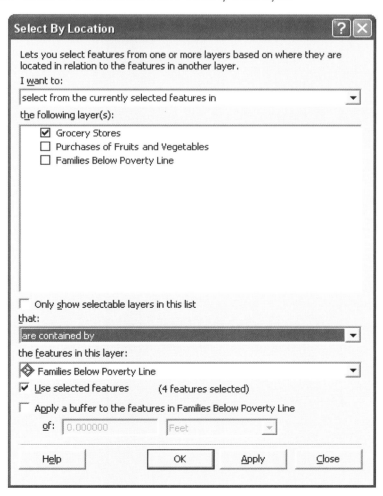

14 **Click Apply to perform the selection, then close the dialog box.**

15 **Restore the Grocery Stores attribute table.**

Note that only the local grocery stores within the four ZIP Codes with the highest percentage of families below the poverty line are selected. Take note of the number of these stores; you will need this information later.

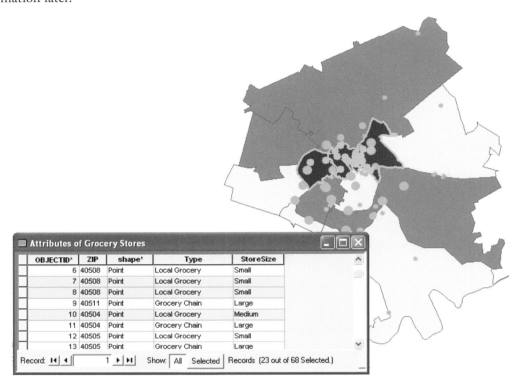

16 **To zoom in to the four selected ZIP Codes, right-click the layer, point to Selection, then click Zoom to Selected Features.**

What do you observe about the distribution of grocery stores within the four lower-income ZIP Codes? Do the selected stores provide adequate coverage for these areas?

Design a map layout

To complete this task, you will design a map layout that displays the Lexington grocery stores you have selected for the push campaign. You will then export this map as a graphics file and include it as exhibit 1 in your report.

1   **Close the Grocery Stores attribute table.**

2   **Click the Layout View button ☐ at the bottom of the ArcMap display area.**

Note that the map remains zoomed into the four lowest-income ZIP Codes and that only the local grocery stores in these ZIP Codes are selected. You will return the map to the original extent and modify the selection.

3   **Click the Full Extent button ● to return the map to its full extent.**

4   **Right-click the Grocery Stores layer, then click Selection > Clear Selected Features to clear the selected grocery stores.**

5   **Click Selection from the main menu bar, then Select by Attributes. Use the Select by Attributes dialog box to select all local grocery stores in the Lexington area. (Note: This is the same selection process you used in steps 1 to 6 of the *Select grocery stores by attribute* task.) Apply the search query, then close the dialog box.**

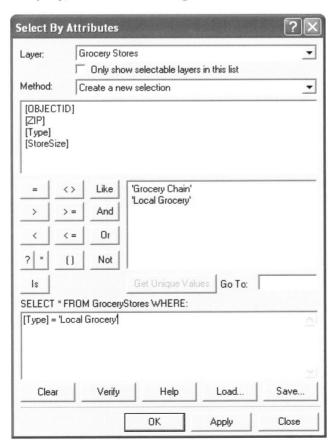

The data frame element is complete but you must edit the text boxes to include your results and to enter your submission and source information.

6 Click the text box to the left of the map to select it, then right-click and click Properties. Replace the ## placeholder text with (1) the number of grocery stores in Lexington, (2) the number of grocery stores you have selected for the campaign, and (3) the number of selected grocery stores located in the lowest-income ZIP Codes. Click OK.

7 Click the submission information text box to select it, then right-click and click Properties. Replace the placeholder text with your name and submission date. Click OK.

8 Click the source text box to select it, then right-click and select Properties. Replace the placeholder text with **ESRI Community Data, 2005**. Click OK.

Export the map

1 From the main menu bar, click File > Export Map to reach the Export Map dialog box. Navigate to your **\GISMKT\CFALexington** folder. For File Name, type **GroceryStores.emf**, then click Save to save the map document as a graphic file in EMF format to include in your report.

Update report and save map document

1 Open CFALexington_ReportTemplate.doc and find the Exhibit 1: Grocery stores heading. Select the instructional text, then from the main menu bar in Microsoft Word, click Insert > Picture > From File. Navigate to your **\GISMKT\CFALexington** folder and select the **GroceryStores.emf** file. Click Insert to insert the picture into the report as exhibit 1. (Note: You may have to select and resize the image to display it on the same page as the title.)

2 Use the map and attribute tables to answer the following questions. Summarize your answers in the appropriate section of the project report template.

How many local grocery stores in the Lexington area are selected for the push campaign? What do you observe about the distribution of grocery stores within the four lower-income ZIP Codes? Do the selected stores provide adequate coverage for these areas?

3 Save the map document as **CFALexington2_fl.mxd** (replace f and l with your first and last initials) in your **\GISMKT\CFALexington** folder.

Exercise 5.3   Select restaurants for the push campaign

The second objective of the CFA push campaign is to identify local restaurants and convince them to include items containing locally produced foods on their menus. Each participating restaurant will be provided with identifying banners and menu stickers to identify the items containing local ingredients. These restaurants will also be featured on the CFA Web site, in its press releases, and its consumer advertising. Therefore, in this exercise you will:

- Display Lexington restaurants by location and size
- Select the restaurants to be approached in the CFA push campaign
- Assess market area coverage of selected restaurants
- Create a map displaying these restaurants

Open an existing map

1   In ArcMap open **CFALexington3.mxd** from your **\GISMKT\CFALexington** folder.

This map displays layers for Lexington's highways and restaurants that overlay a thematic map of purchases at restaurants by ZIP Code. In this exercise you will concentrate on local restaurants that CFA hopes will use locally produced food in their menu items.

Change the display of a map layer

The restaurants layer includes independent operations as well as regional and national chains. While the map displays the location of Lexington's restaurants, it does not indicate their ownership. Your initial step will be to change the display of the grocery stores layer to reflect each restaurant's ownership.

1 Double-click the Restaurants layer (or right-click the layer and select Properties).

2 Click the Symbology tab. In the Show area, click Categories, then Unique values.

3 Select Type in the Value Field drop-down box.

4 Uncheck <all other values>.

5 Click Add All Values to display the values for the Type attribute.

This gives the store unique symbols to indicate type of ownership. Though these symbols display the appropriate data, they are difficult to distinguish on the map. You will choose other symbols to make this layer easier to read.

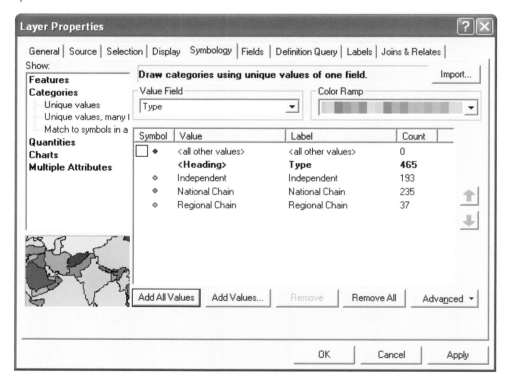

6 Double-click the Independent symbol to display the Symbol Selector dialog box.

7 Click the Square 1 symbol to select it. Select Mars Red (row 3, column 2) for the symbol color and change the size to 8.

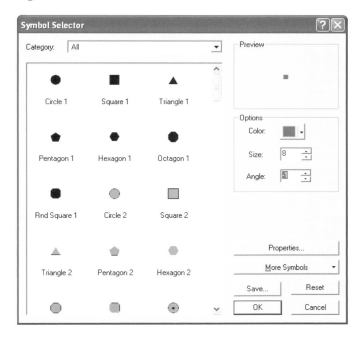

8 Click **OK** to apply these settings and close the Symbol Selector dialog box.

9 Repeat this procedure for the National Chain stores, selecting the Square 1 symbol, Lapis Lazuli color (row 4, column 10), and size 8.

10 Repeat again for the Regional Chain stores, selecting the Square 1 symbol, Solar Yellow color (row 3, column 5), and size 8.

11 Click **OK** to close the Layer Properties dialog box and apply your changes.

The map now displays Lexington's grocery stores with symbols that reflect their ownership.

Select CFA's target restaurants

In its initial program CFA plans to target medium and large independent restaurants. The organization believes that these restaurants are more likely to support a local foods campaign than chain operations would. Further, owners of these restaurants would see participation in this program as a competitive advantage relative to chain competitors.

CFA also wishes to ensure that the restaurants participating in the LIFE program are widely available in Lexington, ensuring that diners have convenient opportunities to patronize restaurants serving local food.

To achieve these objectives you must select the appropriate restaurants for the push campaign and assess the coverage of these restaurants in the Lexington area.

Select restaurants by attribute

1   Right-click the Restaurants layer, then click Open Attribute Table.

2   Click the Options button, then click Select by Attributes option.

3   In the Select by Attributes dialog box, double-click Type to add it to the query box.

4   Click the = button to add it to the query box.

5   Click the Get Unique Values button, then double-click 'Independent' to add it to the query box.

6   Click Apply to run the query.

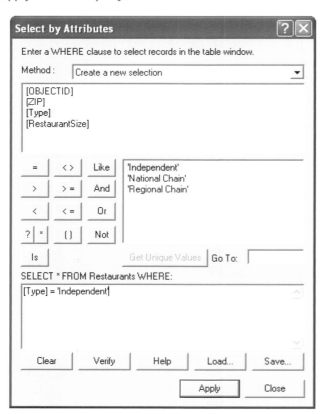

You have selected the appropriate restaurants by ownership type. You will now limit that selection even further to large- and medium-sized independent restaurants.

7   In the Select by Attributes dialog box, choose the "Select from current selection" option in the Method drop-down box.

8   Delete the current query, then use the attribute names, buttons, and values to create the following new query: **[RestaurantSize] = 'Medium' OR [RestaurantSize] = 'Large'**

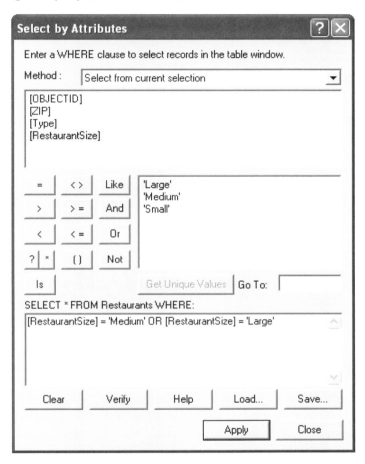

9   Click Apply to run the query and then close the dialog box.

Observe the highlighted records in the table that correspond with the restaurant features highlighted on the map. The numbers at the bottom of the attribute table report how many restaurants are in the Lexington area and how many of them have been selected. Record these numbers, as you will use them later.

10 **Close the attribute table.**

Determine composite coverage area of selected restaurants

You wish to determine if the composite coverage of the selected restaurants sufficiently serves the Lexington area. The composite coverage area is the total geographic area of Lexington which is served by at least one restaurant in the LIFE program. Coverage would be insufficient if any large clusters of restaurants remain outside the composite coverage area of the restaurants you have selected. To make this determination you will assume that diners would be willing to drive an extra mile to a restaurant that offered fresh local foods. If this is true, a LIFE program restaurant would be able to attract patrons from competitors within a one-mile radius of its location. You will use the buffer tool to determine the composite coverage area that includes the geographic area within one mile of any of the selected restaurants.

1 **Click the ArcToolbox button** 🖼️ **on the Standard toolbar.**

2 **In ArcToolbox, expand the Analysis Tools toolbox, then expand the Proximity toolset. Double-click the Buffer tool to open its dialog box.**

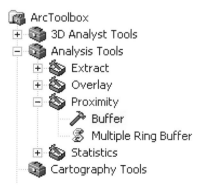

3   In the Buffer tool, select Restaurants in the Input Features drop-down box.

4   Click the Browse button to the right of the Output Feature Class field. Navigate to the **CFALexington.mdb** geodatabase and enter **RestaurantBuffer** for the name of the feature class.

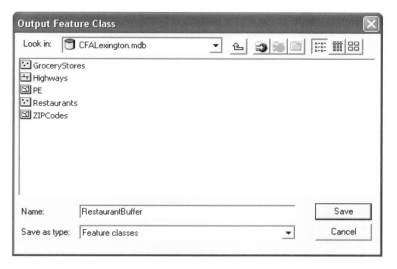

5   Click Save.

6   Select Linear unit for Distance, enter 1 in that field and select Miles in the drop-down box.

You can get help for any parameter in a toolbox's dialog box by clicking on the parameter then looking in the Show Help area. Next you will get help for the Buffer tool's Dissolve parameter.

7   Scroll to the Dissolve type option and click in the field. If the Help panel is not visible on the right of the dialog box, click the Show Help button at the bottom of the box to open it. Review the description of the ALL option in the Help screen to the right of the dialog box. Note that it will produce a single composite coverage area merging the one-mile rings around each of the selected restaurants. This is the option you wish to implement, so select it.

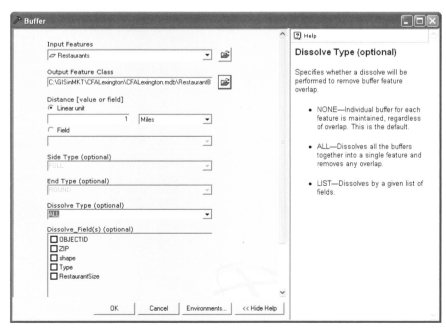

8   Click OK. The buffer operation executes and the new RestaurantBuffer layer appears on your map. Close the progress window and the ArcToolbox window. (Note: You may need to click the Refresh View button ↻ at the bottom of the ArcMap display to see the buffers.)

You will use the Magnifier function to review this map and find any clusters of restaurants that do not include at least one targeted in this campaign. You will use this information to answer the report questions at the end of this exercise.

9   From the main menu bar, click Window > Magnifier to open the Magnifier window.

10 Click and drag the blue bar at the top of the window to move it around the map for a zoomed-in view.

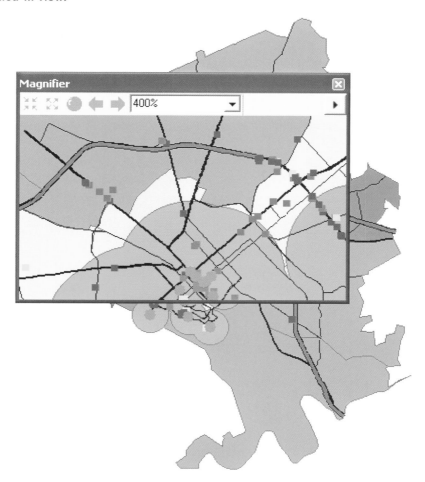

You are looking for clusters of restaurants that fall outside the buffer area. These represent regions in Lexington that offer dining opportunities, but not a restaurant participating in the LIFE program. If these clusters are relatively few in size, coverage of the LIFE program is sufficient. If these clusters are numerous, coverage is insufficient and additional restaurants should be targeted.

11 When you are finished, close the Magnifier window.

Design a map layout

To complete this task, you will design a map that displays the Lexington restaurants you have selected for the push campaign as well as their composite coverage area. You will then export this map as a graphics file and insert it into the appropriate place in your report.

1   Click the Layout View button ⬚ at the bottom of the ArcMap screen.

2   If necessary, move and resize the legend and any other elements that overlap each other.

Note that the restaurant buffer layer somewhat obscures the thematic layer below it. You will correct this by adjusting the display of the buffer layer.

3   Open the RestaurantBuffer Layer Properties.

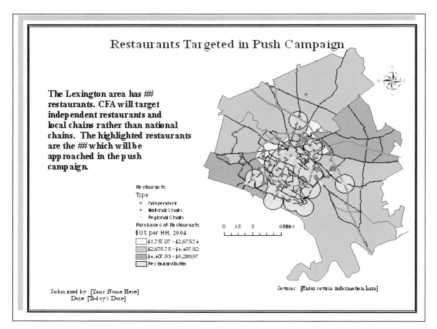

4   Click the General tab and enter **Coverage of Target Restaurants** for the Name.

5   Click the Symbology tab, then click the colored box in the Symbol field to open the Symbol Selector dialog box. Select a light blue fill color and a dark blue 2-point outline. When your dialog box resembles the following graphic, click OK.

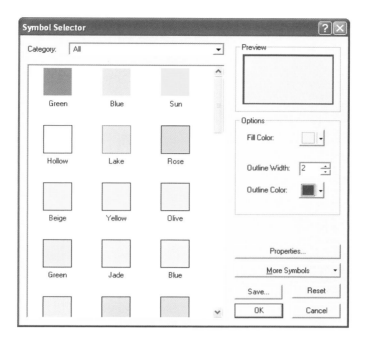

6   Click the Display tab and enter **50** in the Transparent field. When your dialog box looks like the following graphic, click OK to apply the changes.

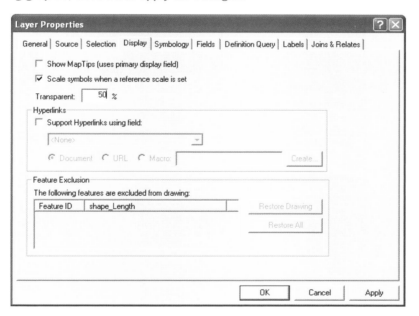

The coverage area buffer is still shaded, but lower layers are visible beneath it.

7   Click the large text box to select it, then right-click and choose Properties. Replace the ## placeholder text with the number of restaurants in Lexington and the number of restaurants you have selected for the campaign.

8   Click the submission information text box to select it, then right-click and choose Properties. Replace the placeholder text with your name and submission date. Click OK.

9   Now click the source text box to select it, then right-click and choose Properties. Replace the placeholder text with **ESRI Community Data, 2005**. Click OK.

Export the map

1 From the main menu bar, click File > Export Map to reach the Export Map dialog box. Navigate to your **\GISMKT\CFALexington** folder. Type **Restaurants.emf** for the file name, then click Save to save the map document as a graphic file in EMF format to include in your report.

Update report and save map document

1 Open the CFALexington_ReportTemplate document and find the Exhibit 2: Restaurants heading. Select the instructional text, and from the main menu bar choose Insert > Picture > From File. Navigate to **Restaurants.emf** and double-click the file name to insert the picture into the report as exhibit 2. (Note: You may have to select and resize the image to display it on the same page as the title.)

2 Use the map and attribute tables to answer the following questions. Summarize your answers in the appropriate section of the project report template.

How many restaurants are in the Lexington area? How many have been selected for this component of the push campaign? Do the selected restaurants provide adequate coverage for the Lexington area? If not, what additional areas require coverage?

3 Save the map document as **CFALexington3_fl.mxd** (replace f and l with your first and last initials) in your **\GISMKT\CFALexington** folder.

Exercise 5.4   Select advertising media using Community Tapestry data

The push portion of the CFA integrated marketing program is designed to increase the availability of locally produced foods in Lexington's grocery stores and restaurants. The pull portion of the campaign is designed to encourage final consumers to seek out and buy these products. To communicate effectively with these consumers you must understand their lifestyles and send your promotional message through the media they prefer. Thus, in this exercise you will:

- Target specific groups of ZIP Codes for customized promotional methods
- Identify the dominant Community Tapestry segments in the targeted ZIP Codes and the lifestyle characteristics of those segments
- Identify the advertising media most often used by the Community Tapestry segments in the targeted ZIP Codes
- Design a map that displays the targeted ZIP Codes and media most appropriate for each group

Open an existing map

1   Open **CFALexington4.mxd**.

The table of contents for this map contains one layer of Lexington's highways, a layer that displays by ZIP Code the percentage of families living below the poverty line, and a third layer that displays purchases at restaurants by ZIP Code. Remember, you can choose which ZIP Code layer you wish to display by turning these layers on or off.

Target ZIP Codes using attribute data

The CFA promotional campaign to consumers is based on the central message that they should increase their consumption of delicious, healthy, local foods. While CFA will use this general approach throughout the Lexington area, it wishes to focus special attention on two specific groups. In lower-income ZIP Codes, the organization will emphasize buying local food products in grocery stores. Its hope is to convince consumers in these lower-income ZIP Codes to eat a more healthy diet using local foods. For the higher income ZIP Codes with high current levels of purchases in restaurants, CFA will emphasize dining at restaurants that serve locally produced food. It wants to convince frequent restaurant diners to seek out restaurants participating in the LIFE program. Any areas that don't clearly fall into either category will be designated as general and receive balanced promotional messages.

Add a layer and add a field

1 Click the Add Data button, navigate to the **CFALexington.mdb** geodatabase, select the **ZIPCodes** layer, and click Add to add this layer to the map.

2 Right-click the ZIPCodes layer, then click Open Attribute Table.

3 Click the Options button, then choose Add Field.

4 Enter **Emphasis** for the Name. Select Text in the Type drop-down box. Change the length to **12** in Field Properties.

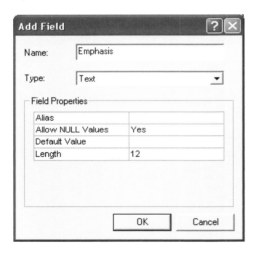

5 Click OK to apply the settings and create the new field.

6 Scroll to the right of the attribute table to locate the new Emphasis field. You will now assign values to this field based on feature attributes.

Select ZIP Codes by attribute and assign to them a Grocery emphasis

Assigning ZIP Codes to segments is a two-step process. First you will select those ZIP Codes that meet the criteria for a specific segment. Second, you will enter the appropriate value for these ZIP Codes in the Emphasis field. You will perform this sequence once for each of the three emphases, beginning with Grocery.

CFA wishes to emphasize a grocery-related message in lower-income ZIP Codes. Thus, you will assign a Grocery emphasis to the four ZIP Codes with the highest percentages of families below the poverty line.

1 Scroll through the attribute table to find PCTFAMBPL. Right-click the column header for the attribute, then click Sort Descending to sort the table by this attribute in descending order.

2 Click the small gray box to the left of the top record in the attribute table to select the record. With the mouse button depressed, drag the mouse to select the top four records. These records are selected in both the table and the map.

3 Right-click the column header of the Emphasis attribute, then click Field Calculator.

4 Click Yes in the warning box to open the Field Calculator dialog box.

5 Select String for the Type.

6 Type **"Grocery"** in the expression box. (Note: Be sure to include the quotation marks, which designate the entry as text rather than numeric data.)

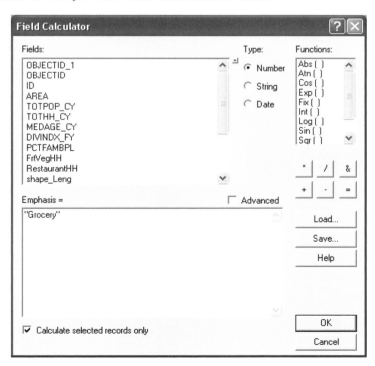

7 Click OK to complete the process.

Observe the Emphasis field of the attribute table, noting that Grocery now appears as the attribute value for all the selected records.

Assign the Restaurant emphasis

CFA wishes to emphasize a restaurant-related message in ZIP Codes with high levels of restaurant purchases. Thus, you will give a Restaurant emphasis to the four ZIP Codes with the highest values for this attribute. You will follow the same procedure you used for the Grocery emphasis, but select features based on a different attribute.

1   Click Options > Clear Selection to clear the current selection.

2   Right-click the column header for the RestaurantHH attribute, then click Sort Descending.

3   Click the small gray box to the left of the top record in the attribute table to select the record. With the mouse button depressed, drag the mouse to select the top four records. These records are now selected in both the table and the map.

4   Right-click the column header of the Emphasis attribute, then click Field Calculator.

5   Click Yes in the warning box to open the Field Calculator dialog box.

6   Select String for the Type.

7   Type **"Restaurant"** in the expression box. (Note: Be sure to include the quotation marks, which designate the entry as text rather than numeric data.)

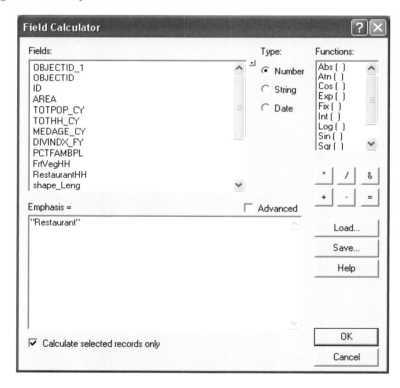

8   Click OK.

Observe the Emphasis field of the attribute table, noting that the value Restaurant now appears as the attribute value for all the selected features.

Assign the General emphasis

Several ZIP Codes have not been assigned to either of the two main emphases. CFA will rely on its general promotional message for these ZIP Codes.

1 Right-click the header cell for the Emphasis attribute, then click Sort Ascending to sort the attributes in ascending order. Note that the features at the top of the table have <Null> values for this attribute.

2 Clear the current selection, then select all rows with <Null> values.

3 Right-click the Emphasis column header, then click Field Calculator.

4 Click Yes in the warning box to open the Field Calculator dialog box.

5 Select String for the Type.

6 Type **"General"** in the expression box. (Note: Be sure to include the quotation marks, which designate the entry as text rather than numeric data.)

7 Click OK.

8 Again clear the selected records, then close the attribute table.

Display the distribution of promotional emphases on a map

You have assigned a promotional emphasis to each of Lexington's ZIP Codes. You will now display the geographic distribution of these emphases on a map by revising the symbology of the ZIPCodes layer.

1 Open the ZIPCodes layer properties.

2 Click the General tab and enter **Promotional Emphasis** as the new layer name.

3 Click the Symbology tab.

4 Select Categories, then Unique values.

5 Select Emphasis for the Value Field.

6 Uncheck <all other values>.

7 Click the Add All Values button to add all the discrete values for this attribute to the classification scheme.

8 Select a color ramp of your choice.

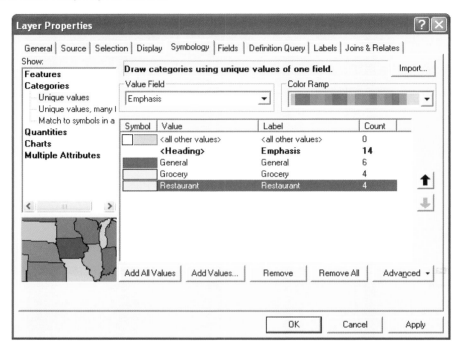

9 Click **OK** to close the Layer Properties dialog box and apply your settings to the map.

10 Change the legend title from Emphasis to **by ZIP Code**.

11 Turn off the Highways layer.

The map now displays Lexington's ZIP Codes with the promotional emphasis assigned to each. You will now identify the dominant Community Tapestry segments in these ZIP Codes to help select appropriate media more precisely.

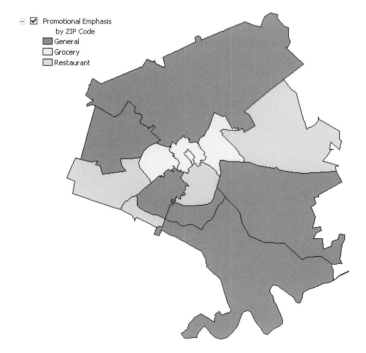

Create a graph

To compare the Community Tapestry segments in the Grocery and Restaurant promotional emphases, you will add data tables to the table of contents and from these design a graph presenting the distribution of Community Tapestry segments.

Add new tables to the map

1   Click the Add Data button. In the Add Data dialog box, navigate to the **CFALexington.mdb** personal geodatabase.

2   Select **EmphasisMPIValues** and **TapestryData** while holding the Ctrl key to select both tables.

3   Click Add to add these tables to the table of contents. Notice the Source tab becomes active so you can see the tables in the table of contents.

TapestryData contains data on the three dominant Community Tapestry segments in the Grocery and Restaurant groups. You will design a graph to display these distributions. EmphasisMPIValues contains data on the media habits of the Community Tapestry segments in the Grocery and Restaurant groups. You will use this information to select the appropriate media for communicating with each group.

Create a graph of Community Tapestry segment distributions

1   From the main menu bar, click Tools > Graphs > Create.

2   In the Create Graph Wizard, maintain the default graph type of Vertical Bar.

3   For the Layer/Table option, choose TapestryData.

4   For the Value field option, choose HH04.

5   For the X label field, choose Emphasis.

6   Choose any custom color you like. Leave all other options set to their default values.

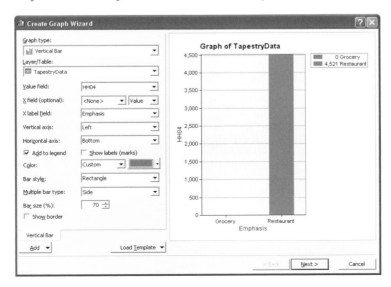

7   At the bottom of the window, click Vertical Bar to make it editable. Replace the default text with **Boomburbs**.

8   Click Add, then choose New Series.

9   Make sure the Layer/Table setting is correct. For Value field, choose HH12. Choose a custom color, then change Vertical Bar to **Up and Coming Families**.

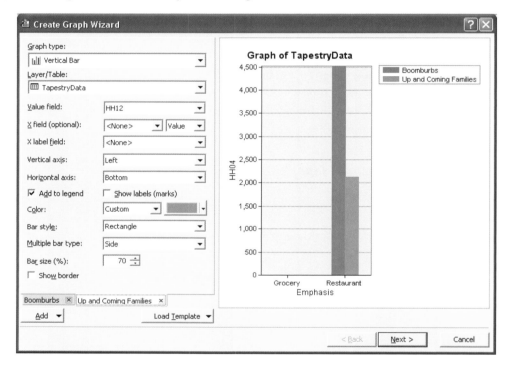

10 Repeat steps 8 and 9 four more times, choosing HH22, HH32, HH33, and HH55 for the value fields. Remember to choose a unique color and rename the bar each time. The new names should be, respectively, **Metropolitans**, **Rustbelt Traditions**, **Midlife Junction**, and **College Towns**.

11 When you're finished, click Next.

12 Change the title to **Community Tapestry Segments by Promotional Emphasis**.

13 Change the left axis title to **Households in each segment**.

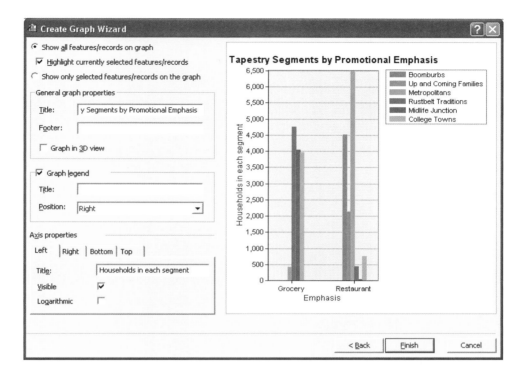

14 Click Finish.

The resulting graph should resemble this one, though your colors will vary. The tallest columns represent the Community Tapestry segments with the most households in each emphasis area.

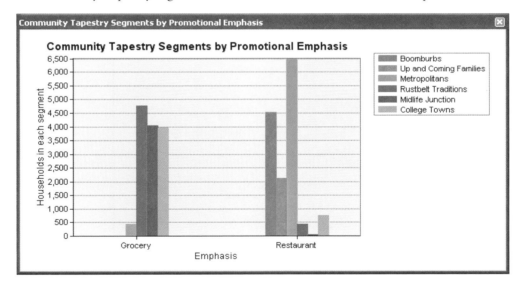

You will insert this graph into your report.

15 Right-click the blue header at the top of the graph, then click Copy as Graphic to copy the graph to the Windows clipboard.

16 In the project report template for this chapter, locate and select the instructional text for exhibit 3. Right-click, then choose Paste to replace this text with the graph.

17 Close the graph in ArcMap.

Your report now graphically displays the three largest Community Tapestry segments for the two areas. The table below identifies these segments and summarizes their characteristics.

Restaurant Emphasis Segments		Grocery Emphasis Segments	
04: Boomburbs		**32: Rustbelt Traditions**	
Segment Number & Name	04 Boomburbs	Segment Number & Name	32 Rustbelt Traditions
LifeMode Group	L1 High society	LifeMode Group	L10 Traditional living
Urbanization Group	U5 Urban outskirts I	Urbanization Group	U5 Urban outskirts I
Household Type	Married-couples with kids	Household Type	Mixed
Median Age	33.8 years	Median Age	35.9 years
Income	High	Income	Middle
Employment	Prof/mgmt	Employment	Skilled/prof/mgmt/svc
Education	Some college; bach./grad degree	Education	HS grad/some college
Residential	Single family	Residential	Single family
Race/Ethnicity	White	Race/Ethnicity	White
Preferences	Play golf; Own common/pref. stock in employers co.; Visit Disney World (FL); Read airline magazines; Own/lease full-size SUV	Preferences	Hunting and shooting; Use credit union; Belong to veterans group; Listen to/watch ice hockey games; Own/lease Pontiac
12: Up and Coming Families		**33: Midlife Junction**	
Segment Number & Name	12 Up and Coming families	Segment Number & Name	33 Midlife junction
LifeMode Group	L9 Family portrait	LifeMode Group	L10 Traditional living
Urbanization Group	U7 Suburban Periphery I	Urbanization Group	U8 Suburban Periphery II
Household Type	Married-couples with kids	Household Type	Mixed
Median Age	31.9 years	Median Age	40.5 years
Income	Upper middle	Income	Middle
Employment	Prof/mgmt	Employment	Prof/mgmt/svc
Education	Some college/bach. degree	Education	Some college
Residential	Single family	Residential	Single family, multiunit
Race/Ethnicity	White	Race/Ethnicity	White
Preferences	Own 2+ dogs; Have mortgage insurance; Visit zoo; Listen to soft. adult contemporary radio; Own/lease SUV	Preferences	Go fishing, play softball; Own CD 6 months or less; Buy children's toys/games; Watch style and QVC on TV; Own/lease Buick
22: Metropolitans		**55: College Towns**	
Segment Number & Name	22 Metropolitans	Segment Number & Name	55 College towns
LifeMode Group	L3 Metropolis	LifeMode Group	L6 Scholars and patriots
Urbanization Group	U3 Metro Cities I	Urbanization Group	U6 Urban Outskirts II
Household Type	Singles, shared	Household Type	Singles, shared
Median Age	37.1 years	Median Age	24.5 years
Income	Middle	Income	Lower middle
Employment	Prof/mgmt	Employment	Students/prof/mgmt/svc
Education	Some college; bach./grad degree	Education	Some college; bach./grad degree
Residential	Single family, multiunit	Residential	Multiunit rentals
Race/Ethnicity	White	Race/Ethnicity	White
Preferences	Visit zoo, museum; Have personal credit line; Go rollerblading; Listen to classical, news-talk radio; Own/lease station wagon	Preferences	Participate in environmental groups; Have personal education loan; Attend college sports events, go to bars; Watch MTV, Comedy Central; Own/lease compact car
Source: ESRI Community Tapestry Demo CD, 2006			

Select media for each promotional emphasis group

1   Open the EmphasisMPIValues data table.

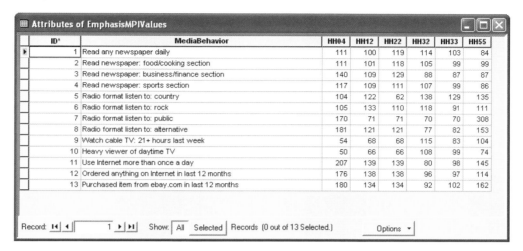

This table contains the MPI values for the six Community Tapestry segments in the Grocery and Restaurant ZIP Codes relative to several media-related behaviors. These values are indexes based on a scale of 100, which is the national average for that behavior. Thus, a segment value of 150 for a behavior, such as watching cable television, indicates that the households in the segment are 50 percent more likely to watch cable television than the average U.S. household.

In this system the most effective media for reaching a segment are indicated by high MPI values. Use this table to answer the report questions below.

Update report and save map document

1   **Use the tables, map, and graph you have created to answer the following questions. Summarize your answers in the appropriate section of the project report template.**

What are the three dominant Community Tapestry segments in the Grocery ZIP Codes? What are the three dominant Community Tapestry segments in the Restaurant ZIP Codes? What three media should CFA use to communicate in the Grocery area? What three media should CFA use to communicate in the Restaurant area? How effective will CFA's Web site be in communicating with these Community Tapestry segments?

2   **Save the map document as CFALexington4_fl.mxd (replace f and l with your first and last initials) in your \GISMKT\CFALexington folder.**

Exercise 5.5   Recommend a media strategy

You have made the integrated marketing communication decisions necessary to implement the full campaign for CFA. You wish to complete your report with a map that displays the distribution of your promotional groups across Lexington's ZIP Codes as well as the media exposure data that supports your recommendations for each group. Thus, in this exercise you will:

- Design a map displaying the promotional emphases for Lexington's ZIP Codes
- Create a table listing the appropriate media for ZIP Codes with a Grocery promotional emphasis
- Create a table listing the appropriate media for ZIP Codes with a Restaurants emphasis

Open an existing map

1   In ArcMap, open **CFALexington5.mxd**.

This map opens in data view. The table of contents contains one layer and two data tables.

2   Click the Source tab to see the tables, if needed.

The Promotional Emphasis layer displays the promotional emphasis you have assigned to each of Lexington's ZIP Codes. The TapestryData table contains data on the Community Tapestry neighborhoods in ZIP Codes assigned to the Grocery and Restaurant emphases. The EmphasisMPIValues table contains the MPI values for various media of each of the Community Tapestry groups in the two promotional emphasis groups. You used this data in the previous exercise to select promotional media for each group. You will use them here to prepare tables in the map document to support your recommendations.

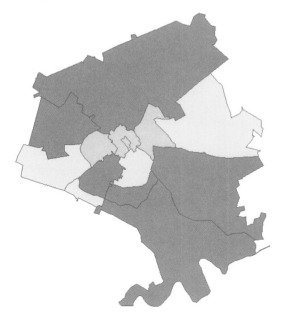

Add and arrange tables on a layout page

Switch to layout view and review map

1   Click the Layout View button ☐ at the bottom of the ArcMap display area.

The map now appears in a data frame in the layout page. The layout includes a legend, scale bar, and north arrow.

Below the map are two areas that describe your media strategy conclusions for ZIP Codes in the Grocery and Restaurant promotional emphasis groups. You will add data tables to these areas to support your media recommendations.

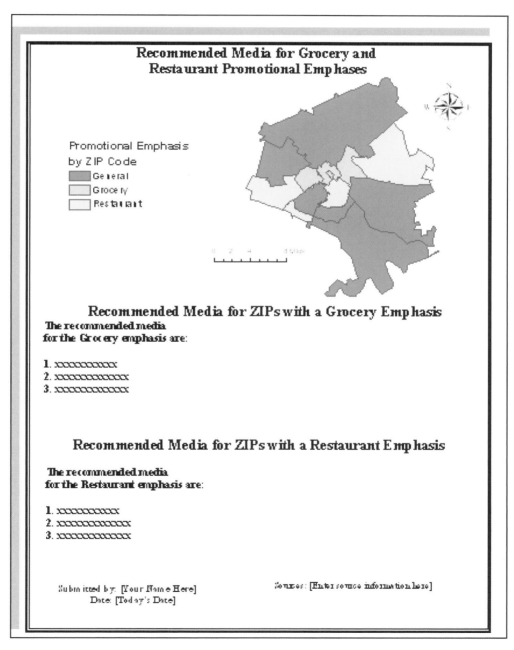

Edit a data table and add it to the layout

1 Open the EmphasisMPIValues table.

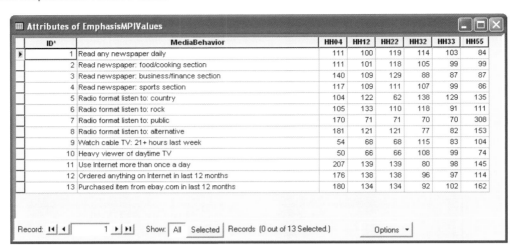

This is the table of MPI values you used to make your media recommendations in the previous exercise. You will edit it here and include it in the map document to support your recommendations.

2 Select the three media behaviors you chose to communicate with the Grocery group in the previous exercise. The three selected records should be highlighted. Click the Selected button at the bottom of the table to display only the selected records.

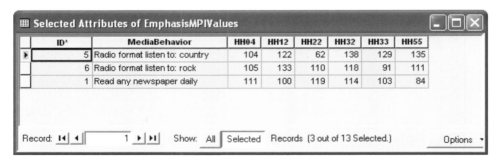

The table displays the records you wish to include, but it also displays attributes for the Community Tapestry segments in the Restaurant emphasis group, which you do not wish to include. You will remove them by editing the table's properties.

3 In the ArcMap table of contents, right-click EmphasisMPIValues, then click Properties to open the Table Properties dialog box.

4   Click the Fields tab if necessary. Select only the attributes MediaBehavior, HH32, HH33, and HH55 (uncheck the others).

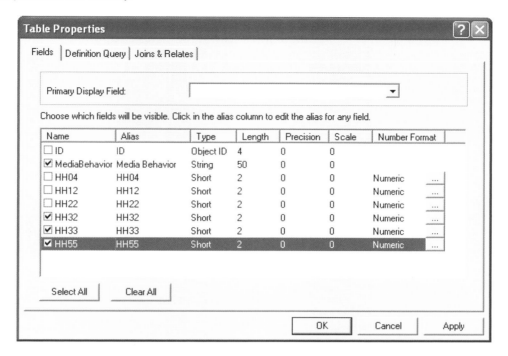

5   Click Apply, then close the Table Properties dialog box.

The data table now includes only the attributes and Community Tapestry segments you have selected.

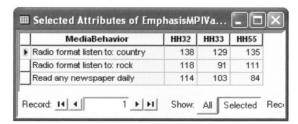

You will now display and format this table in layout view.

6   Click Options at the bottom of the table, then Add Table to Layout.

7   Move the data table so you can see the layout.

The table now appears in layout view, but it is too large and is positioned poorly.

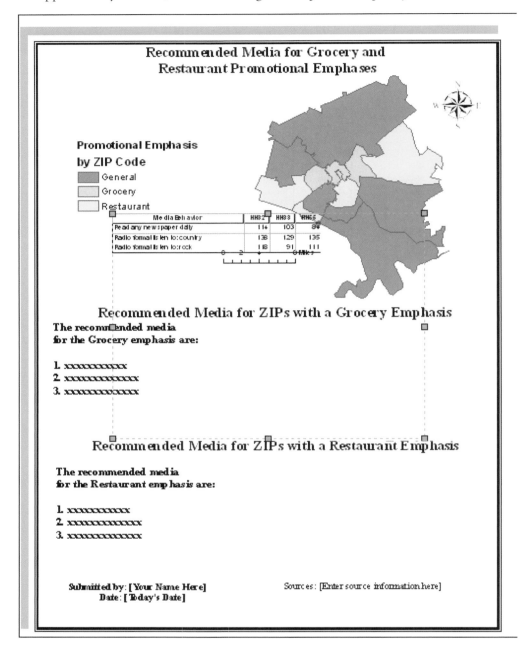

Format table in layout view and edit its descriptive text

1   Use the corner handles to resize the table and move it to the appropriate spot to the right of the text describing the media strategy for the Grocery promotional emphasis.

2   On the layout, right-click the table and click Properties.

3   Select a 2.5-point line in the Border field of the Frame tab as the border for the table.

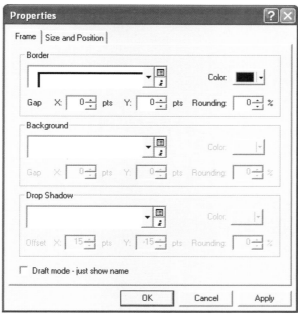

4   Click OK.

5   Click the text box to the left of the table and edit its contents to list the media you have identified for this promotional emphasis.

6   Click the submission information text box to select it, then right-click and click Properties. Replace the placeholder text with your name and submission date. Click OK.

7   Click the sources text box to select it, then right-click and select Properties. Replace the placeholder text with **ESRI Community Data, 2005** and on a second line, **Mediamark Research Inc., Doublebase 2004**.

8   Click OK.

Repeat data table editing, positioning, and formatting steps for the Restaurant emphasis

1   Repeat the basic steps above to produce a corresponding table for the restaurant promotional emphasis. The data table should include only Community Tapestry segments HHO4, HH12, and HH22 and the three media outlets you have determined to be the best mix to reach this group.

2   Add the resulting table to layout view. Close the data table window. Reposition the table in layout view and add a 2.5 point border to it.

3   Edit the text box to the left of the table to list the media you have selected for the Restaurant promotional emphasis.

Export the map

1   From the main menu bar, click File then Export Map to reach the Export Map dialog box. Navigate to the **\GISMKT\CFALexington** folder. Type **PromotionalEmphases.emf** for the file name, then click Save to save the map document as a graphic file in EMF format to include in your report.

Update report and save map document

1   Open the project report template. Locate the page entitled Exhibit 4: Recommended media for grocery and restaurant promotional emphases. Select the instructional text in brackets, and from the main menu in Microsoft Word choose Insert > Picture > From File. Navigate to **PromotionalEmphases.emf** and double-click the file name to insert the picture into the report as exhibit 4. (Note: You may have to select and resize the image to display it on the same page as the title.)

2   Use the maps, tables, and map documents you have created to do the following task. Record your response in the appropriate section of the project report template.

Summarize your recommendations by describing (1) the number and percentage of Lexington's grocery stores you will target, (2) the number and percentage of Lexington's restaurants you will target, (3) the three recommended media for the Grocery promotional emphasis, and (4) the three recommended media for the Restaurant promotional emphasis.

3   Save the map document as **CFALexington5_fl.mxd** (replace f and l with your first and last initials) in your **\GISMKT\CFALexington** folder.

Congratulations! You have completed the Community Farm Alliance project.

Reflect for a moment on what you have achieved in this chapter. You have explored the demographic characteristics of Lexington's ZIP Codes as well as the distribution and characteristics of the city's grocery stores and restaurants. You have targeted businesses for the push component of the CFA integrated marketing communication program, displayed the selected grocery stores and restaurants on the map, and evaluated their geographic coverage of the desired market. For the pull component of the campaign, you have identified two segments to receive customized versions of the program's core message. Further, you have evaluated the Community Tapestry composition of the target groups and used Market Potential Indexes to select the best media to communicate with them. In sum, you have used ArcGIS to implement both components of the CFA integrated marketing communication program.

Additional applications

The potential role of GIS applications in implementing integrated marketing communication programs and promotional programs in general, extends well beyond the scope of this exercise.

In the push component of this exercise, you identified Lexington businesses (grocery stores and restaurants) that were prospective participants in the LIFE program. This selection of potential customers based on attractive features (a process known as qualifying prospects), is an important part of business-to-business marketing. It serves to concentrate the firm's efforts on those businesses that are most likely to respond to promotional or personal selling efforts. It can also function to create a mutual, competitive advantage for the firm and its business customers. In this case, that advantage lay in the ability to provide locally produced food, an advantage shared by this local food cooperative and the locally owned grocery stores and restaurants it targeted. Their combination provides an advantage in local markets over national and regional competitors who, in total, have more market power.

Stella's Kentucky Deli illustrates this advantage.[1] Under new ownership, this established Lexington lunch spot has transformed its menu to feature local produce and meats, much of which is purchased from Community Farm Alliance members. This approach and its creative menu give Stella's a unique appeal in the Lexington lunch scene.

This screening process is more sophisticated when performed in the context of customer relationship management (CRM) systems. CRM systems are comprehensive management tools that allow firms to track contacts, sales, and long-term relationships with their business customers. When integrated with the spatial tools of GIS, they provide greater understanding of the critical success factors in business marketing relationships and, as a result, greater guidance in the prospecting process.

The prospecting and screening processes become even more crucial when a firm assigns its customers to exclusive territories for resale or support functions. In this exercise, CFA could support several grocery stores or restaurants in the same geographic area. However, in some cases, the business assigns each customer to a specific geographic area of responsibility. For CFA, selecting one firm as a customer necessarily entails rejecting all others in that geographic area. GIS systems can be valuable in defining the geographic areas of responsibility and selecting the strongest potential intermediary in each one.

Pull promotional strategies, those aimed at final consumers, also benefit significantly from the application of GIS tools. In this exercise, you used the Market Potential Indexes to select appropriate media to reach the Community Tapestry segments in the Grocery and Restaurant promotional emphasis groups. This system offers substantial potential for expanding this application further.

If you have not done so, review the exercises in chapter 2, which covers the Community Tapestry lifestyle segmentation system. There you will find more extensive listing of MPI behaviors for Community Tapestry segments. In the Media category, for example, the general media descriptions of this exercise appear, but so do many more specific media behaviors, from various types of sporting events to specific network and cable televisions shows. These allow you to refine media selection even further.

In addition, this system includes MPI values for a range of attitudes, leisure and lifestyle activities, and shopping patterns. This information would help you frame a message to appeal to the targeted Community Tapestry segments and what type of buying behavior to seek. For example, a business might target a segment that watches basketball games, reads the newspaper, and seldom uses the Internet with an ad in the sports section of the newspaper that includes a coupon offering discounts at a LIFE program restaurant after basketball games. On the other hand, a business might better reach a segment that attends concert performances and uses the Internet frequently with a banner ad on the local symphony's Web site offering a similar discount after concerts.

GIS applications can also help determine the appropriate media geographically. If a newspaper has limited distribution or a radio/television station limited reach, a company can display that information spatially relative to concentrations of target customers. Thus, media whose reach does not include the targeted customers would be eliminated from consideration.

GIS tools can also be an important part of the promotional message itself. In this case, maps of grocery stores and restaurants participating in the LIFE program will be an important part of any print advertising or mailings. In addition, static or dynamic mapping functions would be included in the CFA LIFE Web site offering users maps and directions to participating outlets. This is a common practice among so-called clicks and mortar retailers. These firms seek to integrate electronic and traditional retailing strategies by using online tools to increase sales and attract customers to existing physical facilities. Mapping tools on the retailer's Web sites support this integrated approach, allowing customers to pick up merchandise purchased online at the nearest retail location. This allows them to pick up the items quickly and save shipping costs. It also affords the retailer an opportunity to add additional items to the customer's purchase with in-store displays and interaction with the sales force. Best Buy[2] is one of the retailers that uses this approach.

Finally, GIS tools can be the central feature of a promotional campaign. Nature Valley is an international brand of granola bars popular with active outdoor-type people. The brand's Web site invites users to identify and describe their own Nature Valley, an outdoor location special to them.[3] GIS Web services allow users to map the location of these sites and share them with other Nature Valley enthusiasts.

In these and other ways, GIS applications can greatly enhance the effectiveness of both the push and pull components of integrated marketing communication programs.

1. Linda Blackford, "Stella's New Groove," *Lexington Herald Leader,* June 16, 2006: 23.

2. Best Buy Web site, *http://bestbuy.com,* offers online shopping, option to pick up locally, as well as a store locator service.

3. Nature Valley Web site, *http://www.wheresyours.com,* allows you to view existing sites and add your own.

CHAPTER 6

Prospect Profiling

Course: Marketing Research/eCommerce/ Internet Marketing

This chapter teaches how to use demographic data for geodemographic profiling. World Treasures* is an online retailer specializing in traditional art objects from around the world. The firm wishes to develop a database marketing program to reach users who are interested in the firm's products but unwilling to buy online. It wishes to test this program in New York, where it has over 30,000 subscribers to its electronic newsletter. Specifically, the firm wishes to profile the demographic characteristics of these subscribers and concentrate its mailing on ZIP Codes that match that profile, thus improving response rates. Toward that end, you will use GIS tools to develop profiles of attractive prospects and focus marketing efforts on concentrations of those prospects.

* This is a fictional company and scenario, created for educational purposes only. Any resemblance to actual persons, events, or corporations is unintended.

Learning objectives

To conduct a prospect profiling market research project in an eCommerce context, you will learn how to use ArcGIS to:

1. Display population demographic information on a map
2. Assign market segment values to ZIP Codes based on the number of subscribers they contain
3. Create demographic profiles of ZIP Code segments and use them to identify attractive prospects
4. Target ZIP Codes that match the profile of attractive prospects
5. Design maps to communicate your customer profiling recommendations

Marketing scenario

World Treasures, Inc. is an electronic retailer specializing in craft products from around the world. It offers items produced by traditional craft masters, primarily in developing countries, through its Web site and eBay store. Though these crafts have long been recognized for their quality and workmanship, the people creating them have not benefited fully from their popularity. The craft masters have typically sold their work to local traders at relatively low prices. The traders then sell the items to distributors and retailers, who offer them to final consumers. Each intermediary added significant price markups as the items moved through the distribution channel. Thus, the craft masters have received a relatively small share of the final price paid by consumers. Further, given their often remote locations and lack of direct access to established distribution channels, they have not had the opportunity to assume more control and reap higher prices from the marketing of their products.

World Treasures offers an electronic alternative to this system. It buys directly from traditional craft masters and sells directly to final consumers through its two electronic outlets. World Treasures provides links to Web sites documenting the quality and value of the items it sells, thus increasing the knowledge base of its customers and, as a result, their willingness to invest in traditional art. By purchasing items directly from craft masters and local craft collectives, World Treasures is able to pass on more of the final price to traditional artists, while still enjoying a reasonable level of return on their operations.

World Treasures wishes to build upon its success and is considering a database marketing program using direct mail to expand its customer base. However, the firm does not wish to invest in a mass mailing effort, which it believes will result in a low response rate and poor net margins on any resulting sales. The firm would rather focus the campaign at specifically targeted prospects in order to increase response rates and sales while lowering the costs of the direct-mail effort. It believes that the subscribers to its electronic newsletter are ideal prospects for this effort. These users often visit the World Treasures Web site and receive weekly information about new offerings. When a subscriber places an order, his or her name is transferred from the subscribers list to a customers list, to which a different monthly electronic newsletter is sent. Thus, the subscribers list includes users who are interested in the firm's products, but have yet to place an order. World Treasures believes that a direct-mail offering might stimulate these users, and other prospects that fit their profile, to make their first purchase. The firm wishes to implement a trial campaign in one of its largest state markets, New York, to test the feasibility and result of this approach with a mailing to about 2,000,000 households.

To summarize, World Treasures wishes to design a demographic profile of its electronic newsletter subscribers and use it to target selected prospects in New York with a direct-mail campaign. However, the firm has no demographic information on subscribers, as the only address information that subscribers provide is their ZIP Code. The pilot project requires that the firm (1) use a geodemographic overlay process to estimate the socioeconomic and demographic profile of its subscribers based on their ZIP Code, (2) use the resulting profile to select geographic areas (in this case ZIP Codes) with similar characteristics, and (3) focus the direct-mail campaign on these areas. A geodemographic overlay assigns demographic values to household records (customers, prospects, or in this case, subscribers) based on their location. In this case, subscribers will be assigned the values for the ZIP Code in which they live.

You have been tasked with carrying this plan out. World Treasures has purchased ESRI demographic data on measures it believes are relevant for its products. In addition to population and household information, these measures include age, household size, disposable income, education, and home ownership. You also have access to a list of the 33,060 electronic newsletter subscribers in New York and their ZIP Codes.

In the following exercises, you will use ArcGIS tools to execute this project for World Treasures and make recommendations for their trial direct-marketing campaign in New York.

Background information

Marketing research encompasses a wide range of tools designed to help firms learn more about their customers. Though many of these tools involve primary research, innovative use of secondary data is also a valuable part of the field. As this data is more readily available, it offers both time and cost advantages that market researchers should exploit. For example, they can analyze demographic information about customers to produce customer profiles. Businesses can use address fields in customer records to attach such information to those records. Even if customer addresses are not available, businesses can use a simple ZIP Code field, as in this exercise, for the same purpose. This might be the case when a business has a subscriber list for an electronic newsletter.

Customer profiles refer to collections of data on the socioeconomic and demographic characteristics of a group of people. Marketers create profiles for current customers, prospective customers, or general market segments to support the development of responsive marketing strategies. Virtually every element of the marketing strategy must take customer characteristics into account. The marketing team designs products to meet the needs of specific groups, creates promotional messages to appeal to customers' values, selects retail sites to match their shopping patterns, and sets prices that reflect their economic situation. Thus, knowledge about the characteristics of target customers is the cornerstone of the marketing effort.

Marketers should draw socioeconomic and demographic information from direct sources whenever possible to ensure the accuracy and currency of data. However, direct access to such information is often not possible. People are hesitant to provide extensive demographic information in response to consumer surveys, and commercial household demographic information is often either unavailable or quite expensive. As a result, marketers seek out alternative methods for acquiring this information. One such method is geodemographic profiling.

Geodemographic profiling is a method for inferring socioeconomic and demographic characteristics of people based on where they live. The technique is based on the premise that populations tend to cluster geographically into groups with relatively similar socioeconomic, demographic, and lifestyle characteristics. The analyst uses the demographic characteristics of the block group, census tract, or ZIP Code in which a household resides as an estimate of the demographic characteristics of that household.

The following exercises illustrate the value of geodemographic profiling. World Treasures is an online retailer that interacts with its subscribers electronically. While it doesn't collect personal information about subscribers, World Treasures seeks some understanding of the socioeconomic and demographic profile of subscribers in order to tailor a direct-mail campaign to them. Though its user base is not limited geographically because they access World Treasures through its Web site, spatial analysis still has potential value for the firm. In this exercise, geodemographic profiling is performed on subscribers' ZIP Codes, the sole piece of spatial information users provide in the subscription process. World Treasures purchased ZIP Code demographic data and assigned values to subscribers living within each ZIP Code. The subscriber profile, in turn, is derived from summary statistics of these values. Finally, the resulting profile allows the firm to selectively target ZIP Codes for its direct-mail campaign.

While geodemographic profiling can be a valuable tool, it has limitations. First and most obvious, it is a technique for demographic estimation, not precise measurement. Assigning a size of 2.49 to a household because that is the average household size of the ZIP Code in which it lies is clearly erroneous. However, when replicated over several households in a list of prospective customers, it can provide a general indication that households tend to be larger or smaller in one ZIP Code than in another. To personalize this dynamic, visit *http://www.esribis.com/reports/ziplookup.html* and enter your ZIP Code to view some summary demographics of your area. How well do these statistics reflect your situation? (Note: You will also view the major Community Tapestry lifestyle segments for the ZIP Code. This segmentation system classifies United States households into 65 distinct lifestyle clusters, each of which has similar demographics, values, and purchasing patterns. This system is a very useful segmentation tool. For additional information, you should complete chapter 2, which provides an orientation to the Community Tapestry system.)

Second, the accuracy of geodemographic profiling estimates increase as the geographic unit employed decreases in size. That is, the degree of homogeneity among households in a compressed census block group of 500 households is likely to be higher than in a census tract of 1,400 households or a ZIP Code of 12,000 households. However, census tracts and block groups are not part of postal addresses. Most people don't know the numbers of the census tract or block group in which they live.

For this reason, marketers must spatially assign household records in a firm's database to their respective census tracts or block groups. This process uses a tool called geocoding. Geocoding uses standard address information to assign each address in a database a pair of latitude and longitude coordinates. Marketers can place this latitude–longitude point within the boundaries of the appropriate census tract or block group. With this link in place, they can attach the demographic values of the census tract or block group to each household contained therein. Though this may sound simple, geocoding involves using extensive collections of street data that marketers must match accurately to the addresses in household records to be successful.

Finally, calculating summary statistics from values assigned by spatial location can create additional inaccuracies. For example, in this exercise, calculating the average percentage of homeownership for a group of ZIP Codes produces an inaccurate result as it does not adjust for differing numbers of households in each ZIP. The calculation for average age also has weaknesses as it is the average of a field that reports median values. These difficulties reemphasize the point that marketers should interpret the values obtained in geodemographic profiling as broad indicators of similarities and differences rather than precise measures of population characteristics.

Given its substantial limitations, how can geodemographic profiling add value to marketing analysis? The answer is that marketing offers targeted on the basis of geodemographic profiling, though imprecise, are more effective than mass random distribution of similar offers. World Treasures's direct mailing to 2,000,000 households is more likely to reach households interested in their products than would a mailing to 2,000,000 random New York households. If the average initial World Treasures order is $50, each 1 percent increase in the response rate to the mailing produces marginal revenue of $1,000,000. If half the new purchasers become loyal customers with yearly purchases of $50, annual revenues will increase by $500,000. These revenue streams represent a substantial return on the investment in data and GIS technology employed in this chapter.

World Treasures New York data dictionary	
Attribute	**Description**
For UsersZIPs	
txtZIP	Subscriber's ZIP Code
For NYZIPDemographics and State	
ZIPCode	ZIP Code number
TOTPOP_CY	Total population, 2004
HHPOP_CY	Population living in households, 2004
TOTHH_CY	Total households, 2004
AVGHHSIZ_CY	Average household size, 2004
MEDAGE_CY	Median age, 2004
AVGDI_CY	Average family disposable income, 2004
PctAssocHigher	Percentage of people > 25 with associate degree or higher, 2004
PctHomeOwner	Percentage of households owning their home, 2004
Source: ESRI Community Data, 2005	

Exercise 6.1   Explore and prepare data

In this project, you will analyze customer data and demographic data at the ZIP Code level. To prepare for this analysis, you must explore a basemap of New York and add the relevant data tables to the map document. You must also prepare customer data for integration with the basemap attribute table. Therefore, in this exercise, you will:

- Explore a basemap of New York and its ZIP Codes
- Add demographic and customer data tables to the project
- Create a summary table of users by ZIP Code to use in your customer profiling analysis

Open an existing map

1   **To start ArcMap, from the Windows taskbar click Start > All Programs > ArcGIS > ArcMap.**

Depending on how ArcGIS and ArcMap have been installed you may have a different navigation path.

2   **If you see a startup window, click the "An existing map" option. Otherwise, click the Open button** 📂 **on the ArcMap Standard toolbar.**

3   **Browse to your \GISMKT\WorldTreasuresNY folder, choose the WorldTreasuresNY1 map document, and click Open.**

The map includes four layers, three of which are visible. The first three, from the bottom up, display the state of New York, its major urban areas, and its interstate highways. The fourth layer, which displays New York's ZIP Codes, is turned off.

Modify the map content

You will examine population information by adding demographic data to the ZIP Code layer and editing its symbology. You can view the ZIP Code layer by turning layers on and off.

Turn layers on and off

1   Check the small white box to the left of the **New York State** layer to turn it off.

2   Check the box to the left of the **New York ZIP Codes** layer to turn it on.

The map now displays the boundaries of New York's ZIP Codes as well as the layers for urban areas and interstate highways. You will use this layer to integrate demographic and customer data into the layer attribute table and display it on the map.

Add tabular data to the table of contents

Demographic data at the ZIP Code level is contained in a table in the WorldTreasuresNY.mdb personal geodatabase. Another table contains the ZIP Codes of subscribers to the World Treasures electronic newsletter in New York. You will add these tables to the table of contents to include them in the analysis.

1   Click the Add Data button. ✛

2   Navigate to the folder where **WorldTreasuresNY.mdb** is stored, and open the geodatabase.

3   Press and hold the Ctrl key, then click the **NYZIPDemographics** and **UsersZIPs** tables to select them.

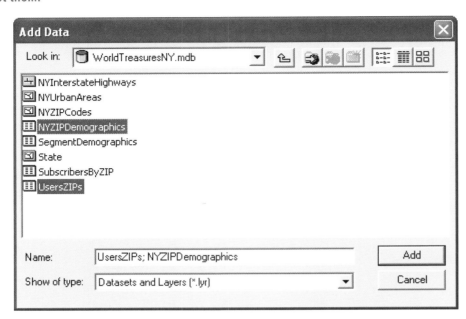

4   Click Add to add the data tables to the table of contents. Notice that when tables are added to the map document, the table of contents switches to the Source tab so the tables can be seen.

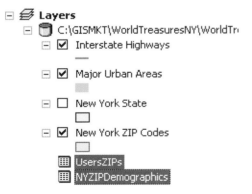

Join tabular data to a feature class attribute table

To design thematic maps that display demographic values for New York's ZIP Codes, you must integrate this data into the attribute table for the basemap layer.

1   Right-click the New York ZIP Codes layer, point to Joins and Relates, then click Join.

2   In the Join Data dialog box, make sure the first option reads "Join attributes from a table."

3   For item 1, choose ZIPCode from the drop-down menu.

4   For item 2, choose NYZIPDemographics.

5   For item 3, choose ZIPCode.

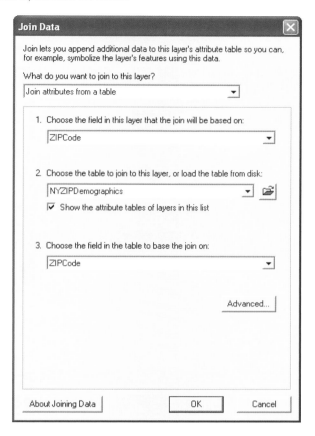

6   Click OK to run the join operation.

The New York ZIP Codes layer now contains data from NYZIPDemographics in addition to its original data. The join operation added the attributes in the demographics table to the features in the New York ZIP Codes layer that have the same ZIP Code.

7   Right-click the New York ZIP Codes layer, then click Open Attribute Table to view the results of your join operation.

The demographic data has been added to the attribute table. You must scroll to the right to see it. Note also that the label for each attribute in the table now displays its home table in addition to its attribute name. For example, NYZIPDemographics.TOTPOP_CY is from the NYZIPDemographics table. This naming convention clearly shows the source of the attributes in the joined table.

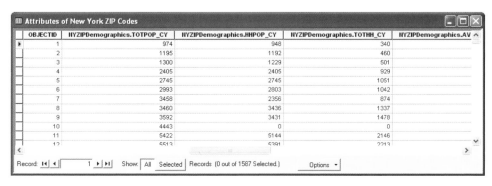

Edit a layer's name and symbology

1   Close the table, then double-click the New York ZIP Codes layer (or right-click the layer and select Properties).

2   Click the General tab and enter **Households by ZIP Code** as the new layer name.

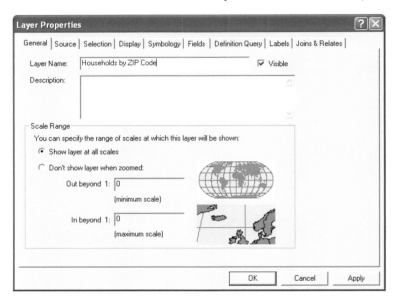

3   Click the Symbology tab. Click Quantities, then Graduated Colors. A random color ramp is assigned to the data.

4   Select the appropriate attribute in the Value field. Use the data dictionary to identify the attribute that reports total households for each ZIP Code. (Note: To see the full attribute name, select an attribute from the drop-down list, then hover your mouse pointer over the value.)

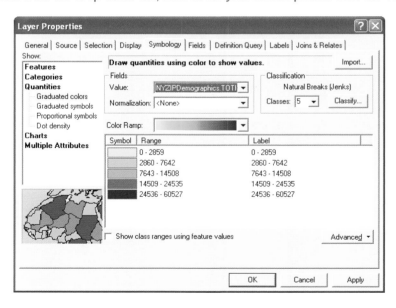

Notice the default classification system in this dialog box. It uses five classes assigned by the natural breaks method, which uses a statistical technique to identify clusters within the attribute's values.

5   Click the Classify button to open the Classification dialog box.

6   For Method, choose Quantile from the drop-down menu.

7   For Classes, choose 3.

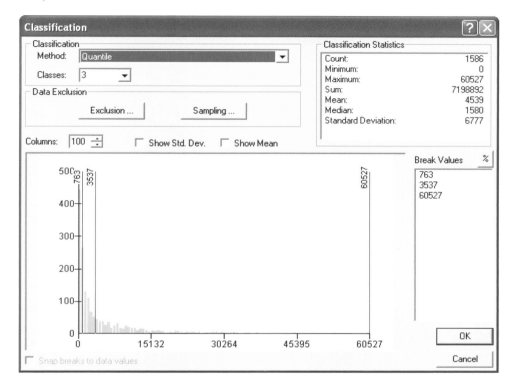

This will cause the map to define three classes with a roughly equal number of ZIP Codes in each. The classifications include the highest, middle, and lowest third of ZIP Codes.

8   Click OK to return to the Symbology tab.

Format classification labels

You will now modify the display of classification labels in the map legend.

1   Click the Label button in the Layer Properties dialog box, then click Format Labels to open the Number Format dialog box. (Note: Do not click the Labels tab at the top of this dialog box. If you do so inadvertently, click the Symbology tab to return.)

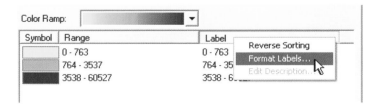

2   Select Numeric in the Category field.

3   Click the **Number of decimal places** radio button, then enter 0 to display values as integers.

4   Check the **Show thousands separators** option, and uncheck any other options if necessary.

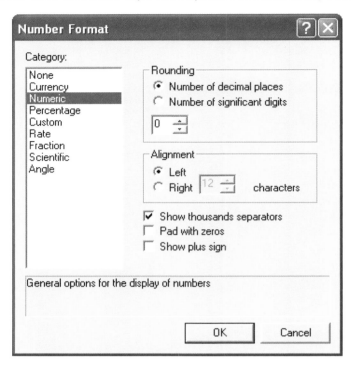

5   Click **OK** to return to the Layer Properties dialog box.

6   Right-click the drop-down arrow in the Color Ramp field, then click **Graphic View** to view the names of the color ramp schemes rather than their color spectra.

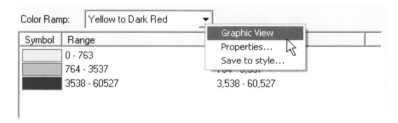

7   Click the drop-down arrow in the Color Ramp field, then click the **Surface** color ramp option.

8   The color ramp should display lower values in lighter colors, higher values in darker ones. If this is not the case, click the Symbol heading, then click **Flip Symbols**.

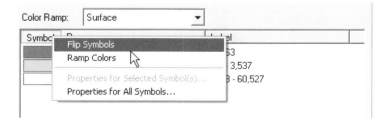

9   Select the "Show class ranges using feature values" option to define classification ranges using actual values from the dataset.

10   Click **OK** to close the Layer Properties dialog box and display the revised settings in the map.

Edit legend title

1   In the table of contents, click the attribute name **NYZIPDemographics.TOTHH_CY** under the title of the layer, then click again to edit it. (Note: If your second click is too quick, the Properties dialog box will open. Click Cancel, then try again, clicking more slowly to reach the edit function.)

2   Replace the existing legend title with **Total households**.

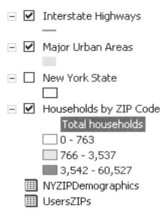

The resulting map displays the number of households in each of New York's ZIP Codes.

Examine layers in detail with ArcMap navigation tools

Next you will use the Zoom In tool to examine specific areas of the state, observing how population concentrations are related to urban areas and major highways. Zoom to specific areas of the map to study these relationships in various regions of the state.

1   Click the Zoom In tool ⊕ to select it. Click and hold the mouse button to draw a box around the area you want to zoom to, then release the mouse button.

2   Click the Pan tool. ✋ Click and hold a point on the map and drag the Pan cursor in one direction to view a different area of the map.

The following map is zoomed to the western portion of the state. Your map will differ based on the area you choose and how far you are zoomed in.

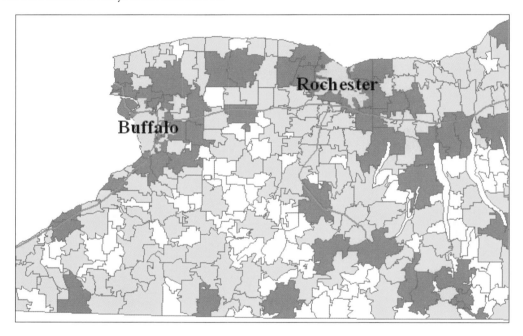

3   When you have completed your examination, click the Full Extent button ⬤ to return the map view to the original full extent of New York.

Use your observations to answer the report question, found at the end of this exercise, about population distribution in New York.

Summarize customer data table

1   **Right-click the UsersZIPs data table, then click Open to open the table and view its contents.**

Note the text at the bottom of the table that reads Records (0 out of *2000 Selected.) The asterisk before the number 2000 indicates that there are additional records in the table.

2   **Click the Last Record button at the bottom of the window to go to the last record in the table.**

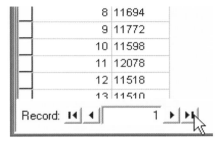

Note that there are 33,060 subscriber records.

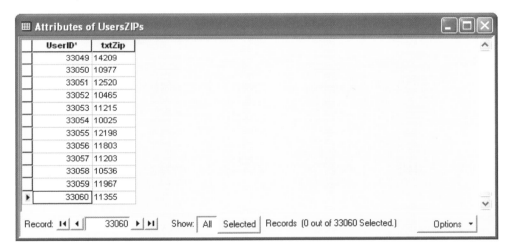

This table has been extracted from the World Treasures electronic newsletter subscription list. It contains one record for each subscriber. As subscriber names are irrelevant for your analysis, they have been deleted from the table.

For this analysis, you require a table that contains the number of subscribers who live in each of New York's ZIP Codes. To create this table, you will perform a summary operation on the UsersZIPs table.

3   Right-click the column header containing the attribute txtZip, then click Summarize to reach the Summarize dialog box.

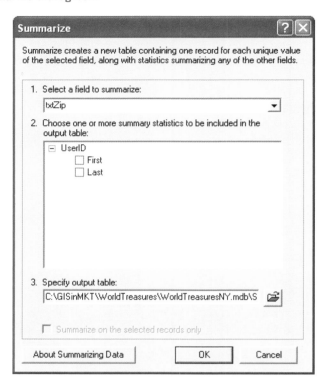

4   Click the Browse button to the right of the Specify output table option to open the Saving Data dialog box.

5   Select File and Personal Geodatabase tables in the Save as type drop-down box.

6   Navigate to and open the **WorldTreasuresNY.mdb** personal geodatabase, and enter **ZIPSummary** for the Name.

This will save the summary table as a personal geodatabase table.

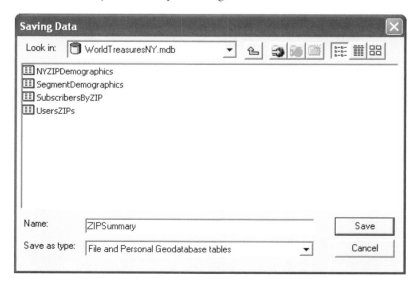

7   Click Save, then OK to perform the summary operation. (As you require only a count of records for each ZIP Code, it is not necessary to summarize any attribute in the table.) When asked if you wish to add the resulting table to the map, click Yes.

8   Close the UsersZIPs table.

The ZIPSummary table now appears in the table of contents.

9   Open the ZIPSummary table.

Note that World Treasures subscribers live in 1,013 of New York's ZIP Codes. The descriptive statistics of the count field will reveal important information about the distribution of these subscribers.

10   Right-click the Count_txtZip column header, then click Statistics to calculate descriptive statistics for this attribute and display the Statistics of ZIPSummary window.

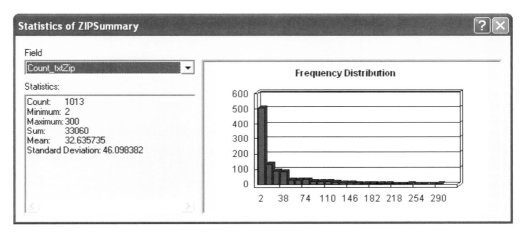

This window contains important information for the rest of your analysis. Note the minimum and maximum values that report the highest and lowest values for the attribute. (There will be several ZIP Codes with no subscribers, but they do not appear in this table, which, by definition, is limited to those ZIP Codes where World Treasures subscribers reside.) The reported sum is 33,060, the number of subscribers in the original table. The mean value is important, as you will use this value to divide ZIP Codes into those with a high number of subscribers and those with a low number. Use this window to answer the report questions on the following page.

Update report and save map document

1 Use the ZIP Code map and data tables to answer the following questions. Summarize your answers in the appropriate section of the project report template (WorldTreasuresNY_ ReportTemplate.doc), which you will find in your \GISMKT\WorldTreasuresNY folder.

What do you observe about the geographic distribution of households relative to New York's urban areas and interstate highways? How many World Treasures subscribers live in New York? How many ZIP Codes have World Treasures subscribers residing in them? What is the highest number of subscribers in any ZIP Code? The lowest? The average number of subscribers per ZIP Code?

2 Save your map file as World TreasuresNY1_fl.mxd (replace f and l with your first and last initials). To do so, click File, then Save As in ArcMap. Navigate to your **\GISMKT\WorldTreasuresNY** folder, type **World TreasuresNY1_fl.mxd** as the file name, and click Save.

Exercise 6.2   Define market segments and assign them to ZIP Codes

The first step in profiling customer segments by ZIP Code is to define appropriate segments and assign them to the correct ZIP Codes. The appropriate segmenting measure for this project is the number of subscribers in each ZIP Code. Thus, in this exercise, you will:

- Define segments based on the number of subscribers
- Assign segment values to New York's ZIP Codes
- Design a map displaying the geographic distribution of these market segments

Open an existing map

1   In ArcMap, open the **WorldTreasuresNY2** map document from your **\GISMKT\WorldTreasuresNY** folder.

This map displays the household population layer you created in the previous exercise and a general layer of New York. The household population data displays values from the NYZIPDemographics table, to which it is joined. The table of contents also includes a new table, SubscribersByZIP.

2   If necessary, click the Source tab on the table of contents to see the tables. Tables are only visible on the Source tab.

The SubscribersByZIP table is the same as the ZIPSummary summary table you created in the previous exercise. It has been renamed to more accurately reflect its contents.

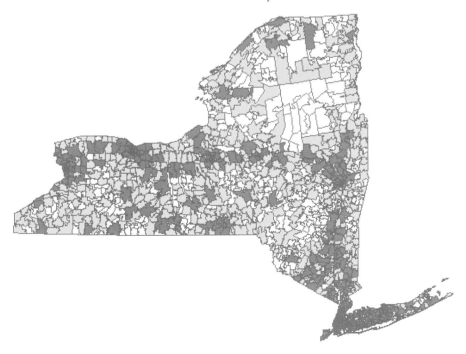

Join data table to map layer

Before you can assign segment values to ZIP Codes based on the number of subscribers they contain, you must join the data in SubscribersByZIP to the ZIP Code map layer.

1   In the table of contents, right-click SubscribersByZIP, then click Open to view its contents.

The table contains the number of newsletter subscribers in New York's ZIP Codes. Note that it contains only those ZIP Codes with some subscribers present. To assign segment values to ZIP Codes and display the subscriber count values, you will join the SubscribersByZIP table to the Households By ZIP Code layer's attribute table.

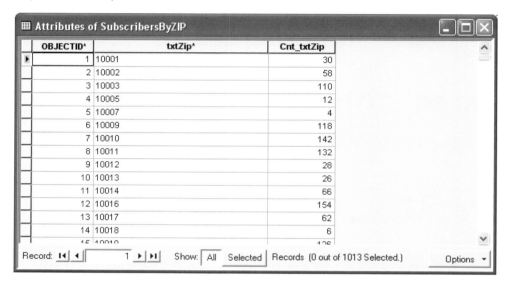

2   Close the table.

3   Right-click the Households By ZIP Code layer, click Joins and Relates, then Join to open the Join Data dialog box.

4   For item 1, choose NYZIPCodes.ZIPCode from the drop-down menu.

5   For item 2, choose SubscribersByZIP.

6   For item 3, choose txtZIP.

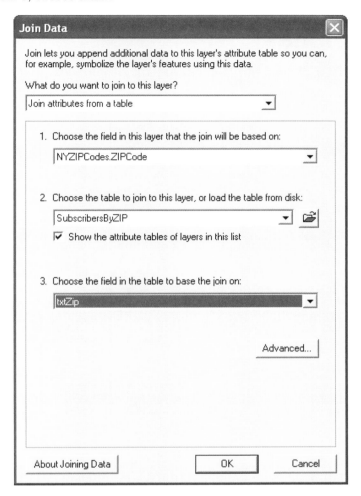

7   Click **OK** to run the join operation.

The Households By ZIP Code layer now contains the subscriber count data from SubscribersByZIP in addition to the demographic data from NYZIPDemographics. You may now explore the relationship between subscriber data and demographic data and use the spatial capabilities of the basemap to display the results geographically.

8   Right-click the **Households By ZIP Code** layer, then click **Open Attribute Table** to view the results of your join operation. Scroll to the right of the table to view the joined data.

Note that several ZIP Codes in the map layer did not have corresponding ZIP Code records in SubscribersByZIP. These records contain <null> values indicating that World Treasures has no subscribers living in these ZIP Codes.

Define segments and assign segment values to ZIP Codes

You wish to use the number of subscribers to divide New York's ZIP Codes into three segments designated as High, Low, and None. Obviously the None segment will include those ZIP Codes with no subscribers. The High segment will include those ZIP Codes with more subscribers than the average value you calculated in the previous exercise. By default, then, the Low segment will include those ZIP Codes with less subscribers than the average value.

In ArcMap, you will select the ZIP Codes for each segment with a series of query operations. You will assign the segment values to the appropriate ZIP Codes by creating a new attribute called Segment and assigning each feature its proper value.

Add a field to a layer's attribute table

1   Click the Options button in the Households By ZIP Code attribute table, then click Add Field to display the Add Field dialog box.

2   For Name, enter **Segment**. In the Type drop-down box, select Text. In Field Properties replace the length of 50 with **12**. This number specifies the number of characters allowed in this text field.

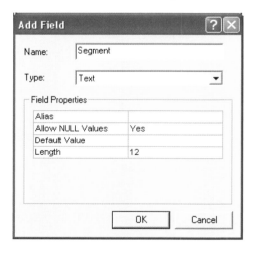

3   Click OK to apply the settings and create the new field.

Scroll through the attribute table to locate the new NYZIPCodes.Segment field. Note that it is created within the original attribute table to which the other two tables were joined. Thus, if you remove the joins, the Segment field and the values assigned to each ZIP Code will remain in the attribute table for the Households By ZIP Code layer.

Select ZIP Codes by attribute and define the High segment

Assigning segment values to ZIP Codes is a two-step process. First, you will select those ZIP Codes that meet the criteria for a specific segment. Second, you will enter the appropriate value for these ZIP Codes in the Segment field. You will perform this sequence once for each of the three segments, beginning with the High segment, which includes those ZIP Codes with a higher-than-average number of subscribers.

1   Click the Options button in the Households by ZIP Code attribute table, then click Select by Attributes to open the Select by Attributes dialog box.

2   In the list of attributes, scroll down until you see SubscribersByZIP.Cnt_txtZip. Double-click this attribute to add it to the query box.

3   Click the greater than (>) button to add it to the query box.

4   Position the cursor after the greater than symbol and type the average value you discovered in the previous exercise.

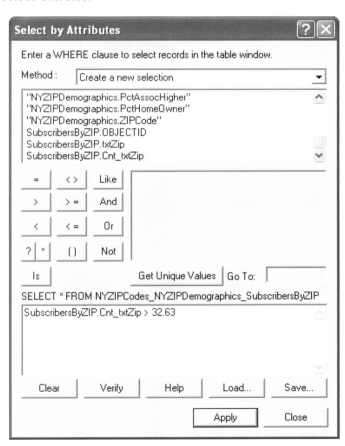

5 Click Apply to run the query.

Observe the number at the bottom of the attribute table that reports how many ZIP Codes have
been selected.

6 In the attribute table, click the Selected button to view only the selected features. You will assign
   these ZIP Codes to the High segment.

7 Right-click the NYZIPCodes.Segment column header, then click Field Calculator.

8 Click Yes if a warning appears.

9 In the Field Calculator, select String for the type, then enter **"High"** in the expression area.
   (Note: Be sure to include the quotation marks, which designate the entry as text rather than
   numeric data.)

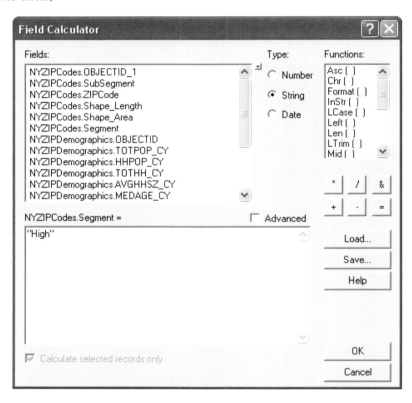

10 **Click OK to complete the process.**

Observe the NYZIPCodes.Segment field of the attribute table, noting that the value High now appears as the attribute value for all the selected features. These ZIP Codes now constitute the High segment.

How many ZIP Codes does the High segment contain?

The following graphic depicts the query and its results in the attribute table and map. You will repeat these steps to create the Low and None segments.

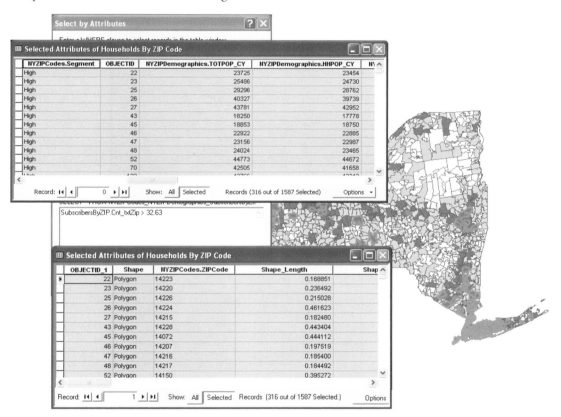

Define the Low segment

The selection procedure for the Low segment involves the same steps you just performed. However, the query is more complex as you must specify a range of values.

1   In the attribute table, click Options > Select by Attributes.

2   Use the attribute names, operators, and your keyboard to enter **SubscribersByZIP.Cnt_txtZip > 1 AND SubscribersByZIP.Cnt_txtZip < 32.63** in the query box.

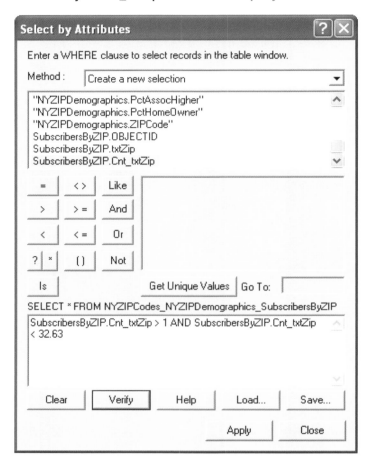

3   Click Apply to run the query.

4   Observe the number at the bottom of the attribute table that reports how many ZIP Codes have been selected. If necessary, click the Selected button to view only the selected features. You will place these ZIP Codes in the Low segment.

5   Right-click the NYZIPCodes.Segment column header, then click Field Calculator.

6   Click Yes if a warning appears.

7   Select String for Type.

8   In the expression area type **"Low"**. (Note: Be sure to include the quotation marks, which designate the entry as text rather than numeric data.)

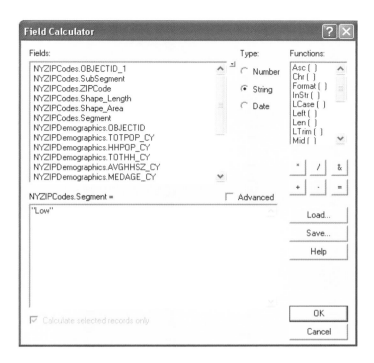

9   Click OK to complete the process.

The selected ZIP Codes have been placed in the Low segment.

   How many ZIP Codes does the Low segment contain?

The map below depicts this query and its results in the attribute table and map.

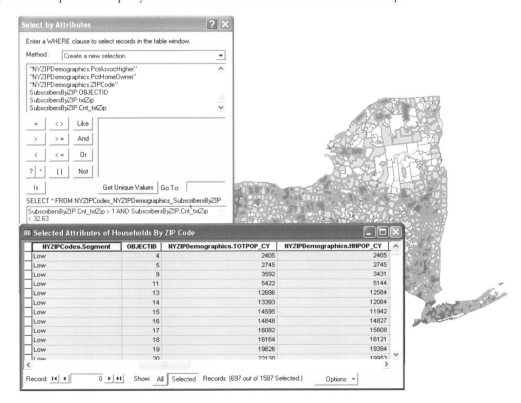

Define the None segment

The ZIP Codes that have not been assigned to the High or Low segments belong to the None segment. This time you will use a different approach for the selection process.

1   Click All at the bottom of the attribute table to show all records.

2   Click the Options button, then choose Select All to select all the records in the table.

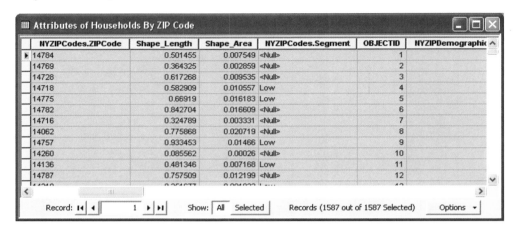

You will now use the Select by Attribute function to remove ZIP Codes from those that have been selected, leaving the ones you will assign to the None segment.

3   Click Options > Select by Attributes.

4   For Method, select the "Remove from current selection" option.

This setting will cause the records that meet the query to be removed from the current selection. By designing a query that removes all ZIP Codes that have been assigned to a segment, you will be left with the ZIP Codes that have not.

5   Use the attributes, operators, and keyboard to enter the following in the query box:
      "NYZIPCodes.Segment" = 'High' OR "NYZIPCodes.Segment" = 'Low'

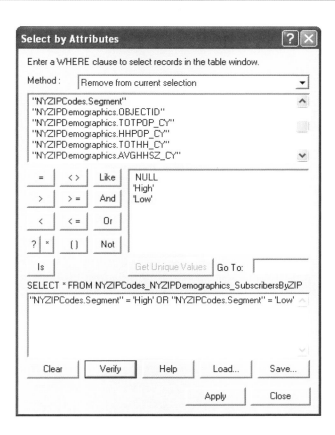

6 Click Apply to run the query and remove the designated ZIP Codes from the selection.

7 Right-click the NYZIPCodes.Segment column header, then click Field Calculator.

8 Click Yes if a warning appears.

9 Select String for Type.

10 Type **"None"** in the expression box. (Note: Be sure to include the quotation marks, which designate the entry as text rather than numeric data.)

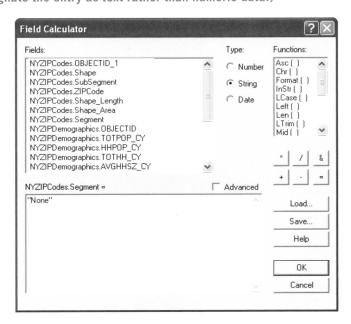

11 **Click OK to complete the process.**

The selected ZIP Codes have been assigned to the None segment.

 How many ZIP Codes does the None segment contain?

The map below depicts this query and its results in the attribute table and map.

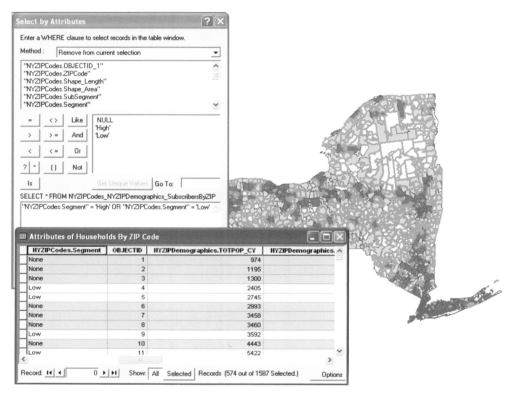

12 **Close the attribute table and the Select by Attributes dialog box.**

13 **From the main menu bar, click Selection > Clear Selected Features.**

Display the distribution of segments on a map

You have assigned each of the New York ZIP Codes to one of three classification segments. You will now display the geographic distribution of these segments on the map by revising the symbology of the Households By ZIP Code layer.

Edit a layer's symbology

1   Double-click the Households By ZIP Code layer (or right-click the layer and select Properties) to open the Layer Properties dialog box.

2   Click the General tab and enter **Segments by ZIP Code** as the new layer name.

3   Click the Symbology tab.

4   Select Categories, then Unique values in the Show box on the left.

5   Select NYZIPCodes.Segment in the Value Field box in the middle.

6   Uncheck <all other values>.

7   Click the Add All Values button below the classification box to add all the values for this attribute to the classification scheme.

8   Double-click the color symbol for the High segment to open the Symbol Selector dialog box.

9   Click the drop-down arrow for the Fill Color field, then select tarragon green (row 5, column 6). Click OK.

10   Repeat this procedure to select lemongrass (row 2, column 6) as the color for the Low segment, and arctic white (row 1, column 1) as the color for the None segment.

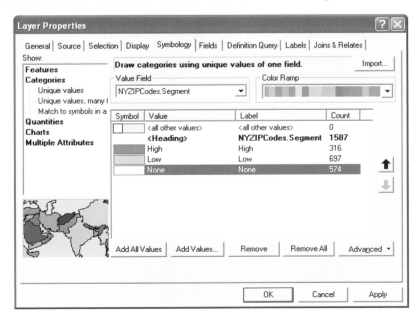

11   Click **OK** to close the Layer Properties dialog box and apply your settings to the map.

12   Click the legend title **NYZIPCodes.Segment** under the title of this layer in the table of contents, then click again to make it editable. Rename it **Subscriber segment**.

The map now displays New York's ZIP Codes by segment class based on the number of subscribers they contain.

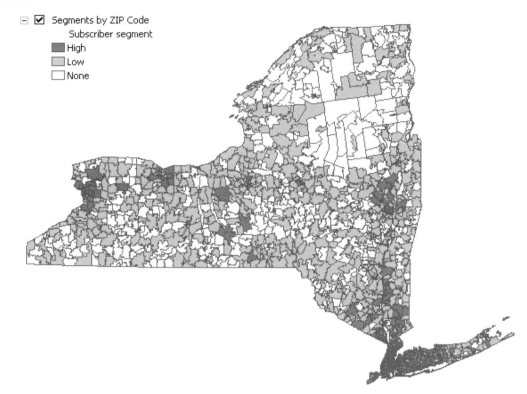

Update report and save map document

1   Use what you've learned in this exercise to answer the questions below. Summarize your answers in the appropriate section of the project report template (WorldTreasuresNY_ReportTemplate.doc), which you will find in your \GISMKT\WorldTreasuresNY folder.

How are the ZIP Code segments defined? What is the threshold for assigning ZIP Codes to the High segment? How many ZIP Codes does each segment contain?

2   Save the map document as **WorldTreasuresNY2_fl.mxd** (replace f and l with your first and last initials) in your **\GISMKT\WorldTreasuresNY** folder.

Exercise 6.3   Profile subscriber segments

Customer profiling involves exploring the characteristics of customer segments and comparing them with each other to identify the characteristics that differentiate segments. Thus, in this exercise, you will:

- Create a summary table of the demographic characteristics of each subscriber segment
- Identify the demographic characteristics that distinguish the High subscriber segment from the other two
- Format a table capturing these values for inclusion in a map layout

Open an existing map

1   In ArcMap, open the **WorldTreasuresNY3** map document from your **\GISMKT\WorldTreasuresNY** folder.

This is a replica of the map you designed in the previous exercise. It displays New York's ZIP Codes and the subscriber segment where each has been assigned. It includes the tables containing demographic and subscriber information for New York's ZIP Codes, and these tables are joined to the layer attribute table to facilitate further analysis. You will create a summary table based on the Segments by ZIP Code layer's attribute table to summarize the demographic characteristics (i.e., the demographic profiles) of the defined segments and to identify the defining characteristics of the High segment.

2   If necessary, click the Source tab at the bottom of the table of contents to view the data tables.

Create a summary table

1   **Open the attribute table for the Segments by ZIP Code layer. Scroll through the table.**

Note that attributes from both the demographic and subscriber tables are visible as they have been joined to the Segments by ZIP Code layer's attribute table. Your summary table will contain information from both joined tables. As you build the summary table, consult with the data dictionary at the beginning of the chapter to ascertain the demographic measures to summarize.

2   **Locate the NYZipCodes.SubSegment field, right-click its header cell, then click Summarize to open the Summarize dialog box.**

Note: Assuming you successfully completed exercise 2, you will see two identical fields: one called Segment, and another called SubSegment, which has been provided for you just in case there were any selection or calculation mistakes and to ensure data consistency. You should work with the SubSegment field from here on.

The Summarize dialog box allows you to specify the attributes to include in the table and the calculations you wish to perform on them.

3   **In section 2, expand NYZIPDemographics.AVGDI_CY in section 2 and check the Average option.**

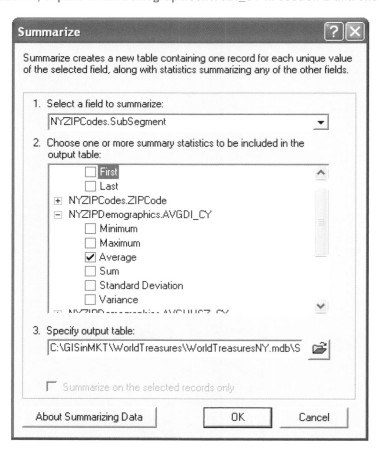

4 Expand NYZIPDemographics.AVGHHSZ_CY and check Average.

5 Repeat this process for each of the following attributes, choosing the Average option
   in each case.
     NYZIPDemographics.MEDAGE_CY
     NYZIPDemographics.PctAssocHigher
     NYZIPDemographics.PctHomeOwner

Taken together, these attributes will allow you to compare average income, household size, age,
education, and home ownership of the three segments.

6 Expand NYZIPDemographics.TOTHH_CY and check Sum.

7 Expand SubscribersByZIP.Cnt_txtZIP and check Sum.

Calculating the sum of these attributes will produce the total number of households and subscribers
in each of the three segments.

8 Click the Browse button 📂 next to the "Specify output table" option.

9 In the Saving Data dialog box, for the "Save as type" option choose File and Personal
   Geodatabase tables.

10 Navigate to and double-click the **WorldTreasuresNY.mdb** personal geodatabase file to view its
    data tables. You will save the summary table within this personal geodatabase.

11 Enter **SegmentDemoSummary** for the name.

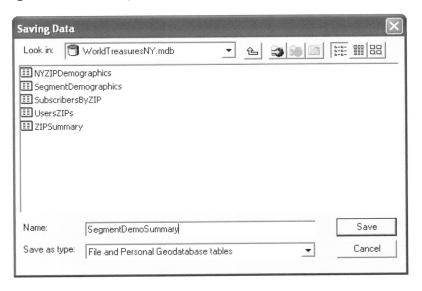

12 Click the Save button to return to the Summarize dialog box.

13 Click OK to perform the specified calculations and create the summary output table. Click Yes
    when asked if you wish to include the summary table in the map.

14 Close the attribute table.

Develop a segment profile from the summary table

The SegmentDemoSummary data table you just created contains comparative demographic data for the three segments you created. You will use this data to complete a demographic profile of the High segment and to identify the two attributes that distinguish it most clearly from the other two segments.

1   Open the SegmentDemoSummary table.

2   Click the right border of each header cell and drag to the left to reduce cell width. This allows you to view the full table.

3   Review the calculated values for each of the three segments. Use this information to answer the report questions below. These values comprise the demographic profile of each segment.

OBJEC	SubSegment	Count_SubSegment	Average_AVGDI_CY	Average_AVGHHSZ_CY	Average_MEDAGE_CY	Average_PctAssocHigher	Average_PctHomeOwner	Sum_TOTHH_CY	Sum_Cnt_txtZip
1	High	316	55595.800633	2.683354	38.256962	40.463308	59.141294	4234723	26294
2	Low	697	44064.007174	2.576040	38.780201	32.300977	61.345118	2523749	6766
3	None	574	37754.410122	2.517592	39.436824	26.715020	58.748564	440420	0

Update report and save map document

1   Use the summary table to answer the following report questions. Summarize your answers in the appropriate section of the project report template. Round your answers to two decimal points.

What are the income, household size, age, education, and home ownership characteristics of the ZIP Codes in the High segment? Which two attributes in the High segment differ most from the other two segments? How many ZIP Codes are in the High segment? How many subscribers?

2   Save the map document as **WorldTreasuresNY3_fl.mxd** (replace f and l with your first and last initials) in your **\GISMKT\WorldTreasuresNY** folder.

Exercise 6.4   Use subscribers' profiles to select target ZIP Codes

You have determined the demographic characteristics that distinguish the High segment from the other two. You will use these characteristics to select ZIP Codes for the direct-mail campaign. Thus, in this exercise, you will:

- Identify ZIP Codes with above-average values for the distinguishing variables
- Calculate the number of households in these ZIP Codes
- Adjust the selection to less than 2,000,000 households, the level dictated by the campaign budget
- Design a map that displays the selected ZIP Codes

Open an existing map

1   Open the **WorldTreasuresNY4** map document.

This map contains one layer that displays the percentage of persons older than 25, with an associate degree or higher, in each of New York's ZIP Codes. This is one of the measures that distinguish the High segment and that you will use to select ZIP Codes for the direct-mail campaign. The map's table of contents also contains the demographic and subscriber tables that you used in the previous exercise. Further, these tables have been joined to the Pct Pop w/Assoc Degree or Higher layer's attribute table to facilitate data analysis.

2   If necessary, click the Source tab at the bottom of the table of contents to see the data tables.

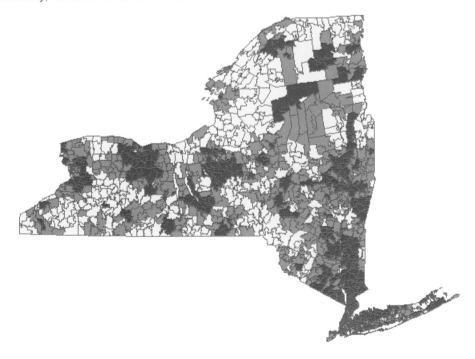

Select features based on demographic attributes

In the previous exercise, you identified the two attributes that most clearly distinguish the High segment from the Low and None segments. You will now identify ZIP Codes with above-average values for these two attributes.

Calculate averages for distinguishing attributes

To select ZIP Codes with above-average values for the distinguishing attributes, you must first determine the average values for those attributes.

1 Open the attribute table for the **Pct Pop w/Assoc Degree or Higher** layer.

2 Locate and right-click the column header for the **NYZIPDemographics.AVGDI_CY** field, then click the Statistics option to display descriptive statistics for this attribute.

3 Note the mean value for this attribute in the Statistics window, and record it below.

The mean value for Average Disposable Income of New York ZIP Codes is $_____.

4 Repeat this procedure for the **NYZIPDemographics.PctAssocHigher** attribute.

The mean value for Percentage of People with Associate Degree or Higher in New York ZIP Codes is _____ %.

These are the values you will use to select attractive ZIP Codes for the direct-mail campaign.

Select features based on distinguishing attributes

To select attractive ZIP Codes, you will formulate a query that identifies features with above-average values for both of the distinguishing attributes.

1   Close the statistics window. In the attribute table, click Options > Select by Attributes.

2   In the Select by Attributes dialog box, use the attribute names, operators, and your keyboard to create the following query:

"NYZIPDemographics.AVGDI_CY" > 44082 AND "NYZIPDemographics.PctAssocHigher" > 31.9

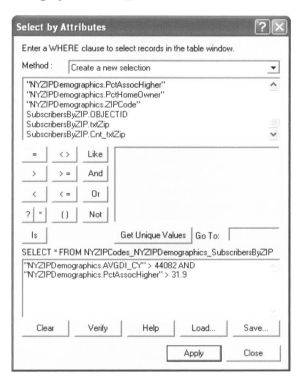

3   Click Apply to make the selection, then close the Select by Attributes dialog box.

Review the layer attribute table, noting the number of ZIP Codes that have been selected. To determine if the campaign will support a mailing to all these ZIP Codes, you must determine the total number of households they contain.

4   Locate and right-click the header cell for the **NYZIPDemographics.TOTHH_CY** field, then click the Statistics option to display descriptive statistics for this attribute.

Observe the Sum figure in the Statistics window. If the sum of households in the selected ZIP Codes is greater than 2,000,000, you must limit the selection further.

   How many total households do the selected ZIP Codes contain?

5   Close the statistics window.

Limit selection based on segment classification

The ZIP Codes that meet your demographic selection criteria contain too many households for the direct-mail campaign. You will limit the selection further by including only those ZIP Codes in the High subscriber segment.

Refine selection based on segment classification

The Pct Pop w/Assoc Degree or Higher layer table should still be open with the ZIP Codes selected above still highlighted. If this is not the case, repeat the Select by Attributes operation.

1   With the attribute table open and the demographically attractive ZIP Codes selected, click the Options button, then Select by Attributes to again open the Select by Attributes dialog box.

2   Click the Method drop-down arrow and choose "Select from current selection."

This setting will cause the records that meet the query criteria to be selected from the current selection. Your query will select those ZIP Codes assigned to the High segment.

3   Delete the existing query, then use the fields, operators, and keyboard as needed to enter the following in the query box: **"NYZIPCodes.SubSegment" = 'High'**

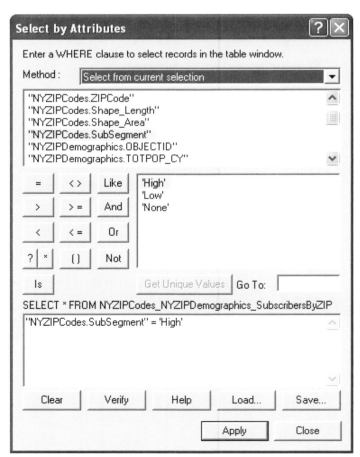

4   Click Apply to run the query and select the designated ZIP Codes from the current selection.

The selection now includes all ZIP Codes that meet the demographic selection criteria and are part of the High subscriber segment. You will determine if this reduction in selected ZIP Codes is now within the 2,000,000 household limit of the direct-mail campaign.

5   Locate and right-click the header cell for the NYZIPDemographics.TOTHH_CY field, then click the Statistics option to display its descriptive statistics.

Observe the Sum figure in the Statistics window. If the sum of households in the selected ZIP Codes is greater than 2,000,000, you must limit the selection further.

 How many total households do the selected ZIP Codes contain?

6   Close the dialog box, statistics window, and attribute table.

Observe the distribution of the highlighted ZIP Codes on the map. These are the ZIP Codes where the direct-mail campaign will be targeted.

 How are the selected ZIP Codes distributed geographically in the state?

To preserve the group of selected ZIP Codes, you will save them as a separate layer.

7   Right-click the Pct Pop w/Assoc Degree or Higher layer, click Selection > Create Layer from Selected Features. This will save the selected ZIP Codes as a new layer in the table of contents.

8   Rename the layer **Selected ZIP Codes** and set its symbol color to Yogo Blue (row 2, column 10) in the Fill Color palette of the Symbol Selector. From the main menu, click Select > Clear Selected Features.

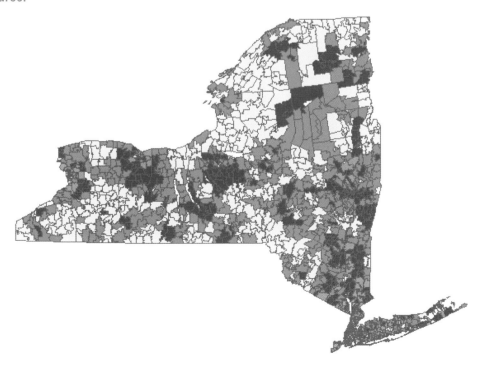

Calculate selection statistics

The purpose of this selection process has been to identify a collection of ZIP Codes with high concentrations of households that fit the target profile. If the process has been successful, the selected ZIP Codes will constitute a relatively small percentage of ZIP Codes and households, but a relatively large percentage of subscribers. In addition, the selected ZIP Codes should have a higher average income, and a greater percentage of persons with associate degrees or higher, than the general New York population. You will calculate these measures to determine if the selected ZIP Codes satisfy these conditions.

1　Open the attribute table for the Selected ZIP Codes layer.

2　Right-click the NYZIPDemographics.TOTHH_CY column header, then click Statistics.

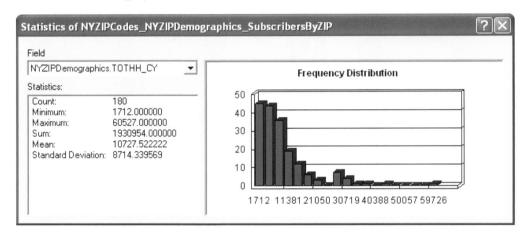

3　Record the Count value in the ZIP Codes row of the table on the following page, under the Selected column. Also record the Sum value in the Households row of the Selected column.

4　Now examine the statistics for the SubscribersByZIP.Cnt_txtZip attribute. To do this, in the Statistics dialog box, in the Field drop-down list choose SubscribersByZIP.Cnt_txtZip. Record the Sum value in the Subscribers row of the Selected column in the table on the following page.

5　Now examine the statistics for the NYZIPDemographics.AVGDI_CY attribute and record the Mean value in the Avg Disposable Income row of the Selected column in the table below.

6　Repeat this operation on the NYZIPDemographics.PctAssocHigher attribute and record the Mean value in the Pct Assoc or Higher row of the Selected column in the table on the next page.

7　Close the Statistics dialog box and the attribute table.

8 Open the attribute table for Pct Pop w/Assoc Degree or Higher. Repeat steps 2 through 5 above and record the results in the appropriate fields of the All ZIP Codes column in the table on the following page.

9 Use the values in the Selected and All ZIP Codes columns to calculate the values in the Selected as % of All ZIP Codes column. To do this, divide the Selected value by the All ZIP Codes value and multiply the result by 100.

	Selected	All ZIP Codes	Selected as % of All ZIP Codes
ZIP Codes			
Households			
Subscribers			
Avg Disposable Income			
Pct Assoc or Higher			

Update report and save map document

1 Use the information you have gathered to answer the following questions. Summarize your answers in the appropriate section of the project report template.

How many ZIP Codes will be included in the mailing? How many households? How are these ZIP Codes distributed in the state? What percentage of New York's ZIP Codes, households, and World Treasures's subscribers will be reached by this campaign? What is the average disposable income of the selected ZIP Codes? The percentage of adults with an associate degree or higher? How do these figures compare with values for all the ZIP Codes in the state?

2 Save the map document as **WorldTreasuresNY4_fl.mxd** (replace f and l with your first and last initials) in your **\GISMKT\WorldTreasuresNY** folder.

Exercise 6.5   Report the analysis results

As the conclusion to your analysis, you will describe how your analysis has improved the potential effectiveness of the direct-mail campaign and design a map that displays targeted ZIP Codes. Thus, in this exercise, you will:

- Explain the attractiveness of the selected ZIP Codes for the campaign
- Explain how this profiling and selection process will improve the effectiveness of the campaign
- Design a map to communicate and support your recommendations

Open an existing map

1   In ArcMap, open **WorldTreasuresNY5.mxd**.

The map opens in layout view and contains two data frames that each have the Subscriber Segments layer. The data frame called Layers is zoomed out to display the entire state of New York while the other data frame, called New York City, is zoomed in on the region around Long Island and Manhattan.

The Layers data frame is active and includes the demographics, subscribers, and segment tables. The ZIP Codes you selected in the previous exercise are highlighted in blue to indicate that they will be targeted with the mailing.

2   If you don't see the tables, click the Source tab at the bottom of the table of contents.

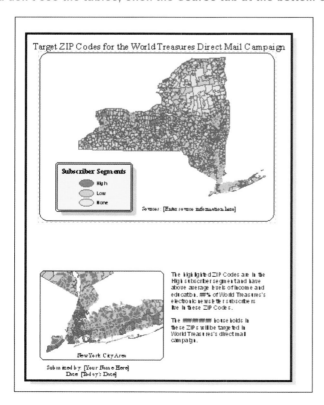

Add cartographic elements to a layout

The Layer data frame displays subscriber segment information for the state of New York. However, it does not have an associated scale bar or north arrow, two important pieces of cartographic information. You will add these to the layout.

1   From the main menu bar, click Insert > North Arrow to open the North Arrow Selector dialog box.

2   Scroll through the list of North Arrows to view them. When you find one that you like, click it to select it and then click OK to add it to the layout.

The north arrow is added to the layout page, but at a random position and possibly overlapping other layout elements.

3   Click the north arrow to select it and then drag it to an appropriate area. For example, move the arrow to a location just above the midpoint between Buffalo and Rochester in the northwestern portion of the state.

You will now insert a scale bar.

4   From the main menu bar, click Insert > Scale Bar to open the Scale Bar Selector dialog box.

5   Scroll through the list of scale bar styles, click on the one you like best, then click OK to add the scale bar of your choice to the layout.

6   Click the scale bar in the layout to select it and move it to the lower right corner of the top data frame and, if you wish, resize it.

7   If the scale bar does not display the map scale in miles, click the scale bar to select it, then right-click and select Properties to open the Properties dialog box. In the Division units drop-down box, select Miles, then click OK to apply the new format.

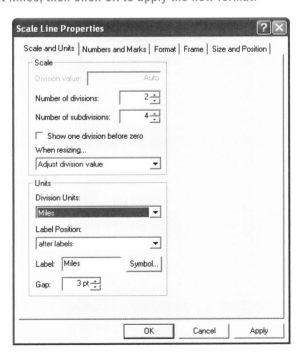

Format a summary table

The SegmentDemographics table in the table of contents duplicates the table you created in exercise 6.3. It summarizes the demographic characteristics of the High, Low, and None segments. It will be a helpful addition to your map. You will revise the table's formatting to increase its communication value for your readers.

1   Right-click the SegmentDemographics table, then click Properties to display the Properties dialog box for the table. Make sure the Fields tab is selected.

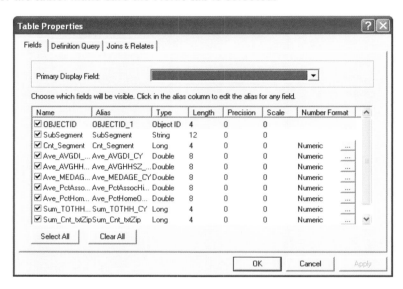

2   Click the boxes to the left of the field names in the Name column to select or unselect them. Only the checked fields will appear when you open a table. (Note: Unchecking fields does not delete them, it simply prevents them from appearing in the visible table.) Choose to have only the following fields displayed in the table:
    SubSegment
    Cnt_Segment
    Ave_AVGDI_CY
    Ave_PctAssocHigher

The Alias column contains the labels that will display in the header cell for each field in the table. By default, a field's alias name is the same as the field's full name. As this name may confuse your readers, you will create alias names for each of the four fields to be displayed in the table.

3   Click SubSegment in the Alias column and rename it **Segment**.

4   Repeat this procedure to rename Cnt_Segment to **ZIPs**, Ave_AVGDI_CY to **Avg Disposable Income**, and Ave_PctAssocHigher to **Pct Assoc or Higher**.

The Number Format column defines the numeric display for each attribute. You will adjust these settings to display the appropriate formats for each attribute.

5   Click the ellipsis button in the Number Format column for the ZIPs attribute to open the Number Format dialog box. If you can't see the Number Format column you can adjust the widths of the other columns to make them smaller. Drag the separator between column headings to resize them.

6   Confirm that the number of decimal places in the Rounding area is set to 0.

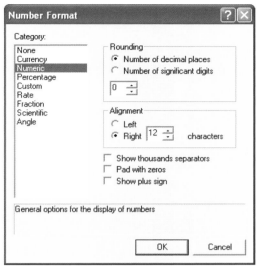

7   Click OK.

8   Change the Number Format for Avg Disposable Income to Currency. Click OK.

9   Change the Number Format for Pct Assoc or Higher to Percentage. Select "The number already represents a percentage." Click the Numeric Options button to open the Numeric Options dialog box. Select Number of decimal places and set the decimal places to 0. If necessary, select Right for the Alignment option.

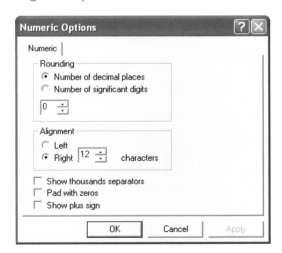

10 Click OK to close the Numeric Options dialog box. Click OK to close the Number Format dialog box. Click OK to close the Table Properties dialog box.

11 Open the SegmentDemographics table. It now reflects your formatting changes and is easier to read.

12 Click Options > Add Table to Layout. The table appears in layout view, but not in an appropriate location. You will adjust it in the next step.

13 Close the table.

Format table in layout

The SegmentDemographics table is now visible in the layout view, but is not properly located or formatted. You will move and resize it, then adjust the table's outline, background color, and drop shadow settings to match those of the legend.

1   On the layout page, click the table to select it, then move it into the space below the top data frame and resize it to display all attributes. If necessary, zoom into the layout using the navigation tools on the Layout toolbar.

2   Open the properties for the layout table (by double-clicking on the table), then click the Frame tab.

3   Select Triple line for the Border.

4   Select Yellow as the background color.

5   Select Med Sand as the drop-shadow color.

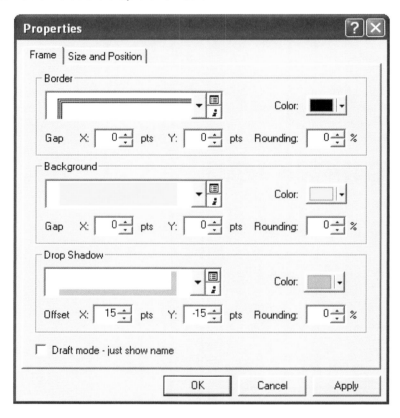

6   Click **OK** to apply the format changes and close the dialog box.

The formatting of the table should now match that of the legend.

7   If necessary, further adjust the sizing and placement of the new elements.

Edit text boxes in layout

1   Double-click the submission information text box at the bottom of the page to open its properties.

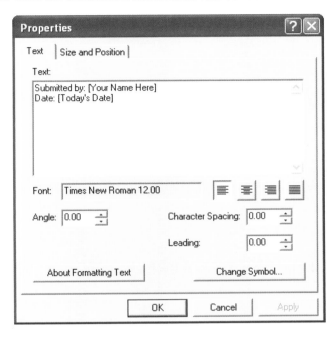

2   Replace the placeholder text with your name and the current date, then click OK.

3   Double-click the large box of explanatory text just below the data table to open its Properties.

4   Replace the #### symbols with the values you calculated for the percentage of subscribers living in the selected ZIP Codes, as well as the total number of households they contain.

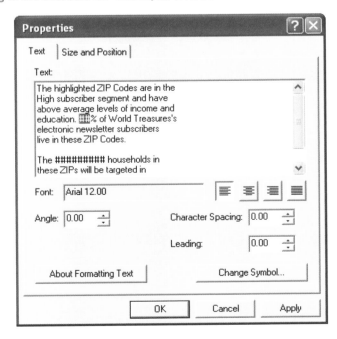

5   Click OK.

6   Double-click the Sources text box below the data table.

7   Replace the placeholder text with **World Treasures Internal Data** and, on a second line, **ESRI Community Data 2005**. Click OK.

You have created a layout that is now ready to print or save as a graphics file.

Export map document and save as exhibit 1

1   From the main menu bar, click File, then Export Map to reach the Export Map dialog box. Navigate to your **\GISMKT\WorldTreasuresNY** folder. Type **TargetedZIPs.emf** for File Name then click Save to save the map document as a graphic file in EMF format to include in your report.

2   Open the report template for this chapter and navigate to the end of the report. Locate the page entitled Exhibit 1: Targeted ZIP Codes, and insert the TargetedZIPs.emf file. (Note: You may have to select and resize the image to display it on the same page as the title.) Exhibit 1 of your report is now complete.

Update report and save map document

1   Use your previous analysis and the map layout you have created to answer the questions below. Summarize your response in the appropriate section of the project report template.

Why are the selected ZIP Codes a more attractive audience for World Treasures's direct-mail campaign than a random selection of 2,000,000 households? How should this profiling and selection process improve the response rates and sales level of the campaign?

2   Save your map file as **WorldTreasuresNY5_fl.mxd** (replace f and l with your first and last initials) in your **\GISMKT\WorldTreasuresNY** folder.

Congratulations! You have completed the World Treasures project.

Take a moment to reflect on what you have learned in this chapter. You integrated demographic data tables with a basemap of New York's ZIP Codes to produce thematic maps of the state's demographic characteristics. You took enterprise data from the World Treasures subscribers database, summarized it, and integrated it with a basemap of ZIP Codes. You used this information to define subscriber segments and generated demographic profiles of those segments. Finally, you used the profiles to select the most attractive ZIP Codes for the firm's direct-mail campaign, communicating your selection in a map document. In short, you have used ArcGIS to improve the effectiveness of a direct-mail campaign through customer profiling.

Additional applications

This exercise illustrates the power of integrating internal data with commercial data and spatial information to gain a more complete understanding of one's customers. In this case, a single piece of spatial data—subscribers's ZIP Codes—allows World Treasures to blend demographic data with its subscriber records to create a user profile and to target attractive prospects. The power of data integration, however, extends well beyond this example.

From a market research perspective, GIS tools provide an additional method for analyzing and understanding internal customer information. Spatial information about customers is inherently valuable for many businesses. The geographic distribution of customers can help firms make site location and routing and market area analysis decisions. In addition, as was done here, spatial location can serve as a link to other types of data about customers. In the World Treasures exercises, the ZIP Code data allowed the firm to target concentrations of potential customers. This type of analysis is more precise when users know full customer addresses rather than only ZIP Codes. This allows for more finely grained profiling and, as a result, more effective prospecting. Ace Hardware uses this approach to identify potential new markets.[1] The Press-Enterprise Co. in Riverside, California uses a similar system, but searches out prospective subscribers based on demographic characteristics in its carrier routes.[2]

These tools become still more powerful when integrated with customer purchasing patterns rather than simple subscriber records. As World Treasures develops its database marketing program, it can use Recency, Frequency, and Monetary analysis[3] to identify its most responsive customer groups. This approach divides customers into segments and evaluates their responsiveness to the firm's offerings using information on the customers' most recent purchases as well the frequency and dollar value of their purchases. Geocoding and profiling processes provide the additional capability of identifying the demographic and lifestyle characteristics of these segments. The *Press-Enterprise* uses this type of system to analyze its geocoded customer base and the demographic characteristics in its carrier routes.[4] Subaru of America incorporates a variety of data sources with lifestyle data from the ESRI Community Tapestry system to identify target groups of customers for its marketing programs.[5]

GIS tools enhance these capabilities by directly accessing organizational databases to enable spatial analysis of that data. For example, ArcSDE software creates direct connections between enterprise Oracle, IBM, and Microsoft databases and ArcGIS systems. This allows users to integrate corporate data with the business, shopping mall, demographic, and lifestyle data provided by the ESRI Business Information Solutions division and other data providers. As in this exercise, a greater understanding of customers allows the firm to serve them better and more easily identify concentrations of prospective customers.

From an eCommerce perspective, this process becomes both more complex and more rewarding. It is more complex in that server log and clickstream information allow the firm to observe customers' purchasing behavior directly. Server logs provide information on the number of times Web sites and individual pages have been accessed, and clickstream data records the sequences with which users navigate Web sites. Taken together, these tools allow Web managers to understand the portions of Web sites that users access most frequently and the sequences they follow in navigating sites and making purchase decisions. Registration systems that collect customers' product preferences supplement this information. Online market research surveys expand the pool of customer information even further. It is more rewarding because by integrating this information with dynamic, data-driven online content, firms can provide personalized online experiences to customers. In this context, the additional insight provided by demographic and lifestyle profiling can improve customer service and prospecting processes significantly.

Business decisions and management tools are increasingly depending on spatial technology. On the one hand, the ESRI ArcGIS Business Analyst extension enables firms to apply market area analysis, customer profiling, and site prospecting tools to their own corporate data.

On the other hand, many business intelligence systems are incorporating spatial tools into their products, applying them to data from enterprise resource planning systems as well as enterprise databases, and including spatial displays in dashboard[6] and other presentation components.[7] Dashboards are compact visual displays within business intelligence systems that present up-to-the-minute performance data to users in a combination of tabular, graphic, and map formats. They allow users to quickly and intuitively assess performance levels in their area of operation.

In an interesting extension of this capability, Aalborg County, Denmark has used ArcIMS—a software package that supports serving map information to Web sites—to access information in an SAS Business Intelligence data warehouse and present it to local decision makers online.[8]

Finally, GIS analysis also improves the effectiveness of promotional campaigns by supporting more precise targeting. *The Arizona Republic,*[10] for example, uses spatial analysis to allow advertisers to target specific ZIP Codes, carrier routes, or households in Maricopa and Pinal counties. The system incorporates multiple sources of corporate, public, and commercial data to facilitate message delivery via mail or newspaper. Advo (www.advo.com) offers similar selective targeting at the national level by mail based on its system of demographically similar, subZIP-Code-level mailing units.

In sum, while eCommerce seems decidedly nonspatial in its appeal, it has, in fact, launched a whole new range of opportunities for GIS analysis. With GIS systems or spatially enabled business intelligence systems, firms can integrate internal data with behavioral Web-based information to significantly improve their understanding of customer purchasing behavior. This, in turn, supports greater service to existing customers and more effective targeting of prospective ones.

1. Christian Harder, *ArcView GIS Means Business,* Redlands, CA: ESRI Press, 1997.

2. *Ibid.*

3. Arthur Hughes, *Strategic Database Marketing,* 3rd ed., New York: McGraw Hill, 2005.

4. *Ibid.*

5. David Huffman, "Subaru of America, Inc. Targets Prime Markets Accurately and Efficiently," *Directions,* February 13, 2005.

6. Ian Clemens, "Towards Enterprise GIS: Utilizing Rich Internet Applications to Drive Adoption," *Directions,* June 9, 2005.

7. James Akright, "Succesful Integration of Business Intelligence and GIS," ESRI GeoInfo Business Summit, April 18–19, 2005. Yuvraj Mathur and Vikas Srivastava, "ArcIntelligence: Spatially Enabled Business Intelligence," ESRI GeoInfo Business Summit, April 18–19, 2005.

8. Peter Gerlich, "Link Between ESRI's ArcIMS and the SAS Data Warehouse," ESRI GeoInfo Business Summit, April 18–19, 2005.

9. Jay Visnansky, "Doing Market Focused Selling at the Arizona Republic," ESRI GeoInfo Business Summit, April 18–19, 2005.

CHAPTER 7

International Market Assessment and Expansion

Course: International/Global Marketing Management

This chapter covers the international market assessment process in global marketing. Personal Management Development, Inc.* is a managerial training firm specializing in preparing women with technical backgrounds to assume managerial positions. It wishes to export its technology-based training tools to countries with attractive combinations of demographic and cultural characteristics. In the process of identifying these countries, you will use GIS tools to screen potential country markets based on demographic characteristics and cultural values in order to identify the most attractive export opportunities.

---

* This is a fictional company and scenario, created for educational purposes only. Any resemblance to actual persons, events, or corporations is unintended.

Learning objectives

To perform international market assessment for a global expansion effort, you will learn how to use ArcGIS to:

1. Display distributions of country demographic and cultural characteristics on a world map

2. Screen potential country markets for favorable technological, economic, and income characteristics

3. Identify countries with appropriate cultural values based on Hofstede's indexes

4. Integrate these criteria to recommend two countries for PMD's international expansion

5. Design a map to communicate and support your recommendations

Marketing scenario

Personal Management Development, Inc. (PMD) specializes in self-training materials for professional women assuming managerial positions for the first time. The founders are women who left successful careers in management to create PMD as a means of supporting other professional women making the transition to management, thus filling a mentoring role that is often lacking.

The customers are professionals with technical training or specialized skills who assume managerial positions as their careers develop. The PMD product line consists of a series of training modules designed to help its customers improve managerial skills and learn how to manage diverse functions within their organizations. Each module contains readings, Web-based chapters, video segments in DVD format, and a series of online case studies covering various managerial issues. Customers use these materials on their own and in online teams of classmates who participate in Web-based simulations that incorporate actual managerial situations and interpersonal interaction into the training process. The PMD products have proven beneficial to new managers who use them to augment organizational training programs and accelerate their development as managers.

Personal Management Development, Inc. wishes to build upon its success in the United States by expanding into select international markets. Because its customers are well-educated professionals with relatively high income levels, the firm wishes to use these factors to screen potential international markets. As PMD's products are technology-based, target countries should also possess a significant level of technology. In addition, PMD is seeking countries where women have opportunities for professional and managerial development. Finally, PMD feels its efforts will be most successful in countries where its people-oriented, collaborative, entrepreneurial, managerial philosophy is highly valued.

In short, the firm wishes to identify potential target countries that meet its demographic criteria, but also possess cultural values consistent with the managerial philosophy of the firm and its training materials. PMD will focus on the two most populous of these countries in its initial international expansion.

In the following exercises, you will use ArcGIS tools to perform this analysis for PMD and to recommend two countries where the firm should focus its marketing efforts.

Background information

Perhaps the most fundamental task in global marketing management is global market assessment. This is the analytical process that identifies marketing opportunities for a firm's products or services. The number of countries in the world, the range of data and data sources available for the analysis, and the high costs associated with market entry errors combine to make this task a challenging one.

Though the formal steps in the process may vary in number and scope, the general pattern of market assessment systems is to move from general to specific data and from secondary to primary data. This allows firms to use widely available, low-cost, secondary information in the initial stages of the process, screening large numbers of potential markets quickly and inexpensively. It also permits firms to commit more time and resources to the selection of final targets from a smaller group of candidate countries using more selective criteria. The early stages of the process use secondary demographic measures to identify the most attractive countries, while the latter stages analyze this smaller group in greater detail to select the target countries for market entry.

The following exercises illustrate that process, showing how the demographic screening process can be tailored to the corporate strategies, competitive positions, and product offerings of specific firms. In the exercises, a variety of demographic data is used to identify a group of attractive countries. Population and income are widely reported measures; however, the other measures—education and technology readiness, female participation in economic activity, and cultural values—are unusual measures, gathered from a variety of sources and selected for relevance to the firm's marketing strategy.

Note that much of the data for this assessment is not available in map-ready format. Thus, you must gather the data from their various sources, integrate it, and match the data to spatial information for the world's countries. These operations have already been performed for the data in the Country-Data feature class. The join operations that underlie this table are the same ones you will use to join the HofstedeClassifications table to a spatial data layer. This process illustrates how the geodatabase can serve as a repository of data from various sources, allowing the analyst to integrate tabular data and display it spatially.

Typically, general demographic screening concentrates the market entry decision on a relatively small group of attractive countries. A more detailed screening process, often using competitive and industry-specific market data, is used to narrow this group further to the specific countries the firm will target. As PMD's product and marketing approach are quite innovative, little competitive market data exists. For that reason, you will use comparative cultural data to screen countries based on their consistency with the core cultural values of PMD's product. To do so, you will employ three of the cultural indexes created by Geert Hofstede[1] in his widely cited work on cultural variations among the world's national cultures.

Hofstede uses multivariate statistical techniques to identify five cultural indexes that reflect cultural variations among nations. Data for the four original indexes—Power Distance, Uncertainty Avoidance, Masculinity, and Individualism—is provided for 87 countries and regions[2] in the HofstedeClassifications table in the PMDGlobal geodatabase. Hofstede subsequently added a fifth index, Long Term Orientation. Less data is available for this measure and it is not included in this study.

The Power Distance index measures the general level of perceived equality in a society as well as the perceived legitimacy of its bureaucratic structures. In countries with a high Power Distance index, social institutions are more often hierarchical in structure, positions of power are based on relatively permanent social distinctions among people, and these distinctions are viewed as legitimate. In countries with a low Power Distance index, people are viewed as being more inherently equal, organizations are typically flatter and more decentralized, and leadership positions are allocated more on the basis of relevant skills rather than permanent social status.

The Uncertainty Avoidance index measures the tolerance of national cultures for uncertainty, risk, and ambiguity. Strong Uncertainty Avoidance cultures tend to avoid risk and are more likely to rely on systems of rules and social conventions to limit uncertain situations. Weak Uncertainty Avoidance countries tend to be more tolerant of risk, more open to variation in personal and group behavior, and more willing to change rule systems to accommodate new conditions. Weak Uncertainty Avoidance countries tend to value entrepreneurship more highly than do strong Uncertainty Avoidance countries.

The Masculinity index measures differences in the perception of emotional gender roles among countries. In Masculine countries, these roles are distinct. Men are supposed to be tougher, more aggressive, and success-oriented, while women are supposed to be more modest, less aggressive, and more concerned with life quality issues. In Feminine countries, the roles overlap and both genders are supposed to be less aggressive, less success-oriented, and equally concerned with the quality of life.[3]

These perceptions include general gender roles but also management styles and decision-making processes. Countries classified as Masculine tend to be more aggressive and to pursue direct, results-oriented solutions to problems, while those classified as Feminine tend toward more collaborative participatory approaches to decision making. Note that while these values may be related to gender roles in management they are not equivalent. Thus, female managers may have Masculine values and managerial styles, while male managers may have Feminine values and managerial styles.

The Individualism index measures the orientation of national cultures relative to individual and group relationships. Countries characterized as Individualist tend to emphasize individual achievement, rights, self-reliance, and personal initiative, while placing less emphasis on the importance of group roles, adherence to group norms, and allegiance to group decisions and power structures. Countries characterized as Collectivist tend to emphasize group allegiance, responsibility, decision making, and the individual's obligation to serve the group and participate appropriately in group activities and initiatives.

In this study, you will use Hofstede's indexes in three ways. First, joining the HofstedeClassifications table with the CountryData table allows you to produce maps displaying the geographic distribution of national cultures on each of the four indexes. Second, the joined tables allow you to compare the demographic characteristics of countries with differing classifications on specific indexes. Third, defining PMD's target market in terms of the values contained in a specific combination of Hofstede indexes allows you to use them as a cultural screening device. This enables PMD to target not only those countries that meet its demographic profile, but to concentrate on those whose cultural values are most attractive for the firm and its products.

In sum, this chapter illustrates the value of GIS tools in global market screening. Standard demographic screening techniques are facilitated by the ability to integrate data from various sources and display the geographic distribution of initial screening results. GIS tools also enable integration of cultural data, exploration of relationships between cultural and demographic measures, and the display of spatial information in the final screening process. Thus, these tools facilitate both the analysis and the visual presentation of this process.

Personal Management Development, Inc. data dictionary	
Attribute	**Description**
For CountryData	
txtCountryName	Name of country
curGDPPC	Gross Domestic Product Per Capita, 2003, CIA
dblFemEcoAct	Percentage of females who are economically active, 2002, ILO
dblTechIndex	Composite index of technological readiness, 2000, WB
dblAvgYrsSchool	Average years in school of persons 15 and older, 2004, WEF
intPopulation	Total population, 2003, ESRI
For tblHofstedeClassifications	
Country	Country name
PDI	Power Distance Index (Small or Large)
MAS	Masculinity Index (Masculine or Feminine)
IDV	Individualism Index (Individualist or Collectivist)
UAI	Uncertainty Avoidance Index (Strong or Weak)
Sources: CIA=CIA World Factbook, ESRI=ESRI Data & Maps, ILO=International Labor Organization, WEF=World Economic Forum, WB=World Bank	

Exercise 7.1 Explore and prepare the global dataset

To begin the country assessment screening process, you should familiarize yourself with the demographic measures you will be using and their distribution around the world. Thus, in this exercise, you will:

- Review, create, and explore thematic world maps
- Explore the global distribution of the dataset's attributes
- Examine attribute values for specific regions and countries

Open an existing map

1   **From the Windows taskbar, click Start > All Programs > ArcGIS > ArcMap.**

Depending on how ArcGIS and ArcMap have been installed or which Windows operating system you are using, there may be a slightly different navigation menu from which to open ArcMap.

2   **If you see an ArcMap start window, click the "An existing map" option. Otherwise, click the Open button 📂 on the ArcMap Standard toolbar.**

3   **Browse to your \GISMKT\PMDGlobal folder, choose the PMDGlobal1 map document, and click Open.**

The table of contents contains a layer displaying the population of the world's countries and three layers displaying the attributes PMD wishes to use as demographic screening attributes.

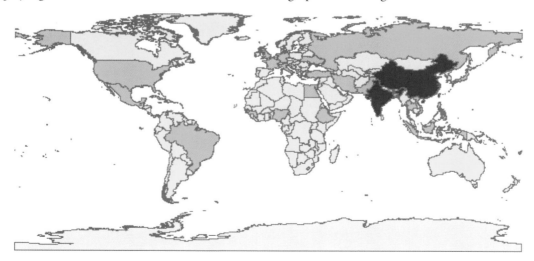

Display and add map layers

You can display layers by turning them on in the table of contents. Remember that layers are displayed from the bottom up, so that you may have to turn off a layer at the top of the table of contents to view a layer that is turned on but is lower in the table of contents.

Turn layers off and on

1   Click the small check box to the left of the Population layer to turn this layer off (the check mark disappears).

2   Click the small check box to the left of the Per Capita Income layer to turn it on (a check mark appears in the check box).

The map reflects the results of these changes: it now displays Per Capita Income for the world's countries in shades of green.

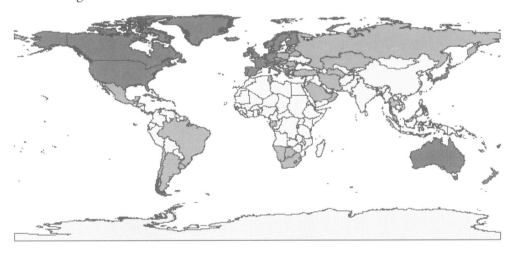

3   Examine the other layers in the map document by turning them on and off.

Add a layer to the map

In addition to population and income layers, the map's table of contents contains layers representing two of the three screening attributes you wish to use. You will add another layer to display the third screening attribute, average levels of education.

1 **Click the Add Data button.**

2 **Navigate to and open the \GISMKT\PMDGlobal folder. Double-click the PMDGlobal.mdb geodatabase file to display the data within it, and click the CountryData feature class to highlight it.**

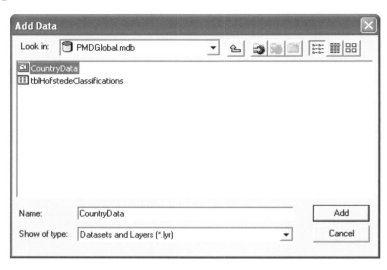

3 **Click Add.**

The new layer is added to the top of the table of contents. It is symbolized with a single color for all countries. You will now revise the properties of that layer to display educational attainment data.

Edit a layer's name and symbology

1   Double-click the CountryData layer (or right-click the layer and select Properties).

2   Click the General tab and enter **Educational Attainment** as the new layer name.

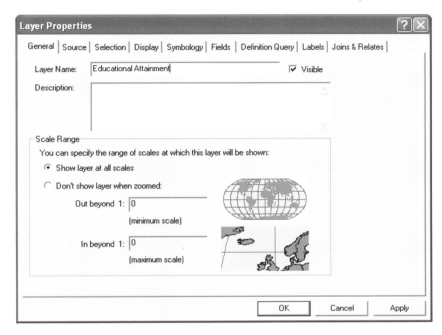

3   Click the Symbology tab. Click Quantities, then Graduated Colors in the Show area.

4   Click the drop-down arrow for the Value field and choose the appropriate option for displaying educational attainment data. (Use the data dictionary to identify the attribute that reports average years in school for persons older than 15.) ArcMap randomly assigns a color ramp, so your colors may be different from those shown in the following graphic.

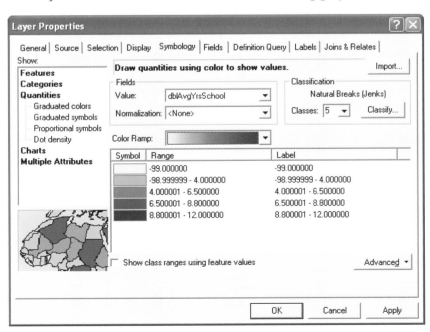

Notice the default classification settings on the Symbology tab. Values are divided into five classes assigned by the natural breaks method. Numbers are shown with six decimal places. There is a class for the value -99, which is the indicator in this dataset for missing values. You will change these settings to achieve consistency with the other layers.

5   Click the Classify button to open the Classification dialog box.

6   For Method, choose Quantile.

7   For Classes, choose 3.

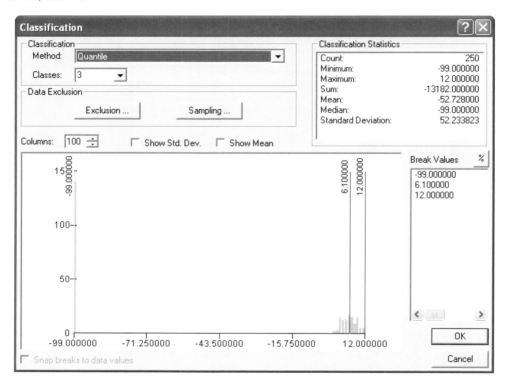

Three classes are defined with an approximate equal number of countries in each, matching the format in which the other demographic layers are displayed.

Identify and display missing values

1   Click the Exclusion button to open the Data Exclusion Properties dialog box. Click the Legend tab.

2   Check the box next to Show symbol for excluded data.

3   Click the Symbol button and in the Fill Color option, change the display color to Gray 10% (row 2, column 1). Click OK.

4   Type **Missing values** for Label.

These settings mean that features that match the exclusion query (which you'll create next) will be clearly shown in the legend and map display as missing values, as is the case with this map's other layers.

5   Click the Query tab.

6   Double-click the [dblAvgYrsSchool] attribute, and then click equal (=) button to add them to the query.

7   Click the Get Unique Values button, then double-click the value -99 to add this value to the query.

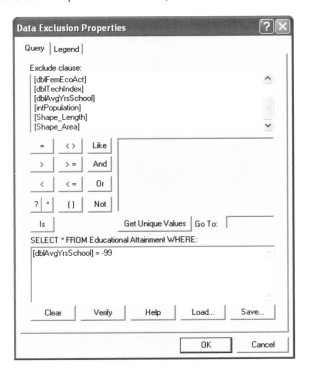

8   Click OK to return to the Classification dialog box.

9   Click OK to return to the Layer Properties dialog box.

Format classification labels

You will now adjust the display of classification labels in the layer's legend.

1   Click the Label column header in the Layer Properties dialog box, then click Format Labels to open the Number Format dialog box. (Note: Do not click the Labels tab at the top of this dialog box. If you do so inadvertently, click the Symbology tab to return.)

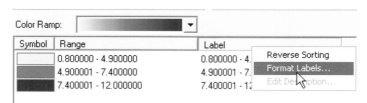

2   Select Numeric in the Category field and reduce the number of decimal places to 1 in the Rounding area.

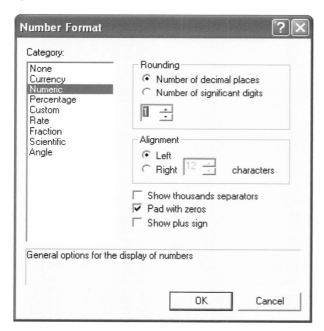

3   Click OK to return to the Layer Properties dialog box.

4   Select a light to dark blue color scheme in the Color Ramp.

5   Select the "Show class ranges using feature values" option to define classification ranges using actual values from the dataset.

6   Click OK to close the Layer Properties dialog box and display the new properties.

Edit legend title

1   In the table of contents, click the attribute name **dblAvgYrsSchool** under the layer name, then click again to make it editable.

2   Replace **dblAvgYrsSchool** with **Average years in school**. (Note: If your second click is too quick, the Layer Properties dialog box will open. Click Cancel, then try again, clicking more slowly to reach the edit function.)

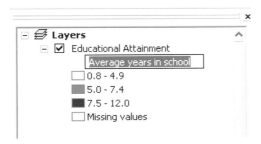

The resulting map displays the average years of education for persons older than 15 in each of the world's countries. This data is for the general population, both male and female. Thus it represents general levels of educational attainment, and must be integrated with other attributes to assess the overall market attractiveness for PMD's training system. You are now ready to analyze this data as well as the other attributes included in the table of contents.

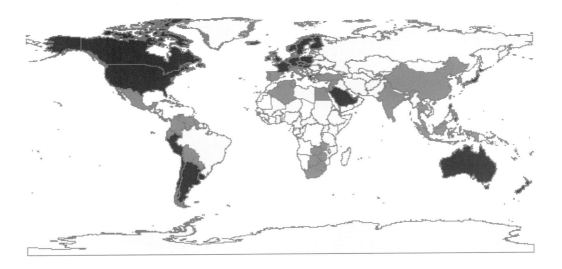

Update report and save map document

1 Use your observations of the map layers you have displayed to answer the following questions. Summarize your answer in the appropriate section of the project report template (PMDGlobal_ ReportTemplate.doc), which you will find in your \GISMKT\PMDGlobal folder.

 What do you observe about the distribution of the map layers' attributes across the globe? What do you notice about female economic activity and high levels of income?

2 Save the map document as PMDGlobal1_fl.mxd (replace f and l with your first and last initials). To do so, from the File menu, choose Save As. Navigate to your **\GISMKT\PMDGlobal** folder, type **PMDGlobal1_fl.mxd** as the file name, and click Save.

Exercise 7.2   Perform demographic screening

PMD wants to target countries with high levels of education, technology readiness, and female participation in the work force. You will identify countries with above-average values on all these measures. Thus, in this exercise you will:

- Calculate global averages for the three attributes deemed most relevant by PMD
- Select countries with above-average values for all three attributes
- Display the selected countries on a map

Open an existing map

1   In ArcMap, open the **PMDGlobal2** map document from your **\GISMKT\PMDGlobal** folder.

This map contains one layer depicting the population of the world's countries. Using this layer as a basemap allows you to compare the market sizes of the countries you select in this exercise. You will use the demographic data in the Population layer's attribute table to screen potential target countries based on their demographic characteristics. You will identify those with above-average values for education, technology readiness, and participation of women in the economy.

This procedure has two steps. First, you will calculate the average values for these attributes. Second, you will design a query to select those countries with above-average values on all three measures.

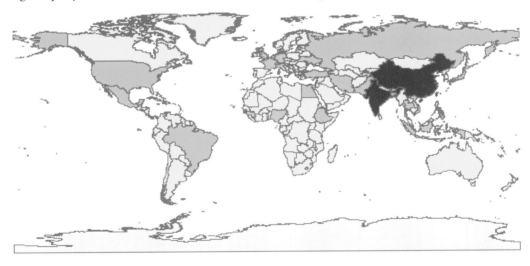

Analyze data in attribute tables

Your first step is to calculate averages for the three screening attributes, ensuring that missing values are excluded from the calculation.

Calculate statistics for attributes

You will begin with the attribute that measures women's participation in economic activity.

1   **Right-click the Population layer, then click Open Attribute Table.**

2   **Click the Options button at the bottom of the attribute table, then click Select by Attributes.**

3   **In the Select by Attributes dialog box, double-click [dblFemEcoAct] and then click the greater-than (>) button to add them to the query.**

4   **Click the Get Unique Values button, double-click the value -99 to add this value to the query, then click Apply.**

Remember that the value -99 indicates missing values. Therefore, you must exclude these countries from the calculation of statistics for this attribute. This query does that by selecting only those countries with values greater than -99.

Review the attribute table. You have selected all countries with actual values for this attribute. You may now calculate statistics for this attribute that are not skewed by countries for which you have no data.

5   **Right-click the header for the dblFemEcoAct field, then click Statistics to display the Selection Statistics window.**

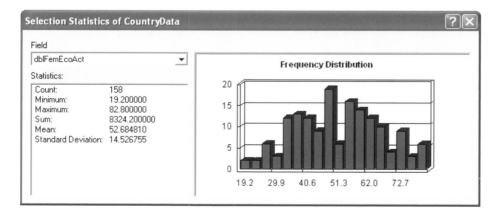

What is the mean value for dblFemEcoAct?

Take note of this number, as you will use it in the next step.

6 Close the statistics window, then in the attribute table click Options > Clear Selection to unselect all features.

7 Repeat the process of excluding missing values then calculating attribute statistics for dblTechIndex. Record the mean value and clear all selected features.

 What is the mean value for dblTechIndex?

8 Repeat the process of excluding missing values then calculating attribute statistics for dblAvgYrsSchool. Record the mean value and clear all selected features.

 What is the mean value for dblAvgYrsSchool?

You now have the values required to perform demographic screening.

Select features based on multiple attributes

1 In the Select by Attributes box, delete the current query. Double-click [dblFemEcoAct] then click the greater-than (>) button to add them to the query box.

2 Click inside the query box to insert the cursor directly following the greater-than symbol and type the mean value you calculated in step 5 above, then click the AND button.

3 Double-click [dblTechIndex], then click the greater-than (>) button. Type the mean value you calculated in step 7 above, then click the AND button.

4   Double-click [dblAvgYrsSchool], then click the greater-than (>) button. Type the mean value you calculated in step 8 above.

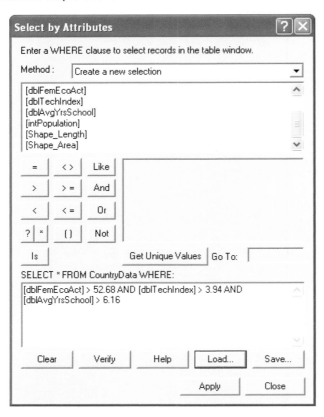

5   To confirm the syntax of the query, click Verify. Click OK in the Verifying expression window. (Note: If an error is detected, edit the query until verification is successful.)

You must save this query as you will use it again in exercise 7.4.

6   In the Query window, click Save, navigate to **PMDGlobal** folder, type the name **PMDDemoScreen**, then click Save to save the query expression.

7   Click Apply to execute the query. At the bottom of the Population attribute table, click the Selected button.

You may view the countries selected by the demographic screening process in the attribute table. They are also highlighted in blue on the map.

8   If you wish, explore the countries more closely using the Zoom In and Identify tools. You may
    have to move the table out of your way to see the map.

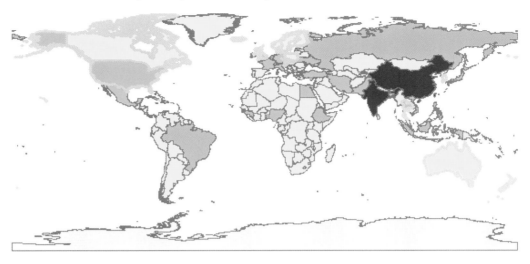

You now have the information you need to complete this exercise.

Update report and save map document

1   Use the Population attribute table and map to answer the following questions. Summarize your
    answers in the appropriate section of the project report template (PMDGlobal_ReportTemplate
    .doc), which you will find in your \GISMKT\PMDGlobal folder.

   *How many countries does this demographic screening process identify? How are these
   countries distributed geographically? List the selected countries.*

2   Save the map document as **PMDGlobal2_fl.mxd** (replace f and l with your first and last initials) in
    your **\GISMKT\PMDGlobal** folder.

Exercise 7.3   Use Hofstede's indexes for cultural analysis

Among the countries identified in the demographic screening process, you wish to select those whose cultural values are consistent with the managerial philosophy of PMD and its training programs. For this purpose, you will use the cultural indexes developed by Geert Hofstede. Thus, in this exercise, you will:

- Integrate Hofstede's classification indexes with country data
- Design maps that show the geographic distribution of countries with different Hofstede index values
- Calculate summary statistics for the three indexes that will be used for cultural screening (Masculinity, Individualism, and Uncertainty Avoidance).

Open an existing map document

1   In ArcMap, open the **PMDGlobal3** map document from your **\GISMKT\PMDGlobal** folder.

In addition to the Population layer, this map displays layers for three of Hofstede's four cultural indexes and a CountryData layer that is undefined. You will use the CountryData layer to symbolize the fourth Hofstede index, the Masculinity index. This data, however, is not included in the attribute table for the CountryData layer, but rather in a separate table called tblHofstedeClassifications. Your first task will be to join this table to the CountryData layer's attribute table, and then use one of the joined attributes to symbolize the layer.

Notice that the thematic layers in this map are symbolized according to category names rather than numerical value ranges as in the previous exercises.

2   If necessary, click the Source tab at the bottom of the table of contents to see the tblHofstedeClassifications table.

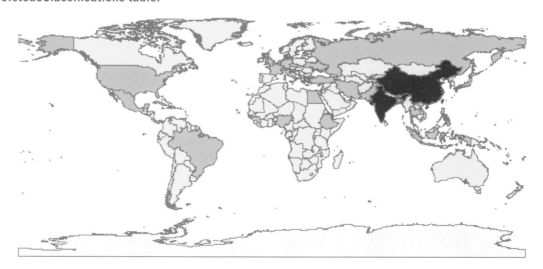

Display tabular data

ArcMap allows you to accumulate data from several different sources, analyze it, and include it in map displays. You will use these capabilities to integrate cultural data into your analysis.

Open a table and join it to a layer attribute table

1   In the table of contents, click the check box next to CountryData to make the layer visible.

2   Right-click tblHofstedeClassification, then click Open to view its contents.

The table contains Hofstede index classifications for 87 countries and regions. Though you can view the data in the table, you cannot display it graphically as it does not contain a Shape field with spatial information. To display this data on a map, you must join it to a layer's attribute table, in this case, the CountryData layer.

3   Close the Hofstede table. Right-click the CountryData layer, click Joins and Relates, then click Join to open the Join Data dialog box.

4   For item 1, choose txtCountryName.

5   For item 2, choose tblHofstedeClassifications.

6   For item 3, choose Country.

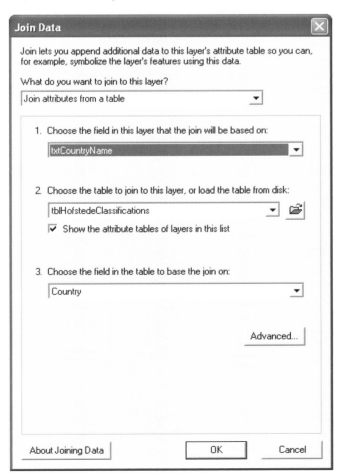

7   Click OK to create the join. Click Yes if prompted to create an index.

The CountryData layer now contains data from tblHofstedeClassifications in addition to its original data. The join operation added the attributes in the Hofstede table to the features in the CountryData layer that have the same country name.

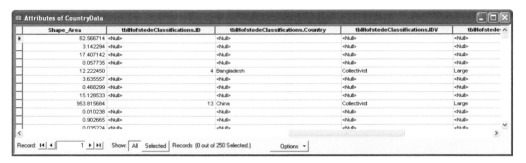

8   Right-click the CountryData layer, then click Open Attribute Table to view the results of your join operation.

The Hofstede data has been added to the CountryData attribute table. In the attribute table, you will have to scroll to the right to see all the extra Hofstede fields. In order to tell which fields come from which tables, each field name is now prefixed with its home table name. Note that while eighty countries have Hofstede values, most do not. When you symbolize the Hofstede data, you will notice this on your map as well.

9   Close the CountryData attribute table.

Display Hofstede Index data in the map

To display Hofstede's cultural indexes you will symbolize the CountryData layer using information in the joined fields.

1   In the table of contents, double-click the CountryData layer name (or right-click and select Properties).

2   Click the General tab and enter **Masculinity** as the new layer name.

3   Click the Symbology tab.

4   Select Categories, then Unique values in the Show area.

5   Select tblHofstedeClassifications.MAS in the Value Field drop-down list.

6   Click the Add All Values button to add all the values for this attribute to the classification scheme.

The two possible values for this attribute (Masculine and Feminine) appear, as does an entry for fields with no data (described as <Null> values). There is also a symbol labeled <all other values>. You will adjust the layer's symbology for easier readability.

7   Click the check box to the left of the <all other values> label to unselect it.

8 Double-click the colored box to the left of the <Null> value to open the Symbol Selector dialog box. For the Fill Color option, select Gray 10% (row 2, column 1), then click **OK** to change the color of this symbol.

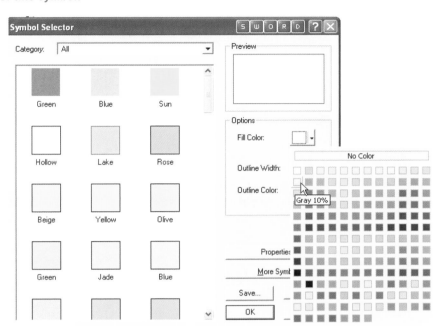

9 Click the <Null> label in the Label column to edit it. Replace it with **Missing values**. With the <Null> row highlighted, use the down arrow to the right of the symbol area to move this symbol to the bottom of the list.

10 Change the color for the Feminine value to Flame Red (row 4, column 3) and the color for the Masculine value to Electron Gold (row 3, column 4).

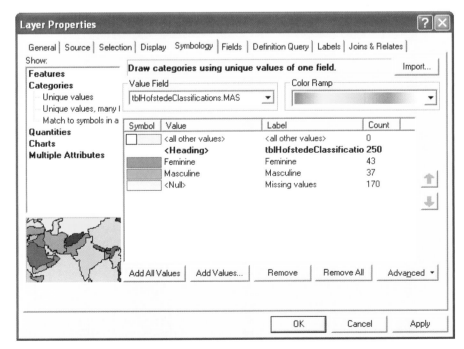

11 Click **OK** to close the Layer Properties dialog box.

12 Click the legend title **tblHofstedeClassifications.MAS** under the layer name, then click again to edit it. Rename it **Hofstede MAS Index**.

The table of contents now has layers for each of Hofstede's indexes. By turning these layers on and off you may view the distribution of each index in turn. Use these layers to analyze the distribution of the cultural values measured by the indexes.

Compare demographics with summary tables

Having examined the global distribution of demographic and cultural characteristics separately, you will now explore the variation of demographic characteristics between countries with different cultural values. Specifically, you will use summary tables to compare demographic measures for countries with Feminine values to countries with Masculine values. You will then make similar comparisons between countries with Individualist values and those with Collectivist values and between countries with Weak Uncertainty Avoidance and those with Strong Uncertainty Avoidance.

Use a query to exclude missing values

As you have noted, several countries in the dataset have missing values for one or more attributes. These missing values are denoted by the value -99. For purposes of accurate comparison, the countries with missing values should be excluded from the summary tables you calculate. You will perform this task with an attribute query.

1   Right-click the Masculinity layer in the table of contents, then click Open Attribute Table.

2   At the bottom of the attribute table, click Options, then Select by Attributes.

3   In the Select by Attributes dialog box, click the Load button, navigate to the **PMDGlobal** folder, click **ExcludeMissing.exp**, then click Open.

The expression is loaded into the query box.

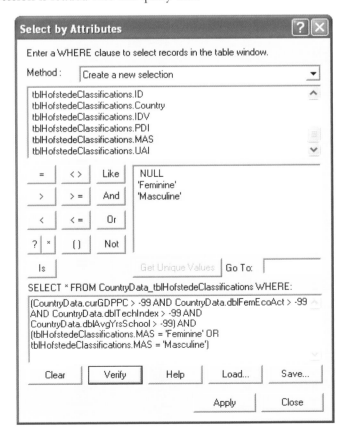

This is a lengthy query but its function is not difficult to understand. Review the portion of the expression in the first set of parentheses. It selects from the dataset all features for which all four key demographic attributes have values greater than -99. This means that each of the summary tables you create will include exactly the same set of countries and that no missing value indicators (values of -99) will be included in any of the calculations.

Review the portion of the expression in the second set of parentheses. It specifies that only those features which have values of "Feminine" OR "Masculine" for the MAS attribute will be selected. As these are the only two values for this attribute, and since all countries with Hofstede values have data for all four of the cultural indexes, this expression ensures that only countries with Hofstede index values will be selected.

Taken together, the two portions of this lengthy expression will select only those countries with Hofstede index values and values for all four demographic measures. This increases the accuracy of the comparisons you will make using the summary tables.

4 Click Apply to run the query and select the countries with valid values for all relevant attributes.

5 Close the Select by Attributes dialog box.

Create summary tables to compare cultural classification data

1 In the attribute table, right-click the column header for the tblHofstedeClassifications.MAS attribute, then click Summarize to open the Summarize dialog box.

2 For option 2, expand CountryData.curGDPPC, then click the check box next to Average.

This setting indicates that you wish to calculate the average per capita gross domestic product of the countries in each of the classifications for this index. Now you want to calculate the averages for other attributes.

3 Expand the CountryData.dblFemEcoAct, CountryData.dblTechIndex, and CountryData. dblAvgYrsSchool categories and select the Average option for each.

4 Click the Browse button 📂 to the right of option 3 to open the Saving Data dialog box.

5 Select the File and Personal Geodatabase tables option in the Save as type drop-down box.

6 Navigate to your **\GISMKT\PMDGlobal** folder and double-click **PMDGlobal.mdb**.

7 Type **MASDemoSummary** for Name, then click Save to return to the Summarize dialog box.

8   Click the check box next to the "Summarize on the selected records only" option.

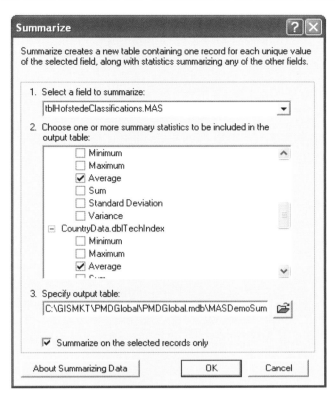

9   Click OK to create the summary table and click Yes when prompted to add the result to the map.

The summary table now appears at the bottom of the table of contents.

10   Open the MASDemoSummary table and examine its contents.

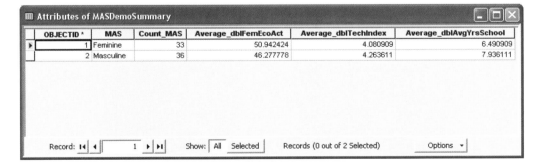

This table reports the average values for each of the four demographic measures for countries classified as Feminine and Masculine on the MAS index. These values allow you to identify general demographic differences between these two groups of countries.

11   Record the attribute values in the MAS rows in the table on the next page. Round income figures to the nearest dollar and all other values to two decimal places.

12 Using the attribute table for the Masculinity layer to retain the current set of selected features, repeat steps 1 through 10 on the tblHofstedeClassifications.IDV attribute to create a summary table named **IDVDemoSummary**, which summarizes the same four attributes. Record the results in the table on the next page.

13 Repeat the procedure a third time on the tblHofstedeClassifications.UAI attribute to create a summary table named **UAIDemoSummary**, which summarizes the same four attributes, and record the results in the following table.

You will use the completed table below and the map to compare the demographic characteristics of countries with Feminine versus Masculine values, Individualist versus Collectivist values, and Weak versus Strong Uncertainty Avoidance values.

Note: If any of your table cells contain negative values, 3 rows, or more than 69 countries, you neglected to limit the summary table to the selected countries. Right-click the erroneous summary table, then click Remove to remove it from the table of contents. Repeat the summary operation and be sure to perform step 9 before clicking the OK button.

	Classification	# of Countries	Per Capita Income	Average Years in School	% Females Economically Active	Technology Index
MAS	Feminine					
	Masculine					
IDV	Collectivist					
	Individualist					
UAI	Strong					
	Weak					

Update report and save map document

1 Use the maps and summary tables you created to answer the following questions. Summarize your answers in the appropriate section of the project report template for this chapter.

What patterns do you see in the geographic distributions of each of Hofstede's Masculinity, Individualism, and Uncertainty Avoidance indexes? What demographic differences do the summary tables for these indexes reveal?

2 Save the map document as **PMDGlobal3_fl.mxd** (replace f and l with your first and last initials) in your **\GISMKT\PMDGlobal** folder.

Exercise 7.4   Perform cultural and demographic screening

The PMD management believes that its managerial style and that of their training program is most consistent with Feminine values on Hofstede's Masculinity (MAS) index, Individualist values on the Individualism (IDV) index, and Weak values on the Uncertainty Avoidance (UAI) index. PMD does not use the Power Distance Index to define its managerial style. Further, they note that the demographic characteristics of Individualist countries (high income and education) combined with the high percentage of economically active women in Feminine countries and in countries with Weak Uncertainty Avoidance measures offer the best opportunities for success. In their international expansion, they wish to focus on countries that share these values. Thus, in this exercise, you will:

- Screen selected countries further based on the values measured in Hofstede's cultural indexes
- Explore the demographic characteristics of the selected countries
- Recommend two specific countries for PMD's expansion

Open an existing map

1   In ArcMap, open **PMDGlobal4.mxd** from your **\GISMKT\PMDGlobal** folder.

This map displays the Economically Active Women layer you created in exercise 7.2, as well as a table called tblHofstedeClassifications.

2   If the table is not visible, click on the Source tab at the bottom of the table of contents to see it.

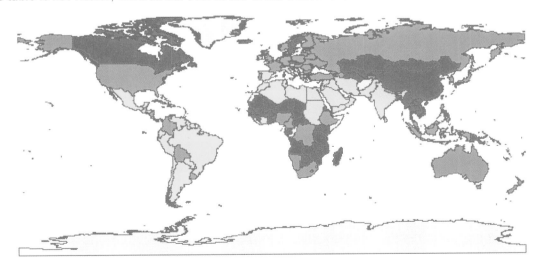

Join tables and perform demographic screening

In this exercise, you will perform a cultural screening to extend the demographic screening process of exercise 7.2. To prepare for that process, you must join tables and then repeat the demographic screening steps from exercise 7.2.

Join layer attribute table with data table

1   In the table of contents, right-click Economically Active Women, then click Joins and Relates > Join.

2   In the Join Data dialog box, for item 1, choose txtCountryName.

3   For item 2, choose tblHofstedeClassifications.

4   For item 3, choose Country.

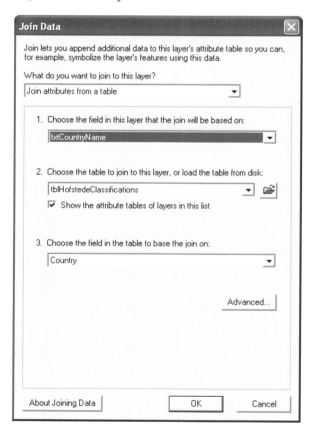

5   Click OK to execute the join operation.

The Economically Active Women layer now contains data from tblHofstedeClassifications in addition to its original data. This will allow you to perform a query operation based on the cultural attributes contained in the Hofstede data table. This query will refine the screening process further by selecting countries with the cultural values PMD is seeking.

Perform demographic screening

1   Open the attribute table for the Economically Active Women layer.

2   Click the Options button, then click Select by Attributes.

3   In the Select by Attributes dialog box, click the Load button, navigate to the **PMDGlobal** folder, and select the **PMDDemoScreen.exp** query you created in exercise 7.2.

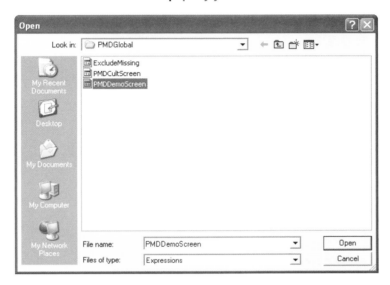

4   Click Open to load the query. (Note: If you did not save the PMDDemoScreen expression, recreate it manually with the help of the graphic below.)

Your query should look exactly like the following graphic.

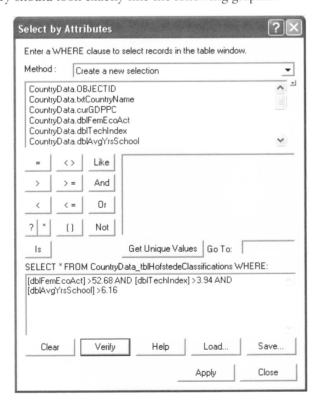

5   **Click Apply to make the selection.**

The countries identified in the demographic screening process are now highlighted. Notice the selection is comprised of 16 countries (this figure is reported at the bottom of the attribute table). You will further refine this selection by applying a cultural screening.

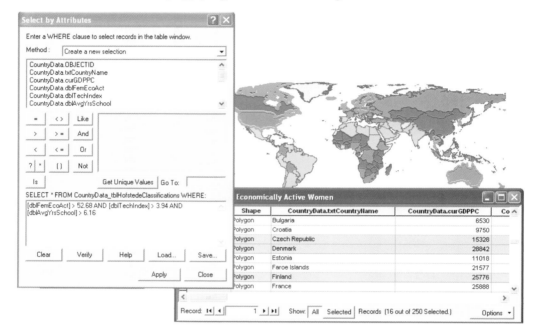

Perform cultural screening

For cultural screening, you will employ the selection technique again. However, this time the criteria will be applied only to those countries identified in the demographic screening process, not the entire dataset. Thus, the selected countries will be those that meet both your demographic and cultural screening criteria.

1   In the Select by Attributes dialog box, for Method, choose Select from current selection.

This option specifies that the query you create will be applied only to those countries already selected in the demographic screening process.

2   Load the **PMDCultScreen.exp** query.

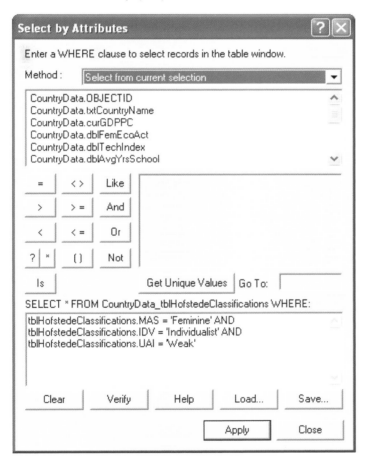

Review the expression. It selects those countries that are classified as Feminine on the MAS index, as Individualist on the IDV index, and as Weak in the UAI. Taken together, these values identify countries that accept a range of managerial values and management styles. They also value individual initiative and are tolerant of risk-taking.

3   Click the Apply button.

 How many countries meet PMD's demographic and cultural criteria?

4   Close the Select by Attributes dialog box.

5   Right-click the Economically Active Women layer, then click Selection > Zoom to Selected Features to better view the selected countries.

6   Right-click the layer again, then click Label Features to display country names on the map.

 What are the names of the selected countries?

Countries that meet all the demographic and cultural screening processes criteria are highlighted. These are the most attractive markets for PMD's initial international expansion. However, this list still includes more than two countries, so you must decide which two of the selected countries to recommend for initial expansion.

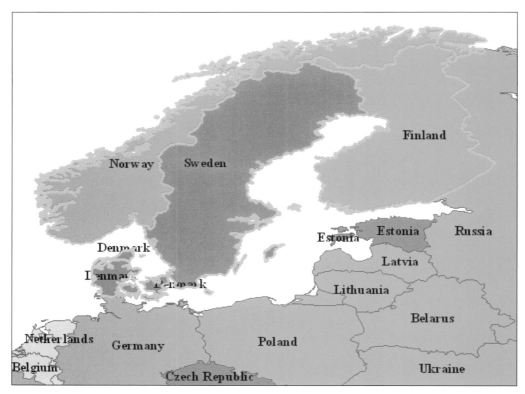

Select countries for final recommendation

Personal Management Development, Inc. plans to enter the two most populous countries that meet its demographic and cultural criteria. You will use the attribute table to select these countries and design a graph to display their populations.

1   In the attribute table Economically Active Women, click the Selected button to display the selected countries.

  Which two countries have the highest populations? These are the countries you will recommend.

Graph the population of the selected countries

To complete your analysis, you will create a graph that displays the populations of the four countries that meet the PMD demographic and cultural screening criteria. You will use the graph to illustrate your selection of the two most populous countries for market entry.

1   From the main menu bar, click Tools > Graphs > Create.

2   In the Create Graph Wizard, maintain the default graph type of Vertical Bar.

3   For the Layer/Table option, choose Economically Active Women.

4   For the Value field option, choose CountryData.intPopulation. (Note: You can see there are too many countries being graphed. You will fix this on the next panel of the wizard.)

5   For X label field, choose CountryData.txtCountryName.

6   Leave all other options set to their default values.

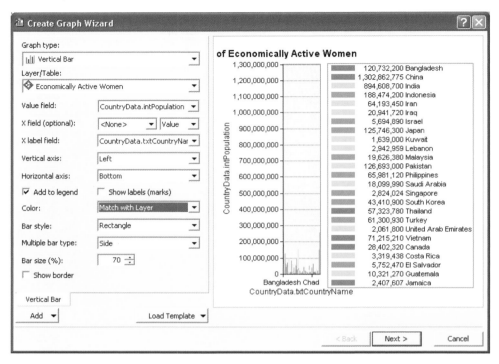

7   Click Next.

8   Choose the option to show only selected features/records on the graph.

9   Under General graph properties, replace the default title with **Population of Selected Countries**.

10 Under Axis properties, delete the left axis title.

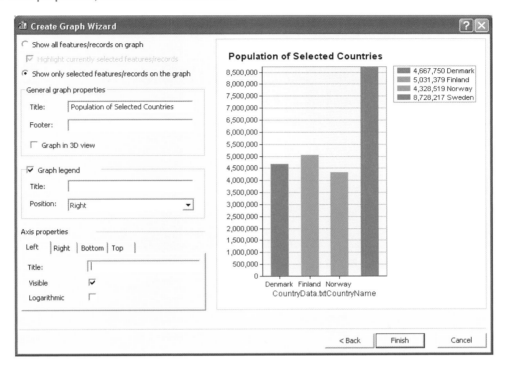

11 Under Axis properties, click the Bottom tab and delete the title there as well.

12 Click Finish.

You will include this graph in your report to support your final recommendation of two countries.

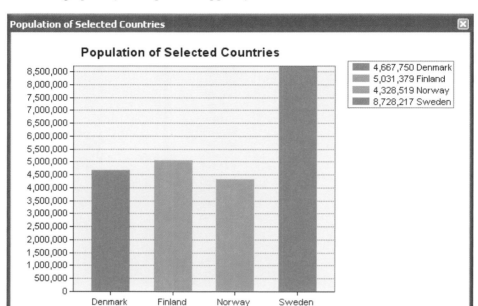

Note that the color of each country's bar in the graph matches the color of that country in the Economically Active Women layer. Thus, the graph displays information for two attributes. The height of each bar represents the population of the country, while the color represents the percentage of women who are economically active as classified in the legend for the Economically Active Women layer.

Update report and save map document

1   Use the map, table, and graph you have created to answer the following questions. Summarize your answers in the appropriate section of the project report template for this chapter.

Which countries are selected by your cultural screening process? What is their geographic distribution? Which two do you recommend for PMD's international expansion? Why?

2   Save the map document as **PMDGlobal4_fl.mxd** (replace f and l with your first and last initials) in your **\GISMKT\PMDGlobal** folder.

Exercise 7.5   Support your expansion recommendations

You have completed the international market assessment process for PMD, using demographic and cultural screening to identify the most attractive markets for the firm's international expansion. To complete your report, you must summarize the process which produced your recommendations and design a map to illustrate and support your recommendations. Thus, in this exercise you will:

- Briefly summarize your demographic and cultural screening processes
- Restate your market expansion recommendations
- Design a supporting map

Open an existing map

1   In ArcMap, open **PMDGlobal5.mxd** from your **\GISMKT\PMDGlobal** folder.

The map opens in layout view and contains a legend, title, north arrow, scale bar, and text boxes that explain the map.

The map displays the Economically Active Women layer, highlighting the countries that were selected during the demographic screening process. Another layer, CountryData, is not turned on. The map also includes the table with which you're now familiar, tblHofstedeClassifications.

2   If you don't see the table, click the Source tab at the bottom of the table of contents.

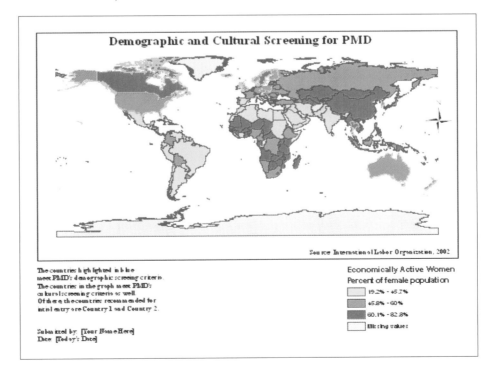

Add a graph to the layout

The map displays the results of the demographic screening process, but not those of the cultural screening process. Nor does it identify the two countries you will recommend based on their populations. You will provide this information by adding a graph to the layout.

1   From the main menu bar, click Tools > Graphs > Population of Selected Countries to open this graph. Note that it is the same graph you designed in exercise 7.4.

2   Right-click the title bar at the top of the graph window and select Add to Layout. Close the graph window.

The graph has been added to the center of the layout, and not in an optimal location. You can drag the graph to a new location or move any of its eight selection handles (the eight tiny squares that surround the graph) to resize it.

3   Click on the graph in layout view to select it if it isn't already. Click and drag the graph to the empty space at the bottom of the layout and resize it to fit as needed. (Use the graphic shown below as a guide.)

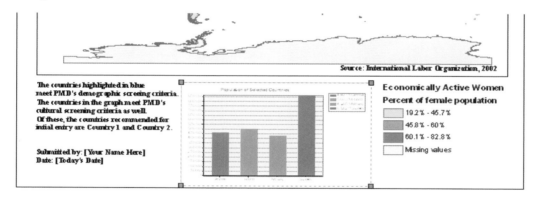

The graph is now in its proper place. You will now edit the two text boxes to complete the map.

Edit layout text boxes

1   Right-click the text box at the bottom of the page that includes the Submitted by and Date elements, then click Properties.

2   In the Properties dialog box, replace the placeholder text with your name and today's date, then click OK.

3   Select the large text box with the explanatory paragraph, then right-click and choose Properties.

4   Delete the text Country 1 and Country 2 and enter the names of the two countries you recommend for initial market entry, then click OK.

You have now completed the map that you will use as exhibit 1 in your report. You will save it as a graphic file and insert it into the report template.

Export map document and insert it into a report

1   From the main menu bar, click File > Export Map. In the Export Map dialog box, navigate to the **\GISMKT\PMDGlobal** folder. Type **CountryRec.emf** for File Name, then click Save to save the map document as an EMF graphic file to include in your report.

2   Open the report template and navigate to the end of the report. Locate the page entitled Exhibit 1: Market Entry Recommendations, and insert the EMF file. (Note: You will have to select and resize the image to make it readable.)

Exhibit 1 of your report is now complete.

Update report and save map document

1   Use your previous analysis and the map layout you have created to complete the following task. Summarize your response in the appropriate section of the project report template.

Restate your recommendations briefly. Describe the role of demographic screening in the selection process. Describe the role of cultural screening in the selection process.

2   Save your map file as **PMDGlobal5_fl.mxd** (replace f and l with your first and last initials) in your **\GISMKT\PMDGlobal** folder.

Congratulations! You have completed the PMD Global project.

Take a moment to think about what you accomplished in this chapter. You integrated demographic data for the world's countries into spatial data and displayed the dataset's global distribution using thematic maps. You calculated threshold values for the attributes critical to PMD's expansion strategy and used them to perform demographic screening in search of the most attractive markets. You integrated a table of Hofstede's cultural indexes into a global basemap, displayed the distribution of these indexes, and examined the relationship between the cultural and demographic attributes in the dataset. Finally, you refined the demographic screening process with a cultural screening operation, chose the most attractive country markets from the final candidates, and designed a map document to communicate and support your recommendations. In short, you have used ArcGIS to select the most attractive countries for international expansion through the process of demographic and cultural screening.

Additional applications

As the previous exercises illustrate, GIS tools are useful in the global market assessment process. They allow managers to integrate data from disparate sources, explore relationships between different types of information, and view spatial dimensions of demographic, socioeconomic, and cultural data. In addition, these tools provide effective communication capabilities by integrating maps, graphs, and tables to illustrate important points.

In this marketing application, the real strength of GIS is the ability to integrate data from a wide range of sources. This allows a marketing manager to tap the vast collection of international statistical data and accumulate relevant information within a single system.

Among the most commonly used international statistical resources are the World Bank and the CIA World Factbook. The World Bank provides a wealth of statistical information on economic and social development indicators. Its datasets include several country-level reports that include comparative as well as country-specific data. Its World Development Indicators package offers an extensive collection of this data and also includes tables of comparative data across countries. These data tables are especially useful for the comparative dimensions of market assessment analysis. The Web-based Quick Query function allows users to extract data from this dataset for a customized list of countries, statistical measures, and dates.[4] Users may view query results online, print them as reports, and save them as Microsoft Excel files. The latter option allows users to integrate the data into the personal geodatabase and use in ArcGIS applications.

The CIA World Factbook offers a useful collection of current demographic, political, and socioeconomic information for most of the world's countries. It also includes a collection of Rank Order statistics that ranks these countries on key statistical measures. This data is also provided in tab-delimited format for use in standard statistical and database programs.[5] In this form, it can be readily integrated into the ArcGIS personal geodatabase format.

NationMaster.com[6] is an excellent example of this type of resource. It accumulates statistics and qualitative data from an array of original sources and makes them available through a common Web-based interface. This site offers simple mapping capabilities and displays results in graphs and tables. In addition, it offers correlation charts that illustrate the relationship (based on the R^2 correlation coefficient) between any two variables in its collection. Integration of this data into ArcGIS allows users to incorporate the data into other datasets.

Other resources focus on specific dimensions of country comparisons and provide both information and analysis on that topic. WorldAudit.org, for example, assesses the status of key democratic institutions in the world's countries and provides results in online data tables and downloadable Microsoft Excel files.[7] Similarly, the Heritage Foundation/Wall Street Journal Index of Economic Freedom[8] provides data and rankings of the world's countries on several dimensions of economic freedom. It provides data in Excel format, with longitudinal data available from 1995 to 2006. The online GlobalEdge's *Market Potential Indicators for Emerging Markets* index provides a different focus.[9] This portion of the GlobalEdge site provides a statistical index measuring market potential in a range of emerging markets. Historical data is also provided.

Although it was the focus of this chapter, GIS applications in international marketing do not end with the selection of target countries. Indeed, all of the U.S.-focused chapters in this book contain concepts and techniques that are relevant to similar challenges in international markets. They require only the addition of local basemaps and detailed local data on consumers, businesses, and demographic and lifestyle measures. While the availability and quality of such data around the world is inconsistent, effective GIS analysis can be performed for many of the world's major markets.

1. Hofstede, Geert and Gert Jan Hofstede. *Cultures and Organizations: Software of the Mind.* New York: McGraw Hill, 2005.
Hofstede, Geert. *Culture's Consequence: Comparing Values, Behaviors, Institutions, and Organizations Across Nations.* 2nd Ed. Newbury Park, CA: Sage Publications, 2003.

2. Hofstede and Hofstede's *Cultures and Organizations* lists values for 74 countries and regions. For the data table in this exercise, three multicultural regions (Arab countries, East Africa, and West Africa) are removed and the values assigned to each of the 14 countries which comprise them. Two countries, Belgium and Switzerland, are divided into two regions each. These regions are included in the data table, but the overall national values for these countries, which appeared in Hofstede's previous work, are also included. *Cultures and Organizations* also includes national values for Canada and separate values for Quebec. This produces the total of 87 countries and regions contained in the HofstedeClassifications data table.
For each index, countries are assigned to classifications based on their numeric values. High Uncertainty Avoidance countries are those with UAI values greater than 62. Masculine countries are those with MAS values greater than 50. High Power Distance countries are those with PDI values greater than 50. Individualist countries are those with IDV values greater than 50.

3. Hofstede and Hofstede, *Cultures and Organizations,* 120.

4. The World Bank, *Data and Statistics: Quick Query: http://web.worldbank.org/WBSITE/EXTERNAL/ DATASTATISTICS/0,contentMDK:20535285~menuPK:1390200~ pagePK:64133150~piPK:64133175~theSitePK:239419,00.html*

5. The CIA World Factbook, *Guide to Rank Order Pages: http://www.odci.gov/cia/publications/factbook/ docs/rankorderguide.html*

6. NationMaster.com: *http://www.nationmaster.com/index.php*

7. World Audit.org: *http://www.worldaudit.org/home.htm*

8. Heritage Foundation/Wall Street Journal, Index of Economic Freedom: *http://www.heritage.org/ research/features/index/*

9. Michigan State University Center for International Business Education and Research, GlobalEdge, *Market Potential Indicators: http://globaledge.msu.edu/ibrd/marketpot.asp*

CHAPTER 8

Retail Site Selection

Course: Retailing/Retail Management

Better Books* is a book retailer with two stores in the San Francisco area. The company wants to build on its success by opening a third store in the city. It is seeking a location that serves a customer base similar to that of its most successful store, while minimizing the sales the new location will draw from the two existing stores. You will use GIS tools to help Better Books profile the characteristics of its current market areas and identify a third location that will meet the company's objectives.

* This is a fictional company and scenario, created for educational purposes only. Any resemblance to actual persons, events, or corporations is unintended.

Learning objectives

To perform retail site selection analysis in San Francisco, you will learn how to use ArcGIS to:

1. Create maps that illustrate characteristics of stores, competitors, and population demographics
2. Create buffers around store locations to define market areas
3. Analyze the demographic characteristics of the market areas and key customers
4. Apply several market area models and select the most appropriate one
5. Display alternative sites for new stores, evaluate their attractiveness, and select the most favorable site
6. Design a map that supports your recommendation

Marketing scenario

Better Books is a family-owned book retailer with two stores in the San Francisco area, both of which have been in operation for more than forty years. The firm refers to these outlets as the Steiner and Bosworth stores, named for the streets where they are located. They are popular within their respective market areas, each relying upon repeat sales to a loyal base of customers for success. While the firm carries new and modern titles, much of its business is selling used, historical, and collectible books to an established customer base. Many of its customers buy books as investments, hoping they will increase in value among avid collectors.

Both stores have been financially successful and the firm is considering how to build upon that success. It has implemented an Internet operation, but found price pressures too great to support profitable operation on such a small scale. It has considered catalog sales, but believes the market to be relatively small for the used and collectible books it carries. Therefore, Better Books believes the best growth option is expansion to a third outlet in the San Francisco area.

While San Francisco is an affluent market, there are many competing bookstores. In addition, real estate is quite expensive and rental rates are high; thus, opening a new store involves significant financial risk, and failure would harm Better Books's reputation in the community. Better Books wishes to open a new store by purchasing one of six available properties in the San Francisco area. It wishes to find the location that best matches the demographic profile of its most successful store while minimizing potential cannibalization, which occurs when sales at a firm's new store decrease sales at existing stores.

Toward this end, the firm has hired you to analyze the market areas for its existing stores and select one of them as the ideal profile for a new store. You will then analyze the six properties available for a new store, and eliminate those which might cannibalize sales of existing stores. Finally, you will perform a market analysis of the remaining potential sites and select the one that is most attractive according to the ideal profile you have defined. To support your efforts, Better Books has purchased demographic data at the census block group level for San Francisco. In addition to demographic information on population, households, and household size, the dataset also contains measures of income, education, net worth, and home value. Better Books believes these last measures to be particularly important for identifying customers who purchase books as investments or collectibles. These customers tend to value personalized treatment and are willing to pay significantly higher prices for rare or historical books.

Better Books does not have address information on all its customers. However, the firm has provided you with data from BB's Book Lovers club files. Book Lovers are the firm's best customers and buy books on a regular basis. Better Books sends them monthly newsletters, offers club discounts on featured books, and provides free home delivery service, which is available to other customers at a fee.

In the following exercises, you will use ArcGIS tools to analyze this data for Better Books and make a recommendation for their acquisition of an available property to house their new store.

Background information

Site selection is a key function—perhaps the most important function—of retail management. It is also one of the most common and successful GIS applications in the field of marketing. Though GIS analysis informs site decisions for production facilities, distribution centers, and customer service centers, its most common application is retail site selection. Location is a significant factor in successful retailing strategies that match merchandising and promotional programs to the store's customer base. It is also a major consideration in retail expansion strategies where firms place new stores in market areas similar to those that have been profitable for existing stores.

Site selection is a complex process that involves consideration of customer characteristics, market area definition, competitive conditions, and constantly changing consumer preferences. Analytical tools range from the simple market area definitions to complex models of competitive influence, consumer preferences, and the gravity of retail centers. Gravity is the ability of a retail site to draw customers based on distance and attractiveness factors. While the approach in this exercise is relatively straightforward, it illustrates the basic philosophy and procedures of the site selection process.

In the following exercises, the site selection process involves selecting a model store, then identifying available properties whose market area characteristics resemble those of the model. The first step in that process is to define market areas for existing stores, determine their characteristics, and evaluate store performance in each. Specifically, you will evaluate the merits of three methods of defining market areas.

While market areas can be defined in several ways, the simplest methods assume that consumers will select the store that is most convenient to them. One surrogate measure for convenience is physical distance, which for our purposes is illustrated with a simple one-mile ring around each store.

Another surrogate measure is drive time, which assumes that in assessing a store's convenience, consumers consider the time it takes to reach a store rather than the physical distance. For our purposes, this approach is reflected in the drive-time market areas, with 1- and 3-minute boundaries. Note that this approach produces uneven polygons elongated upon more rapidly moving roads and streets. Which of these measures do you consider most important in your shopping decisions? Do your drive-time estimates vary with time of day? Do you consider parking opportunities, time, and expense in your assessment? How does the highly congested San Francisco traffic situation compare with the traffic patterns in the areas where you shop?

The third market area definition in this project is customer concentration, which is not a measure of convenience, but the actual geographic compression of total store sales. In this model, the inner polygon contains 60 percent of each store's sales and the outer polygon 80 percent. The tighter the pattern of these polygons around a store, the more concentrated is the store's base of sales. However, you will see that many customers live beyond any of the defined market areas. It is best to view market area definitions as approximations of customer behavior, not absolute boundaries.

Once you have defined the market areas, you must determine their demographic characteristics. You do that by calculating the appropriate measures for the people (not just customers) living in each market area. In this project, you will manually calculate Average Household Income for households in the selected block groups. You will also estimate Average Home Value for those households by calculating the average of the selected block group values for this attribute. Note two computational difficulties: First, some selected block group boundaries extend beyond the ring, thus skewing your results. However, were you to select only block groups that are "completely within" the ring, you would exclude households in block groups intersecting the ring, also skewing the results. Second, in the Average Home Value operation you are calculating the simple average of a field that is already an average value for households within each block group. Your calculation is not weighted, as it should be, by the number of home-owning households in each block group. Therefore, manual calculations resulting from this method are approximations, rather than precise measures, of market area characteristics.

For these reasons, precise market area profiling requires the more sophisticated analysis provided by ArcGIS Business Analyst, which produced the reports contained in this project. Using more accurate techniques applied to smaller units (block points), Business Analyst produces more precise and finely grained profiles for market areas. Note, for example, that the Drive Time and Percentage of Customers reports provide distinct profiles for both of the polygons in each market area. As the values are based on block points rather than block groups, they reduce the impact of geographic approximation.

The next step in the site selection process is to select a model store with which to evaluate the market areas of available sites. You will perform this task using sales characteristics as criteria. These characteristics include factors such as total sales, total orders, sales and orders per customer, and number of customers.

Once the model store is identified, the next step is to find locations that match its market area profile. These locations become potential sites for the third store. Then you will evaluate the potential sites to determine which ones to eliminate. For example, some of the available sites may be in an area of the city that is zoned for residential use and not commercial. Some sites may be too close to your existing stores, creating the threat of cannibalization.

The final step is to compare the market areas of available sites with that of the model store. This comparison, combined with an assessment of the competitive environment in each of the available market areas, forms the basis for selecting the best new retail site.

Better Books San Francisco data dictionary	
Attribute	**Description**
For SFBlockgroups (ESRI)	
TOTPOP_CY	Population, 2003
TOTHH_CY	Households, 2003
AVGHHSZ_CY	Average Household Size, 2003
POPGRW00FY	Projected Annual Population Growth Rate, 2000–03
MEDAGE_CY	Median Age, 2003
DIVINDX_CY	Ethnic diversity index, higher is more diverse, USA Avg = 54.6
AVGHHINC_CY	Average Household Income, 2003
AVGNW_CY	Average Net Worth, 2003
AVGVAL_CY	Average Home Value, 2003
PCTSMCOL	Percent of Population Over 25 with Some College Education, 2003
PCTOWN	Percent of Households Owning Home, 2003
TotHHIncome	Total Income of all Households, 2003
For BBStores (Hypothetical)	
STORENAME	Name of the store location
ADDRESS	Store address in San Francisco
SALES	Sales in $US last year
For BBClubMembers (Hypothetical)	
CUST_ID	Customer's loyalty club identification number
NumOrders	Total number of orders by customer last year
TotPurchases	Total purchases by customer last year in $US
Store	Store location where customer buys
For SFBookstores (Hypothetical)	
SalesLevel	Approximate sales range last year in $US
StoreType	Type of ownership: independent, local/regional chain, or national chain
For AvailableProperties (Hypothetical)	
LOCATION	Location of property
SQFEET	Area of property in square feet
ZONED	Zoning classification of property
Source: ESRI Community Data, 2004; hypothetical data for this exercise	

Exercise 8.1 Explore demographics and competition in San Francisco

Before assessing available properties, you want to familiarize yourself with Better Books's competitive environment and San Francisco's demographic characteristics. Thus, in this exercise you will:

- Map the location of San Francisco's Better Books stores
- Map the location and sales levels of competing bookstores
- Explore key demographic characteristics of the San Francisco area with thematic maps

Open an existing map

1   **From the Windows taskbar, click Start > All Programs > ArcGIS > ArcMap.**

Depending on how ArcGIS and ArcMap have been installed or which Windows operating system you are using, there may be a slightly different navigation menu from which to open ArcMap.

2   **If you see an ArcMap startup window, choose "An existing map" and click OK. Otherwise, click the Open button 📂 on the Standard toolbar.**

3   **Browse to your \GISMKT\BetterBooksSF folder and open the BetterBooksSF1 map document.**

The initial map contains five layers. The Better Books Stores layer displays the location of these stores in San Francisco. The second displays the location of competing bookstores, and the three remaining layers display demographic characteristics of San Francisco at the block group level. Only the uppermost of these three layers is currently visible; the others are obscured by the layer above.

Edit a layer's symbology

While the map displays the location of competing bookstores, it does not reflect their competitive strength. You will edit the symbology of this layer to display stores by their level of sales.

1 In the table of contents, right-click the Competitor Stores layer and select Properties (or double-click the layer).

2 Click the Symbology tab.

3 In the Show area, click Categories, then Unique values.

4 In the Value Field area, click the drop-down arrow and choose SalesLevel from the list.

5 Uncheck <all other values>.

6 Click the Add All Values button to display the values for the SalesLevel field.

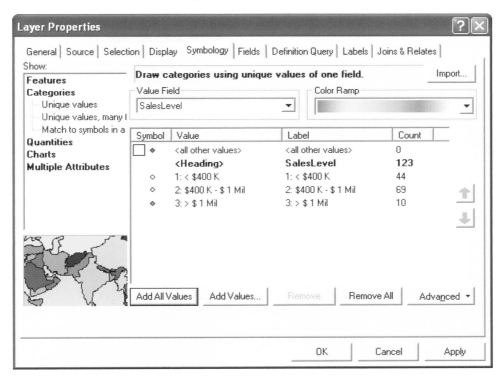

Your settings display stores by sales level using the small circles indicated. Though these symbols display the appropriate data, they are difficult to distinguish on the map. You will choose other symbols to make this layer more clear.

7 Double-click the symbol next to 1: < $400 K to display the Symbol Selector dialog box.

8 Click the Triangle 1 symbol to select it. Select Spruce Green (column 6, row 6) as the color, set the size to 10, and click OK.

9   Repeat this procedure for the remaining two symbols, selecting the same symbol and color in the Symbol Selector window. Set the size to 14 for the second symbol and 18 for the third symbol.

10 Click **OK** to close the Layer Properties dialog box.

The map now displays San Francisco bookstores with symbols that reflect their sales levels. This information allows you to more accurately assess the intensity of competition in a geographic area.

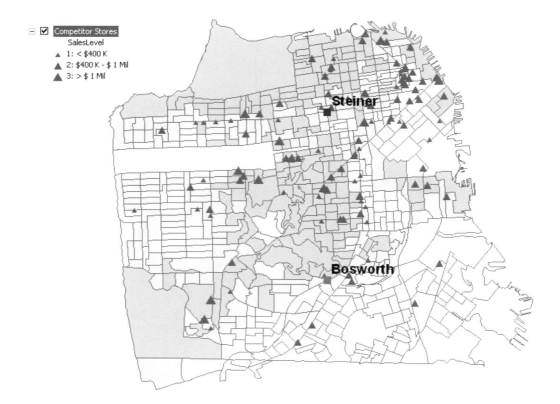

Add and display layers

Add a layer to the map

The table of contents contains thematic layers for three relevant demographic measures. However, a fourth measure, the average net worth of households, may influence the sales of collectible books in this market. You will add a layer to the map and symbolize it based on average net household worth.

1   Click the Add Data button. ✛

2   In the resulting window, navigate to **\GISMKT\BetterBooksSF\BetterBooksSF.mdb**. Double-click this geodatabase file to display the feature classes within it, then click the **SFBlockgroups** feature class.

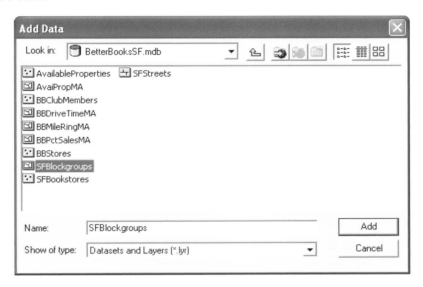

3   Click Add to add SFBlockgroups to the map.

The new layer is added to the table of contents and displays with a single color. You will now revise the layer properties to display average household net worth.

Rename and symbolize a layer

1   Open the properties of the SFBlockgroups layer.

2   Click the General tab and type **Average Household Net Worth** as the new layer name.

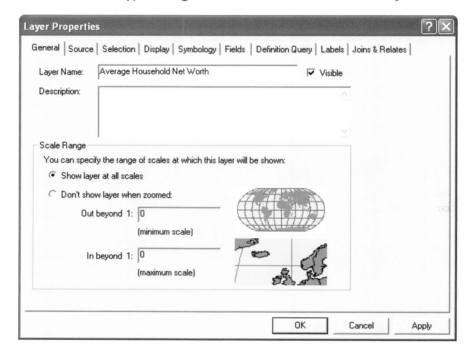

3   Click the Symbology tab.

4   In the Show area, click Quantities, then Graduated Colors.

5   In the Fields area, click the Value drop-down arrow and select the appropriate attribute from the list. (Use the data dictionary at the beginning of the chapter to identify the attribute that reports average net worth.)

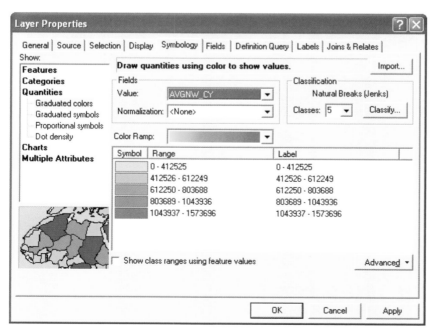

6 ArcMap randomly assigns a color scheme, and it might not be the best fit. Since this layer deals with money, you want to choose a graduated green color ramp. Right-click the color ramp, uncheck Graphic View, and from the Color Ramp drop-down list, select Green Bright.

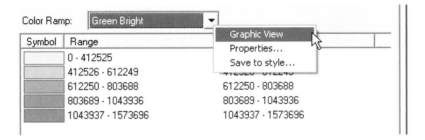

7 Click the Classify button to open the Classification dialog box.

Notice the default classification system in this dialog box. It uses five classes assigned by the natural breaks method, which creates classification ranges in the data based on inherent groupings of data points for the attribute. You will change these settings to achieve consistency with the other map layers.

8 From the drop-down menu for Method, select Quantile.

9 From the drop-down menu for Classes, select 3.

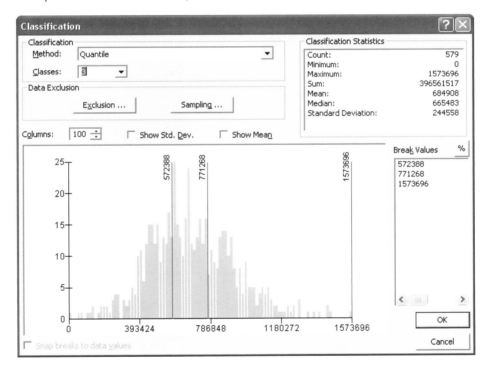

The quantile method will attempt to put an equal number of features (block groups) into each class. For example, there are 3 classes, and if there were 30 block groups, the quantile method would put 10 block groups into each class. So the color coding would show you the 10 highest block groups in one color, then the 10 middle ones in another color, and finally the lowest 10 in yet another color.

10 Click OK to return to the Symbology tab.

Change legend label format

You will now adjust the labels that will appear in the layer's legend. Since the values represent dollars, you will format the labels to look like currency.

1 Click the Label column heading, then click Format Labels to open the Number Format dialog box. (Note: Do not click the Labels tab at the top of the Layer Properties dialog box. If you do so inadvertently, click the Symbology tab to return.)

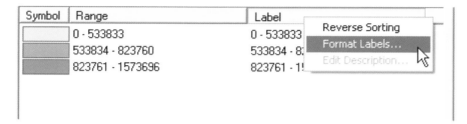

2 In the Category field, select Currency.

3 Click OK to return to the Symbology tab.

4 Check the "Show class ranges using feature values" box to define classification ranges using actual values from the dataset.

5 Click OK to close the Layer Properties dialog box and display the revised settings in the map.

Rename legend title

1   In the table of contents, click the AVGNW_CY heading under the layer name, then click again to edit it. (Note: If your second click is too quick, the Properties dialog box will open. Click Cancel, then try again, clicking more slowly to reach the edit function.)

2   Replace AVGNW_CY with **$US per household**.

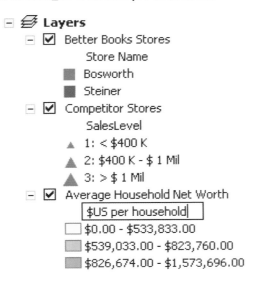

The resulting layer displays the average net household worth in each of San Francisco's block groups. This type of map, which displays the distribution of attribute data over a geographic area, is called a thematic map. It is commonly used to identify and illustrate patterns of variation in demographic data.

Visually analyze data

1   Visually compare the four demographic layers. Since some of the layers are on top of each other, you should turn off all the layers and then turn them back on one at a time. (Do this by clicking the check boxes in the table of contents to toggle the visibility.)

Notice the location of the Steiner and Bosworth stores. Note the predominant demographic characteristic near each store. For example, compare the average net household worth values around each store. Are the block groups around each store in the high, medium, or low range for this variable? Or are the stores in a mixed area?

Make sure to examine the competition. Where are the competing stores with high sales levels, and are they surrounded by similar demographic characteristics?

Your observations will help you answer the project report questions posed below.

Update report and save map document

1   Use the map layers to answer the following questions. Summarize your answers in the appropriate section of the project report template (BetterBooksSF_ReportTemplate.doc), which you will find in your \GISMKT\BetterBooksSF folder.

What do you observe about the geographic distribution of demographic measures in the San Francisco area and near the Better Books stores? About the distribution and sales levels of competing bookstores in the city and near the Better Books stores?

2   Save the map file as BetterBooksSF1_fl.mxd (replace f and l with your first and last initials). To do so, in ArcMap click File, then Save As. Navigate to your **\GISMKT\BetterBooksSF** folder, type **BetterBooksSF1_fl.mxd** as the file name, and click Save.

Exercise 8.2   Analyze customer and market area characteristics

To understand Better Books's current competitive position in San Francisco, you must analyze the firm's stores, their customers, and the market areas they serve. In this exercise, you will:

- Examine the geographic distribution and buying patterns of store customers
- Display a simple one-mile ring market area around each store
- Compare the demographic characteristics of the market areas of the two stores

Open an existing map

1   In ArcMap, open the **BetterBooksSF2** map document from your **\GISMKT\BetterBooksSF** folder.

The Better Books Stores layer displays the Steiner and Bosworth stores. The Percent with Some College layer displays by block group the percentage of persons with some college education. Two other layers are included in the map but are turned off: one depicting the location of Book Lovers Club members, and the other, one-mile market area rings around the Bosworth and Steiner stores.

Create a data summary table

Open a layer attribute table to display its contents

1 **Turn on the Book Lovers Club Members layer.**

This layer displays the residential location of each member of the Books Lovers Club with markers color-coded to indicate each customer's store preference.

The attribute table for the Book Lovers Club Members layer contains sales data for each club member. Performing a summary operation on this table will allow you to analyze this data.

2 **Right-click the Book Lovers Club Members layer, then click Open Attribute Table.**

The table displays the attributes for each club member. Note that the store affiliation of each member is captured in the Store attribute. You will use this attribute to create a summary table of the purchasing patterns of the members affiliated with each store.

Summarize feature attributes

1   Right-click the column header for the Store attribute, then click Summarize to open the Summarize dialog box.

2   Confirm that Store is listed as the summary field in step 1.

3   In step 2, expand NumOrders, then select Sum.

This setting indicates that you wish to calculate the total number of orders made by club members for each of the two stores.

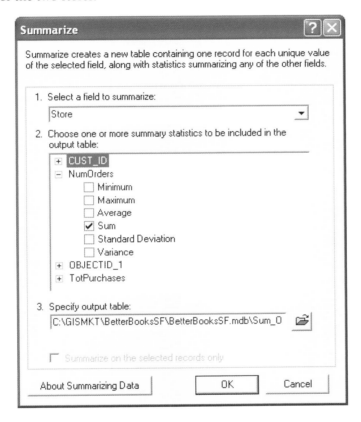

4   Now expand TotPurchases and select Sum.

5   Click the Browse button to the right of step 3 to open the Saving Data dialog box.

6   For the Save as type option, choose File and Personal Geodatabase tables.

7   Navigate to the **\GISMKT\BetterBooksSF** folder and double-click **BetterBooksSF.mdb**.

8 Replace the default name with **StoreSalesSummary**, then click Save to return to the Summarize dialog box.

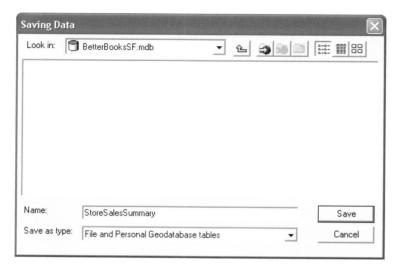

9 Click OK to create the summary table.

10 Click Yes when asked if you want to add the result table to the map.

11 Close the attribute table.

The summary table now appears in the table of contents as StoreSalesSummary.

12 Right-click the StoreSalesSummary table, then click Open to view the number of members in each store's book club as well as comparative sales data for them.

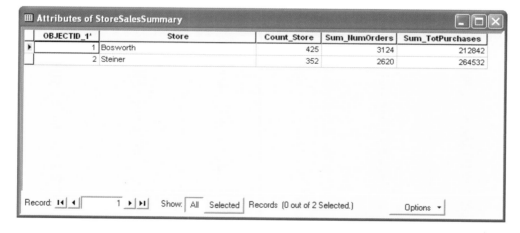

In this table, the Count_Store field reports the number of Book Lovers in the club for each store. The Sum_NumOrders field reports the number of orders they have placed with that store and Sum_TotPurchases reports the dollar value of those purchases.

13 Close the table.

Explore market areas

A retail store's market area is the geographic region from which it draws most of its customers. As you can see on the current map, Book Lovers Club members are distributed across San Francisco, but they are more heavily clustered in the vicinity of the store in which they shop. Several different market area models are used in retail site analysis. The most basic is a simple buffer ring at a specified distance from the store. You will employ that approach in this task with a simple one-mile ring. You will then compare the market areas of the two stores by selecting the block groups they include and calculating demographic measures for them.

Select club members within the market areas

1 Turn on the BB Stores Market Area layer.

A circle now appears at a constant one-mile radius around each store. This is the simple ring definition of the stores' market areas.

While many club members live outside these rings, it appears that most of them live within the market areas. You will determine the percentage of Book Lovers living within the market areas with a selection query based on location.

2 From the main menu bar, click Selection > Select by Location.

3 In the Select by Location dialog box, create a statement that says: *I want to select features from the Book Lovers Club Members layer that are completely within the BB Stores Market Area layer.*

The Select by Location dialog box should look like the following graphic.

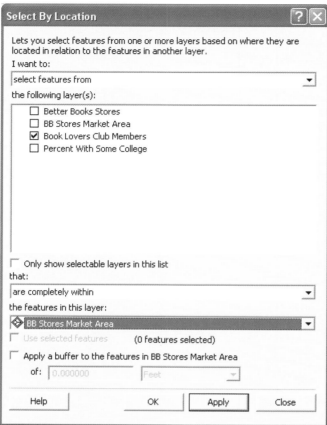

4   **Click Apply, then Close to perform the selection.**

5   **Open the attribute table for the Book Lovers Club Members layer. Note the number of features in the layer and the number of selected features at the bottom of the table. Use this figure to calculate the percentage of club members living within the two market areas. To do so, divide the number of selected features by the total number of features.**

 The percentage of Book Lovers Club members living within the two market areas is ___ percent.

6   **At the bottom of the attribute table, click Options > Clear Selection, then close the table.**

7   **Zoom in on the Steiner market area at the top of the screen.**

Notice that some of the club members in the Steiner area are actually affiliated with the Bosworth store, though they don't live in the market area for that store. In fact, seventeen club members fall into this category, which somewhat reduces the percentage you calculated above; however, the fact is a substantial majority of club members live within the market areas of their affiliated stores, so the percentage is fairly accurate.

Select block groups within the market areas

1   **Turn off the Book Lovers Club Members layer.**

This allows you to see the block groups in each market area more clearly. Using the Steiner store as an example, you will select the block groups within the store's market area and use them to estimate the demographic characteristics of the market area.

2   **Right-click the BB Stores Market Area layer, then click Selection > Make This The Only Selectable Layer.**

This setting allows you to select features from this layer without simultaneously selecting features from other layers.

3   **On the Tools toolbar, click the Select Features tool.**

4   **Click on the Steiner store ring outline to select it. (If you miss, click it again.)**

The one-mile ring of the Steiner market area is now highlighted, indicating that it is selected. You will now create a selection of block groups whose centers fall within this boundary. The majority of the area of the selected block groups will lie within the market area, though some portions will be beyond it.

5   **From the main menu bar, click Selection > Select by Location.**

6 In the Select by Location dialog box, create a statement that says: *I want to select features from the Percent With Some College layer that have their centroid in the BB Stores Market Area layer.*

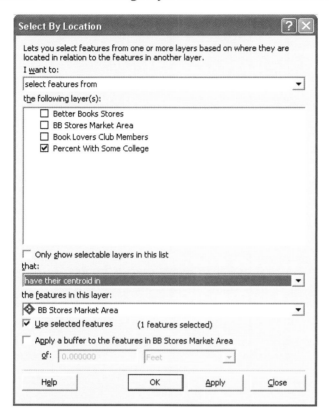

All the block groups with a center within the highlighted ring on the map will be selected.

7 Make sure that the Use selected features option is checked, click Apply to perform the operation, then click Close.

The block groups within the highlighted circular market area are now highlighted. You will now estimate the demographic characteristics for this market area by performing calculations on the attributes of the selected block groups.

Perform calculations on selected features

1   Open the attribute table for the Percent with Some College layer, then click the Selected button at the bottom of the table to display only the 82 selected records.

2   Scroll to the right of the table to find the TotalHHIncome attribute. Right-click the column header for this attribute, then click Statistics to calculate statistics for the selected features.

The descriptive statistics are reported in the Selection Statistics window.

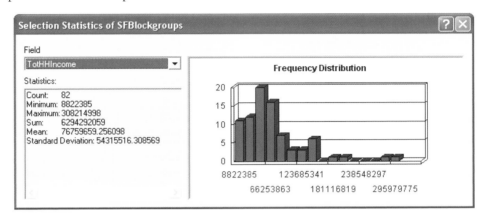

3   Record the Sum value as the total income for the selected features below.

4   Now calculate statistics for the TOTHH_CY field. Record the Sum value as total households for the selected features below. On your own, calculate the average household income for households in the selected block groups.

For the selected block groups around the Steiner store,
total income is _____,
the total number of households is _____, and
average household income is _____ (total income divided by total households).

While it was easy to figure out average household income for the selected block groups, it is more difficult to determine other statistics. For example, a precise calculation for average home value would be considerably more involved. Instead, you will estimate this value by calculating the mean of the average home value attribute among the selected block groups.

5   Right-click the column header for the AVGVAL-CY attribute, then click Statistics. Record the Mean of this field for the selected features below.

For the selected block groups, the average value for the AVGVAL_CY attribute is $ ____.

This is your estimate for average home value for the Steiner market area. This estimate is subject to the computational limitations identified in the introduction. As an unweighted average of block group values, this estimate can only approximate the true average home value of households in this area. However, it can still be useful in revealing general patterns of variation between demographic characteristics of the two market areas.

6   Close the statistics window and attribute table.

7   In the map, compare the boundaries of the market area and the selected block groups.

Portions of some selected block groups lie outside the market area. Households in these areas are included in the demographic calculations, but should not be. In addition, some block groups are not selected even though portions of them lie within the market area. Households in these areas should be included in the demographic calculations, but are not. As a result, the demographic calculations you have made do not cover the exact set of households in the designated market area.

To obtain more precise measures of its market area characteristics, Better Books has obtained market area reports from ArcGIS Business Analyst. These reports are based on smaller geographic units, and therefore offer more precise estimates. The report for the one-mile ring market area definition for these two stores follows. Use it to compare the demographic characteristics of the market areas for the Steiner and Bosworth stores.

Market area report Better Books San Francisco: Site selection project Market area definition: One-mile ring		
Population measures	**Steiner** One-mile ring	**Bosworth** One-mile ring
Total population	88,502	41,789
Annual population growth rate	0.6%	0.1%
Households	46,839	14,791
Average household size	1.81	2.78
Median age	37.5	39.1
Diversity index	47.7	49.6
Income and wealth measures		
Average household income	$103,188	$96,268
Average net worth	$739,566	$631,537
Average home valuation	$637,353	$421,505

Update report and save map document

1   Use the map and market area report to answer the questions below. Summarize your answers in the appropriate section of the project report template (BetterBooksSF_ReportTemplate.doc), which you will find in your \GISMKT\BetterBooksSF folder.

How densely are customers clustered around the store where they shop? Is there any geographic crossover between the stores? How do the purchase patterns of Book Lovers Club members differ between the Steiner and Bosworth stores? How do the demographic characteristics of one-mile ring market areas differ between the two stores?

2   Save your map file as **BetterBooksSF2_fl.mxd** (replace f and l with your first and last initials) in your **\GISMKT\BetterBooksSF** folder.

Exercise 8.3   Review other market area models and select model store

Market areas may be defined in different ways, with different models more relevant to specific firms and situations. You should consider several market area approaches in your analysis. Therefore, in this exercise you will:

- Display two additional market area models on your map
- Review market area reports based on these models
- Identify the most appropriate approach, then select one of the Better Books stores to serve as a model for evaluating prospective sites

Open an existing map

1   In ArcMap open **BetterBooksSF3.mxd** from your **\GISMKT\BetterBooksSF** folder.

This map displays the Better Books stores, one-mile ring market areas, and Book Lovers Club members over a thematic map of household income for San Francisco's block groups. Two other layers in the table of contents contain market area models based on sales and drive-time, but they are not displayed.

You have already reviewed the market area report for the one-mile ring model. You will now examine the visual representation of a second and third approach to market area definition, and then review the reports that correspond to those approaches.

The second approach defines market areas by the percentage of Better Books's total sales that they contain. You will find this approach represented on the map by the BB Stores Sales Market Areas (Percent of sales) layer.

Display and modify layers

1   **Turn on the BB Stores Sales Market Areas 2 layer (Percent of sales).**

The layer is composed of two irregular polygons surrounding the Bosworth and Steiner stores. For each store, 60 percent of club sales are made to members in the inner polygon and another 20 percent to members in the outer. Taken together, the two polygons account for 80 percent of sales to club members.

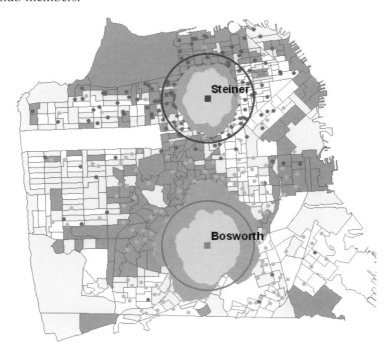

As this layer is represented in solid colors, it obscures the point symbols representing the customers. You will adjust the transparency of this layer to make lower layers visible.

2   **Right-click the layer name in the table of contents, then click Properties (or double-click the layer) to open the Layer Properties dialog box.**

3   **Click the Display tab.**

4   **Change the transparency to 33%.**

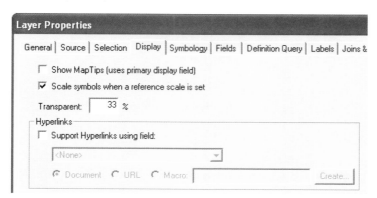

5 **Click OK to close the dialog box and apply the transparency to the map.**

The market area polygons are now semitransparent, revealing the customer and block group layers beneath them.

6 **Zoom in on one market area, and then pan to the other to see each in more detail. Note their geographic area relative to the one-mile rings.**

 How do the sizes of the sales-related market areas compare with the one-mile ring market areas?

Review the market area report for this model on the following page. Note that, in this report, attribute values are reported separately for each polygon. That is, the values in the 0–60% column are for households located within the inner polygon. Those in the 60–80% column are for households located beyond the boundary of the inner polygon, but within the boundary of the second.

 What conclusions can you draw about the differences in the percentage of sales market areas for the two stores?

Better Books San Francisco site selection project Market area definition: Percentage of store club sales				
Population measures	**Steiner**		**Bosworth**	
	0–60%	**60–80%**	**0–60%**	**60–80%**
Total population	32,919	19,626	38,247	26,420
Annual population growth rate	1.2%	0.0%	0.0%	0.2%
Households	17,487	10,444	15,406	9,046
Average household size	1.84	1.82	2.47	2.86
Median age	39.0	36.9	39.1	38.8
Diversity index	50.1	31.4	40.5	46.1
Income and wealth measures				
Average household income	$95,438	$116,812	$106,704	$93,007
Average net worth	$759,420	$754,691	$660,690	$632,204
Average home valuation	$601,062	$448,241	$332,565	$423,537

The third market area model is based on drive time. It assumes that accessibility of a retail location is not based on geographic distance, but on travel time to get to that location. It assumes further that most customers will drive to the location rather than walk or use public transportation. If these assumptions are true for Better Books's retail locations, then drive time is a reasonable measure of the accessibility of that location.

7   Turn off the BB Stores Market Areas 2 layer, and turn on the BB Stores Market Areas 3 layer (Drive Time Polygons).

8   If necessary, zoom out to the full extent of the map.

9   Open the layer properties for the BB Stores Market Area 3 layer, and click the Display tab.

10   Change the transparency to **50**%. Click OK to close the dialog box and apply the transparency to the layer.

The drive-time layer is now semitransparent. Note the shape of its polygons relative to the other market area models.

What produces the irregular shape of the drive-time polygons? Do they reflect the geographic distribution of store customers?

Review the market area report for this model. Note that, in this report, attribute values are reported for each polygon separately. That is, the values in the 1–3 minutes column are for households located beyond the boundary of the inner polygon but within the boundary of the second.

Better Books San Francisco site selection project				
Market area definition: Drive time				
Population measures	**Steiner**		**Bosworth**	
	0–1 minute	**1–3 minutes**	**0–1 minute**	**1–3 minutes**
Total population	12,745	128,366	4,074	59,073
Annual population growth rate	1.4%	0.5%	0.2%	0.1%
Households	6,466	69,923	1,539	21,803
Average household size	1.91	1.76	2.62	2.68
Median age	37.3	37.6	39.8	38.4
Diversity index	48.8	47.4	36.3	52.2
Income and wealth measures				
Average household income	$80,034	$94,974	$100,960	$95,119
Average net worth	$692,544	$691,732	$614,901	$640,345
Average home valuation	$532,245	$589,419	$422,310	$377,294

Make a recommendation

1 Review the three market area models you have seen. You will record your recommendation in the project report. Which of the three market area models reflects the distribution of Book Lovers Club members most accurately? The concentration of sales? This is the most appropriate market area model for your project.

To evaluate new sites, you must select a model store with which to compare them. Which store, Steiner or Bosworth, do you recommend for this purpose? To make this decision, compare the stores' number of club members, orders, and total sales. Which store is the most productive in sales, sales per order, and sales per member? Examine the demographic characteristics in the market area reports as well. Which store has higher population and number of households? The more rapidly growing population? Which has the higher levels of household income? Which has the higher levels of net worth, which might be relevant for collectors who buy collectible books as investments? Based on all these factors, decide which store you will recommend as the model store.

Update report and save map document

1 Use the map layers, reports, and your conclusions about the relative competitive environments of the stores to answer the following questions. Summarize your answers in the appropriate section of the project report template.

How do the market areas for the two stores differ? Which market area approach is most appropriate for this analysis? Why? Which of the two stores should serve as the "model store" for the firm's planned new store? Why?

2 Save the map document as **BetterBooksSF3_fl.mxd** (replace f and l with your first and last initials) in your **\GISMKT\BetterBooksSF** folder.

Exercise 8.4   Evaluate available properties and their market areas

You have determined the demographic characteristics of existing stores and identified the model store. You are ready to evaluate the attractiveness of available properties in the San Francisco area. Thus, in this task, you will:

- Identify available properties and display their locations
- Eliminate properties that are improperly zoned or too close to existing stores
- Create one-mile ring market areas for the remaining properties and evaluate their characteristics
- Select the property you will recommend for the third Better Books store

Open an existing map

1   Open **BetterBooksSF4.mxd** from your **\GISMKT\BetterBooksSF** folder.

This map contains six layers. They display the two Better Books stores and the book club members per store. The one-mile rings for the two stores are also displayed. Though possibly not your preferred method, these rings do account for more than 80 percent of the club member sales at the Steiner store and more than 60 percent at the Bosworth store. It is also the method that will be used to evaluate candidate sites for the third store, as these sites lack comparable sales data. There is also a layer of competing bookstores, as well as a layer for available commercial sites for the third Better Books store.

Examine map features

1 Take a look at the Available Properties layer, which displays the commercial properties available for purchase or lease in San Francisco.

There are six properties, each labeled with its location. Your first step is to eliminate from consideration those properties that are not zoned retail or that are too close to existing stores.

2 Right-click Available Properties in the table of contents, then click Open Attribute Table to view the attributes of the features in this layer.

3 Find the feature that is zoned as industrial and click in the small gray box to the left of this feature to select it. Move the table, if necessary, to view the map, noting that this site is highlighted on the map as well as in the table.

Make a note of this feature and do not include it in the remaining steps of your analysis.

OBJECTID_1	Shape*	SQFEET	ZONED	Location
1	Point	2500	Retail	Northwest
2	Point	3385	Retail	Southeast
3	Point	2268	Retail	Southwest
4	Point	3250	Retail	Northeast
5	Point	9054	Industrial	North Central
6	Point	2157	Retail	East Central

4 Examine the layer more closely, using the Zoom, Pan, and Identify tools as needed.

Do any properties fall within the one-mile ring market areas of the Steiner or Bosworth stores? If so, eliminate them from consideration as well.

 Which stores will be excluded from consideration?

Having eliminated three locations from consideration, you will create and evaluate market areas for the remaining three.

Select potential sites and create market areas for them

You want to create one-mile market area rings for the three available properties. To do so, you must select those locations, then use the Buffer tool to create the market area for them.

Make a selection

1 In the attribute table, click the small box to the left of one of the properties you wish to select. Confirm that this layer is highlighted on the map.

2 Depress and hold the Ctrl key. Click the small box to the left of the second property you wish to select. Confirm its selection on the map. Select the third property in the same way. (Note: If you select a property in error, simply click it again to unselect it.)

The attribute table and map both highlight the sites for which you wish to create market area rings.

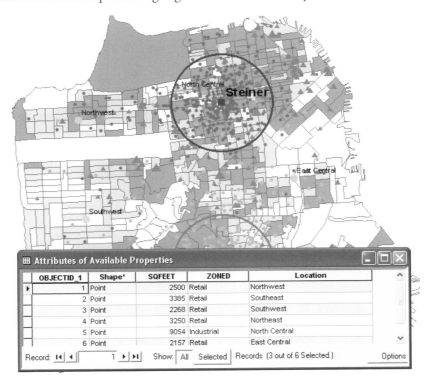

3 Close the attribute table.

Create buffers

You will now create a one-mile market area ring for each of the selected properties using the Buffer tool from ArcToolbox.

1 Click the ArcToolbox button 🎲 on the Standard toolbar to open ArcToolbox.

2 Expand Analysis Tools, then expand the Proximity toolset to view the Buffer tool.

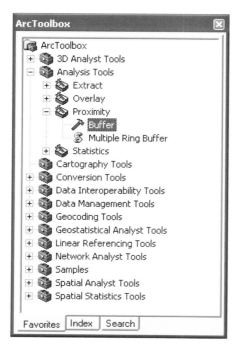

3 Double-click the Buffer tool to open its dialog box.

4 For Input Features, click the drop-down arrow and choose Available Properties.

5 For Output Feature Class click the Browse button and navigate to the **BetterBooksSF.mdb** personal geodatabase.

6 Type **AvailablePropertiesMA** in the Name field.

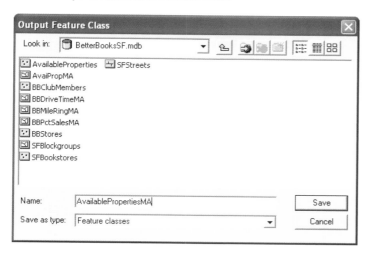

7 Click Save.

8 Under Distance, for Linear unit type **1**, and in the drop-down menu, select Miles.

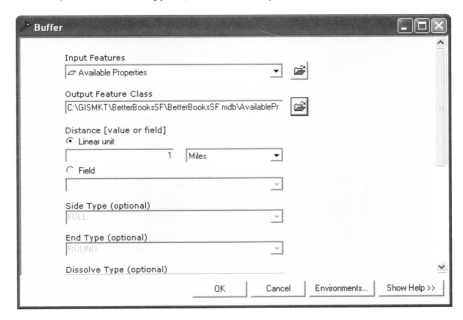

9 Click **OK** to execute the Buffer operation. When the operation is complete, close the progress window if necessary. Close ArcToolbox as well.

The new layer appears in the table of contents and is displayed on the map in solid circles of a single color. (Your color may differ from the following graphic.) Next you will revise the display properties of this layer to make it clearer.

10   In the table of contents, click the symbol under AvailablePropertiesMA to open the Symbol Selector dialog box.

11   For Fill Color, select No Color. Set the Outline Width setting to 2. For Outline Color, select Seville Orange (row 4, column 4).

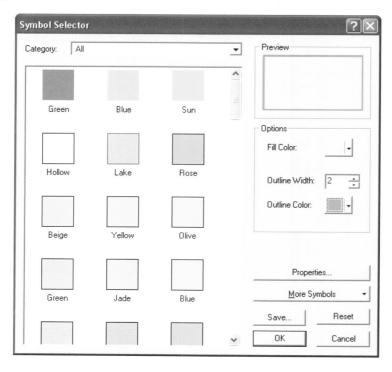

12   Click OK to apply the new settings.

13   Click the layer name in the table of contents, then click it again to edit it. Change the name to **Available Properties Market Areas**. (Note: If your second click is too quick, the Properties dialog box will open. Click Cancel, then try again, clicking more slowly to reach the edit function.)

14   Click the empty text box next to the new buffer symbol, then click again to reach the edit function. Enter **One-mile rings** for the legend title.

The map now displays a one-mile ring market area around each of the three properties still under consideration for the third store. To select the site for the third store, you will review the characteristics of the block groups in each of these three market areas. The market area report, following, contains this data.

Better Books San Francisco site selection project		
Market areas for available sites		
Market area definition: One-mile ring		
Population measures	**Southwest**	**Northwest**	**East Central**
	One-mile ring	One-mile ring	One-mile ring
Total population	52,618	46,567	61,836
Annual population growth rate	0.16%	0.06%	0.8%
Households	18,406	18,812	21,630
Average household size	2.52	2.36	2.55
Median age	37.0	38.7	30.9
Diversity index	51.0	56.6	74.9
Income and wealth measures			
Average household income	$80,135	$91,742	$82,990
Average net worth	$588,466	$682,075	$552,539
Average home valuation	$401,716	$544,172	$464,133

Update report and save map document

1 Use the map and table you have created to answer the following questions. Summarize your answers in the appropriate section of the project report template.

What differences do you find between the market area characteristics of the three potential sites? Which site's market area most closely resembles that of the model store?

2 Save your map file as **BetterBooksSF4_fl.mxd** (replace f and l with your first and last initials) in your **\GISMKT\BetterBooksSF** folder.

Exercise 8.5 Recommend a new site

As the conclusion to your analysis, you must recommend one of the three eligible sites for the new Better Books store in San Francisco. Therefore, in this exercise, you will:

• Review the comparative market area and competitive data you have analyzed
• Identify the property you selected for the third Better Books store in San Francisco
• Design a supporting map

Open an existing map

1   In ArcMap, open **BetterBooksSF5.mxd** from your **\GISMKT\BetterBooksSF** folder.

This map opens in layout view. The table of contents displays two data frames, each of which contains several layers. The upper data frame displays layers for available properties and associated market areas as well as the Steiner and Bosworth stores and their market areas. It also displays a Competitor Stores layer and a demographic layer depicting the number of households by block group. The lower data frame duplicates several of these layers. The use of two data frames in the table of contents supports two different map images on the layout page. Right now, these images appear identical. You will change the lower data frame to display your recommended location for the third Better Books store.

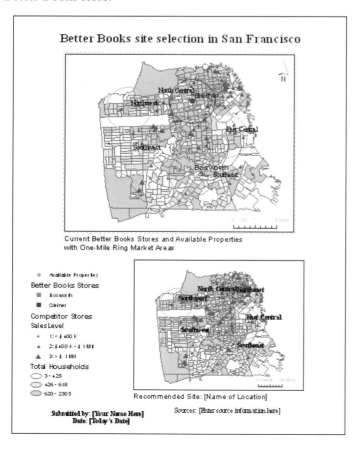

Change map extent in layout view

The data frame in the lower right portion of the layout is designed to display a zoomed-in view of the location you will recommend to Better Books for expansion. You will zoom to that location to display it on the map.

1 **On the Tools toolbar, click the Zoom In tool.** ⊕ **(Note: You should not use the Zoom In tool on the Layout toolbar for this step.)**

2 **Use the Zoom In tool to make a box around your recommended location's one-mile buffer circle in the lower data frame. (Note: Your location may differ from that shown in the following graphics.)**

The lower data frame is now zoomed to the area you designated. If this is not the result you desire, adjust the display with the navigation tools or click the Full Extent button to return to the original display and repeat the zoom operation.

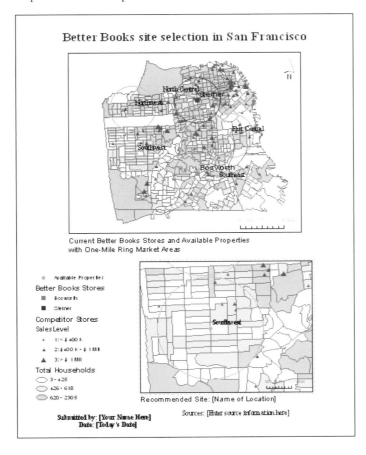

Edit text boxes in layout

1   Click the Select Elements tool. At the bottom of the page, click the text box that includes the Submitted by and Date elements.

2   Right-click the text box, then click Properties.

3   In the Properties dialog box, replace the placeholder text with your name and today's date, then click OK to accept the changes.

4   Now select the Sources text box, then right-click and choose Properties.

5   Replace the placeholder text with **Better Books Internal Data** on the first line and, on the next line, **ESRI Community Data, 2005**.

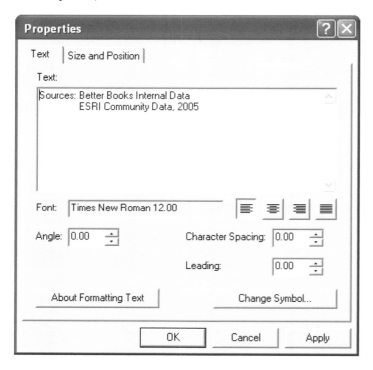

6   Click OK to accept the changes.

7   Open the properties for the Recommended Site text box, and replace the placeholder text with the name of the location you will recommend to Better Books. Click OK to accept the changes.

The layout is now ready to be presented as exhibit 1 in your report. You will save it as a graphic file and insert it into the report template.

Export map and insert it into a report

1   From the main menu bar, click File > Export Map to reach the Export Map dialog box. Navigate to the **\GISMKT\BetterBooksSF** folder. For File Name, type **SiteRec.emf**, then click Save to save the map document as a graphic file in EMF format to include in your report.

2   Open the report template and navigate to the end of the report. For exhibit 1, select the instructional text, then from the main menu bar in Microsoft Word click Insert > Picture > From File. Navigate to the **\GISMKT\BetterBooksSF** folder and select the **SiteRec.emf** file. Click Insert to insert the picture into the report as exhibit 1. (Note: You may have to select and resize the image to display it on the same page as the title.)

Exhibit 1 of your report is now complete.

Update report and save map document

1   Use your previous analysis and the map you have created to answer the questions below. Summarize your response in the appropriate section of the project report template.

Based on market area comparisons and the competitive environment, which property do you recommend for Better Books's third retail location in San Francisco? Why?

2   Save the map document as **BetterBooksSF5_fl.mxd** (replace f and l with your first and last initials) in your **\GISMKT\BetterBooksSF** folder.

Congratulations! You have completed the Better Books project.

Stop for a minute or two to reflect on what you accomplished in this chapter. You displayed the demographic characteristics of San Francisco and the competitive strength of its retail bookstores on a map. You learned three different ways of defining the market area of a retail store and how to compare the demographic characteristics of multiple stores. You evaluated the attractiveness of alternative locations for new stores and matched them with a model store whose market area characteristics you wished to duplicate. In brief, you have learned how to use ArcGIS in the retail site selection process.

Additional applications

Though this exercise illustrates the general process of site selection, it has some weaknesses. First, it ignores features such as parks, limited street access, and bodies of water that might impact accessibility within market areas. Second, it does not include quantitative estimates of the drawing power of Better Books and competitors' stores. This can be a function of each store's presence and appeal within an attractive concentration of stores (e.g., malls, shopping centers, galleries, pedestrian areas). Third, it assumes that consumers shop in only one bookstore. How many different bookstores (or restaurants, theaters, clothing, or music stores for that matter) do you frequent? Fourth, it assumes that cannibalism of sales from existing stores should eliminate prospective sites. While this assumption sounds reasonable, it is not always applicable. For example, a nearby site with favorable demographics may well reduce sales in existing stores. While this is not the optimal result, these sales are still to Better Books. However, if a competitor bought this site, a third Better Books store would not get these sales, but a competitor would. Which is the better option—internal cannibalization or sales lost to a competitor?

More sophisticated site selection tools improve the process by addressing these factors. Retail gravity models use the relationship between some attractiveness measure (such as square feet of shopping area) and some distance measure (such as geographic distance and drive time) to predict shopping patterns between stores. Gold's Gym has used this type of approach to evaluate the attractiveness and potential internal cannibalization of adding new locations to markets with existing franchises.[1]

Other approaches incorporate data on the daytime population of an area (i.e., persons who work in the area rather than live there) to include purchasing behavior during working hours. Chase Manhattan Bank used this approach to expand its services to the daytime population of its service areas.[2]

Market penetration approaches such as the Huff model[3] integrate survey data on consumer shopping preferences with multiattribute models of store attractiveness to analyze probabilities that consumers will shop at one store rather than another. The Credit Union of Texas used this type of approach to locate new branches with the dual objective of attracting new customers and reducing traffic at existing branches that customers perceived as overcrowded.[4]

Specialized site selection software providers and GIS software firms offer packages that have borne fruit for firms such as Dunkin Brands, the parent company of Dunkin' Donuts, Baskin-Robbins and Togo's, and Carvel Ice Cream.[5]

The ESRI ArcGIS Business Analyst system offers an impressive array of trade area analysis and site selection features. It allows firms to integrate their internal sales and customer records with a substantial collection of demographic and lifestyle data for consumers to perform customer profiling. It also contains data on businesses and shopping centers to facilitate competitive analysis. Once they use these tools to understand the characteristics of existing stores, customers, and trade areas, firms can then use Business Analyst segmentation and prospecting tools to find attractive potential sites across town or across the United States.[6]

Recent trends in retailing have included the growth of electronic retailing and the integration of eCommerce operations within traditional retailing strategies, a "clicks and mortar" approach. The major appeals of electronic shopping include the ability to shop from home (or quite commonly, it seems, from the office) and the ability to compare prices from geographically disbursed sellers and order the most favorable combination of product, delivery, and customer service. In this context, location has seemingly disappeared from the retail equation. This is not, however, the case. Traditional retailers such as Circuit City[7] use Web-based GIS applications to help customers identify and find their local stores. Some retailers offer customers the option of shopping electronically and picking up purchases at their local store. Even purely electronic retailers can use GIS systems to profile customers and Web site users in order to devise more effective marketing strategies. The World Treasures scenario in chapter 6 illustrates this GIS application.

1. Christian Harder, *ArcView GIS Means Business,* Redlands, CA: ESRI Press, 1997.

2. Harder, Ibid.

3. Ela Dramowicz, "Retail Trade Area Analysis Using the Huff Model," *Directions,* June 29, 2005.

4. David Boyles, *GIS Means Business: Volume Two,* Redlands, CA: ESRI Press, 2002.

5. Ryan Chittum, "Location, Location, Technology," *The Wall Street Journal,* July 18, 2005.

6. Gary Burgess and David Huffman, "Introducing ArcGIS9 Business Analyst," ESRI GeoInfo Business Summit, April 18–19, 2005.

7. Circuit City's site locator service is at the following URL: *http://www.circuitcity.com/ccd/locator.do*

CHAPTER 9

Managing Sales Territories

Course: Personal Selling/Sales Management

This chapter covers the process of defining and managing sales territories. Northwest's Best (NWB)* is a new wine distributor in Portland, Oregon. It specializes in fine wines from Washington and Oregon vineyards. The firm plans to sell these wines to liquor stores and restaurants in the Portland area through a three-person sales team. The firm must define the territories to balance the sales potential and workload equitably among the sales representatives. In this process, you will use GIS tools to map the geographic distribution of businesses and wine consumers, assess alternative sales territory systems to identify the best one, and determine the optimal route for a series of sales calls.

* This is a fictional company and scenario, created for educational purposes only. Any resemblance to actual persons, events, or corporations is unintended.

Learning objectives

To manage NWB's sales territory system in Portland, you will learn how to use ArcGIS to:

1. Symbolize wine purchasing patterns and business prospect characteristics on a map
2. Select prospects and assign them to territories
3. Evaluate alternative territory systems with summary tables and visual analysis
4. Create a map to communicate territory characteristics and support recommendations
5. Use network functionality to determine the optimal driving route for sales calls

Marketing scenario

Mark Carter is the owner of Northwest's Best, Inc. He has experience as a buyer for a large wine retailer in San Francisco. In that capacity he became acquainted with a number of wines and vineyards in the Pacific Northwest. Convinced that consumers underappreciated these high-quality wines, Carter left his position, moved to Portland, and founded a distributorship that specializes in wines from vineyards in Washington and Oregon. He believes that these wines will become more popular as consumers and restaurant owners become familiar with their quality and value. He hopes to hasten that process by promoting them exclusively, resulting in higher sales and wider distribution for his firm and the vineyards he represents.

Carter has convinced several Washington and Oregon vintners to give Northwest's Best exclusive distribution rights for their products in the Portland metropolitan area. His goal is to demonstrate the success and profitability of his business model in this area, then expand to other markets through internal growth and franchising. His market is Portland-area liquor stores and full-service restaurants that serve alcoholic beverages. The restaurant data in this project includes only those in this category.

Having secured distribution rights from an impressive selection of vineyards, Carter has hired you to manage the firm's sales operations. As sales manager, you must identify prospective customers in the Portland area and assign them to sales territories. At your request, he has acquired consumer purchasing data as well as sales potential data for area liquor stores and restaurants. Based on this data, you estimate that an initial staff of three sales representatives is necessary to serve the market effectively. Your next task is to define three sales territories, with one sales representative servicing each.

In designing a territory system, your primary objective is to balance the workload and income opportunities among the sales staff. Your guidelines are that the number of prospects in the three territories should vary by no more than two and that no territory should have total sales potential more than 5 percent above or below the territory average. Your secondary objective is to achieve driving efficiency within territories. Driving efficiency is high if there are few prospects in a territory located away from major highways and if the most direct driving routes between prospects lie within their assigned territory.

Once sales territories are established and accounts assigned, you must implement a routing system to help sales representatives minimize driving time. The initial emphasis will be on prospects with the largest sales potential. Using the one sales territory as an example, you will determine the best route to reach the 10 largest accounts.

To accomplish these tasks, you will use ArcGIS tools to define Northwest's Best's sales territories in the Portland market area, and the ArcGIS Network Analyst extension to solve the sales call routing problem.

Background information

Sales territory creation, revision, and management are among the key responsibilities of a sales manager. They impact all aspects of sales performance. Territories that are too geographically dispersed are inefficient, requiring excessive travel time. When businesses create territories with workload demands that are beyond the resources of their sales representatives, they risk underserved customers, lost potential sales, and frustrated sales reps. Unbalanced sales potential among territories can lead to a disgruntled and unmotivated sales force. Territory adjustments that are not sensitive to established personal and professional relationships create difficulties with both sales representatives and customers.

Spatial analysis capabilities provided by GIS tools are a valuable resource in this vital function. They allow sales managers to visually understand the relationship between territory boundaries, travel routes, customers, and sales potential in a specific territory structure. GIS users can immediately see the impact of adjusting boundaries on a map. Moreover, as users link the visual data to underlying data tables of historical and potential sales, they can measure the impact quantitatively as well. Thus, the sales manager is able to evaluate alternative sales territory structures or revisions quickly and comprehensively. For large organizations, GIS extensions designed specifically for territory management automate much of this process, allowing sales managers to administer more extensive territory structures effectively.

Within sales territories, sales call routing is a key function of sales management. Efficient routes reduce transportation costs, increase the ratio of selling time to driving time, and increase the number of calls a sales representative can make. When integrated with customer data and information on account characteristics, it also has a role in the broader tasks of scheduling customer contacts and prioritizing accounts. In addition, implementation of routing systems within mobile networking and Global Positioning System (GPS) tracking systems allows sales representatives and managers to manage these tasks minute-by-minute throughout the workday.

In short, designing sales territory systems that match the organization's objectives and optimize the efficiency of sales call routes are important goals of sales managers. In the following exercises, you will pursue these goals using the tools and functions available in ArcGIS.

Northwest's Best Portland Metro Area data dictionary	
Attribute	**Description**
For CensusTracts (ESRI)	
NAME	Census tract
TOTHH_CY	Households, 2004
AVGHHSIZ_CY	Average household size, 2004
RestaurantsHH	Total purchases of meals at restaurants, 2004
AlcBevHH	Total purchases of alcoholic beverages, 2004
For MajorRoads (ESRI)	
OBJECTID	Road identification number
Name	Road name
Type	Limited access, primary highway, or secondary highway
For Prospects (Hypothetical)	
OBJECTID	Identification number for the store
SalesPotential	Estimated potential annual purchases from NWB
Type	Liquor store or restaurant
For NETerritoryStreets and associated network dataset	
OBJECTID	Street identification number
Name	Street name
Source: ESRI Community Data, 2005; hypothetical data for this exercise	

Exercise 9.1   Explore purchasing patterns and sales outlets

You have been tasked to create sales territories in the Portland metropolitan area. To do so you must be familiar with the population distribution in the area, wine purchasing patterns of households in the area, and the locations of the liquor stores and restaurants that are Northwest's Best (NWB) prospective customers. Therefore, in this exercise you will:

- Load and explore a basemap of Portland, Oregon, depicting the number of households in its census tracts
- Display prospective customer stores by location and store type
- Explore average household restaurant and liquor store purchases by census tract
- Calculate estimates of wine purchases by households for Portland's census tracts

Open an existing map

1   From the Windows taskbar, click Start > All Programs > ArcGIS > ArcMap.

Depending on how ArcGIS and ArcMap have been installed, or which Windows operating system you are using, there may be a slightly different navigation menu from which to open ArcMap.

2   If you see an ArcMap start window, click the "An existing map" option. Otherwise, click the Open button 📂 on the Standard toolbar.

3   Browse to the location of the GISMKT folder (e.g., **C:\ESRIPress\GISMKT**), double-click the **NWBPortland** folder, then click the **NWBPortland1** map document and click Open.

The map opens with three of its seven layers turned on. It shows the Portland, Oregon metropolitan area, along with its major highways and customer prospects for NWB's wine distribution enterprise. The center of the city is near the confluence of highways in the central part of the map, but the market area includes surrounding suburban areas as well.

Display layers

The map displays the census tracts in the Portland metropolitan area classified by the number of households in each. It also displays the area's major highways and a layer labeled Prospects. For NWB, prospects are liquor stores and restaurants that are prospective customers for their wines. The table of contents also contains layers depicting liquor store purchases per household, restaurant purchases per household, and a general CensusTracts layer, though these layers are not currently turned on.

1 Click the small check box to the left of the Households by Census Tract layer to turn it off (the check mark disappears from the check box).

2 Click the box to the left of the Restaurant Purchases layer to turn it on.

The map now displays information about the amount spent in restaurants per household.

3 Click the box to the left of the Liquor Store Purchases layer to turn it on and display the distribution of that attribute.

4 Turn the Liquor Store Purchases layer off and on again to compare it to the Restaurant Purchases layer. What do you notice about the two layers?

Edit a layer's symbology

The Prospects layer uses a single symbol, though it includes both liquor stores and restaurants. As the buying patterns of the two groups differ, you wish to distinguish between them in the map display.

1 Double-click Prospects in the table of contents (or right-click the layer and select Properties).

2 In the Layer Properties dialog box, click the Symbology tab. Click Categories, then Unique values in the Show area.

3 Select StoreType from the Value Field drop-down list.

4 Click the box next to <all other values> to uncheck it.

5 Click the Add All Values button to display the values for the StoreType attribute.

The display shows the two categories of competitors, Liquor Store and Restaurant, with a unique color for each point symbol. This creates the distinction you want, but the current point symbols are very small, which makes them difficult to distinguish on a map. You will choose larger symbols that are easier to see.

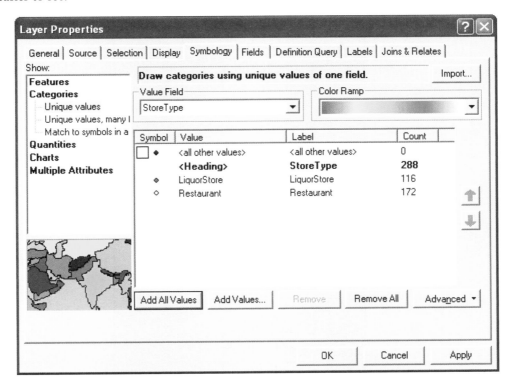

6 Double-click the small circle to the left of the LiquorStore heading to display the Symbol Selector dialog box.

7　Click More Symbols, then choose Public Signs. Scroll toward the bottom of the list and click the Bar, Cocktails symbol. Change the size to 12. (To speed your search, click the Category drop-down arrow and click Services. Bar, Cocktails will then be the seventh symbol in the list.)

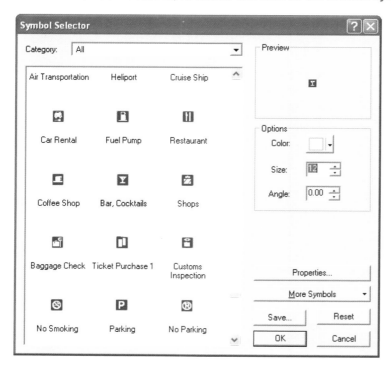

8　Click OK.

9　Double-click the circle symbol next to Restaurant. Again scroll down toward the bottom of the list and click the Restaurant symbol to select it. Change the size to 12.

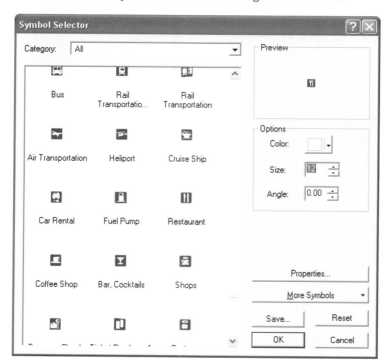

10 **Click OK, then click OK again to close the Layer Properties and display your changes.**

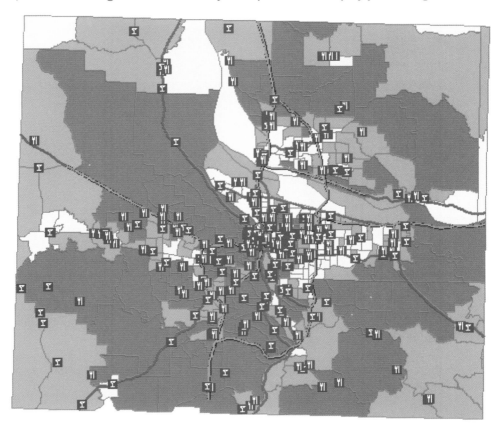

Now you can easily distinguish liquor store prospects from restaurant prospects.

Create and display new attribute data

Though liquor store and restaurant purchases are clearly relevant to NWB's potential sales, it would be better to display a measure of wine purchase per household. Though this data was not available for purchase, you can estimate it. Wine industry publications report that wine accounts for about 18 percent of retail liquor store purchases nationwide. Restaurant industry data indicates that for restaurants that serve alcohol beverages, wine represents about 6 percent of total sales. You will use these figures to calculate estimates of wine purchases by household for Portland's census tracts and display this information on the map.

The table of contents includes a CensusTracts layer. You will use this layer to calculate and display wine purchases by household.

Create a new attribute field

1   Turn on the CensusTracts layer.

2   Right-click the CensusTracts layer, then click Open Attribute Table.

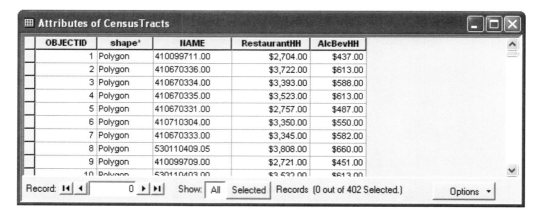

The layer's attribute table opens revealing values for liquor store and restaurant purchases by household. You will use these values to calculate estimated wine purchases by household. You must create a new field in the table to store your calculated values.

3   Click the Options button at the bottom of the attribute table, then click Add Field to open the Add Field dialog box.

4   Enter **WineHH** in the Name field and select Double from the Type drop-down box.

5   Click OK.

If you scroll to the right of the attribute table, you will see the WineHH attribute field has been added, with all its values set to <null>. You will now calculate estimated values for this attribute using other attributes in the table.

Calculate attribute values

1   Right-click the header cell for the WineHH column, then click Calculate Values. Click Yes in the Field Calculator warning box.

The Field Calculator allows you to enter an expression that calculates values to be stored in this field. Note the WineHH = notation above the empty expression box. You will complete the expression using two other attributes and the figures you acquired from industry sources. Specifically, you will estimate wine purchases per household as 18 percent of liquor store purchases plus 6 percent of restaurant purchases.

2   Enter the following in the expression box: **([AlcBevHH] * .18) + ([RestaurantHH] * .06)**
Be sure to include the parentheses to specify calculation order. To avoid mistyping, you may enter the attribute names and mathematical operators by clicking the items in the dialog box.

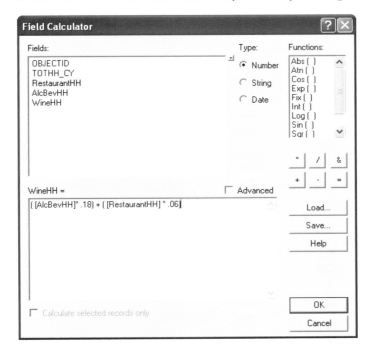

3   Click OK to perform the calculation and close the Field Calculator.

The values for WineHH have been added for each census tract. You are now ready to display this information on the map.

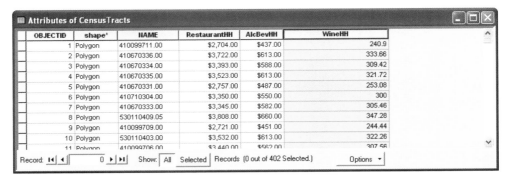

OBJECTID	shape'	NAME	RestaurantHH	AlcBevHH	WineHH
1	Polygon	410099711.00	$2,704.00	$437.00	240.9
2	Polygon	410670336.00	$3,722.00	$613.00	333.66
3	Polygon	410670334.00	$3,393.00	$588.00	309.42
4	Polygon	410670335.00	$3,523.00	$613.00	321.72
5	Polygon	410670331.00	$2,757.00	$487.00	253.08
6	Polygon	410710304.00	$3,350.00	$550.00	300
7	Polygon	410670333.00	$3,345.00	$582.00	305.46
8	Polygon	530110409.05	$3,808.00	$660.00	347.28
9	Polygon	410099709.00	$2,721.00	$451.00	244.44
10	Polygon	530110403.00	$3,532.00	$613.00	322.26
11	Polygon	410099706.00	$3,440.00	$562.00	307.56

4   Close the CensusTracts attribute table.

Edit a layer's symbology

1   In the table of contents, double-click CensusTracts (or right-click the layer and select Properties) to open the Layer Properties dialog box.

2   Click the General tab and enter **Wine Purchases** as the new layer name.

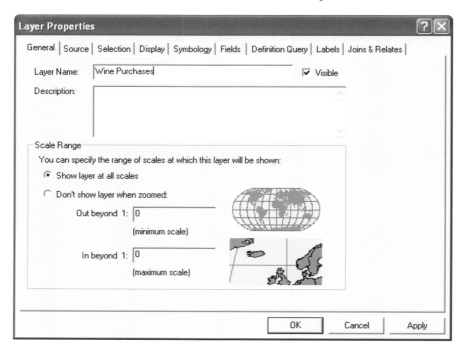

3   Click the Symbology tab. Select Quantities in the Show area, then select Graduated colors.

4   Select WineHH in the Value drop-down list.

5   Select the light-red-to-blue color scheme in the Color Ramp drop-down list.

6   Click the Symbol box, then Flip Symbols to display lower values in blue and higher values in red.

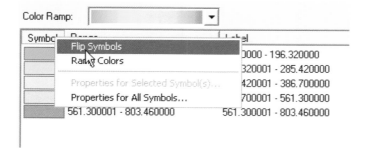

These settings specify which data values will be displayed in this layer and how it will appear. You may also designate how many classes will be used to display the data and how they will be defined.

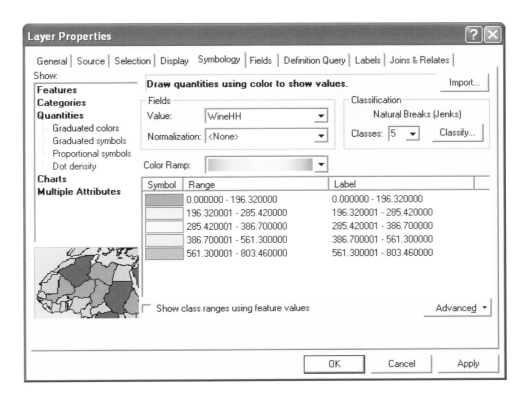

7   Click the Classify button to display the Classification dialog box.

8   Select Quantile in the Method drop-down box.

9   Select 3 in the Classes drop-down box.

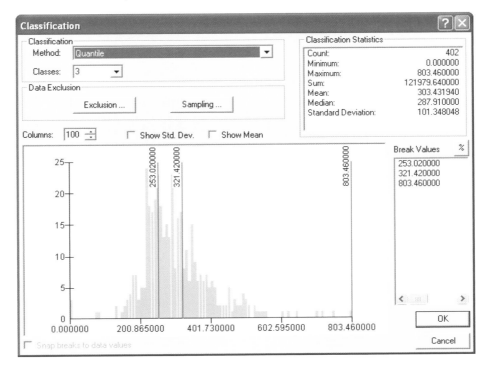

This classification scheme divides the census tracts into three groups, with roughly an equal number of census tract polygons in each group.

10 Click OK to return to the Symbology tab.

You will now adjust the display of classification labels in the map legend.

11 Click the Label heading, then click Format Labels to open the Number Format dialog box. (Note: Do not click the Labels tab at the top of this dialog box. If you do so inadvertently, click the Symbology tab to return.)

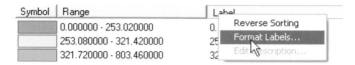

12 Select Currency in the Category field.

13 Click OK to return to the Symbology tab.

14 Check the box next to "Show class ranges using feature values" to define classification ranges using actual values from the dataset.

☑ Show class ranges using feature values

15 Click OK to close the Layer Properties dialog box and display the revised settings in the map.

Change legend title

1   In the table of contents, click the attribute name WineHH under the layer name, then click again to edit it. Replace WineHH with **$US per HH, 2004**. (Note: If your second click is too quick, the Properties dialog box will open. Click Cancel, then try again, clicking more slowly to reach the edit function.)

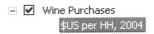

The resulting map reflects all your changes. It displays the average wine purchases by household as well as the location and type of each of NWB's prospective customer stores.

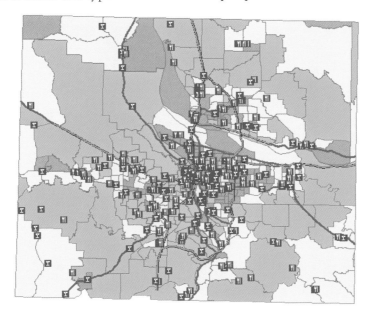

The map now contains all the information you need to answer the report questions below and complete this exercise.

Update report and save map document

1   Use the map you have designed to answer the following questions. Summarize your answers in the appropriate section of the project report template (NWBPortland_ReportTemplate.doc), which you will find in your \GISMKT\NWBPortland folder.

What do you observe about the geographic distribution of households and their restaurant, liquor store, and wine purchases in the Portland area? What do you observe about the distribution of liquor stores and restaurants relative to these purchasing patterns?

2   Save your map file as NWBPortland1_fl.mxd (replace f and l with your first and last initials). To do so, click File, then Save As in ArcMap. Navigate to your **\GISMKT\NWBPortland** folder, type **NWBPortland1_fl.mxd** as the file name, and click Save.

Exercise 9.2　Assign prospective customers to sales territories

Your first approach to territory design will seek to maximize the balance in prospects and sales potential among three territories. To do so, you will identify three geographic clusters with equal numbers of prospects and draw sales territories around them. Thus, in this exercise you will:

- Add a territory attribute to each feature in the Prospects layer
- Select groups of prospects based on their geographic location
- Assign prospects to territories

Open an existing map

1　In ArcMap, open the **NWBPortland2** map document from your **\GISMKT\NWBPortland** folder.

The map displays the census tracts in the Portland metropolitan area, classified by wine purchases per household in 2004. It also displays a layer that identifies the location and type of prospective customers, and a layer representing the area's major highways. There is also a layer outlining the region of the Portland metropolitan area for which Northwest's Best has the opportunity for distribution.

Your first task in assigning territories is to determine target values for the number of prospects and the level of sales potential. You will calculate these values from the Prospects layer attribute table.

Calculate target values for sales territories

NWB wishes to balance the workload and sales potential in its market area among three territories. This means that each territory should include roughly one-third of the prospects and estimated sales potential. Specifically, the number of prospects should not vary by more than two among territories and the level of sales potential should not vary more than 5 percent above or below the average of the territories.

1 Right-click the Prospects layer in the table of contents, then click Open Attribute Table.

The number of features—in other words, prospects—is reported at the bottom of the table. Record this number below and use it to set the target and range values for this attribute. To maintain a range of no more than two prospects between territories, the upper and lower ranges are the average value plus or minus one.

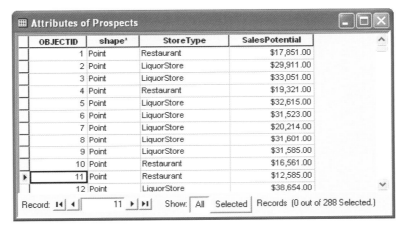

	OBJECTID	shape'	StoreType	SalesPotential
	1	Point	Restaurant	$17,851.00
	2	Point	LiquorStore	$29,911.00
	3	Point	LiquorStore	$33,051.00
	4	Point	Restaurant	$19,321.00
	5	Point	LiquorStore	$32,615.00
	6	Point	LiquorStore	$31,523.00
	7	Point	LiquorStore	$20,214.00
	8	Point	LiquorStore	$31,601.00
	9	Point	LiquorStore	$31,585.00
	10	Point	Restaurant	$16,561.00
▶	11	Point	Restaurant	$12,585.00
	12	Point	LiquorStore	$38,654.00

Record: ◄◄ ◄   11 ► ►◄   Show: All | Selected   Records (0 out of 288 Selected.)

How many prospects are there? What is the target level of prospects for each territory? What is the highest acceptable number of prospects in any territory? What is the lowest acceptable number of prospects in any territory?

To calculate the target value and acceptable range of sales potential per territory, you must first determine the total sales potential of the market area.

2 In the table, right-click the SalesPotential column header, then click Statistics.

This command calculates descriptive statistics for this attribute and reports them in the Statistics window.

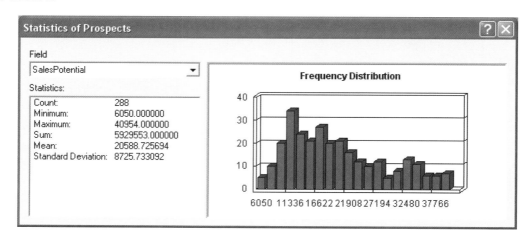

Record the Sum of the SalesPotential attribute below and use it to set target and range values for this attribute. To determine the target value for each territory's sales potential, divide this number by three. To achieve territory values within 5 percent of the target value, multiply the target value by 1.05 for the highest acceptable value and .95 for the lowest acceptable value.

What is the Sum of the SalesPotential attribute? What is the target level of sales potential for each territory? What is the highest acceptable sales potential in any territory? What is the lowest acceptable sales potential in any territory?

You will use these values to balance the workload and sales potential of the territories you design.

3 **Close the Statistics window.**

Assign prospects to territories

You will create sales territories by selecting geographic clusters of prospects and assigning them to a territory. To accomplish this task, you will first add a new field to the Prospects attribute table.

Add a field and calculate values

1   In the Prospects attribute table, click Options > Add Field.

2   In the Add Field dialog box, enter **Territory** for the Name.

3   Select Text from the Type drop-down box.

4   Enter **10** in the Length field.

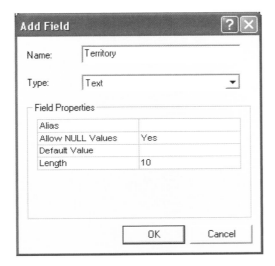

5   Click OK to add the field, which is populated with <null> values.

6   Right-click the Territory column header, click Field Calculator, and click Yes in the warning box to open the Field Calculator.

7   Click the String option in the Type field.

8 Enter **"None"** in the expression box (make sure to include the quotation marks).

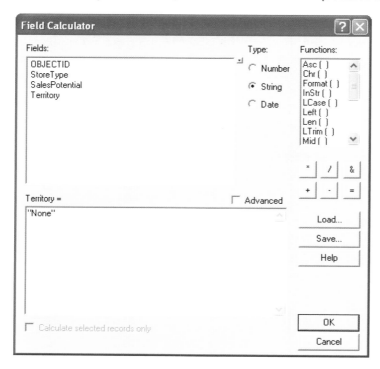

9 Click OK to complete the calculation.

Each feature now has a value of None in the Territory field. You will adjust these values as prospects get assigned to distinct sales territories.

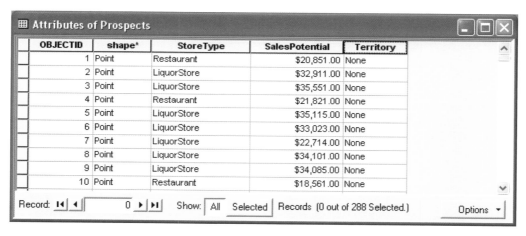

10 Close the attribute table.

Use the Select Features tool

To assign sales territories you will select prospect features manually and enter a common name for the Territory attribute. You will select about 96 features for each territory. Remember, you can select as few as 95 or as many as 97 and still be within the acceptable range. You will make the selections manually with the Select Features tool. But first you'll want to practice the technique.

1 Turn off the Major Highways and Wine Purchases layers, and turn on the Portland Metropolitan Area layer.

The map now displays only a rectangular outline of the Portland Metropolitan Area layer and point symbols for liquor stores and restaurants in the area.

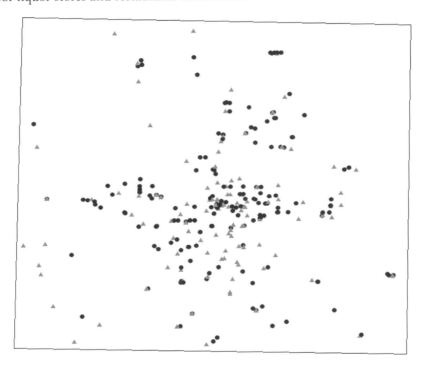

2 From the main menu bar, click Selection > Set Selectable Layers. In the Set Selectable Layers dialog box, check the Prospects layer and clear the other layers. Click Close.

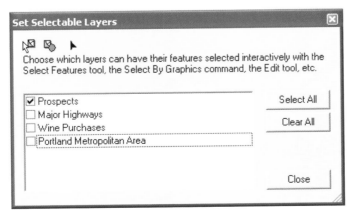

This allows you to select features from the Prospects layer without selecting features from other layers.

3 Click the Select Features tool to activate it.

This tool allows you to select features individually or collectively with a click or a drag of the mouse.

4 Move the mouse pointer into the map, then click and drag a rectangular area. Release the mouse button.

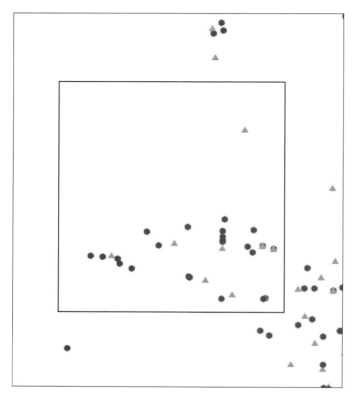

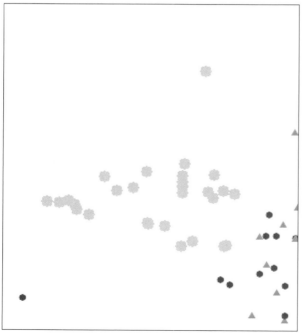

5 Open the Prospects layer attribute table and observe that the features are selected in the table as well as the map. Close the table.

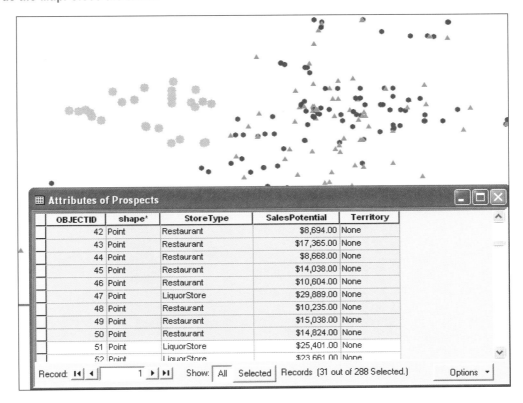

6 Move to another area of the map and repeat this process.

Note that the second selection replaces the first. That is, the features in the new rectangle are selected, while the previously selected features are cleared.

You may use the Shift key with the Select Features tool active to select features in different areas of the map.

7 With your last selection highlighted, press and hold the Shift key and click and drag over another cluster of prospects, then release the Shift key.

This action selects the second group of features while retaining the first selection. Note that the total number of selected features is reported in the status bar below the table of contents.

8 Move the mouse pointer to an empty area of the map and click to remove all selections. No prospects should be selected at this time.

9   Click and drag a new selection anywhere you like, press and hold the Shift key and click and drag a new area that overlaps the selected features, as shown in the following graphic.

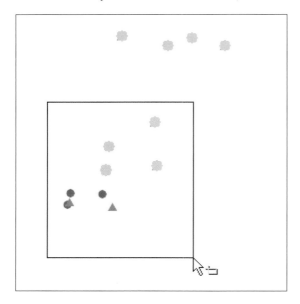

10   Release the mouse button. Your screen should now resemble the graphic below (but you'll likely be working with a different set of points).

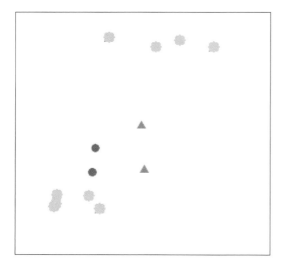

In this operation, the actual effect of the Shift–Select Features operation becomes apparent. It reverses the selection status of the features within the area defined with the Shift key depressed. Thus, all previously selected features in the overlap area were removed from the selection, while all previously unselected features were added to it.

11   Again click in an open area to clear all selections.

You've had enough practice; you are now ready to use the Select Features tools to create territories by selecting prospect features.

Select features and assign them to the West territory

Your goal in this task is to create three sales territories—West, Northeast, and Southeast—with 96 prospects each.

Visual examination of the map reveals that prospect features are somewhat more concentrated in the eastern half of the area than in the western half. For that reason, you will create one larger territory in the western portion of the Portland metropolitan area and two smaller ones in the eastern portion.

1   Open the attribute table for the Prospects layer. Move the table so it doesn't obscure the map.

2   Click the Select Features tool to activate it if necessary. Click and drag to select prospects in roughly the western half of the Portland metropolitan area.

3   Press and hold the Shift key and use the Select Features tool to adjust the number of selected features to 96. You can see the number of selected features at the bottom of the attribute table or in the status bar below the table of contents.

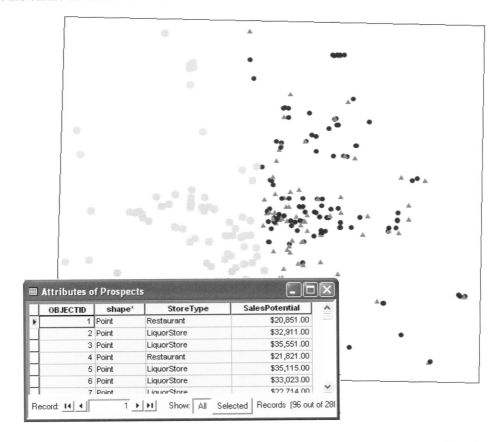

If your original selection contained more than 96 features, use the Select Features tool to clear features. If it contained fewer than 96 features, use the Select Features tool to select additional features. Make these adjustments on the eastern edge of the selected area to maintain the geographic integrity of the territory. Continue this process until you have selected exactly 96 features.

Your selection now meets the objective for the number of prospects in the territory. You will determine if it meets the objective for sales potential.

4   In the attribute table, right-click the SalesPotential column header and click Statistics to calculate and display the summary statistics of the selected records for this field.

Observe the Sum field that reports the total sales potential of the selected features. If this value is within the range you calculated earlier, you have met the sales potential objective. It not, continue to clear and select features until you meet this objective.

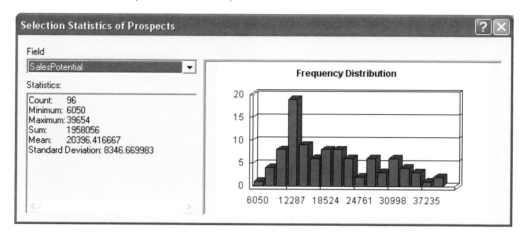

5   Close the Statistics window.

When you have achieved a selection that meets both objectives, you are ready to assign the selected prospects to a territory.

6   With the features still selected, right-click the Territory column header, and open the Field Calculator. If prompted, click Yes in the warning box.

7   Select String as the Type and enter **"West"** in the formula box. (Be sure to include the quotation marks.)

8   Click OK to enter this value as the Territory attribute for the selected features.

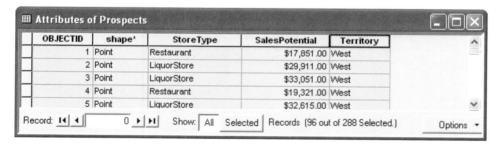

9   Click an open area of the map to clear the selected features.

Select features and assign them to the Northeast territory

You will repeat the selection process for the prospects in the northeastern portion of the map and assign them to a Northeast territory. However, the process is complicated by two factors. First, you wish to ensure that you do not include any prospects already assigned to the West territory. Second, as prospects are clustered more tightly in this area, you may need to zoom in so you can discern distinct prospect features.

1   Use the Select Features tool to select a large group of features in the northeast corner of the Portland metropolitan area. Don't worry if you select some features that were already assigned to the West territory; you will remove those shortly. Determine the number of selected features by observing the bottom of the attribute table.

2   Click the Selected button at the bottom of the attribute table to display only selected records.

3   Right-click the Territory column header and click Sort Descending.

Observe the first few records in the table. If you have selected any prospects previously assigned to the West territory they will appear here. You will clear these features with a Select by Attributes operation.

4   Click the Options button at the bottom of the attribute table and click Select by Attributes to open the dialog box.

5   For the Method option, choose Remove from current selection.

6   Enter **[Territory] = 'West'** in the Query box.

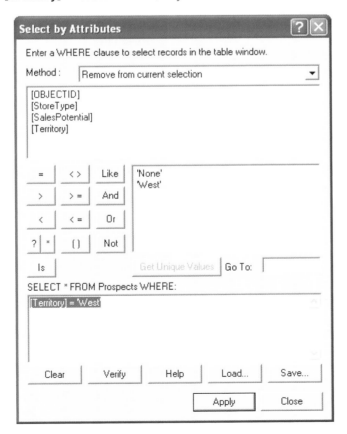

7 Click Apply to remove the features assigned to the West territory from the current selection. Close the Select by Attributes dialog box.

8 Continue selecting and clearing features until you reach the objective of 95 to 97 selected prospects. Remember to keep the Shift key pressed continuously throughout this procedure to avoid clearing the selected features.

As features are clustered tightly at the bottom of your selection, you should use the Fixed Zoom In tool to help distinguish them.

9 To see features in greater detail, click the Fixed Zoom In button ⋰⋰ as many times as necessary. (Note: Clicking this button does not deactivate the Select Features tool.)

10 To see other portions of the zoomed in map, click the Pan tool 🖑 then click and drag the map to see additional features. (Note: Clicking the Pan tool deactivates the Select Features tool. Thus, you must click this tool again to resume selecting or clearing features.)

11 When you have completed the selection of features, right-click the column header for the SalesPotential attribute and click Statistics to calculate and display summary statistics for this attribute.

If the Sum of the selected records is within the sales potential range you established earlier, your selection process for the Northeast territory is complete. If not, continue the clearing and selecting process until you meet this objective.

12 Use the Field Calculator to assign a value of "Northeast" to the Territory field of the selected features.

Select features and assign them to the Southeast territory

The Southeast territory is the last one to assign values to. All features not assigned to the West or Northeast territories should be assigned to it. You will use the Select by Attributes tool and the Field Calculator to do this.

1   Click the Options button in the Prospects attribute table and click Select by Attributes to open the Select by Attributes dialog box.

2   Make sure the Method is set to Create a new selection. In the Query field, enter **[Territory] = "None"** and click Apply to select those features not assigned to the West or Northeast territories. Close the dialog box.

3   Right-click the SalesPotential column header and click Statistics to calculate and display summary statistics for this attribute.

If the Sum of the selected records is within the sales potential range you established earlier, your selection is complete. If not, use the Select Features and Field Calculator functions to select and reassign prospects to different territories until you meet this objective.

4   Use the Field Calculator to assign a value of **"Southeast"** to the Territory field of the selected features.

5   Close the Prospects attribute table.

6   Click on the map to unselect the points, and zoom back out to the full extent of the map if necessary.

You have assigned all of NWB's prospective customers to three sales territories. You will now change the symbology of the Prospects layer to display each prospect's sales territory on the map.

Change the display of a layer

The Prospects layer currently displays the location and type of store for each feature. You will edit the symbology of this layer to display the territory to which each feature has been assigned.

1   Double-click the Prospects layer in the table of contents (or right-click the layer and select Properties).

2   In the Layer Properties dialog box, click the Symbology tab.

3   Select Territory in the Value Field drop-down list.

4   If necessary, check the box next to <all other values> to uncheck it, then click the Add All Values button to display the values for the Territory attribute.

5   Edit the symbols for each layer to Circle 1 and Size 10. Select a different dark, distinctive color for each of the three territories. Click OK to apply the changes.

6   Turn on the Major Highways layer to view the distribution of sales territories relative to Portland's highway system.

Your map may be slightly different depending on which points you chose for each territory.

Summarize attributes

To demonstrate that your territory scheme balances the number of prospects and sales potential within acceptable ranges, you will create a summary table.

1   Open the Prospects attribute table.

2   Right-click the Territory column header and click Summarize to open the Summarize dialog box.

3   For step 1, choose Territory.

4   For step 2, expand the SalesPotential attribute and check the Sum box.

5   For step 3, click the Browse button to open the Saving Data dialog box. For the Save as type option, choose File and Personal Geodatabase tables. Navigate to the **NWBPortland.mdb** geodatabase and enter **TerritorySummary** as the data table name.

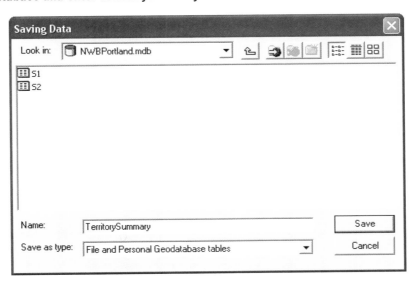

6   Click Save.

The Summarize dialog box should look like this.

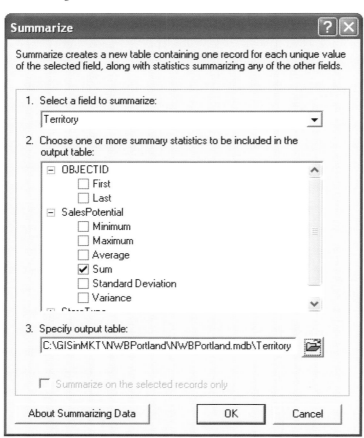

7   **Click OK to create the summary table, then click Yes to add it to the table of contents.**

8   **Close the attribute table, and open the TerritorySummary table to review its contents.**

Use the summary table to answer the following report questions.

Update report and save map document

1   Use the maps you have designed to answer the following questions. Summarize your answers in the appropriate section of the project report template (NWBPortland_ReportTemplate.doc), which you will find in your \GISMKT\NWBPortland folder.

   How many total prospects are in the Portland metropolitan area? What is their total sales potential? What are the target levels and acceptable ranges for the number of prospects in each of the three territories and the sales potential of the territories? Complete the table below with the actual values for these measures among the territories you defined.

Territory	Number of Prospects	Total Sales Potential
West		
Northeast		
Southeast		

2   Save the map document as **NWBPortland2_fl.mxd** (replace f and l with your first and last initials) in your **\GISMKT\NWBPortland** folder.

Exercise 9.3   Display and assess two territory systems

You have assigned all existing prospects to sales territories. In this exercise you will display and evaluate two alternative sales territory systems. Both have been created by drawing three polygons on a map of sales prospects. The first is similar to the one you designed in the previous exercise. The second system uses major highways in Portland to define territory boundaries. You must assess each system for balance of prospects and sales potential and for driving efficiency. Thus, in this exercise you will:

- Use group layers to organize two territory system alternatives
- Display alternative territory systems on a map of prospects and area highways
- Use summary tables to assess the balance of prospects and sales potential in each system
- Use the map to visually assess the driving efficiency of the territories

Open an existing map

1   In ArcMap, open the **NWBPortland3** map document from your **\GISMKT\NWBPortland** folder.

The map displays an outline of the Portland metropolitan area, along with its major expressways and primary highways. The table of contents also contains territory and prospect layers for two sales territory systems. The first, Territories 1, is similar to the one you created. The second, Territories 2, is an alternative design. These layers are turned off. Finally there are summary tables, S1 and S2, which contain prospect and sales potential information for the two systems.

2   Click the Source tab at the bottom of the table of contents to see the S1 and S2 data tables.

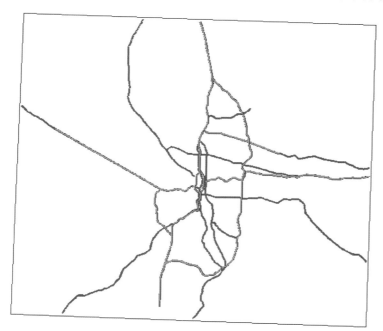

Use group layers to organize a table of contents

The table of contents is confusing, as it is not clear how the layers relate to each other. You will create a group layer for each territory system, label it, and move appropriate layers into it. This will allow you to simultaneously turn on and off the layers associated with each alternative.

1   Click the Display tab at the bottom of the table of contents.

2   Right-click the Sales Territory Alternatives data frame title, then click New Group Layer.

3   Repeat this procedure to create a second new group layer.

4   Double-click the first group layer to open its properties. On the General tab, enter **Alternative 1** as the name for the group layer.

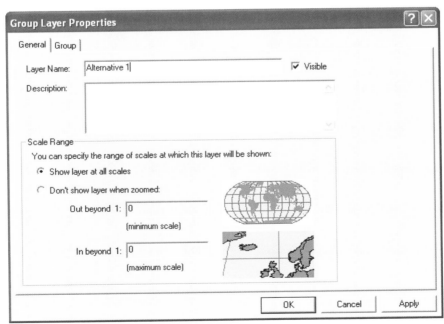

5   Click OK to apply the new name. Repeat this procedure for the second group layer, naming it **Alternative 2**.

6   Drag and drop the Territories 1 and Prospects 1 layer below the Alternative 1 group layer.

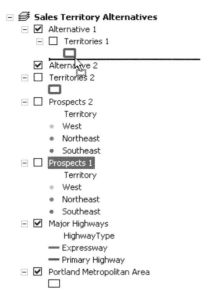

7   Drag and drop the Territories 2 and Prospects 2 layer below the Alternative 2 group layer.

The territories and prospects layers should be below and indented from their respective Alternative group layers in the table of contents.

8   Turn on the Territories 1, Prospects 1, Territories 2, and Prospects 2 layers.

9   Turn off and on the Alternative 1 and Alternative 2 group layers to compare the two. If you have difficulty discerning the difference between the two systems, turn off the Major Highways layer for a moment.

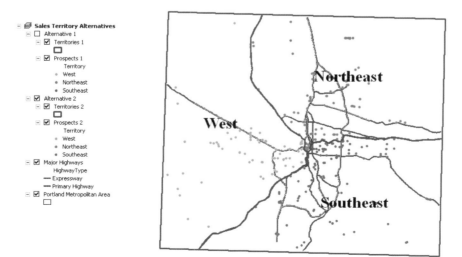

Notice that each group layer displays both of its component layers when it is on and neither when it is off. This allows you to move quickly between complete displays of both alternatives.

Assess alternative systems

1   Turn on Alternative 1 and turn off Alternative 2.

2   Click the Source tab at the bottom of the table of contents, then open the S1 data table to display prospect and sales potential data for this territory system.

This system resembles the system you created in exercise 9.2. Prospects are assigned to territories based on their geographic proximity, and territory borders are drawn around each group of prospects. Use the map and table to answer the following questions.

Based on the values in the data table, does the Alternative 1 territory system meet the balance guidelines for number of prospects and sales potential? Based on your visual assessment, how do you evaluate the driving efficiency of each of the territories in Alternative 1?

3   Go back to the Display tab. Turn on Alternative 2, and turn off Alternative 1.

4   From the Source tab, open the S2 table to display prospect and sales-potential data for this territory system.

Examine the territory map closely. Note that territory boundaries in this system follow major highways, allowing easier access to prospects within the territories. In this system, territories are drawn based on highway access and prospects are assigned to the geographic territory in which they are located. Use the map and table to answer the following questions.

Based on the values in the data table, does the Alternative 2 territory system meet the balance guidelines for number of prospects and sales potential? Based on your visual assessment, how do you evaluate the driving efficiency of each of the territories in Alternative 2?

Review the territory maps, summary tables, and your conclusions about the two alternatives. Using this information, answer the report questions below.

Update report and save map document

1   Use the map document in your report to answer the following questions. Summarize your answers in the appropriate section of the project report template.

Which territory system offers the better balance of prospects and sales potential among territories? Explain your answer. Which territory system offers the better driving efficiency? Explain your answer.

2   Save your map file as **NWBPortland3_fl.mxd** (replace f and l with your first and last initials) in your **\GISMKT\NWBPortland** folder.

Exercise 9.4 Recommend a territory system

You have evaluated two alternative sales territory systems. Based on your comparative analysis, you will recommend one of them to NWB's owner, Mr. Carter. To support your recommendation, you will append to your report a map depicting the characteristics of the territory system you recommend. Thus, in this exercise, you will:

- Decide which territory system you will recommend to Northwest's Best
- Design a map layout depicting the system and its characteristics

Open an existing map and display relevant data

1 In ArcMap, open **NWBPortland4.mxd** from your **\GISMKT\NWBPortland** folder. If necessary, click the Display tab.

The map displays an outline of the Portland metropolitan area as well as its major expressways and primary highways. The table of contents also contains group layers for the two territory systems you evaluated in the previous exercise. These layers are turned off.

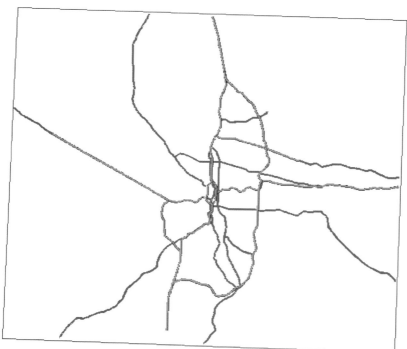

Review NWB's priorities for its territory management system. Compare these priorities with your assessment of Alternative 1 and Alternative 2 at the end of the previous exercise.

 Based on your assessment, which territory system do you recommend? Why?

2   In the table of contents, turn on the territory system you recommend.

Create graphs and add to layout

1   Click the Layout View button ▯ at the bottom of the display to switch to layout view.

The map layout includes a data frame that displays the territory alternative you will recommend. It also contains a legend, title, north arrow, scale bar, an author information text box, and a source information text box. Below the data frame are two empty squares that you will use to display graphs with information about the territory system you have chosen. You will create one graph depicting the number of prospects in each territory and another depicting the sales potential of each.

2   Open the attribute table for the Territories layer of the recommended alternative and examine its attributes. Close the table when you're finished.

Though it is possible to display the values for prospects and sales potential on a single graph, it would be difficult to read because the values for prospects are so much lower than those for sales potential. For this reason, you will design a graph for each attribute.

3   From the main menu bar, click Tools > Graphs > Create.

4   In the Create Graph Wizard, maintain the default graph type of Vertical Bar.

5   For the Layer/Table option, choose the Territories layer you recommend.

6   For the Value field option, choose Prospects.

7   For X label field, choose Territory.

8　For Color, choose Palette, then choose the Solid option. Leave all other options set to their default values. (You may have some differences from the following graphics.)

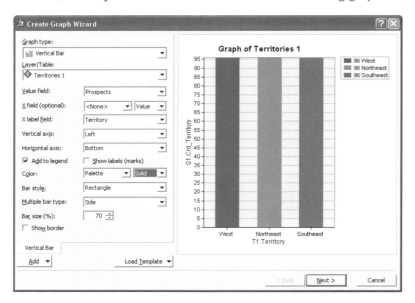

9　Click Next.

10　For Title, enter **Prospects By Territory**.

11　For Axis properties, on the Left tab enter **Count** for the title. Then click the Bottom tab and enter **Territory**.

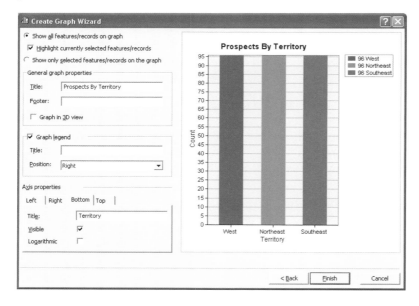

12　Click Finish.

13　Right-click the title bar of the graph window and choose Add to Layout, then close the graph window.

14　The graph should appear in the center of the layout page.

15　Click and drag the graph to the empty box on the left. Adjust the graph size as necessary.

16 Repeat this procedure to create a graph for the sales potential attribute. Choose the same color scheme. For title, enter **Sales Potential By Territory**. For left axis title, enter **Sales Potential**, and for bottom axis title enter **Territory**. Once the graph is created, position it correctly in the empty box on the right of the layout and resize it as necessary.

Edit layout elements

1 Select and right-click the author information text box at the bottom left of the map document, then click Properties to open its Properties dialog box. Replace the placeholder text with your name and today's date, then click OK.

2 Now open the properties for the source information text box. Replace the placeholder text with **ESRI Community Data, 2005** and click OK.

Your map is complete. You will export it and insert it into your report.

Export the map document

1 From the main menu bar click File > Export to open the Export Map dialog box. Navigate to the **NWBPortland** folder and enter **NWBPortland1.emf** in the File Name field. Click Save to save the map and close the dialog box.

2 Open the project report template for this chapter and find the Exhibit 1: Recommended sales territory system heading.

3 Select the instructional text, then from the main menu bar click Insert > Picture > From File. Navigate to your **\GISMKT\NWBPortland** folder and select the **NWBPortland1.emf** file. Click Insert to insert the picture into the report as exhibit 1. (Note: You may have to select and resize the image to display it on the same page as the title.)

Update report and save map document

1 Use the map document to answer the following questions. Summarize your answers in the appropriate section of the project report template.

Which territory system do you recommend to Northwest's Best? How do the map and charts in exhibit 1 explain the benefits of this system relative to NWB's territory management objectives and guidelines?

2 Save your map file as **NWBPortland4_fl.mxd** (replace f and l with your first and last initials) in your **\GISMKT\NWBPortland** folder.

Exercise 9.5 Determine optimal route for sales calls

With territories established, each representative now has an assigned set of prospects within a specified geographic area. To serve this client base most efficiently, each representative should determine the most efficient route for each day's sales calls. You wish to illustrate the value of GIS systems in sales call routing to the sales force and Mr. Carter. You will use the Northeast territory as an example. Thus, in this exercise, you will:

- Identify the 10 prospects with the highest sales potential in the Northeast territory
- Use the ArcGIS Network Analyst extension to determine the best driving route for sales calls on these prospects
- Create a map of the optimal route
- Create driving directions for use in following this route

Open an existing map and change the display of a layer

1   In ArcMap, open **NWBPortland5.mxd** from your **\GISMKT\NWBPortland** folder.

The map focuses on the Northeast sales territory. It displays an outline of the territory and layers for prospects and major highways. In addition the Sales Rep's Home layer displays the home address of Jason Porter, the newly hired representative for this territory. Three other layers, Streets, StreetsNetwork_ND_Junctions, and StreetsNetwork_ND_Edges are also in the table of contents, but not currently visible in the map. Network Analyst uses these layers in routing applications.

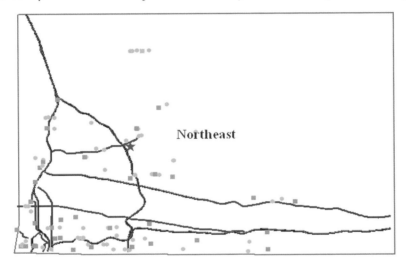

2   Check the box to the left of the Streets layer to turn it on.

The streets layer displays, but its dark color makes the rest of the map difficult to see. You will change the color of the line symbol to correct this problem.

3   Click the line symbol for the Streets layer to open the Symbol Selector dialog box. Change the color for the line symbol to Gray 20%.

The streets layer is still visible, but does not obscure the other layers in the map.

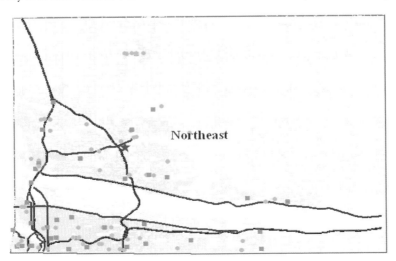

Use Network Analyst for sales call routing

Network Analyst is an extension to ArcGIS. This means that it offers functionality that builds upon ArcGIS technology but is not included in the basic system. To work with this functionality, the Network Analyst extension must be enabled and the Network Analyst toolbar turned on.

1   To confirm activation of the Network Analyst extension, click the Tools menu from the main menu bar, then Extensions. If it is not checked, click the check box to the left of the Network Analyst extension to activate it.

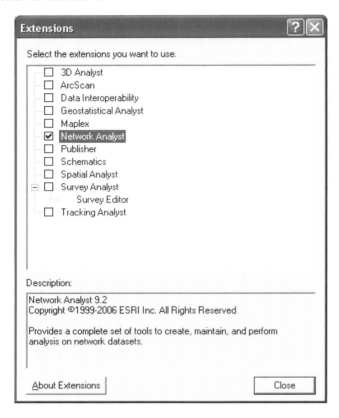

2   Click Close.

3   To open the Network Analyst toolbar, click View from the main menu bar, then Toolbars, then Network Analyst.

The Network Analyst extension is now activated and the extension's toolbar is visible. You may dock the toolbar anywhere on the ArcMap interface.

4   Click the Show Network Analyst window button 🗗 on the Network Analyst toolbar. The window will be empty.

Start a new route

1   On the Network Analyst toolbar, click the Network Analyst menu and choose New Route to add layers for Stops, Barriers, and Routes to the table of contents and similar items to the Network Analyst window.

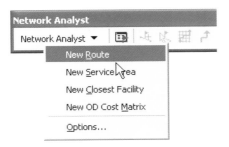

You are ready to begin selecting the data points for the routing application. The sales representative for the Northeast territory is Jason Porter. You want him to begin work in the new territory by calling on the prospects with the largest sales potential. Using Network Analyst, you will determine the optimal route for these sales calls, beginning at Mr. Porter's home and including the 10 designated prospects. The first step is to designate Mr. Porter's home as the beginning point for the route.

2   In the Network Analyst window, right-click the Stops layer, then click Load Locations to open the Load Locations dialog box.

3   Select Sales Rep's Home in the Load From field. In the Location Position area select Use Geometry and set the search tolerance to 50 Meters.

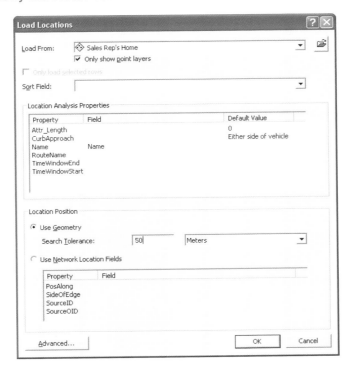

4   Click OK.

5   If necessary, expand the Stops layer in the Network Analyst window.

Note that Mr. Porter's home now appears as a stop. Look at the map. A circle labeled "1" now appears at the location of Mr. Porter's home, indicating that this is the first location in the route. The circle is green in this graphic, but could be a different color on your screen.

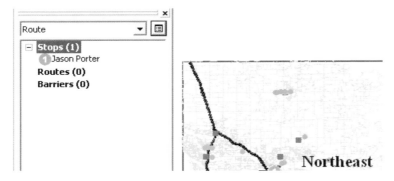

Select prospects for sales calls

You will select prospects for Mr. Porter's initial sales calls by identifying the 10 prospects with the highest sales potential and adding them as stops on the route.

1 In the table of contents, right-click the **NE Territory Prospects** layer, then click **Open Attribute Table.**

2 In the table, right-click the **Sales Potential** column header, then click **Sort Descending** to sort the features in descending order of sales potential.

3 Click the gray box to the left of the first record in the table to select it. Hold the mouse button down and drag it until you have selected 10 features. (Note: If your initial selection does not contain 10 features, depress the Ctrl key and click the gray box to select or unselect additional records.)

The features are selected in the map as well as in the table. These are the 10 prospects you wish to include in the route.

4 Close the attribute table.

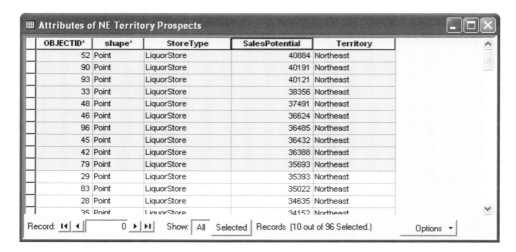

5   Right-click the Stops layer in the Network Analyst window, then click Load Locations to open the
    Load Locations dialog box.

6   In the Load From field, select the NE Territory Prospects layer. Just below that field, confirm that
    the "Only load selected rows" option is checked to limit the locations to the 10 prospects you
    have selected.

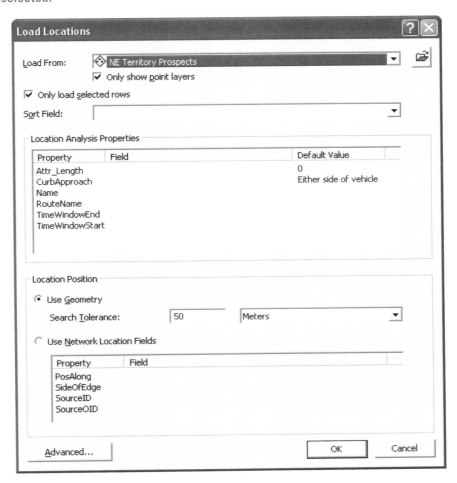

7   Click OK.

The 10 prospects have been added to the stops list and are also highlighted on the map.

8   In the table of contents, right-click the NE Territory Prospects layer, then click Selection > Zoom
    to Selected Features to zoom the map display to the selected prospects.

9   On the main menu bar, click Selection > Clear Selected Features to clear the selection.

With the highlighting removed from the selected prospects on the map, they now appear
as numbered stops in colored circles. By default, they are listed in ascending order of the
OBJECTID field of the attribute table. These are the stops on the sales call route for Mr. Porter's
first day in the field.

Determine the optimal route

1   On the Network Analyst toolbar, click the Solve button to calculate a route for the selected stops in their order of appearance in the Stops list.

2   If you want to change the color of the route feature that has just been drawn on the map, click the symbol for the Routes layer in the table of contents to open the Symbol Selector dialog box. Select a distinctive color in which to display the new route.

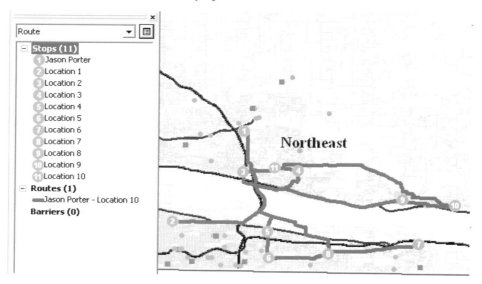

Review the default route. Note that it moves along the stops in sequence of their numeric order in the database. Note that the route seems circuitous and redundant; it often doubles back on itself. You will use the Directions button to determine the length of the current route.

3   In the Network Analyst Toolbar, click the Directions window button to open the Directions window.

The Directions window displays detailed driving directions for the route and the length of each segment.

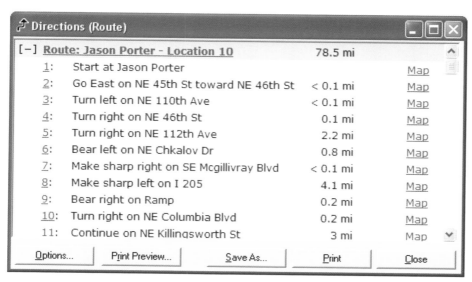

At the top of the Directions window, the total length of this route is reported.

What is the length of the default route?

4   **Close the Directions window.**

If you want to improve the default route, you may adjust the properties of the route to search for the optimal route among the selected stops.

5   **Click the Properties button** ▦ **at the top right of the Network Analyst window to open the Properties dialog box.**

6   **Click the Analysis Settings tab and check the box next to Reorder Stops to Find Optimal Route. Make sure the Preserve First Stop box is checked and that the Preserve Last Stop box is unchecked.**

With these settings, Network Analyst will start with the first stop in the list (Mr. Porter's home), and then find the route that reaches the remaining stops in the most efficient path possible, with no restrictions on the specified order of stops or the location of the final stop.

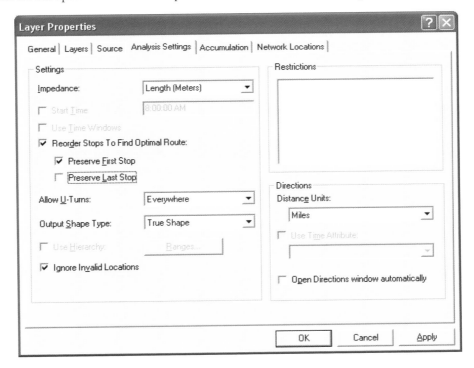

7   **Click OK to apply the settings and close the dialog box.**

8   **Click the Solve button on the Network Analyst toolbar.**

In a moment, the optimal route is calculated with the new property settings. Note that the new route appears more compact and efficient.

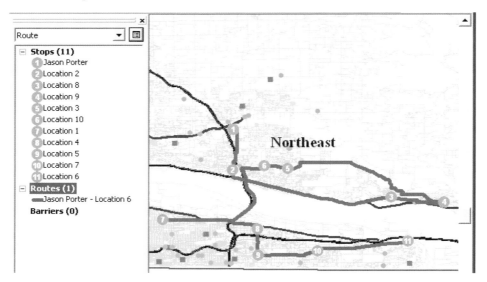

9 **Open the Directions window to determine the length of the optimal route.**

 What is the length of the optimal route? How does the length of this route compare with that of the default route?

Consider for a moment the implications of this improved efficiency. First, it lowers the transportation component of sales costs for the territory. Though this reduction seems modest, a similar result in each of the three territories on each of the 200 annual work days would produce substantial savings. More significantly, if this reduction in route length enables each sales representative to make only one more sales call each day, the result would be 600 additional sales calls annually. Whether allocated to existing customers or to the search for new accounts, this would be a significant resource.

Print route map and driving directions

To follow the optimal route, Mr. Porter must be able to access the route map and directions in the field. The Directions window enables you to print detailed directions for this purpose.

1   In the Directions window, click the Options button in the lower left corner to open the Directions Options dialog box. Click the Printing tab and select the Include all option, then choose Overview Maps and Stop Vicinity Maps.

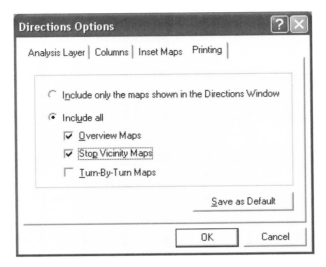

2   Click OK.

3   In the Directions window, click the Print Preview button.

The Print Preview window indicates that the document is 12 pages in length. The first page displays a map of the overall route.

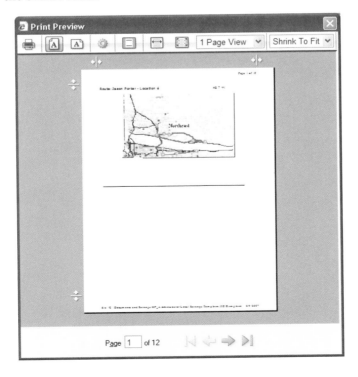

4   Click the Next arrow ⇒ to move to the second page. This page displays detailed instructions for the first segment of the route with a map indicating the location of the first stop at the bottom of the page. Examine the remaining pages, noting that each one provides directions for one route segment and a vicinity map of the destination stop.

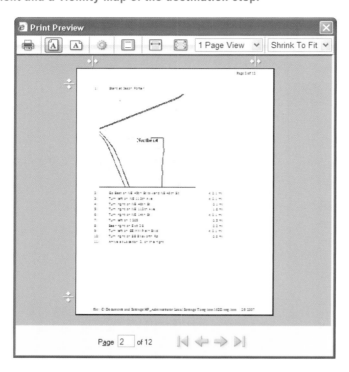

This document provides a comprehensive, segment-by-segment field guide to direct Mr. Porter along the optimal route. You will print the first two pages of this document and attach them to your report for this chapter.

5   In the Print Preview window, click the print button in the upper left corner. Select a printer. Print *only pages one and two of the document*. Include them in your report as attachment 1.

Update report and save map document

1   Use the map document to answer the following questions. Summarize your answers in the appropriate section of the project report template.

How do the lengths of the default and optimal routes compare? How can shortening sales routes improve the efficiency and effectiveness of this sales representative? Of the overall sales force?

2   Save your map file as **NWBPortland5_fl.mxd** (replace f and l with your first and last initials) in your **\GISMKT\NWBPortland** folder.

Congratulations! You have completed the Northwest's Best project.

Take a moment to consider what you have learned in this chapter. You used thematic maps to explore demographic patterns and wine purchasing behavior in the Portland area, calculating wine purchase estimates based on industry data. You created sales territories to achieve a specific set of objectives, evaluated alternative territory systems, and recommended the best system relative to those objectives. Finally, you used network analysis to determine the optimal route to serve a select set of sales prospects. In sum, you have learned how to use ArcGIS to support sales territory design and management applications.

Additional applications

In this chapter, you performed sales territory development in a basic implementation. The system was new, with no existing customers or boundaries to consider. NWB's objectives and their relative priority were clear and the guidelines for the most important criteria were precisely defined.

Even in this simplified environment, however, the complexity of this process is obvious. You used two different techniques for assigning and drawing territories. However, you evaluated only one possible system from each technique. Within either, several different systems are possible depending upon how prospects are grouped in the first instance and which highways are selected as boundaries in the second. Indeed, as you no doubt observed, relatively minor adjustments to the second alternative you explored in this chapter might well produce a system that performs well on all three criteria. Thus, with the tools you used, further improvement are possible in this effort to address Northwest's Best's desire to create balanced sales territories.

To understand additional complexities of territory management, consider the situation the firm hopes to face in three years' time. Assume there have been three years of successful performance, significant sales growth, and a broader product line as more vintners have become attracted to NWB's business model. At that time, the firm will have a large customer base, greater knowledge of the monthly contact time required for each customer, better estimates of the resources required to secure new customers, a larger product line requiring extended knowledge by sales representatives, and more extensive sales reporting requirements to capture the information that sales reps obtain from their customers. At that point, sales growth and customer demands may well require additional sales representatives, each with a new territory. This will likely involve reassigning some customers to new sales reps, disrupting established relationships and accounts.

Obviously, this scenario greatly complicates the territory management process. GIS tools have a significant role to play in managing this more complex environment. First, GIS systems can incorporate and integrate the account data captured in the firm's sales management or customer relationship management systems. Second, by tying this information to the location of each customer, GIS systems allow managers to view the geographic distribution of their best customers and their worst, their most time-consuming customers and their most efficient. Third, by matching territory information with other spatial data, GIS systems can improve the efficiency with which sales representatives service their territories. In this chapter, you evaluated driving efficiency visually and with the Network Analyst extension. By integrating drive time and highway construction information into the analysis, this process can be refined considerably. In a distributed system in which representatives have continuous access to enterprise information resources, real-time information on traffic flows and accident reporting can be used to improve efficiency on a daily basis. As an example, in this chapter you assumed that expressways and primary highways offer the most efficient routes to prospects. This might not, however, be the case, especially during periods of heavy traffic. On a longer term basis, chronic bottlenecks or extended construction projects might affect drive time measures. On a daily basis, accidents or temporary detours might dictate other routes. GIS tools can integrate these factors into short- and long-term planning. ESRI Business Analyst, which includes the Network Analyst extension and drive time data, provides support for this level of territory management.

Ink Tech's experience illustrates the value of using GIS tools in territory management. The firm, a Florida-based producer of specialty inks, applied these tools to increase the effectiveness of its sales force in the Chicago area.[1] The firm's consultant studied the spatial characteristics and sales behavior of customer accounts to identify inefficiencies in the firm's existing systems, then realigned sales territories by building groups of contiguous ZIP Codes around the homes of sales reps. Though the resulting territories differed significantly in size, they balanced the workload among sales representatives more efficiently. Sound familiar?

Western Exterminator is a pest control firm headquartered in Irvine, California.[2] It services residential accounts in three western states and commercial accounts across the United States. As the firm took on new residential accounts, the routes and territories of its service personnel began to overlap. GIS analysis allowed the firm to reduce the geographic size of territories and concentrate the number of accounts in each. In this system, technicians service existing accounts, but do not have responsibility for developing new ones. Western Exterminator also uses GIS analysis for this purpose, by identifying areas with high levels of home sales but low volume for the firm's inspection service. These areas are opportunities for sales expansion for this service.

As the territory management task grows in scope and complexity, many firms turn to consultants and/or specialized software for solutions. Mapping Analytics[3] provides territory management and alignment consulting services to help clients achieve maximum efficiency and profitability. The firm also offers ProAlign, an extension of ArcGIS, to firms who wish to implement territory management systems of their own. Based on the ArcGIS platform, it provides advanced, specialized territory management functions.

Routing applications are another significant component of sales territory management. The project you just completed used sales potential to identify the highest priority prospects in a new territory and efficiently routed sales calls to them. In more mature territories, the routing task assumes greater complexity. Sales managers allocate resources to established accounts based on historical purchases, profitability, and level of required service. Customer relationship management software provides a comprehensive framework for managing contacts, sales, service, and support transactions between a firm and its customers. Sales managers and representatives use this information to assign priority to accounts, schedule contacts, and allocate sales time. This information can be integrated with GIS routing applications to prioritize and schedule sales calls.

In addition, GIS routing applications have relevance beyond sales call routing. Morey's Seafood International, a distributor of seafood products to customers across the United States, uses GIS tools to manage routing and scheduling for delivery and service calls.[4] Yale Appliance and Lighting, a large New England retailer, has implemented a similar system and realized substantial cost savings as a result.[5] In more complex applications, information on the capabilities of technicians is matched with demands of each customer's situation to ensure that technicians have the skill and materials necessary to solve the customer's problem quickly. The U.S. Postal Service has implemented such a system for delivery applications and route analysis.[6]

In short, GIS technologies can contribute significantly to territory design and sales call routing, two critical tasks of the sales management function.

1. Christian Harder, *ArcView GIS Means Business,* Redlands, CA: ESRI Press, 1997.

2. David Boyles, *GIS Means Business: Volume Two,* Redlands, CA: ESRI Press, 2002.

3. Mapping Analytics Consulting Services Web site: *http://www.mappinganalytics.com/consulting/sales-territory-design.html*

4. Boyles, *GIS Means Business: Volume Two.*

5. Lewis Frazer and Don Kushto, "Daily Route Optimization of Service and Delivery Fleets," ESRI GeoInfo Business Summit, April 30–May 2, 2006.

6. Harder, *ArcView GIS Means Business.*

Appendix A

Data License Agreement

Important:
Read carefully before opening the sealed media package

ENVIRONMENTAL SYSTEMS RESEARCH INSTITUTE, INC. (ESRI), IS WILLING TO LICENSE THE ENCLOSED DATA AND RELATED MATERIALS TO YOU ONLY UPON THE CONDITION THAT YOU ACCEPT ALL OF THE TERMS AND CONDITIONS CONTAINED IN THIS LICENSE AGREEMENT. PLEASE READ THE TERMS AND CONDITIONS CAREFULLY BEFORE OPENING THE SEALED MEDIA PACKAGE. BY OPENING THE SEALED MEDIA PACKAGE, YOU ARE INDICATING YOUR ACCEPTANCE OF THE ESRI LICENSE AGREEMENT. IF YOU DO NOT AGREE TO THE TERMS AND CONDITIONS AS STATED, THEN ESRI IS UNWILLING TO LICENSE THE DATA AND RELATED MATERIALS TO YOU. IN SUCH EVENT, YOU SHOULD RETURN THE MEDIA PACKAGE WITH THE SEAL UNBROKEN AND ALL OTHER COMPONENTS TO ESRI.

ESRI License Agreement

This is a license agreement, and not an agreement for sale, between you (Licensee) and Environmental Systems Research Institute, Inc. (ESRI). This ESRI License Agreement (Agreement) gives Licensee certain limited rights to use the data and related materials (Data and Related Materials). All rights not specifically granted in this Agreement are reserved to ESRI and its Licensors.

Reservation of Ownership and Grant of License: ESRI and its Licensors retain exclusive rights, title, and ownership to the copy of the Data and Related Materials licensed under this Agreement and, hereby, grant to Licensee a personal, nonexclusive, nontransferable, royalty-free, worldwide license to use the Data and Related Materials based on the terms and conditions of this Agreement. Licensee agrees to use reasonable effort to protect the Data and Related Materials from unauthorized use, reproduction, distribution, or publication.

Proprietary Rights and Copyright: Licensee acknowledges that the Data and Related Materials are proprietary and confidential property of ESRI and its Licensors and are protected by United States copyright laws and applicable international copyright treaties and/or conventions.

Permitted Uses: Licensee may install the Data and Related Materials onto permanent storage device(s) for Licensee's own internal use.

Licensee may make only one (1) copy of the original Data and Related Materials for archival purposes during the term of this Agreement unless the right to make additional copies is granted to Licensee in writing by ESRI.

Licensee may internally use the Data and Related Materials provided by ESRI for the stated purpose of GIS training and education.

Uses Not Permitted: Licensee shall not sell, rent, lease, sublicense, lend, assign, time-share, or transfer, in whole or in part, or provide unlicensed Third Parties access to the Data and Related Materials or portions of the Data and Related Materials, any updates, or Licensee's rights under this Agreement.

Licensee shall not remove or obscure any copyright or trademark notices of ESRI or its Licensors.

Term and Termination: The license granted to Licensee by this Agreement shall commence upon the acceptance of this Agreement and shall continue until such time that Licensee elects in writing to discontinue use of the Data or Related Materials and terminates this Agreement. The Agreement shall automatically terminate without notice if Licensee fails to comply with any provision of this Agreement. Licensee shall then return to ESRI the Data and Related Materials. The parties hereby agree that all provisions that operate to protect the rights of ESRI and its Licensors shall remain in force should breach occur.

Disclaimer of Warranty: THE DATA AND RELATED MATERIALS CONTAINED HEREIN ARE PROVIDED "AS-IS," WITHOUT WARRANTY OF ANY KIND, EITHER EXPRESS OR IMPLIED, INCLUDING, BUT NOT LIMITED TO, THE IMPLIED WARRANTIES OF MERCHANTABILITY, FITNESS FOR A PARTICULAR PURPOSE, OR NONINFRINGEMENT. ESRI does not warrant that the Data and Related Materials will meet Licensee's needs or expectations, that the use of the Data and Related Materials will be uninterrupted, or that all nonconformities, defects, or errors can or will be corrected. ESRI is not inviting reliance on the Data or Related Materials for commercial planning or analysis purposes, and Licensee should always check actual data.

Data Disclaimer: The Data used herein has been derived from actual spatial or tabular information. In some cases, ESRI has manipulated and applied certain assumptions, analyses, and opinions to the Data solely for educational training purposes. Assumptions, analyses, opinions applied, and actual outcomes may vary. Again, ESRI is not inviting reliance on this Data, and the Licensee should always verify actual Data and exercise their own professional judgment when interpreting any outcomes.

Limitation of Liability: ESRI shall not be liable for direct, indirect, special, incidental, or consequential damages related to Licensee's use of the Data and Related Materials, even if ESRI is advised of the possibility of such damage.

No Implied Waivers: No failure or delay by ESRI or its Licensors in enforcing any right or remedy under this Agreement shall be construed as a waiver of any future or other exercise of such right or remedy by ESRI or its Licensors.

Order for Precedence: Any conflict between the terms of this Agreement and any FAR, DFAR, purchase order, or other terms shall be resolved in favor of the terms expressed in this Agreement, subject to the government's minimum rights unless agreed otherwise.

Export Regulation: Licensee acknowledges that this Agreement and the performance thereof are subject to compliance with any and all applicable United States laws, regulations, or orders relating to the export of data thereto. Licensee agrees to comply with all laws, regulations, and orders of the United States in regard to any export of such technical data.

Severability: If any provision(s) of this Agreement shall be held to be invalid, illegal, or unenforceable by a court or other tribunal of competent jurisdiction, the validity, legality, and enforceability of the remaining provisions shall not in any way be affected or impaired thereby.

Governing Law: This Agreement, entered into in the County of San Bernardino, shall be construed and enforced in accordance with and be governed by the laws of the United States of America and the State of California without reference to conflict of laws principles. The parties hereby consent to the personal jurisdiction of the courts of this county and waive their rights to change venue.

Entire Agreement: The parties agree that this Agreement constitutes the sole and entire agreement of the parties as to the matter set forth herein and supersedes any previous agreements, understandings, and arrangements between the parties relating hereto.

Appendix B

Installing the Data and Software

GIS Tutorial for Marketing includes one CD with exercise data and one DVD with ArcGIS 9.2 Desktop (ArcView license, Single Use, 180-day trial) software. You will find both in the back of this book.

Installation of the exercise data CD takes approximately five minutes and requires around 300 megabytes of hard disk space.

Installation of the ArcGIS Desktop software DVD with extensions takes approximately 25 minutes and requires at least 1.5 GB of hard disk space. Installation times will vary with your computer's speed and available memory.

If you already have a licensed copy of ArcGIS 9.2 installed on your computer (or accessible through a network), do not install the software DVD. Use your licensed software to do the exercises in this book. If you have an older version of ArcGIS installed on your computer, you must uninstall it before you can install the software DVD that comes with this book.

The exercises in this book only work with ArcGIS 9.2 or higher.

Installing the exercise data

Follow the steps below to install the exercise data.

1   Put the data CD in your computer's CD drive. A splash screen will appear.

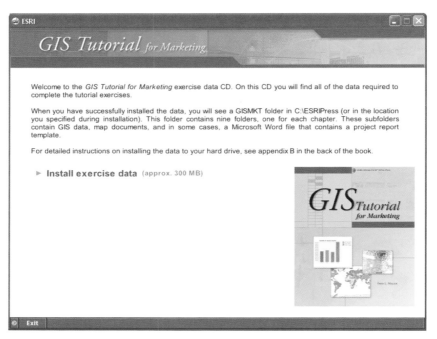

2   Read the welcome, then click the Install exercise data link. This launches the Setup wizard.

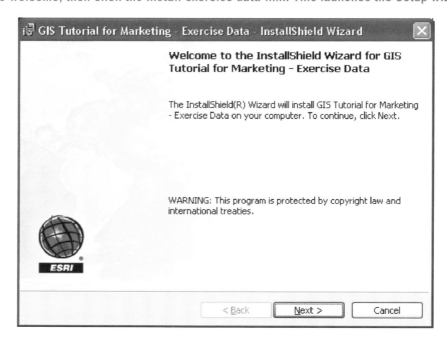

3   Click Next. Read and accept the license agreement terms, then click Next.

4   Accept the default installation folder or click Change and navigate to the drive or folder location where you want to install the data. If you choose an alternate location, please make note of it.

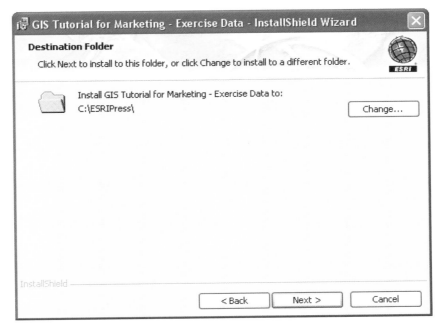

5   Click Next. The installation will take a few moments. When the installation is complete, you will see the following message:

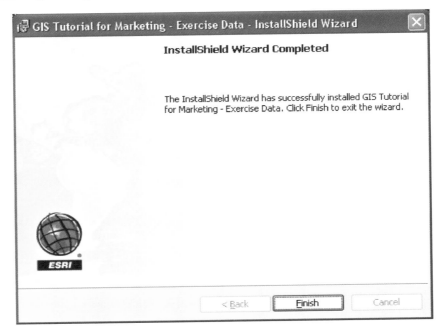

6   Click Finish. The exercise data is installed on your computer in a folder called GISMKT.

Uninstalling the exercise data

To uninstall the exercise data from your computer, open your operating system's control panel and double-click the Add/Remove Programs icon. In the Add/Remove Programs dialog box, select the following entry and follow the prompts to remove it:

GIS Tutorial for Marketing - Exercise Data

Installing the software

The ArcGIS software included on this DVD is intended for educational purposes only. Once installed and registered, the software will run for 180 days. The software cannot be reinstalled nor can the time limit be extended. It is recommended that you uninstall this software when it expires.

Follow the steps below to install the software.

1   Put the software DVD in your computer's DVD drive. A splash screen will appear.

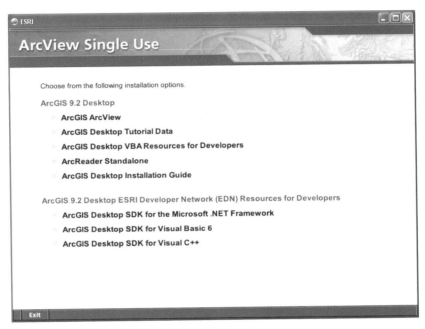

2   Click the ArcGIS ArcView installation option. On the Startup window, click Install ArcGIS Desktop. This will launch the Setup wizard.

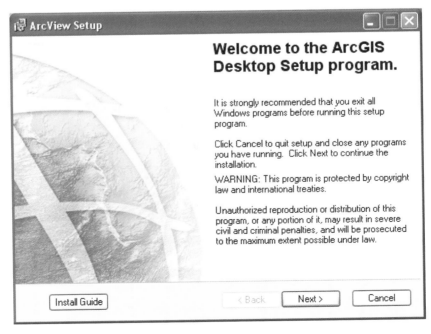

3   Read the Welcome, then click Next.

4   Read the license agreement. Click "I accept the license agreement" and click Next.

5   The default installation type is Typical. You must choose the Complete install, which will add extension products that are used in the book. Click the button next to Complete install.

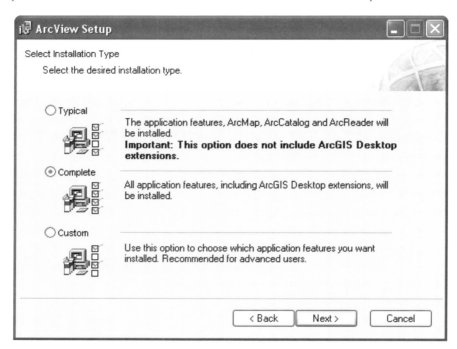

6   Click Next. Accept the default installation folder or click Browse and navigate to the drive or folder location where you want to install the software.

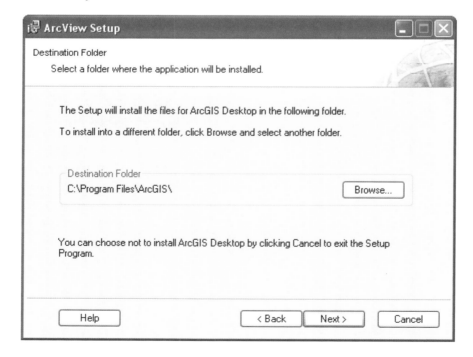

7   Click Next. Accept the default installation folder or navigate to the drive or folder where you want to install Python, a scripting language used by some ArcGIS geoprocessing functions. (You won't see this panel if you already have Python installed.) Click Next.

8   The installation paths for ArcGIS and Python are confirmed. Click Next. The software will take several minutes to install on your computer. When the installation is finished, you see the following message:

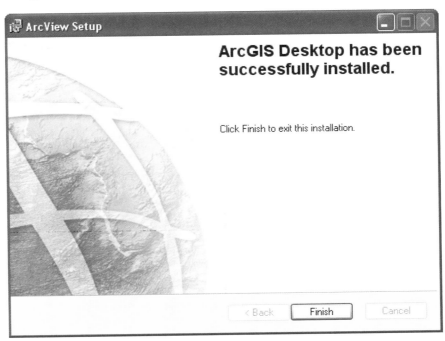

9   Click Finish.

10   On the next panel, click Register Now and follow the registration process. The registration code is located at the bottom of the software DVD jacket in the back of the book. Be sure to register the Network Analyst extension as well as any other extensions you might be interested in exploring. (You will use the Network Analyst extension in chapter 9 of this book.)

If you have questions or encounter problems during the installation process, or while using this book, please use the resources listed below. (The ESRI Technical Support Department does not answer questions regarding the ArcGIS 9 software DVD, the *GIS Tutorial for Marketing* exercise data CD, or the contents of the book itself.)

• To resolve problems with the trial software or exercise data, or to report mistakes in the book, send an e-mail to ESRI workbook support at *workbook-support@esri.com*.

• To stay informed about exercise updates, FAQs, and errata, visit the book's Web page at *www.esri.com/esripress/gistutorialmarketing.*

Uninstalling the software

To uninstall the software from your computer, open your operating system's control panel and double-click the Add/Remove Programs icon. In the Add/Remove Programs dialog box, select the following entry and follow the prompts to remove it:

ArcGIS Desktop

Data Source Credits

Chapter 1 data sources include:
\GISMKT\SilverStonesSF\SilverStonesSF1.mxd

Major Highways from ArcGIS Business Analyst 8.3, courtesy of Tele Atlas North America, Inc.

Population by Census Tract, 2004, from ESRI Business Information Solutions,[1] 2005, courtesy of U.S. Census.

\GISMKT\SilverStonesSF\SilverStonesSF.mdb

Jewelry HH from ESRI Business Information Solutions, 2005, courtesy of U.S. Census.

SantaFeStreets from ArcGIS Business Analyst 8.3, courtesy of Tele Atlas North America, Inc.

\GISMKT\SilverStonesSF\SilverStonesSF2.mxd

Major Highways from ArcGIS Business Analyst 8.3, courtesy of Tele Atlas North America, Inc.

Jewelry Purchases, 2004, from ESRI Business Information Solutions, 2005, courtesy of U.S. Census.

Population by Census Tract, 2004, from ESRI Business Information Solutions, 2005, courtesy of U.S. Census.

Chapter 2 data sources include:
\GISMKT\CommunityTapestry\ESRI.exe

Community Tapestry Demonstration CD, from ESRI BIS, courtesy of MediaMark Data.

U.S. Map courtesy of U.S. Census.

Chapter 3 data sources include:
\GISMKT\OutdoorLivingFL\OutdoorLivingFL1.mxd

State from ArcGIS Business Analyst 8.3, courtesy of Tele Atlas North America, Inc.

ZIP Codes from ArcGIS Business Analyst 8.3, courtesy of Tele Atlas North America, Inc.

Hillsborough Census Tracts from ArcGIS Business Analyst 8.3, courtesy of Tele Atlas North America, Inc.

Major Cities from ArcGIS Business Analyst 8.3, courtesy of Department of Commerce, Census Bureau.

Total Population by County, from ArcGIS Business Analyst 8.3, courtesy of Tele Atlas North America, Inc.

Average Family Size by County, from ArcGIS Business Analyst 8.3, courtesy of Tele Atlas North America, Inc.

Tampa Area per Capita Income, 2004, from ArcGIS Business Analyst 8.3, courtesy of Tele Atlas North America, Inc.

Per Capita Income by County, from ArcGIS Business Analyst 8.3, courtesy of Tele Atlas North America, Inc.

1. ESRI Business Information Solutions is currently known as ESRI Community Data

\GISMKT\OutdoorLivingFL\OutdoorLivingFL2.mxd

Major Cities from ArcGIS Business Analyst 8.3, courtesy of Department of Commerce, Census Bureau.

State from ArcGIS Business Analyst 8.3, courtesy of Tele Atlas North America, Inc.

\GISMKT\OutdoorLivingFL\OutdoorLiving.mdb

Counties from ArcGIS Business Analyst 8.3, courtesy of Tele Atlas North America, Inc.

\GISMKT\OutdoorLivingFL\OutdoorLivingFL3.mxd

Major Cities from ArcGIS Business Analyst 8.3, courtesy of Department of Commerce, Census Bureau.

ZIP Codes from ArcGIS Business Analyst 8.3, courtesy of Tele Atlas North America, Inc.

State from ArcGIS Business Analyst 8.3, courtesy of Tele Atlas North America, Inc.

\GISMKT\OutdoorLivingFL\OutdoorLivingFL4.mxd

Hillsborough Census Tracts from ArcGIS Business Analyst 8.3, courtesy of Tele Atlas North America, Inc.

State from ArcGIS Business Analyst 8.3, courtesy of Tele Atlas North America, Inc.

\GISMKT\OutdoorLivingFL\OutdoorLivingFL5.mxd

Counties from ArcGIS Business Analyst 8.3, courtesy of Tele Atlas North America, Inc.

Major Cities from ArcGIS Business Analyst 8.3, courtesy of Department of Commerce, Census Bureau.

State from ArcGIS Business Analyst 8.3, courtesy of Tele Atlas North America, Inc.

ZIP Codes from ArcGIS Business Analyst 8.3, courtesy of Tele Atlas North America, Inc.

Chapter 4 data sources include:

\GISMKT\MeiersChicago\MeiersChicago1.mxd

State from ArcGIS Business Analyst 8.3, courtesy of Tele Atlas North America, Inc.

Family Households by Census Tract, 2004, from ArcGIS Business Analyst 8.3, courtesy of Tele Atlas North America, Inc.

Average Family Income by Census Tract, 2004, from ArcGIS Business Analyst 8.3, courtesy of Tele Atlas North America, Inc.

Major Roads from ArcGIS Business Analyst 8.3, courtesy of Tele Atlas North America, Inc.

\GISMKT\MeiersChicago\MeiersChicago.mdb

Census Tracts from ArcGIS Business Analyst 8.3, courtesy of Tele Atlas North America, Inc.

\GISMKT\MeiersChicago\MeiersChicago2.mxd

Census Tracts from ArcGIS Business Analyst 8.3, courtesy of Tele Atlas North America, Inc.

Major Roads from ArcGIS Business Analyst 8.3, courtesy of Tele Atlas North America, Inc.

MeiersMarketAreaTapestry from Community Tapestry Demonstration CD, courtesy of MediaMark Data.

MeiersMarketAreaDemographics table from Community Tapestry Demonstration CD, courtesy of MediaMark Data.

\GISMKT\MeiersChicago\MeiersChicago3.mxd

Census Tracts from ArcGIS Business Analyst 8.3, courtesy of Tele Atlas North America, Inc.

Major Roads from ArcGIS Business Analyst 8.3, courtesy of Tele Atlas North America, Inc.

MeiersMarketAreaTapestry from Community Tapestry Demonstration CD, courtesy of MediaMark Data.

\GISMKT\MeiersChicago\MeiersChicago4.mxd

Census Tracts from ArcGIS Business Analyst 8.3, courtesy of Tele Atlas North America, Inc.

Major Roads from ArcGIS Business Analyst 8.3, courtesy of Tele Atlas North America, Inc.

MarketPotentialIndices from Community Tapestry Demonstration CD, courtesy of MediaMark Data.

\GISMKT\MeiersChicago\MeiersChicago5.mxd

Census Tracts from ArcGIS Business Analyst 8.3, courtesy of Tele Atlas North America, Inc.

Major Roads from ArcGIS Business Analyst 8.3, courtesy of Tele Atlas North America, Inc.

MarketPotentialIndices from Community Tapestry Demonstration CD, courtesy of MediaMark Data.

MeiersMarketAreaTapestry from Community Tapestry Demonstration CD, courtesy of MediaMark Data.

Chapter 5 data sources include:

\GISMKT\CFALexington\CFALexington1.mxd

Highways from ArcGIS Business Analyst 8.3, courtesy of Tele Atlas North America, Inc.

ZIP Codes from ArcGIS Business Analyst 8.3, courtesy of Tele Atlas North America, Inc.

Purchases of Fruits & Vegetables, 2004, from ArcGIS Business Analyst 8.3, courtesy of Tele Atlas North America, Inc.

Families Below Poverty Line, 2004, from ArcGIS Business Analyst 8.3, courtesy of Tele Atlas North America, Inc.

ZIP Codes from ArcGIS Business Analyst 8.3, courtesy of Tele Atlas North America, Inc.

\GISMKT\CFALexington\CFALexington2.mxd

ZIP Codes from ArcGIS Business Analyst 8.3, courtesy of Tele Atlas North America, Inc.

Purchases of Fruits & Vegetables, 2004, from ArcGIS Business Analyst 8.3, courtesy of Tele Atlas North America, Inc.

Families Below Poverty Line, 2004, from ArcGIS Business Analyst 8.3, courtesy of Tele Atlas North America, Inc.

\GISMKT\CFALexington\CFALexington3.mxd

Highways from ArcGIS Business Analyst 8.3, courtesy of Tele Atlas North America, Inc.

ZIP Codes from ArcGIS Business Analyst 8.3, courtesy of Tele Atlas North America, Inc.

Purchase at Restaurants per HH, 2004, from ArcGIS Business Analyst 8.3, courtesy of Tele Atlas North America, Inc.

\GISMKT\CFALexington\CFALexington4.mxd

Highways from ArcGIS Business Analyst 8.3, courtesy of Tele Atlas North America, Inc.

ZIP Codes from ArcGIS Business Analyst 8.3, courtesy of Tele Atlas North America, Inc.

Families Below Poverty Line, 2004, from ArcGIS Business Analyst 8.3, courtesy of Tele Atlas North America, Inc.

Purchase at Restaurants per HH, 2004, from ArcGIS Business Analyst 8.3, courtesy of Tele Atlas North America, Inc.

\GISMKT\CFALexington\CFALexington.mdb

ZIP Codes from ArcGIS Business Analyst 8.3, courtesy of Tele Atlas North America, Inc.

TapestryData, from Community Tapestry Demonstration CD, courtesy of MediaMark Data.

EmphasisMPIValues, from Community Tapestry Demonstration CD, courtesy of MediaMark Data.

\GISMKT\CFALexington\CFALexington5.mxd

EmphasisMPIValues, from Community Tapestry Demonstration CD, courtesy of MediaMark Data.

Promotional emphasis from ArcGIS Business Analyst 8.3, courtesy of Tele Atlas North America, Inc.

TapestryData, from Community Tapestry Demonstration CD, courtesy of MediaMark Data.

Chapter 6 data sources include:

\GISMKT\WorldTreasuresNY\WorldTreasuresNY1.mxd

Interstate Highways, from ArcGIS Business Analyst 8.3, courtesy of Federal Highway Administration, Bureau of Transportation Statistics and Geosystems Global Corporation in association with National Geographic Maps and Melcher Media, Inc.

Major Urban Areas from ArcGIS Business Analyst 8.3, courtesy of Department of Commerce, Census Bureau, Geography Division.

State from ArcGIS Business Analyst 8.3, courtesy of Tele Atlas North America, Inc.

ZIP Codes from ArcGIS Business Analyst 8.3, courtesy of Tele Atlas North America, Inc.

\GISMKT\WorldTreasuresNY\WorldTreasures.mdb

NYZIPDemographics from ArcGIS Business Analyst 8.3, courtesy of Tele Atlas North America, Inc.

NYZIPCodes from ArcGIS Business Analyst 8.3, courtesy of Tele Atlas North America, Inc.

\GISMKT\WorldTreasuresNY\WorldTreasuresNY2.mxd

Households by ZIP Code from ArcGIS Business Analyst 8.3, courtesy of Tele Atlas North America, Inc.

State from ArcGIS Business Analyst 8.3, courtesy of Tele Atlas North America, Inc.

ZIP Codes from ArcGIS Business Analyst 8.3, courtesy of Tele Atlas North America, Inc.

NYZIPDemographics from ArcGIS Business Analyst 8.3, courtesy of Tele Atlas North America, Inc.

\GISMKT\WorldTreasuresNY\WorldTreasuresNY3.mxd

Households by ZIP Code from ArcGIS Business Analyst 8.3, courtesy of Tele Atlas North America, Inc.

State from ArcGIS Business Analyst 8.3, courtesy of Tele Atlas North America, Inc.

ZIP Codes from ArcGIS Business Analyst 8.3, courtesy of Tele Atlas North America, Inc.

NYZIPDemographics from ArcGIS Business Analyst 8.3, courtesy of Tele Atlas North America, Inc.

\GISMKT\WorldTreasuresNY\WorldTreasuresNY4.mxd

Households by ZIP Code from ArcGIS Business Analyst 8.3, courtesy of Tele Atlas North America, Inc.

State from ArcGIS Business Analyst 8.3, courtesy of Tele Atlas North America, Inc.

ZIP Codes from ArcGIS Business Analyst 8.3, courtesy of Tele Atlas North America, Inc.

NYZIPDemographics from ArcGIS Business Analyst 8.3, courtesy of Tele Atlas North America, Inc.

\GISMKT\WorldTreasuresNY\WorldTreasuresNY5.mxd

Households by ZIP Code from ArcGIS Business Analyst 8.3, courtesy of Tele Atlas North America, Inc.

State from ArcGIS Business Analyst 8.3, courtesy of Tele Atlas North America, Inc.

ZIP Codes from ArcGIS Business Analyst 8.3, courtesy of Tele Atlas North America, Inc.

NYZIPDemographics from ArcGIS Business Analyst 8.3, courtesy of Tele Atlas North America, Inc.

Chapter 7 data sources include:

\GISMKT\PMDGlobal\PMDGlobal1.mxd

GlobalData basemap from ESRI ArcMap global template in GCS, WGS, 1984.

GlobalData, country demographics, courtesy of NationMaster.com.

\GISMKT\PMDGlobal\PMDGlobal2.mxd

GlobalData basemap from ESRI ArcMap global template in GCS, WGS, 1984.

GlobalData, country demographics, courtesy of NationMaster.com.

\GISMKT\PMDGlobal\PMDGlobal3.mxd

GlobalData basemap from ESRI ArcMap global template in GCS, WGS, 1984.

GlobalData, country demographics, courtesy of NationMaster.com.

tblHofstedeClassifications, courtesy of Hofstede, Geert and Gert Jan Hofstede (2005), Cultures and Organizations: Software of the Mind: 2nd Edition, McGraw Hill, New York.

\GISMKT\PMDGlobal\PMDGlobal4.mxd

GlobalData basemap from ESRI ArcMap global template in GCS, WGS, 1984.

GlobalData, country demographics, courtesy of NationMaster.com.

tblHofstedeClassifications, extracted with permission from Geert Hoftede BV, Geert and Gert Jan Hofstede (2005), Cultures and Organizations: Software of the Mind: 2nd Edition, McGraw Hill, New York.

\GISMKT\PMDGlobal\PMDGlobal5.mxd

GlobalData basemap from ESRI ArcMap global template in GCS, WGS, 1984.

GlobalData, country demographics, courtesy of NationMaster.com.

tblHofstedeClassifications, courtesy of Hofstede, Geert and Gert Jan Hofstede (2005), Cultures and Organizations: Software of the Mind: 2nd Edition, McGraw Hill, New York.

Chapter 8 data sources include:

\GISMKT\BetterBooksSF\BetterBooksSF1.mxd

Better Books Stores, courtesy of ArcGIS Business Analyst 8.3 Tutorial Data.

Competitor Stores, courtesy of ArcGIS Business Analyst 8.3 Tutorial Data.

\GISMKT\BetterBooksSF\BetterBooksSF.mdb

SFBlockgroups, courtesy of ArcGIS Business Analyst Tutorial Data.

\GISMKT\BetterBooksSF\BetterBooksSF2.mxd

Book Lovers Club Members, courtesy of ArcGIS Business Analyst Tutorial Data.

Better Books Stores, courtesy of ArcGIS Business Analyst 8.3 Tutorial Data.

SFBlockgroups, courtesy of ArcGIS Business Analyst Tutorial Data.

SFStreets, courtesy of ArcGIS Business Analyst Tutorial Data.

\GISMKT\BetterBooksSF\BetterBooksSF3.mxd

Book Lovers Club Members, courtesy of ArcGIS Business Analyst Tutorial Data.

Better Books Stores, courtesy of ArcGIS Business Analyst 8.3 Tutorial Data.

SFBlockgroups, courtesy of ArcGIS Business Analyst Tutorial Data.

SFStreets, courtesy of ArcGIS Business Analyst Tutorial Data.

\GISMKT\BetterBooksSF\BetterBooksSF4.mxd

Available Properties, courtesy of ArcGIS Business Analyst Tutorial Data.

Book Lovers Club Members, courtesy of ArcGIS Business Analyst Tutorial Data.

Better Books Stores, courtesy of ArcGIS Business Analyst 8.3 Tutorial Data.

SFBlockgroups, courtesy of ArcGIS Business Analyst Tutorial Data.

Competitor Stores, courtesy of ArcGIS Business Analyst 8.3 Tutorial Data.

SFStreets, courtesy of ArcGIS Business Analyst Tutorial Data.

\GISMKT\BetterBooksSF\BetterBooksSF5.mxd

Available Properties, courtesy of ArcGIS Business Analyst Tutorial Data.

Book Lovers Club Members, courtesy of ArcGIS Business Analyst Tutorial Data.

Better Books Stores, courtesy of ArcGIS Business Analyst 8.3 Tutorial Data.

SFBlockgroups, courtesy of ArcGIS Business Analyst Tutorial Data.

Competitor Stores, courtesy of ArcGIS Business Analyst 8.3 Tutorial Data.

Chapter 9 data sources include:

\GISMKT\NWBPortlans\NWBPortland1.mxd

Census Tracts from ArcGIS Business Analyst 8.3, courtesy of Tele Atlas North America, Inc.

Major Highways from ArcGIS Business Analyst 8.3, courtesy of Tele Atlas North America, Inc.

\GISMKT\NWBPortlans\NWBPortland2.mxd

Census Tracts from ArcGIS Business Analyst 8.3, courtesy of Tele Atlas North America, Inc.

Major Highways from ArcGIS Business Analyst 8.3, courtesy of Tele Atlas North America, Inc.

\GISMKT\NWBPortlans\NWBPortland3.mxd

Major Highways from ArcGIS Business Analyst 8.3, courtesy of Tele Atlas North America, Inc.

\GISMKT\NWBPortlans\NWBPortland4.mxd

Major Highways from ArcGIS Business Analyst 8.3, courtesy of Tele Atlas North America, Inc.

\GISMKT\NWBPortlans\NWBPortland5.mxd

Major Highways from ArcGIS Business Analyst 8.3, courtesy of Tele Atlas North America, Inc.

Related titles from ESRI Press

GIS Tutorial: Workbook for ArcView 9, Second Edition
ISBN 978-1-58948-178-7

GIS Tutorial for Health
ISBN 978-1-58948-148-0

ArcView GIS Means Business
ISBN 978-1-87910-251-4

GIS Means Business, Volume Two
ISBN 1-58948-033-3

A to Z GIS: An Illustrated Dictionaryof Geographic Information Systems
ISBN 978-1-58948-140-4

ESRI Press publishes books about the science, application, and technology of GIS. Ask for these titles at your local bookstore or order by calling 1-800-447-9778. You can also read book descriptions, read reviews, and shop online at www.esri.com/esripress. Outside the United States, contact your local ESRI distributor.

The ArcView 9.2 software accompanying this book is provided for educational purposes only. For use beyond the 180-day time limit, users must obtain fully licensed ArcView 9.x software.

For information about purchasing a fully licensed version of ArcView 9.x, visit *www.esri.com/software/arcgis/about/how-to-buy.html*.

For help with installing this book's software and data, e-mail *workbook-support@esri.com*.

Purchaser may not redistribute the software or data packaged with this book. Libraries purchasing this book are subject to the following restrictions: discs may not be loaned; software cannot be downloadable to anyone other than the purchaser; and discs must be removed before books are placed in circulation.